REFORMED READER: A SOURCEBOOK IN CHRISTIAN THEOLOGY

VOLUME 2

Contemporary Trajectories, 1799 to the Present

Edited by

GEORGE W. STROUP

D0945227

WESTMINSTER/JOHN KNOX PRESS
Louisville, Kentucky

Book design by Publishers' WorkGroup

First edition

Published by Westminster/John Knox Press
Louisville, Kentucky

This book is printed on acid-free paper that meets the American National Standards Institute Z39.48 standard.

PRINTED IN THE UNITED STATES OF AMERICA

2 4 6 8 9 7 5 3 1

Library of Congress Cataloging-in-Publication Data
(Revised for volume 2)

Reformed reader.

   Vol. 2 edited by George Stroup.
   Includes bibliographical references and index.
   Contents: v. 1. Classical beginnings, 1519–1799—
v. 2. Contemporary trajectories, 1799–present.
   1. Theology, Doctrinal—History—Modern period,
1500–   . 2. Reformed Church—Doctrines. I. Johnson,
William Stacy. II. Leith, John H. III. Stroup,
George W., date–   .
BT27.R39   1993   230'.42   92-46620
ISBN 0–664–21957–8 (v. 1 : alk. paper)
ISBN 0–664–21958–6 (v. 2 : alk. paper)

REFORMED READER:
A SOURCEBOOK IN CHRISTIAN THEOLOGY

For
Lucille Elizabeth Stroup
and
Andrew Wells Stroup

CONTENTS

CONTENTS

ACKNOWLEDGMENTS

Acknowledgment is made to the following publishers and authors for permission to reprint selections from copyrighted material:

The American Tract Society. Excerpts from Philip Schaff, *The Person of Christ: The Miracle of History* (Boston: The American Tract Society, 1865).

Augsburg Fortress Publishers. Reprinted from *The Future of Creation* by Jürgen Moltmann, copyright © 1979 Fortress Press. *The Uses of Scripture* by David H. Kelsey, copyright © 1975 Fortress Press. *The Faith We Confess* by Jan Milic Lochman, copyright © 1984 Fortress Press. *On Human Dignity* by Jürgen Moltmann, translated by M. Douglas Meeks, copyright © 1984 Fortress Press. *The Experiment Hope* by Jürgen Moltmann, copyright © 1975 Fortress Press. Used by permission of Augsburg Fortress.

The Banner of Truth Press. Excerpts from Robert L. Dabney, *Systematic Theology*, second edition (Edinburgh: The Banner of Truth Trust, 1985). Herman Bavinck, *The Doctrine of God*, translated by William Hendriksen (Edinburgh: The Banner of Truth Trust, 1977).

Corpus Books. Excerpts from Rubem Alves, *A Theology of Human Hope* (Washington: Corpus Books, 1969).

Crossroad Publishing Company. Excerpt from *A Land Flowing with Milk and Honey: Perspectives on Feminist Theology* by Elisabeth Moltmann-Wendel, translation © John Bowden 1986. Reprinted by permission of the Crossroad Publishing Company.

Doubleday & Co., Inc. Karl Barth, "The Christian Community and the Civil Community," in *Community, State, and Church* (Garden City, N.Y.: Doubleday & Co., 1960).

William B. Eerdmans Publishing Company. Excerpts from Charles Hodge, *Systematic Theology*, 3 volumes. Hendrikus Berkhof, *Christian Faith: An Introduction to the Study of the Faith*, translated by Sierd Woudstra, revised edition. Jacques Ellul, *The Ethics of Freedom*, translated by Geoffrey W. Bromiley. Otto Weber, *Foundations of Dogmatics*, 2 volumes, translated by Darrell L. Guder. Lesslie Newbigin, *Foolishness to the Greeks: The Gospel and Western Culture*. G. C. Berkouwer, *Divine Election*, translated by Hugo Bekker. G. C. Berkouwer, *The Providence of God: Studies in Dogmatics*, translated by Lewis Smedes. G. C. Berkouwer, *The Church*, translated by James E. Davison. Geoffrey W. Bromiley, *Children of Promise: The Case for Baptising Infants*. Thomas F. Torrance, "The Paschal Mystery of Christ and the Eucharist," in *Theology in Reconciliation*. Louis Berkhof, *Systematic Theology*. Karl Barth, *Evangelical Theology: An Introduction*, translated by Grover Foley.

Faber and Faber Limited. Excerpts from Donald M. Baillie, *The Theology of the Sacraments* (New York: Charles Scribner's Sons, 1957). Donald M. Baillie, *God Was in Christ: An Essay on Incarnation and Atonement* (New York: Charles Scribner's Sons, 1948).

HarperCollins Publishers Inc. Excerpts from *The Trinity and the Kingdom* by Jürgen Moltmann, English translation copyright © 1977 by SCM Press Ltd. *The Way of Jesus Christ* by Jürgen Moltmann, copyright © 1990 by Margaret Kohl. *God in Creation* by Jürgen Moltmann, English translation copyright © 1965 by SCM Press. *The Church in the Power* by Jürgen Moltmann. *The Responsible Self* by H. Richard Niebuhr, copyright © 1963 by Florence M. Niebuhr. *An Interpretation of Christian Ethics* by Reinhold Niebuhr, copyright © 1935 by Harper & Row, Publishers, Inc. *Evil and the God of Love* by John Hick. *Death and Eternal Life* by John Hick, copyright © 1976 by John Hick. Ethics in a *Christian Context* by Paul Lehmann, copyright © 1963 by Paul Lehmann. *The Crucified God* by Jürgen Moltmann, English translation copyright © 1974 by SCM Press. *On Religion* by Friedrich Schleiermacher, copyright © 1958 by Harper & Row, Publishers, Inc., copyright renewed 1986 by Harper & Row, Publishers, Inc. Pages 45–46 from *Essentials of Evangelical Theology*, Volume One: *God, Authority and Salvation* by Donald G. Bloesch, copyright © 1979 by Donald G. Bloesch. *The Purpose of the Church* by H. Richard Niebuhr, copyright © 1956 by Harper & Row, Publishers, Inc. Reprinted by permission of HarperCollins, Publishers, Inc.

Professor John Hick. Excerpts from John Hick, *Evil and the God of Love* (London: Collins, 1974). John Hick, *Death and Eternal Life* (London: Collins, 1974). Used by permission of the author.

Hodder & Stoughton Publishers. Excerpts from Karl Barth, *Credo* (New York, Scribner's 1962). George S. Hendry, *God the Creator* (London: Hodder & Stoughton Publishers, 1937).

Lutterworth Press. Excerpts from Emil Brunner, "The Christian Doctrine of the Church, Faith, and Consummation," in *Dogmatics*, 3 volumes, translated by David Cairns and T.H.L. Parker. Emil Brunner, "The Christian Doctrine of God," in *Dogmatics*, 3 volumes, translated by Olive Wyon. Emil Brunner, "The Christian Doctrine of Creation and Redemption," in *Dogmatics*, 3 volumes, translated by Olive Wyon.

Macmillan Ltd. Excerpts from John McLeod Campbell, *The Nature of the Atonement and Its Relation to Remission of Sins and Eternal Life* (London: Macmillan & Co., 1915).

Macmillan Publishing Company. Reprinted with the permission of Charles Scribner's Sons, an imprint of Macmillan Publishing Company: Excerpts from Claude Welch, *The Reality of the Church*, copyright © 1958 Claude Welch; copyright renewed 1986. Reinhold Niebuhr, *The Nature and Destiny of Man*, Volume 2, copyright 1943, © 1964 Charles Scribner's Sons; copyright renewed 1971 Reinhold Niebuhr. Reinhold Niebuhr, *Moral Man and Immoral Society*, copyright 1932 Charles Scribner's Sons; copyright renewed © 1960 Reinhold Niebuhr. Reinhold Niebuhr, *Faith and History*, copyright 1949 Charles Scribner's Sons; copyright renewed © 1977 Ursula M. Niebuhr. D.M. Baillie, *God Was in Christ*, copyright 1948 Charles Scribner's Sons; copyright renewed © 1976 Ian Fowler Baillie. D.M. Baillie, *The Theology of the Sacraments*, copyright 1957 John Baillie; copyright renewed 1985 Ian Fowler Baillie. Karl Barth, *Church Dogmatics*, Volume I, Part 2, translated by G.T. Thomason and Harold Knight (New York, 1956). Reprinted with the permission of Macmillan Publishing Company: Excerpts from Reinhold Niebuhr, *The Nature and Destiny of Man*, Volume 1, copyright 1941, © 1964 Charles Scribner's Sons; copyright renewed 1969 Reinhold Niebuhr. H. Richard Niebuhr, *The Meaning of Revelation*, copyright 1941 by Macmillan Publishing Company; copyright renewed 1969 by Florence Niebuhr, Cynthia M. Niebuhr, and Richard R. Niebuhr.

The Edwin Mellen Press. Excerpts from Arnold A. van Ruler, *Calvinist Trinitarianism and Theocentric Politics: Essays Toward A Public Theology*, translated by John Bolt, Toronto Studies in Theology, volume 38 (Lewiston/Queenston/Lampeter: The Edwin Mellen Press, 1989).

Ursula M. Niebuhr. Excerpts from Reinhold Niebuhr, "The Christian Church in a Secular Age" in *The Essential Reinhold Niebuhr,* edited by R. M. Brown (New Haven: Yale University Press, 1986).

Northwestern University Press. Excerpts from Paul Ricoeur, *The Conflict of Interpretations,* edited by Don Ihde. Copyright © 1974 Northwestern University Press.

Orbis Books. Excerpts from Allan Boesak, "Black and Reformed: Contradiction or Challenge," in *Black and Reformed: Apartheid, Liberation and the Calvinist Tradition,* edited by Leonard Sweetman. Chung Hyun Kyung, *Struggle to Be the Sun Again: Introducing Asian Women's Theology.* C. S. Song, *The Compassionate God.* Hyun Young-hak, "A Theological Look at the Mask Dance in Korea," in *Minjung Theology: People as the Subjects of History,* edited by The Commission on Theological Concerns of the Christian Conference of Asia. Used by permission of the publisher.

Oxford University Press. Excerpts from Thomas F. Torrance, *Space, Time, and Incarnation* (Oxford: Oxford University Press, 1969). *The Mercersburg Theology,* edited by James Hastings Nichols, copyright 1966 by Oxford University Press, Inc. Reprinted by permission of Oxford University Press.

Presbyterian and Reformed Publishing Company. Excerpts from Benjamin Breckinridge Warfield, "Predestination," in *Biblical Doctrine* (New York: Oxford University Press, 1929).

Presbyterian Church (U.S.A.). Excerpts from Jorge Lara-Braud, *What Is Liberation Theology? Answers from Within and Reflections from the Reformed Tradition* (Atlanta: General Assembly Mission Board of the Presbyterian Church in the United States, 1980). "The Theological Declaration of Barmen," in *The Book of Confessions,* of the Presbyterian Church (U.S.A.) (Louisville, Ky.: The Office of the General Assembly, Presbyterian Church (U.S.A.), 1991). "The Confession of 1967," in *The Book of Confessions,* Part 1 of The Constitution of the Presbyterian Church (U.S.A.) (Louisville, Ky.: The Office of the General Assembly, Presbyterian Church (U.S.A.), 1991). "A Declaration of Faith" of The Presbyterian Church in the United States (Atlanta: Stated Clerk of the General Assembly, Presbyterian Church in the U.S., 1977). *Biblical Authority and Interpretation* (New York: Advisory Council on Discipleship and

Worship, The United Presbyterian Church in the United States of America, 1982). *A Brief Statement of Faith*, in *The Book of Confessions*, Part 1 of The Constitution of the Presbyterian Church (U.S.A.) (Louisville, Ky.: The Office of the General Assembly, Presbyterian Church (U.S.A.), 1991). "A Theological Understanding of the Relationship Between Christians and Jews," in *Minutes: 199th General Assembly; Part I: Journal* (New York; Atlanta: Office of the General Assembly, 1987). "The Confession of 1967," in *The Book of Confessions* of the Presbyterian Church (U.S.A.) (New York: The Office of the General Assembly, 1983). "Christian Faith and Economic Justice," in *Minutes of the General Assembly, Part 1 (1984)* (Louisville, Ky.: Office of the General Assembly, Presbyterian Church (U.S.A.), 1984).

Princeton Seminary Bulletin. Excerpts from George S. Hendry, "The Life Line of Theology" in *The Princeton Seminary Bulletin* 65, no. 2 (December, 1972).

The Regina Press. Excerpts from Horace Bushnell, *Forgiveness and Law: Grounded in Principles Interpreted by Human Analogies* (Hicksville, N.Y.: The Regina Press, 1975).

Fleming H. Revell Publishers. Excerpts from Abraham Kuyper, *Calvinism*.

Scholars Press. Excerpts from Friedrich Schleiermacher, *Hermeneutics: The Handwritten Manuscripts*, edited by Heinz Kimmerle, translated by James Duke and Jack Forstman. Paul Ricoeur, "Biblical Hermeneutics," in *Paul Ricoeur on Biblical Hermeneutics*, edited by John Dominic Crossan, *Semeia* 4.

SCM Press Ltd. Excerpts from John Hick, *The Myth of God Incarnate*. John McIntyre, *The Shape of Christology*. Chung Hyun Kyung, *Struggle to Be the Sun Again: Introducing Asian Women's Theology*. Jürgen Moltmann, *Theology of Hope*, translated by James W. Leitch. Jürgen Moltmann, *God in Creation: A New Theology of Creation and the Spirit of God*, translated by Margaret Kohl. C. S. Song, *The Compassionate God*. Jürgen Moltmann, *The Trinity and the Kingdom: The Doctrine of God*, translated by Margaret Kohl. Jürgen Moltmann, *The Crucified God*, translated by R. A. Wilson and John Bowden. Jürgen Moltmann, *The Church in the Power of the Spirit*, translated by Margaret Kohl. Used by permission of SCM Press, Ltd.

T. & T. Clark. Excerpts from Karl Barth, *Church Dogmatics*, volume 1/part 1, edited by G. W. Bromiley and T. F. Torrance (Edinburgh: T. & T. Clark, 1975). Karl Barth, *Church Dogmatics*, volume 1/part 2, translated by G. T. Thomson and Harold Knight (New York: Charles Scribner's Sons, 1956). Karl Barth, *Church Dogmatics*, volume 1/part 2, translated by G. T. Thomson and Harold Knight (Edinburgh: T. & T. Clark, 1956). Karl Barth, *Church Dogmatics*, volume 2/part 1, translated by T.H.L. Parker, W. B. Johnson, Harold Knight, J.L.M. Haire (Edinburgh: T. & T. Clark, 1957). Karl Barth, *Church Dogmatics*, volume 2/part 1, edited by G. W. Bromiley and T. F. Torrance (Edinburgh: T. & T. Clark, 1957). Karl Barth, *Church Dogmatics*, volume 2/part 2, edited by G. W. Bromiley and T. F. Torrance (Edinburgh: T. & T. Clark, 1957). Karl Barth, *Church Dogmatics*, volume 3/part 1, edited by G. W. Bromiley and T. F. Torrance (Edinburgh: T. & T. Clark, 1958). Karl Barth, *Church Dogmatics*, volume 3/parts 2 and 3, edited by G. W. Bromiley and T. F. Torrance (Edinburgh: T. & T. Clark, 1960). Karl Barth, *Church Dogmatics*, volume 3/part 4, edited by G. W. Bromiley and T. F. Torrance (Edinburgh: T. & T. Clark, 1961). Karl Barth, *Church Dogmatics*, volume 4/part 1, edited by G. W. Bromiley and T. F. Torrance (Edinburgh: T. & T. Clark, 1956). Karl Barth, *Church Dogmatics*, volume 4/part 2, edited by G. W. Bromiley and T. F. Torrance (Edinburgh: T. & T. Clark, 1958). Karl Barth, *Church Dogmatics*, volume 4/part 4, edited by G. W. Bromiley and T. F. Torrance (Edinburgh: T. & T. Clark, 1969). Friedrich Schleiermacher, *The Christian Faith*, edited by H. R. Mackintosh and J. S. Stewart (Edinburgh: T. & T. Clark, 1968).

Theology Today. Excerpts from Joseph L. Hromadka, "Social and Cultural Factors in Our Divisions," in *Theology Today* 9, no. 4 (January 1953). H. Richard Niebuhr, "The Doctrine of the Trinity and the Unity of the Church," in *Theology Today* 3, no. 3 (October 1946).

The University of Chicago Press. Excerpts from James M. Gustafson, *Ethics from a Theocentric Perspective*, 2 volumes, copyright © The University of Chicago Press 1981.

World Alliance of Reformed Churches. Excerpts from "Confession of Faith (1977)" of the Reformed Presbyterian Church of Cuba, in *Reformed Witness Today*, edited by Lukas Vischer (Bern: Evangelische Arbeitsstelle Oekumene Schweiz, 1982). "A Declaration of Faith (1967)" of the Congregational Church in England and Wales, in *Reformed Witness Today*, edited by Lukas Vischer (Bern: Evangelische Arbeitsstelle Oekumene Schweiz, 1982). "New Confession (1972)" of the Presbyterian Church in the Republic of Korea, in *Reformed Witness Today*, edited by Lukas Vischer (Bern: Evangelische Arbeitsstelle Oekumene Schweiz, 1982). "A Creed (1980)" of the United Church of Canada in *Reformed Witness Today*, edited by Lukas Vischer (Bern: Evangelische Arbeitsstelle Oekumene Schweiz, 1982).

ACKNOWLEDGMENTS

Yale University Press. Excerpts from Hans W. Frei, *The Eclipse of Biblical Narrative: A Study in Eighteenth and Nineteenth Century Hermeneutics,* copyright © 1974 Yale University.

ABBREVIATIONS AND SHORT TITLES

Barth, *Church Dogmatics*

Karl Barth, *Church Dogmatics*. Edited by G. W. Bromiley and T. F. Torrance. Edinburgh: T. & T. Clark, 1936–77.

Berkhof, *Christian Faith*

Hendrikus Berkhof, *Christian Faith: An Introduction to the Study of the Faith*. Revised edition. Translated by Sierd Woudstra. Grand Rapids: Wm. B. Eerdmans, 1986.

Book of Confessions

The Book of Confessions. Part I of The Constitution of the Presbyterian Church (U.S.A.). Louisville: The Office of the General Assembly, 1991.

Brunner, *Dogmatics*

Emil Brunner, *The Christian Doctrine of God*. Dogmatics: Volume I. Translated by Olive Wyon. Philadelphia: Westminster, 1950.
Emil Brunner, *The Christian Doctrine of Creation and Redemption*. Dogmatics: Volume II. Translated by Olive Wyon. Philadelphia: Westminster, 1952.
Emil Brunner, *The Christian Doctrine of the Church, Faith, and the Consummation*. Dogmatics: Volume III. Trans. David Cairns and T.H.L. Parker. Philadelphia: Westminster Press, 1962.

Declaration of Faith

A Declaration of Faith. Louisville: The Office of the General Assembly of the Presbyterian Church (U.S.A.), 1991.

Gustafson, *Ethics*

James Gustafson, *Ethics from a Theocentric Perspective*. Volume 1: Theology and Ethics. Volume 2: Ethics and Theology. Chicago: The University of Chicago Press, 1981 and 1984.

Hodge, *Systematic Theology*

Charles Hodge, *Systematic Theology*. 3 Volumes. New York: Charles Scribner and Company, 1872.

Lehmann, *Ethics*

Paul Lehmann, *Ethics in a Christian Context*. New York and Evanston: Harper & Row, 1963.

Lochman, *The Faith We Confess*

Jan Milič Lochman, *The Faith We Confess*. Translated by David Lewis. Philadelphia: Fortress Press, 1984.

Moltmann, *The Church*

Jürgen Moltmann, *The Church in the Power of the Spirit: A Contribution to Messianic Ecclesiology*. Translated by Margaret Kohl. New York: Harper & Row, 1977.

Moltmann, *Crucified God*

Jürgen Moltmann, *The Crucified God: The Cross as the Foundation and Criticism of Christian Theology*. Translated by R. A. Wilson and John Bowden. London: SCM, 1974.

Moltmann, *Theology of Hope*

Jürgen Moltmann, *Theology of Hope: On the Ground and the Implications of a Christian Eschatology*. Translated by James W. Leitch. London: SCM, 1967.

Moltmann, *The Trinity and the Kingdom*

Jürgen Moltmann, *The Trinity and the Kingdom: The Doctrine of God*. Translated by Margaret Kohl. San Francisco: Harper & Row, 1981.

Niebuhr, *The Purpose of the Church*

H. Richard Niebuhr, in collaboration with Daniel Day Williams and James M. Gustafson, *The Purpose of the Church and Its Ministry*. New York, Evanston, and London: Harper & Row, 1956.

Niebuhr, *Nature and Destiny*

Reinhold Niebuhr, *The Nature and Destiny of Man*. Volume I: Human Nature. Volume II: Human Destiny. New York: Charles Scribner's Sons, 1964.

Reformed Witness Today

Lukas Vischer, ed., *Reformed Witness Today: A Collection of Confessions and Statements of Faith Issued by Reformed Churches*. Bern: Evangelische Arbeitsstelle Oekumene Schweiz, 1982.

Schleiermacher, *Christian Faith*

Friedrich Schleiermacher, *The Christian Faith*. Edited by H. R. Mackintosh and J. S. Stewart. Edinburgh: T. & T. Clark, 1976.

Weber, *Foundations*

Otto Weber, *Foundations of Dogmatics*. 2 Volumes. Translated by Darrell L. Guder. Grand Rapids: Wm. B. Eerdmans, 1981.

PREFACE

Longer ago than I care to remember, Dr. James J. Heaney, at that time editor of Westminster Press, asked Professor Alasdair I.C. Heron of the University of Erlangen and myself if we would put together a one-volume survey of Reformed theology that would demonstrate its continuity and significant developments. We began work on the book, but developments in our professional lives and two changes in the editorial office at Westminster led us to put the project aside for several years. In 1990, Dr. Davis Perkins, now director of Westminster/John Knox Press, expressed an interest in having the project completed. At that time, Professor Heron had assumed a number of responsibilities that made it impossible for him to complete the work and he graciously stepped aside. Dr. Perkins then decided that it would be best to divide the project into two volumes and invited Dr. John H. Leith, recently retired from Union Theological Seminary in Richmond, Virginia, and William Stacey Johnson, at that time a graduate student at Harvard University, to assume responsibility for the first volume, which would cover the classical period from 1519–1799. I agreed to edit the second volume, which would cover the development of Reformed theology from the publication of Friedrich Schleiermacher's *Speeches* in 1799 until the present.

I am indebted to a number of people for their assistance in the completion of this project. Professor Heron played an important role in the conception and initial effort to develop the book. I am especially indebted to John Leith and to Stacey Johnson, now Assistant Professor of Theology at Austin Presbyterian Theological Seminary, for the fine work they did on the first volume and for their advice in regard to the second.

I am also grateful to Davis Perkins for his remarkable patience and persistence. There were many occasions when it appeared that this project, or at least the second volume, might not be completed, but Davis never wavered in his support and enthusiasm. A major difficulty in completing the second volume has been securing permissions to use material under copyright from a large number of publishers. I am grateful to Westminster/John Knox Press for being able to find funds in addition to those stipulated in the original contract to cover the fees associated with the permissions and to Dr. Geoffrey Green of T. & T. Clark for his kind permission to use a large amount of material from Barth's *Church Dogmatics* and Schleiermacher's *The Christian Faith*. William B. Eerdmans was also most cooperative.

I am especially grateful to Robin Andres of Westminster/John Knox Press who labored at great length to obtain permissions from those publishers who had not responded to my initial requests or whom I had been unable to locate. Ms. Andres also prepared the acknowledgments for this volume, and I am much in her debt.

Phyllis Carson of Publishers' WorkGroup edited the manuscript and significantly improved it.

Several students at Columbia Theological Seminary assisted in the collection of material included in this volume: Evan Campbell, J. Michael Castronis, Robert Earl Madsen, and Melana Scruggs.

The two volumes in this project attempt to demonstrate that Reformed theology is a living tradition that depends, first and foremost, on the continuing grace of God, but, second, relies on the commitment of each generation to pass along that tradition to its children. It is in that spirit that this volume is dedicated to Lucy and Andrew Stroup.

George W. Stroup
Columbia Theological Seminary
Decatur, Georgia

INTRODUCTION:
REFORMED THEOLOGY
IN THE MODERN AGE

The two volumes of *Reformed Reader* describe the development of Reformed theology during nearly five hundred years. Volume 1, subtitled *Classical Beginnings, 1519–1799*, presents many of the texts that shaped early Reformed theology. These writings express the distinctive concerns and emphases of Reformed belief: a commitment to the catholic (universal) character of Christian faith, the authority of the Bible, the sovereignty of God, the lordship of Jesus Christ, the prevenience of God's grace, and the call to Christian individuals and communities to glorify and serve God in the world.

Volume 2, subtitled *Contemporary Trajectories, 1799 to the Present*, discusses Reformed theology in the nineteenth and twentieth centuries and attempts to demonstrate the living character of the Reformed tradition. On the one hand, contemporary Reformed theology continues many of its classical predecessors' distinctive themes. On the other hand, Reformed theologians have often been reluctant simply to repeat an earlier theology in response to the new challenges and demands confronting them. For example, most Reformed theologians of the nineteenth and twentieth centuries have affirmed biblical authority and God's sovereignty and thus have maintained their predecessors' commitments. In the modern (post-Enlightenment) era, however, the Bible's authority often stems not from a property such as inerrancy, but from the Bible's function as the indispensable witness to Christ. In the same way, God's sovereignty may be described not in terms of God's decrees or God's will as in classical theology, but in terms of God's suffering love. This paradigm shift from will to suffering love reflects an important development in contemporary Christianity. Many people no longer ask about God's role in the lives of individuals and communities; they ask in what sense, if any, God is present.

Whether one thinks of these changes as unfortunate distortions of authentic Christian faith or as creative advancements of it—the vitality of Reformed theology is obvious. Because God's Word reforms Christian faith, this faith must in principle remain open to new reformations through God's Word and Spirit. Consequently, no theological statement or formula can be absolutized as true for all times, people, and places. Faith—trust in God's faithfulness— may abide, but the interpretation of faith changes in response to the new things God does in the world. Further, the development and vitality of Reformed theology spring not from tradition, but from the living God who promises to do "new things" and to create "a new heaven and a new earth." The changes in Reformed theology have not always been constructive nor always the work of God's Spirit. They are, however, attempts to remain faithful to God, who is at work in the world in ways the church comprehends only belatedly and partially.

In order to understand what has happened to Reformed theology in the nineteenth and twentieth centuries, one must review briefly some major events.

NINETEENTH- AND TWENTIETH-CENTURY THEOLOGY

The period covered by volume 2 begins with Friedrich Schleiermacher's *On Religion: Speeches to Its Cultured Despisers*, published in the summer of 1799. *Speeches* is an appropriate beginning for study of contemporary Reformed theology because Schleiermacher is often described as the first parent of modern theology. In *Speeches* he attempted to reinterpret Christian faith after the Enlightenment's devastating criticism of classical theology. As the book's subtitle states, the readers Schleiermacher hoped to address were not believing Christians but religion's "cultured despisers," those poets, writers, and artists in Germany at the beginning of the nineteenth century who had turned their backs on traditional forms of religion. Schleiermacher argued that religion in general and Christian faith in particular are rooted neither in reason nor in morality—two central themes in Enlightenment religion. Instead, they arise from the affective dimension of human existence, from a sense of and taste for the infinite.

Schleiermacher's major contribution to the development of Reformed theology was his dogmatics, *The Christian Faith*, first published in 1821–1822. Although he affirmed that Christian faith is based on redemption from sin, which is mediated by Jesus Christ in the church's life, Schleiermacher proposed new metaphors and paradigms for interpreting Christian faith. His christology provided the basis for the subsequent development of modern theology. Rather than relying on the classical categories of nature and substance, Schleiermacher described Jesus Christ in terms of his "perfect God-consciousness." This shift from the categories of classical metaphysics to the psychological idiom of consciousness illustrates the emphasis on hermeneutics—the reinterpretation of Christian faith by means of categories borrowed from contemporary culture—in nineteenth- and twentieth-century theology.

Not every modern Reformed theologian shares Schleiermacher's commitment to the reform and reinterpretation of Christian faith for the sake of proclaiming the Gospel more intelligibly. Some worry that the emphasis on relevance at times overshadows the equally worthy concern for the truth of the Christian tradition. The struggles between New School and Old School Presbyterians in the United States in the nineteenth century, and between fundamentalists and modernists in the twentieth century, were debates about the viability of classical Reformed theology in a modern setting. In response to new discoveries in science, especially the controversy over evolution, and to the emergence of historical-critical interpretations of the Bible, the so-called Princeton School (led by Charles Hodge and B. B. Warfield) tried in the nineteenth century to defend classical Reformed theology by appealing both to the authority of the Bible and to John Calvin and the Westminster Confession of Faith. The debate between New School theologian Nathaniel Taylor and Hodge about the nature of sin and the interpretation of the atonement foreshadowed many future debates between those who wanted to unite Christian faith with contemporary experience and those who refused to sacrifice the objective claims of the Gospel and of the tradition for intelligibility's sake.

In the last half of the nineteenth and the first half of the twentieth centuries, many Reformed theologians in North America and Europe joined movements like Protestant Liberalism and the Social Gospel. Whereas Protestant liberals tried to make Christian faith compatible with new discoveries in science, history, and the social sciences, Social Gospel theologians insisted that faith in the kingdom of God is not simply a pious hope for the hereafter but a call to Christians to address social injustice.

The First World War created a major crisis for Protestant Liberalism. A then unknown Swiss Reformed pastor, Karl Barth, watched in horror as the fighting began and as many of his former teachers signed a statement supporting the German government. In 1918 Barth published a commentary on Paul's Epistle to the Romans in which he discarded many theological tenets of liberalism. Although Protestant Liberalism rejected a supernatural interpretation of God, Barth affirmed a God who is "wholly other" than the world, and who in Jesus Christ stands in gracious judgment of it. Protestant Liberalism celebrated the goodness of human beings and worked to transform society, but Barth emphasized the reality of sin and humanity's utter dependence on God's grace.

Barth was the central figure in the movement known as neo-orthodoxy. From 1918 to the 1960s, Barth and others such as Emil Brunner forged versions of a theology that returned to some classical Reformed themes, although reinterpreting them so as to address the social chaos of the first half of the twentieth century. Neo-orthodox theologians insisted that theology begin not with human experience or natural theology but with the Word of God. Unlike some of their predecessors, they understood the Word to refer first to Jesus Christ and second to the Bible. The Bible is authoritative for faith and life not because of properties like infallibility or inerrancy, but because it is the unique witness to God's Word made flesh in the man Jesus of Nazareth. Neo-orthodox theologians also tried to recover what they believed to be the dialectics of the Gospel and of classical Reformed theology by stressing that God's "yes" (God's grace in Jesus Christ) to the world comprised God's "no" (God's judgment on human sin).

In the United States, neo-orthodox theology influenced the Christian realism of Reinhold Niebuhr, who also rejected Protestant Liberalism's naive optimism and affirmed that all human beings are equally sinful and in need of God's grace, if not equally guilty in their abuse of power and privilege. Niebuhr returned to the classical symbol of original sin, although without claiming that the fall was a historical event. He argued that Christian faith paradoxically confesses that all people are sinful, yet each is responsible for his or her sinfulness. Like Calvin, Niebuhr believed that, without God's grace, all human thoughts, acts, and deeds are tainted by sin.

The 1950s and 1960s witnessed the emergence of process theology, which drew upon the philosophies of Alfred North Whitehead and Charles Hartshorne. Reformed theologians feared that this new theology, along with other forms of panentheism that considered God to be internally related to creation, undercut the biblical interpretation of God's sovereignty.

The neo-orthodox consensus—if it had existed—began to unravel in the 1960s. Theologians like Jürgen Moltmann argued that neo-orthodoxy is inadequate on several grounds. First, it is insufficiently eschatological. Moltmann's theology of hope was an attempt to rethink Christian faith in light of the Bible's claim that resurrection faith lives in anticipation of the second parousia. Second, neo-orthodoxy and Christian realism were insufficiently political because they are blind to the meaning of Jesus' crucifixion: suffering is a part of God's life and God identifies not with the powerful but with those who suffer in the world. Third, because its emphasis on christology borders on christomonism, neo-orthodoxy is insufficiently trinitarian. The church needed an interpretation of the triune God that stressed the reality of the Holy Spirit.

Reformed theology, as well as the remaining Protestant and Roman Catholic systems of belief, began to splinter in the 1960s into many so-called genitive theologies—theologies of hope, play, third-world liberation, feminism, black liberation, gays, and lesbians. These new movements asserted that neo-orthodox and other theologies had failed to acknowledge their cultural, racial, class, and gender captivity and had excluded other voices, experiences, and points of view. In the last forty years of the twentieth century, Reformed theology has occupied itself above all with the meaning of Christian faith for those contexts and communities formerly excluded from articulating theological paradigms. What does the Gospel mean when interpreted not exclusively by men but also by women? What is Christian faith that reflects not only the experience of white churches in western Europe and North America, but also the faith and experiences of African American churches and churches in Asia, Africa, Latin America, and the rest of the non-Western world? At the close of the twentieth century, these questions are only partly answered, but Reformed theology in the twenty-first century will clearly differ from anything that has preceded it. Furthermore, the import of these recent developments is difficult to assess. The events of the late twentieth century may represent a new chapter in the history of Reformed theology or only a continuation of Protestant Liberalism, which began with Schleiermacher and was briefly interrupted by neo-orthodoxy.

In any case, the development of Reformed theology in the nineteenth and twentieth centuries demonstrates one of that tradition's deepest convictions. This convoluted story, full of new discoveries, mistakes, and blind alleys, reveals a theology whose vitality is grounded in its faith in a living God continuously doing new things in the world. Reformed not just once in the sixteenth century but repeatedly throughout its history, this theology refuses to absolutize any one interpretation of the Gospel and remains open to new reformations by God's Word. The history of Reformed theology demonstrates the conviction that *ecclesia reformata semper reformanda* (the church reformed and always to be reformed).

THEMES AND ISSUES

Reformed theology during the nineteenth and twentieth centuries has been characterized not only by individuals and movements, but also by discussions of theological issues. The major issues are too numerous to discuss at length, but some areas of continuing reinterpretation include the following: (1) the authority of the Bible; (2) the role of experience in theology; (3) God's nature; (4) the meaning of salvation; (5) the church's relation to society; and (6) the identity of Reformed faith and theology.

The Authority of the Bible

As indicated above, some Reformed theologians argued against Protestant Liberalism by appealing to the infallibility and/or inerrancy of the Bible. In neo-orthodox theology, however, the interpretation of the Bible changed significantly. The Bible, Barth argued, is not the Word of God in the same sense as is Jesus Christ. Jesus Christ is "the Word made flesh," and Christians believe they are saved by Christ, not by the Bible. But the Bible is authoritative for Christian faith and theology in a derivative and functional sense, as the unique, irreplaceable witness to Jesus Christ.

Far from being new, Barth's interpretation of the relation between Jesus Christ and the Bible and the role of each in Christian theology reverts to the biblical interpretation of Martin Luther and, to an extent, of John Calvin. Barth's position departs from that of Luther, however, in that Luther's appeal to the Bible as Christ's cradle stemmed from a theology and a piety emphasizing biblical authority. Unfortunately, neo-orthodox interpretations of the Bible are not always allied with a similar piety. In the second half of the twentieth century, few Reformed churches pursue the study of the Bible and the recovery of the Gospel within it; more and more they grow biblically illiterate. Although most Reformed denominations in Europe and North America affirm a neo-orthodox interpretation of the Bible's authority, the daily life of their congregations suggests that the Bible is authoritative in word only. This is not surprising in light of the collapse of almost all traditional authority in Western culture in the last half of the twentieth century, the triumph of individualism, and, according to some literary critics, the emergence of the reader as the final authority, if not the only reality, for interpreting texts.

The Role of Experience

Barth, as well as many other neo-orthodox theologians, insisted that Protestant Liberalism was less theology than anthropology with a loud voice or anthropology masquerading as theology. Christian faith and theology must begin not with human subjectivity, Barth argued, but with the objective reality of God's self-revelation in Jesus Christ. In the last half of the twentieth century, however, new theological voices have begun to question the existence and nature of this objective reality to which Christian faith refers. Liberation theologians in oppressed communities ask how both classical and neo-orthodox theologians could have failed to discern, in the objective reality of God's self-revelation, God's preferential option for the poor. Feminist, African American, and non-Western theologians argue that neo-orthodox interpretations of the objective reality of God's self-revelation reflect the biases of white, affluent, male theologians rather than the biases of the Gospel. A Reformed theology relevant to non-male, non-white, oppressed people is necessary, they urge.

On the other hand, those Reformed theologians who still subscribe to neo-orthodoxy fear that liberation theologians risk repeating the error of Protestant Liberalism by neglecting the sinfulness pervading all interpretations of the Bible, including those of oppressed communities; by making experience normative for theology, liberation theology may give up the check (once provided by the Bible and by tradition) against the idolatrous construction of God from projected human needs.

Neo-orthodoxy so feared the threat of anthropological reduction that it allowed almost no room for a theology of the Holy Spirit that values the subjectivity of revelation and the human experience of God's grace. The legacy of neo-orthodoxy is a theology without a correlative piety, a theology that views piety itself as an adversary. Theology detached from piety soon falls victim to intellectual reduction and loses sight of Calvin's claim that in Christian faith knowledge of the head must not be separated from knowledge of the heart. Consequently, contemporary Reformed theology seeks a new piety or, in the idiom of our day, a new spirituality.

The Nature of God

Classical Reformed theology described God in terms of sovereign will. The Christian life was a call to obey and serve God's will in the world, and Reformed Christians believed that, by means of the Holy Spirit and the Bible, they could know God's will. In the twentieth century, Reformed theologians frequently describe God's sovereignty in terms of love rather than will—a significant shift in interpretation. Human experience in the twentieth century may stop Reformed theologians from saying much about what God does in the world, but not from affirming God's presence in the suffering of the crucified Christ.

In light of the horrors of twentieth-century history, the theological issue has become not so much God's activity in history as it is the sense, if any, in which God is present in the world. Classical Reformed theology described God's providence in terms of conservation, concurrence, and governance. Contemporary interpretations say little about God's governance or rule; rather, they appeal to the cross as the basis for claiming God's presence in the world with those who suffer. Similarly, although classical theology affirmed God's sovereignty by means of a doctrine of election or predestination, many contemporary Reformed confessions of faith omit any reference to predestination.

The Meaning of Salvation

Reformed theology has various interpretations of the atonement, but it joins the rest of the Christian tradition in affirming that Jesus is savior. Contemporary Reformed theology, however, is less clear than was classical theology about the meaning of salvation and the life and death of Jesus Christ as the means of salvation.

Protestant Liberalism rejected most classical theories of the atonement (cosmic conflict, substitutionary, and penal) because they presupposed cosmologies, worldviews, and images no longer intelligible to a post-Enlightenment world. In their place were proposed various subjective or moral-influence interpretations of the atonement. In the last half of the twentieth century, Reformed churches in North America and western Europe have translated the moral-influence tradition into political images, thereby reducing the biblical symbols of shalom and the kingdom of God to the code words of peace and justice. Those Reformed churches reducing salvation to social and political causes have lost many members. Whether the latter results from the former is open to debate, but although salvation may mean more (but not less) than a particular political agenda—although it may be a reality established by Jesus' death and resurrection—contemporary Reformed theology, like the rest of mainline Protestantism, has difficulty defining salvation.

The Church's Relation to Society

Although the Reformed mainstream has believed in the sinfulness of individuals and societies, it has also argued that God calls Christians not to shun a sinful world, but to serve God in it in order to witness to and take part in God's transformation of it. Consequently, most Reformed theologians have rejected the proposal that the church live on the margins of, and in opposition to, sinful society. Rather, the church must live out its faith amid the public arena. As many Reformed theologians have recognized, this transformation model risks allowing the Gospel to be identified with and determined by society.

In the last half of the twentieth century, more and more Reformed theologians think that the church, especially the church in North America and western Europe, must depart from its traditional location in the center of society and identify with those people and causes on the margins. This would move Reformed theology toward a more sectarian, anabaptist position. Advocates of this change sometimes suggest that the church has no choice because Western societies increasingly oppose Christian communities critical of the dominant order's values and policies.

On the other hand, some Reformed theologians reject, for two reasons, this proposal to abandon the transformation model. First, in the tradition of Reinhold Niebuhr, they suspect that those proposing a Christ-against-culture model harbor the traditional liberal assumption that a sectarian church is less sinful than one at society's center. Second, they wonder whether liberationists recognize that such a change entails the reinterpretation not only of the church's social policy, but of its liturgy, hymnody, piety, and theology as well.

The Identity of Reformed Faith and Theology

These theological issues in contemporary Reformed theology are only five of many areas of discussion, but together they point to a larger issue undergirding all of them—the question of Reformed identity. In light of the developments in the nineteenth and twentieth centuries, what, if anything, gives Reformed theology its identity?

Some theologians have argued that essential tenets of doctrine can identify authentic forms of Reformed theology. Unfortunately for those who support this position, the various confessions of Reformed churches, both classical and contemporary, do not speak about these essential tenets, and theologians vigorously disagree about which are essential and which are not. Others suggest that the very notion of essential tenets and Reformed theology is a non sequitur. A truly Reformed theology is always open to reformation by means of God's Word and, as such, cannot affirm any doctrine to be essential, except perhaps that of reform itself. This debate raises the question of whether Reformed belief still has an identifiable theological common ground, or whether Reformed theology acquires its identity only from its polity and perhaps from a social and political perspective shared by some leaders of the various denominations.

WHO SPEAKS
FOR REFORMED THEOLOGY?

This volume contains two kinds of texts. Most selections were written by theologians in the nineteenth and twentieth centuries, but several texts from study papers and confessions of faith by Reformed denominations have been included.

Volume 2 seeks to demonstrate two points. First, although Reformed theology changed during the nineteenth and twentieth centuries, common themes persisted. Along with volume 1, this volume shows readers the ideas that give Reformed theology its identity throughout its history. Although interpreted in various ways, certain themes or symbols often appear in discussions of the meaning of Christian faith. These themes are not so much fixed and eternal truths as they are characteristics of Reformed theology. In order to document both the continuity and the development of Reformed theology, several theologians appear often, especially Friedrich Schleiermacher, Karl

Barth, and Jürgen Moltmann. When these three are compared to classical theologians, such as John Calvin and Jonathan Edwards, and then compared to one another, some of the significant changes in Reformed theology become apparent.

Second, one of the major developments in Reformed theology during the last half of the twentieth century is its geographical, racial, and gender diversification. Schleiermacher, Barth, and Moltmann are European white males. In the twentieth century, Reformed theology has been articulated in new forms, not only in North America and Europe, but also in Latin America, Asia, Africa, and other non-Western contexts, and not only by white European males, but also by women and by theologians from various races and cultures.

These new voices demonstrate the diversity and vitality of recent Reformed theology. Because of this diversity, however, and because of page limitations, many influential European and North American theologians, especially those of the nineteenth and early twentieth centuries, have been omitted. In addition, the writers are of disparate theological significance. A feminist, liberation, or third-world theologian of the stature of Schleiermacher or Barth has yet to appear in the Reformed tradition. No doubt such theologians will emerge. In this volume, however, some writers are included because they represent new developments rather than because they may be seen to have made lasting contributions when the next generation assesses them. Finally, volume 2 emphasizes Reformed theology in North America, in part because many readers of this volume will be North Americans.

What is and is not Reformed is extraordinarily difficult to determine. The concept has no self-evident boundaries; one can argue that all Protestant theology is reformed. In this volume the term *Reformed* refers to Reformed, Presbyterian, and Congregationalist denominations and to united churches that include these traditions, but not to Lutheran, Methodist, Baptist, Restoration, and Episcopal traditions. Also included are a few theologians who are not Reformed but who write from Reformed perspectives or who have significant things to say about the Reformed tradition.

1

CONCERNS AND
METHODS OF THEOLOGY

One of the distinctive characteristics of modern theology (that is, theology written in the nineteenth and twentieth centuries) is its preoccupation with the problems of methodology. The consequences of the Enlightenment were devastating for traditional forms of theology; many of the assumptions and categories of classical theology were subjected to unrelenting criticism in the seventeenth and eighteenth centuries. Two common arguments in classical theology for the truthfulness of Christian faith were the reality of miracles and the fulfillment of prophecy. During the Enlightenment both of these arguments were rendered null and void.

Theologians working in the aftermath of the Enlightenment found themselves facing questions and problems that had been of only minor importance to their classical predecessors, questions such as: Is theology possible? What is the subject matter of theology? What is the epistemological status of theological claims? At the beginning of his *Institutes of the Christian Religion*, John Calvin argued that knowledge of God and knowledge of self are closely related. But Calvin did not feel the need to demonstrate that knowledge of God is possible. He simply assumed it. Few modern theologians, however, have thought they could assume the reality of knowledge of God.

The reasons for this important difference between classical and modern theology are both numerous and complex. Modern science and its discoveries about the nature of the universe and the human creature, coupled with the development of historical-critical methods for reading and interpreting the Bible, sharply challenged some of the assumptions that had informed the work of earlier theologians. More than anything else, however, it was the cumulative attack on Christianity during the Enlightenment of the seventeenth and eighteenth centuries that devastated traditional forms of theology. The history of theology in the nineteenth and twentieth centuries is the story of a search for new methods, idioms, and paradigms by which to do theology.

1

FOR FURTHER STUDY

For surveys of the development of theology, especially Protestant and Reformed Theology, in the nineteenth and twentieth centuries, see the following: Karl Barth, *Protestant Theology in the Nineteenth Century: Its Background and History* (Valley Forge: Judson, 1972). Hendrikus Berkhof, *200 Yahre Theologie: Ein Reisebericht* (Neukirchen-Vluyn: Neukirchener Verlag, 1985). G. C. Berkouwer, *A Half Century of Theology: Movements and Motives*, trans. Lewis B. Smedes (Grand Rapids: Wm. B. Eerdmans, 1977). B. A. Gerrish, *Tradition and the Modern World: Reformed Theology in the Nineteenth Century* (Chicago and London: University of Chicago Press, 1978). Alasdair I. C. Heron, *A Century of Protestant Theology* (Philadelphia: Westminster, 1980). Hugh Ross Mackintosh, *Types of Modern Theology: Schleiermacher to Barth* (New York: Charles Scribner's Sons, n.d.). Claude Welch, *Protestant Thought in the Nineteenth Century*, 2 vols., Vol. 1: 1799–1870; Vol. 2: 1870–1914 (New Haven and London: Yale University Press, 1972, 1985).

THE TASK OF THEOLOGY

Theology in the nineteenth and twentieth centuries is a series of attempts to reconstruct the interpretation of faith in such a manner that it is intelligible to contemporary culture and responsive to its challenges, but also congruent with the faith of the church through the ages. That is no small undertaking.

The most important attempts to reconstruct theology in the Reformed tradition differ to a remarkable extent. Friedrich Schleiermacher (1768–1834) and Karl Barth (1886–1968) dominate the period. Both were Reformed theologians, but they constructed theology very differently, in part because they perceived the world in which they lived and the task of theology from quite different perspectives.

In the last half of the twentieth century, most Reformed theologians became acutely aware of the perspectival and cultural contexts in which all theology is written. As new voices began to be heard in both the larger church and Reformed communities—voices of women, African Americans, theologians from oppressed communities—theologians came to recognize that Reformed theology, if it is to be true to its deepest convictions concerning the openness of the church to God's reforming activity, had not only to rethink its assumptions about theological method, but also to listen to quite different proposals about the meaning of the gospel.

FOR FURTHER STUDY

Karl Barth, *Anselm: Fides Quaerens Intellectum (Faith in Search of Understanding)*, trans. Ian W. Robertson (Cleveland and New York: World, 1960). Hendrikus Berkhof, *Introduction to the Study of Dogmatics*, trans. John Vriend (Grand Rapids: Wm. B. Eerdmans, 1985). Edward Farley, *Ecclesial Reflection: An Anatomy of Theological Method* (Philadelphia: Fortress, 1982). Douglas John Hall, *Thinking the Faith: Christian Theology in a North American Context* (Minneapolis: Augsburg, 1989). Hans Küng and David Tracy, eds., *Paradigm Change in Theology: A Symposium for the Future*, trans. Margaret

Kohl (New York: Crossroad, 1991). Jürgen Moltmann, *Theology Today: Two Contributions Toward Making Theology Present*, trans. John Bowden (London: SCM, and Philadelphia: Trinity, 1988). Dietrich Ritschl, *The Logic of Theology: A Brief Account of the Relationship Between Basic Concepts in Theology*, trans. John Bowden (Philadelphia: Fortress, 1986). Friedrich Schleiermacher, *Brief Outline on the Study of Theology*, trans. Terrence N. Tice (Richmond: John Knox, 1966). Juan Luis Segundo, S.J., *The Liberation of Theology*, trans. John Drury (Maryknoll, N.Y.: Orbis, 1976). David Tracy, *Blessed Rage for Order: The New Pluralism in Theology* (New York: Seabury, 1975).

Dogmatics and Piety

Friedrich Schleiermacher is usually described as the founder of modern theology, and appropriately so. In 1799, Schleiermacher published *On Religion: Speeches to Its Cultured Despisers*, in which he sought to make religion intelligible to those artists and intellectuals of his day who could no longer accept Christian faith in its traditional language and form. In 1810, Schleiermacher became dean of the theological faculty of the University of Berlin, and in 1821–22, published *The Christian Faith*, one of the most important texts in Reformed theology in the modern period. It is a remarkable book in several respects. In it Schleiermacher constructs a new idiom—religious self-consciousness—for the interpretation of Christian faith, and he insists that Christian doctrines are inseparable from the affective life of the religious self-consciousness.

SOURCE
Schleiermacher, *Christian Faith*, 76–78.

FOR FURTHER STUDY
Karl Barth, *The Theology of Schleiermacher: Lectures at Göttingen, Winter Semester of 1923/24*, ed. Dietrich Ritschl, trans. Geoffrey W. Bromiley (Grand Rapids: Wm. B. Eerdmans, 1982). James O. Duke and Robert F. Streetman, eds., *Barth and Schleiermacher: Beyond the Impasse?* (Philadelphia: Fortress, 1988). B. A. Gerrish, "Continuity and Change: Friedrich Schleiermacher on the Task of Theology," in *Tradition and the Modern World*, 13–48. Richard R. Niebuhr, *Schleiermacher on Christ and Religion* (New York: Charles Scribner's Sons, 1964). Martin Redeker, *Schleiermacher: Life and Thought*, trans. John Wallhausser (Philadelphia: Fortress, 1973).

IV. THE RELATION OF DOGMATICS TO CHRISTIAN PIETY.

§ 15. Christian doctrines are accounts of the Christian religious affections set forth in speech.

NOTE.—Cf. § 3, 5.

1. All religious emotions, to whatever type and level of religion they belong, have this in common with all other modifications of the affective

self-consciousness, that as soon as they have reached a certain stage and a certain definiteness they manifest themselves outwardly by mimicry in the most direct and spontaneous way, by means of facial features and movements of voice and gesture, which we regard as their expression. Thus we definitely distinguish the expression of devoutness from that of a sensuous gladness or sadness, by the analogy of each man's knowledge of himself. Indeed, we can even conceive that, for the purpose of maintaining the religious affections and securing their repetition and propagation (especially if they were common to a number of people), the elements of that natural expression of them might be put together into sacred signs and symbolical acts, without the thought having perceptibly come in between at all. But we can scarcely conceive such a low development of the human spirit, such a defective culture, and such a meagre use of speech, that each person would not, according to the level of reflection on which he stands, become in his various mental states likewise an object to himself, in order to comprehend them in idea and retain them in the form of thought. Now this endeavour has always directed itself particularly to the religious emotions; and this, considered in its own inward meaning, is what our proposition means by an account of the religious affections. But while thought cannot proceed even inwardly without the use of speech, nevertheless there are, so long as it remains merely inward, fugitive elements in this procedure, which do indeed in some measure indicate the object, but not in such a way that either the formation or the synthesis of concepts (in however wide a sense we take the word "concept") is sufficiently definite for communication. It is only when this procedure has reached such a point of cultivation as to be able to represent itself outwardly in definite speech, that it produces a real doctrine (*Glaubenssatz*), by means of which the utterances of the religious consciousness come into circulation more surely and with a wider range than is possible through the direct expression. But no matter whether the expression is natural or figurative, whether it indicates its object directly or only by comparison and delimitation, it is still a doctrine.

2. Now Christianity everywhere presupposes that consciousness has reached this stage of development. The whole work of the Redeemer Himself was conditioned by the communicability of His self-consciousness by means of speech, and similarly Christianity has always and everywhere spread itself solely by preaching. Every proposition which can be an element of the Christian preaching (κήρυγμα) is also a doctrine, because it bears witness to the determination of the religious self-consciousness as inward certainty. And every Christian doctrine is also a

4

part of the Christian preaching, because every such doctrine expresses as a certainty the approximation to the state of blessedness which is to be effected through the means ordained by Christ. But this preaching very soon split up into three different types of speech, which provide as many different forms of doctrine: the poetic, the rhetorical (which is directed partly outwards, as combative and commendatory, and partly inwards, as rather disciplinary and challenging), and finally the descriptively didactic. But the relation of communication through speech to communication through symbolic action varies very much according to time and place, the former having always retreated into the background in the Eastern Church (for when the letter of doctrine has become fixed and unalterable, it is in its effect much nearer to symbolic action than to free speech), and having become ever more prominent in the Western Church. And in the realm of speech it is just the same with these three modes of communication. The relation in which they stand to each other, the general degree of richness, and the amount of living intercourse in which they unfold themselves, as they nourish themselves on one another and pass over into one another—these things testify not so much to the degree or level of piety as rather to the character of the communion or fellowship and its ripeness for reflection and contemplation. Thus this communication is, on the one hand, something different from the piety itself, though the latter cannot, any more than anything else which is human, be conceived entirely separated from all communication. But, on the other hand, the doctrines in all their forms have their ultimate ground so exclusively in the emotions of the religious self-consciousness, that where these do not exist the doctrines cannot arise.

The Inductive Method

Charles Hodge (1797–1878) taught theology at Princeton Theological Seminary for almost fifty years and is one of the major figures in what came to be known as the "Princeton school of theology." By virtue of his position at Princeton and his frequent writing in *The Biblical Repertory and Princeton Review*, Hodge exercised enormous influence on American Presbyterianism. He was a staunch defender of old school Calvinism. His three-volume *Systematic Theology* (1872–73), published near the end of his life, continued his influence into the late nineteenth and early twentieth centuries. At the beginning of his *Systematic Theology*, Hodge describes his approach to theology as an "inductive method." By inductive he meant, however, not an appeal to experience, but a theology that begins with the "facts" contained in the Bible.

SOURCE

Hodge, *Systematic Theology*, 2:10–12.

FOR FURTHER STUDY

Jacks B. Rogers and Donald K. McKim, *The Authority and Interpretation of the Bible: An Historical Approach* (New York: Harper & Row, 1979), 274–98. David F. Wells, *Reformed Theology in America: A History of Its Modern Development* (Grand Rapids: Wm. B. Eerdmans, 1985), 35–59.

A. THE INDUCTIVE METHOD AS APPLIED TO THEOLOGY

The Bible is to the theologian what nature is to the man of science. It is his store-house of facts; and his method of ascertaining what the Bible teaches, is the same as that which the natural philosopher adopts to ascertain what nature teaches. In the first place, he comes to his task with all the assumptions above mentioned. He must assume the validity of those laws of belief which God has impressed upon our nature. In these laws are included some which have no direct application to the natural sciences. Such, for example, as the essential distinction between right and wrong; that nothing contrary to virtue can be enjoined by God; that it cannot be right to do evil that good may come; that sin deserves punishment, and other similar first truths, which God has implanted in the constitution of all moral beings, and which no objective revelation can possibly contradict. These first principles, however, are not to be arbitrarily assumed. No man has a right to lay down his own opinions, however firmly held, and call them "first truths of reason," and make them the source or test of Christian doctrines. Nothing can rightfully be included under the category of first truths, or laws of belief, which cannot stand the tests of universality and necessity, to which many add self-evidence. But self-evidence is included in universality and necessity, in so far, that nothing which is not self-evident can be universally believed, and what is self-evident forces itself on the mind of every intelligent creature.

Facts to Be Collected

In the second place, the duty of the Christian theologian is to ascertain, collect, and combine all the facts which God has revealed concerning himself and our relation to Him. These facts are all in the Bible. This is true, because everything revealed in nature, and in the constitution of man concerning God and our relation to Him, is contained and authenticated in Scripture. It is in this sense that "the Bible, and the Bible alone, is the religion of Protestants." It may be admitted that the truths which the theologian has to reduce to a science, or, to speak more humbly, which he has to arrange and harmonize, are revealed partly in the external works of God, partly in the constitution of our nature, and partly in the religious experience of believers; yet lest we should err in our inferences from the works of God, we have a clearer revelation of all that nature reveals, in his word; and lest we should misinterpret our own consciousness and the laws of our nature, everything that can be legitimately learned from that source will be found recognized and authenticated in the Scriptures; and lest we should attribute to the teaching of the Spirit the operations of our own natural affections, we find in the Bible the norm and standard of all genuine religious experience. The Scriptures teach not only the truth, but what are the effects of the truth on the heart and conscience, when applied with saving power by the Holy Ghost.

The Theologian to Be Guided by the Same Rules as the Man of Science

In the third place, the theologian must be guided by the same rules in the collection of facts, as govern the man of science.

1. This collection must be made with diligence and care. It is not an easy work. There is in every department of investigation great liability to error. Almost all false theories in science and false doctrines in theology are due in a great degree to mistakes as to matters of fact. A distinguished naturalist said he repeated an experiment a thousand times before he felt authorized to announce the result to the scientific world as an established fact.

2. This collection of facts must not only be carefully conducted, but also comprehensive, and if possible, exhaustive. An imperfect induction of facts led men for ages to believe that the sun moved round the earth, and that the earth was an extended plain. In theology a partial induction of particulars has led to like serious errors. It is a fact that the Scriptures attribute omniscience to Christ. From this it was inferred that He could not have had a finite intelligence, but that the Logos was clothed in Him with a human body with its animal life. But it is also a Scriptural fact that ignorance and intellectual progress, as well as omniscience, are ascribed to our Lord. Both facts, therefore, must be included in our doctrine of his person. We must admit that He had a human, as well as a divine intelligence. It is a fact that everything that can be predicated of a sinless man, is in the Bible, predicated of Christ; and it is also a fact

that everything that is predicated of God is predicated of our Lord; hence it has been inferred that there were two Christs,—two persons,— the one human, the other divine, and that they dwelt together very much as the Spirit dwells in the believer; or, as evil spirits dwelt in demoniacs. But this theory overlooked the numerous facts which prove the individual personality of Christ. It was the same person who said, "I thirst," who said, "Before Abraham was I am." The Scriptures teach that Christ's death was designed to reveal the love of God, and to secure the reformation of men. Hence Socinus denied that his death was an expiation for sin, or satisfaction of justice. The latter fact, however, is as clearly revealed as the former; and therefore both must be taken into account in our statement of the doctrine concerning the design of Christ's death.

The Revealed Word of God

The most important Reformed theologian in the twentieth century was the Swiss theologian Karl Barth (1886–1968). Barth's theology marked a clear break with the theological liberalism that had dominated so much of nineteenth- and early-twentieth-century theology. His experience as pastor of a small Swiss congregation, combined with the intellectual and physical devastation of World War I, led Barth to seek some basis for constructing theology other than on human experience and its "religious dimension." In contrast to a liberalism that emphasized God's immanence, Barth wrote a commentary on Paul's letter to the church at Rome that announced a God who is wholly other than the world. Later, in the early 1930s, Barth published a commentary on Anselm in which he insisted that theology must begin with what God has revealed and not with some innate human capacity for the infinite. This emphasis on the objective reality of revelation was also a major principle in Barth's monumental work, *Church Dogmatics*, at the beginning of which he states that the task of theology is critical reflection on the language and activity of the church.

SOURCE

Barth, *Church Dogmatics*, I/1:3–4.

FOR FURTHER STUDY

Eberhard Busch, *Karl Barth: His Life from Letters and Autobiographical Texts*, trans. John Bowden (Philadelphia: Fortress, 1976). George Hunsinger, *How to Read Karl Barth: The Shape of His Theology* (New York: Oxford University Press, 1991). Eberhard Jüngel, *Karl Barth: A Theological Legacy*, trans. Garrett E. Paul (Philadelphia: Westminster, 1986).

§ I.

The Task of Dogmatics

As a theological discipline dogmatics is the scientific self-examination of the Christian Church with respect to the content of its distinctive talk about God.

I. The Church, Theology, Science

Dogmatics is a theological discipline. But theology is a function of the Church.

The Church confesses God as it talks about God. It does so first by its existence in the action of each individual believer. And it does so secondly by its specific action as a fellowship, in proclamation by preaching and the administration of the sacraments, in worship, in its internal and external mission including works of love amongst the sick, the weak and those in jeopardy. Fortunately the reality of the Church does not coincide with its action. But its action coincides with the fact that alike in its existence in believers and its communal existence as such it speaks about God. Its action is "theology" in both the broader and the narrower sense. . . .

But as it confesses God the Church also confesses both the humanity and the responsibility of its action. It realises that it is exposed to fierce temptation as it speaks of God, and it realises that it must give an account to God for the way in which it speaks. The first and last and decisive answer to this twofold compulsion consists in the fact that it rests content with the grace of the One whose strength is mighty in weakness. But in so doing it recognises and takes up as an active Church the further human task of criticising and revising its speech about God. This brings us to the concept of theology in the third, strictest and proper sense of the word. . . .

Theology as a science, in distinction from the "theology" of the simple testimony of faith and life and the "theology" of the service of God, is a measure taken by the Church in relation to the vulnerability and responsibility of its utterance. It would be meaningless without justifying grace, which here too can alone make good what man as such invariably does badly. But it can be meaningful as an act of obedience to this grace, i.e., of the obedience in which here too man may believe that he is doing well even though he does not see it. . . .

The Church produces theology in this special and peculiar sense by subjecting itself to self-examination. It puts to itself the question of truth, i.e., it measures its action, its talk about God, against its being as the Church. Thus theology exists in this special and peculiar sense because before it and apart from it there is in the Church talk about God. Theology follows the talk of the Church to the extent that in its question as to the correctness of its utterance it does not measure it by an alien standard but by its own source and object. Theology guides the talk of the Church to the extent that it concretely reminds it that in all circumstances it is fallible human work which in the matter of relevance or irrelevance lies in the balance, and must be obedience to grace if it is to be well done. Theology accompanies the utterance of the Church to the extent that it is itself no more than human "talk about God," so that with this talk it stands under the judgment that begins at the house of God and lives by the promise given to the Church.

The work in which the Church submits to this self-examination falls into three circles which intersect in such a way that the centre of each is also within the circumference of the other two, so that in view of that which alone can be the centre it is as well neither to affirm nor to construct a systematic centre, i.e., the centre of a circle embracing the other three. The question of truth, with which theology is concerned throughout, is the question as to the agreement of the Church's distinctive talk about God with the being of the Church. The criterion of past, future and therefore present Christian utterance is thus the being of the Church, namely, Jesus Christ, God in His gracious revealing and reconciling address to man. Does Christian utterance derive from Him? Does it lead to Him? Is it conformable to Him? None of these questions can be put apart, but each is to be put independently and with all possible force. Hence theology as biblical theology is the question of the basis, as practical theology the question of the goal and as dogmatic theology the question of the content of the distinctive utterance of the Church.

The Crisis of Identity and Relevance

Four years before Barth died in 1968, Jürgen Moltmann (b. 1926) published *Theology of Hope*, a book which in many ways continued the Barthian tradition, but which also attempted to come to terms with themes, such as eschatology, to which Barth had not given a great deal of attention. The sequel, *The Crucified God*, demonstrated Moltmann's sensitivity to the events that took place in World War II and amidst the social chaos of the 1960s. Theology must attend to the situation in which it finds itself, Moltmann argued, if it is to be relevant, and, yet, at the same time it must be faithful to the gospel if it is to maintain its authentic Christian identity. For Moltmann, this meant that theology must place the cross at the center of its understanding of God and rethink its interpretation of the Trinity. It is the crucified and suffering Christ who enables the church to address the suffering and oppression rampant in the world with a word of hope.

SOURCE

Moltmann, *Crucified God*, 7.

FOR FURTHER STUDY

Moltmann, *Theology of Hope*. Idem, *The Church*. Idem, *The Trinity and the Kingdom*.

THE IDENTITY AND RELEVANCE
OF FAITH

If it is true that the inner criterion of whether or not Christian theology is *Christian* lies in the crucified Christ, we come back to Luther's lapidary statement: *Crux probat omnia*. In Christianity the cross is the test of everything which deserves to be called Christian. One may add that the cross alone, and nothing else, is its test, since the cross refutes everything, and excludes the syncretistic elements in Christianity. This is a hard saying. To many it sounds unattractive and unmodern, and to others rigid and orthodox. I will try to disappoint both.

We may want to make Christian theology reveal that it is Christian, but this cannot be done in abstract and timeless terms, or from the mere desire for self-assertion. It has a definable and circumscribed place amongst modern problems. The Christian life of theologians, churches and human beings is faced more than ever today with a double crisis: the *crisis of relevance* and the *crisis of identity*. These two crises are complementary. The more theology and the church attempt to become relevant to the problems of the present day, the more deeply they are drawn into the crisis of their own Christian identity. The more they attempt to assert their identity in traditional dogmas, rights and moral notions, the more irrelevant and unbelievable they become. This double crisis can be more accurately described as the *identity-involvement dilemma*. We shall see how far, in these specific experiences of a double crisis, reflection upon the cross leads to the clarification of what can be called Christian identity and what can be called Christian relevance, in critical solidarity with our contemporaries.

The Challenge of Liberation Theology

In the last third of the twentieth century, a new theological movement known as "liberation theology" emerged in Latin America and other parts of the

Third World and among African Americans and feminists in North America. Liberation theology argues that despite its claim to place the Bible at the center of its faith and life, Western Christianity had ignored some obvious themes in the Bible, the most important of which was God's "preferential option for the poor." Western Christianity, blinded by its comfort and self-interest, had failed to heed the call of the gospel to commit itself to solidarity with the poor and oppressed of the world. It had failed to do so in part because it continued to understand theology to be a matter of theory and practice (application) rather than a matter of praxis in which reflection emerges out of the prior commitment to and participation in God's liberating activity among the oppressed.

In order to clarify its understanding of liberation theology and the relation between liberation theology and Reformed theology, the Presbyterian Church in the United States, through its Council on Theology and Culture, commissioned Jorge Lara-Braud to write a monograph on these issues. It was published in 1980 under the title *What Is Liberation Theology? Answers from Within and Reflections from the Reformed Tradition*.

SOURCE

Jorge Lara-Braud, *What Is Liberation Theology? Answers from Within and Reflections from the Reformed Tradition* (Atlanta: General Assembly Mission Board of the Presbyterian Church in the United States, 1980), 36–38.

FOR FURTHER STUDY

José Míguez Bonino, *Doing Theology in a Revolutionary Situation: Toward a Christian Political Ethics* (Philadelphia: Fortress, 1975). James H. Cone, *God of the Oppressed* (New York: Seabury, 1975). Gustavo Gutiérrez, *A Theology of Liberation*, trans. Sister Caridad Inda and John Eagleson (Maryknoll, N.Y.: Orbis, 1973). Letty M. Russell, *Human Liberation in a Feminist Perspective—A Theology* (Philadelphia: Westminster, 1974).

REFLECTIONS FROM THE
REFORMED TRADITION

. . . Latin American liberation theology desires to contribute to the life and reflection of the universal Christian community. . . . This invitation to dialogue encourages us as members of the Presbyterian Church in the U.S. to listen to liberation theology and then to pose our own questions to the challenge of our Latin American colleagues and to that of U.S. liberation theologies, whether Black, feminist, or some other. There are six areas in which the dialogue for us Presbyterians will be especially demanding, even painful.

First we may begin by remembering that the methodological principle of Reformed theology is *ecclesia reformata semper reformanda*, the church reformed and always to be reformed, according to the Word of God. Our tradition is one that calls for perennial reformation, not unlike what liberation theology calls permanent transformation. The Reformed tradition also recognizes that all theologies are human creations, historically conditioned and subject to correction in the light of God's self-revelation. That revelation is given in Jesus Christ, is mediated in Scripture, and is constantly re-presented to us by the Holy Spirit, who brings us new light on the Word. So we can hear liberation theology as stressing again the growing, changing, historically relative character of theology based on revelation.

At the same time we may raise questions about the tendency to stress ideology in both non-pejorative and pejorative senses. Sometimes it sounds not only as if there is no escaping the relativity of interpretation but also as if there is no true or continuing content to revelation. So ideology in the non-pejorative sense means the relativizing of all doctrine and every ethical principle. For the Reformed tradition, the link between the Bible and human understanding and human action as an expression of faith is considerably more than an ideology and certainly more than a "learning to learn" (Segundo). For us in the Reformed faith, the Bible provides theological principles and ethical paradigms which may not be timeless, but which withstand the test of time.

Liberation theologians are further contending that any theology not born from "sharing in the sufferings of God in the world" (Bonhoeffer) is ideology in the pejorative sense. Reformed theology has also understood that theology written in books must be written in lives, the truest test of a person's faith being love for the neighbor. The Reformed tradition has also held that believers are called to transform society in accordance with the purpose of God. Calvin wrote: "Tyrants and their cruelty cannot be endured without great weariness and sorrow . . . for God hears the cries and groanings of those who cannot bear injustice." At the same time Reformed theology will call into question the tendency to call pejoratively ideology any theology but one's own or to suggest that the situation of the poor and oppressed is somehow free from the taint of sin, selfishness, and loveless disregard for others.

Second, central to the method of liberation theology is the hermeneutical circle. That such a circle, involving the Word of God, especially Scripture, in interaction with the life and experience of the believer (and the believing community), exists cannot be denied. We always come to the Word from our own experience as well as take the Word to our experience. The liberation theologians, however, do not seem really to have a hermeneutical *circle*, for they talk about the "ideological suspicion" in experience leading to a new system and then to a new exegesis. In actuality they seem to be calling for a theology based more on experience than on the Word, which for Reformed theology is an inversion of norms. So, while we are reminded properly by liberation theologians of the inevitable role of experience against our tendency to naive biblicism, we must also remind them of the need to have experience corrected and transformed by the living Word in the listening to Scripture.

Third, we may also note some themes common to both liberation theology and Reformed theology: the sovereignty of God over all existence; Jesus Christ as the Savior and the Lord of history; the Holy Spirit as the one who constitutes the Church and works within and beyond the Church; the triumph of the grace of God in Christ in the forgiveness of sin and the removal of its consequences; the Church as a sign of the reality, present and future, of God's new creation, marked by the holiness which is the gift and call of the Spirit to believers and the Church. We can rejoice in the new insights into these common convictions that liberation theologians bring us and in the call that comes through their earnestness and their witness to realize these convictions more adequately and truly in our individual lives and our common life as the Church.

Fourth, the three-fold characterization of liberation as involving human action, as this-worldly, and as intended for all people raises serious challenges to Reformed theology as commonly understood in our church. We have been careful to claim that true liberation is God's work of realizing the kingdom. Perhaps we need to be reminded that the kingdom is also our human task to realize, and that God may use people and movements that do not acknowledge the lordship of Christ to accomplish His purpose on earth. At the same time we need to remind liberation theology that our ultimate trust and the ultimate power of liberation does not reside in human movements or in our power to accomplish good ends, but in God.

We also need to be reminded that despite the common American orthodox and evangelical attempts to deny it, Reformed faith along with liberation theology has always seen liberation and salvation as transforming life in this world—providing new life and new conditions of life for persons and societies. To be recalled from an excessive otherworldliness to our expectation and responsibility for this life is at once realistic, biblical, and Reformed. Yet we must recall for liberation theologians that while utopian visions may enable the translation of biblical understandings into concrete ethical and political action, still every utopia is flawed by human sin, and every achievement of justice and love is partial, incomplete, and even distorted. Realization of the kingdom in truth and full power lies beyond the present age in which we have only its partial presence and its first-fruits at best.

Further, we need to hear that both the power and love of God and the full incarnation and atonement of Jesus Christ imply that the promised liberation is not limited to some favored group but is for all people. Too often we have used our rationalized theology to restrict salvation to some chosen group, certainly including us and our kind of people and exclusive of those who are different. We thus seek to limit God's grace in a way that has no warrant in Scripture, and we limit the power of Christ's atoning work, which involves all human beings and indeed the whole created order. We are too fearful of what we call "universalism" lest we have nothing of value to offer in evangelism at home and abroad. The fact is that powerful evangelism and authentic mission involve not the giving of something we possess but the announcing of what God has done, is doing, and will do. At the same time, that announcement involves and must never obscure the centrality, sufficiency, and indispensability of Jesus Christ. All liberation and salvation is through him and his work, even when that is hidden and unacknowledged.

A fifth issue is liberation theology's perplexing use of Marxist theory not only to analyze and repudiate capitalism, but also to opt for the socialist alternative as a structure more akin to the demands of God's kingdom. The actual socialist societies we know about are uniformly authoritarian, if not totalitarian, with a consequent loss of basic democratic freedoms (as Moltmann underscores in his "Open Letter to Míguez Bonino"). Yet, Latin American theologians insist there are no "third ways" so that they leave no room for European-style democratic socialism or for a representative democracy based on a possible, but as yet unknown economic democracy. Their faith in the human capacity for good is not matched by its actual record whether in socialist or capitalist societies, a Calvinist would observe. The Latin American reply is, of course, that socialism is yet to be built, to be indigenized, and even when it does begin, it will be a process of permanent self-correction.

A derivative question from the "instrumental use of Marxism" is really whether it is Marxist theory only which comes to the aid of theology, or something beyond theory, Marxist philosophy *as a system*. In the latter case Reformed theology would question whether the case for a specifically *Christian* theology of liberation can still be made. The recently adopted Confession of Faith of the Reformed Presbyterian Church of

Cuba is a case in point. For American Calvinists it might be too much of a concession to Marxist socialism to build an account of Christian faith on the notion of God as worker and the human being also as worker. For other Calvinists, certainly for those of Cuba who adopted the Confession, it is the only responsible way to give the account of their faith.

Finally, we are troubled by the ecclesiology of liberation theology, which sees the church in conflictive categories. Here Latin American, Black, and feminist theologians alike challenge what we have always understood about the unity and catholicity of the Church. Now we are confronted in the interest of a new understanding of holiness and apostolicity in terms of the oppressed and their interests with the demand for struggle and division in the Church. That demand seems to deny or destroy the unity and catholicity of the Church. Liberation theologians would remind us, however, that the disunity already exists and the catholicity is already denied by the exclusion of persons by class or race or sex. They would remind us further that unity at the expense of justice is not Christian or biblical.

In other ways than these, too, we can and shall enter the dialogue with these liberation theologians. If we listen with care, we can, however painfully, shed our innocence as we receive new light from God's Word in the struggle with this theology of liberation. And we can in the integrity of our Reformed faith and the power of the Spirit seek to do God's will and thus come to know God's doctrine (John 7:17).

THE AUTHORITY OF SCRIPTURE

During the nineteenth and twentieth centuries one of the most basic convictions of Reformed theology—that, in the words of the Westminster Confession of Faith, the books of the Bible "are given by inspiration of God, to be the rule of faith and life"—was both challenged and reinterpreted within the Reformed community. In the last half of the nineteenth century, the fear of Darwinism in the United States and England prompted some Reformed theologians, especially those associated with the Princeton school to argue a "high" interpretation of the authority of scripture. The Bible was without error because it was authored by God. Apparent errors and contradictions were just that, only apparent; and if the original biblical texts or "autographs," now lost, could be recovered, the contradictions would be shown to be errors of transmission.

In the twentieth century, new developments in biblical criticism and theology forced a significant revision of Westminster's understanding of the authority of scripture. Karl Barth, among others, argued that there is only one Word of God—that is, Jesus Christ, the Word incarnate—and that the Bible consists of human words which, through the work of the Spirit, may become the unique and authoritative witness to Jesus Christ.

While nineteenth-century interpretations of Westminster suggested that the Bible's authority was some property it possessed, such as infallibility or inerrancy, theologians in the twentieth century, who followed Barth, understood the Bible to be authoritative not because of what it is, but because of what it does or how it functions, as the unique and indispensable witness to Jesus Christ.

FOR FURTHER STUDY

G. C. Berkouwer, *Holy Scripture*, trans. Jack B. Rogers (Grand Rapids: Wm. B. Eerdmans, 1975). Edward Farley and Peter C. Hodgson, "Scripture and Tradition," in *Christian Theology: An Introduction to Its Traditions and Tasks*, Peter C. Hodgson and Robert H. King, eds. (Philadelphia: Fortress, 1982), 35–61. Robert Clyde Johnson, *Authority in Protestant Theology* (Philadelphia: Westminster, 1959). Jack B. Rogers and Donald K. McKim, *The Authority and Interpretation of the Bible: An Historical Approach* (San Francisco: Harper & Row, 1979). Benjamin Breckinridge Warfield, *The Inspiration and Authority of the Bible*, ed. Samuel G. Craig (Philadelphia: The Presbyterian and Reformed Publishing Company, 1948).

The Lost Autographs of Scripture

While Charles Hodge and Benjamin Breckinridge Warfield (1851–1921) are the names best known from the Princeton school of theology, Hodge's son, Archibald Alexander Hodge (1823–86), named after the first professor of theology at Princeton, took the interpretation of biblical authority even one step further than had his illustrious father. In the second edition (1879) of his *Outlines of Theology*, A. A. Hodge argued that the original autographs of the Bible were indeed infallible.

SOURCE

A. A. Hodge, *Outlines of Theology: For Students and Laymen* (Grand Rapids: Zondervan, 1879), 66–69.

STATEMENT OF THE CHURCH DOCTRINE
OF INSPIRATION

In what sense and to what extent has the Church universally held the Bible to be inspired?

That the sacred writers were so influenced by the Holy Spirit that their writings are as a whole and in every part God's word to us—an authoritative revelation to us from God, indorsed by him, and sent to us as a rule of faith and practice, the original autographs of which are absolutely infallible when interpreted in the sense intended, and hence are clothed with absolute divine authority.

What is meant by "plenary inspiration"?

A divine influence full and sufficient to secure its end. The end in this case secured is the perfect infallibility of the Scriptures in every part, as a record of fact and doctrine both in thought and verbal expression. So that although they come to us through the instrumentality of the minds, hearts, imaginations, consciences, and wills of men, they are nevertheless in the strictest sense the word of God.

What is meant by the phrase "verbal inspiration," and how can it be proved that the words of the Bible were inspired?

It is meant that the divine influence, of whatever kind it may have been, which accompanied the sacred writers in what they wrote, extends to their expression of their thoughts in language, as well as to the thoughts themselves. The effect being that in the original autograph copies the language expresses the thought God intended to convey with infallible accuracy, so that the words as well as the thoughts are God's revelation to us.

That this influence did extend to the words appears—1st, from the very design of inspiration, which is, not to secure the infallible correctness of the opinions of the inspired men themselves (Paul and Peter differed, Gal. ii.11, and sometimes the prophet knew not what he wrote), but to secure an infallible record of the truth. But a record consists of language.

2d. Men think in words, and the more definitely they think the more are their thoughts immediately associated with an exactly appropriate verbal expression. Infallibility of thought can not be secured or preserved independently of an infallible verbal rendering.

3d. The Scriptures affirm this fact, 1 Cor. ii. 13; 1 Thess. ii. 13.

4th. The New Testament writers, while quoting from the Old Testament for purposes of argument, often base their argument upon the very words used, thus ascribing authority to the word as well as the thought.— Matt. xxii. 32, and Ex. iii.6, 16; Matt. xxii. 45, and Psalms cx.1; Gal. iii.16, and Gen. xvii. 7.

By what means does the Church hold that God has effected the result above defined?

The Church doctrine recognizes the fact that every part of Scripture is at once a product of God's and of man's agency. The human writers have produced each his part in the free and natural exercise of his personal faculties under his historical conditions. God has also so acted concurrently in and through them that the whole organism of Scripture and every part thereof is his word to us, infallibly true in the sense intended and absolutely authoritative.

God's agency includes the three following elements:

1st. His PROVIDENTIAL agency in producing the Scriptures. The whole course of redemption, of which revelation and inspiration are special functions, was a special providence directing the evolution of a specially providential history. Here the natural and the supernatural continually interpenetrate. But, as is of necessity the case, the natural was always the rule and the supernatural the exception; yet as little subject to accident, and as much the subject of rational design as the natural itself. Thus God providentially produced the very man for the precise occasion, with the faculties, qualities, education, and gracious experience needed for the production of the intended writing. Moses, David, Isaiah, Paul, or John, genius and character, nature and grace, peasant, philosopher, or prince, the man, and with him each subtile personal accident, was providentially prepared at the proper moment as the necessary instrumental precondition of the work to be done.

2d. REVELATION of truth not otherwise attainable. Whenever the writer was not possessed, or could not naturally become possessed, of the knowledge God intended to communicate, it was supernaturally revealed to him by vision or language. This revelation was supernatural, objective to the recipient, and assured to him to be truth of divine origin by appropriate evidence. This direct revelation applies to a large element of the sacred Scriptures, such as prophecies of future events, the peculiar doctrines of Christianity, the promises and threatenings of God's word, etc., but it applies by no means to all the contents of Scripture.

3d. INSPIRATION. The writers were the subjects of a plenary divine influence, called inspiration, which acted upon and through their natural faculties in all they wrote, directing them in the choice of subject and the whole course of thought and verbal expression, so as while not interfering with the natural exercise of their faculties, they freely and spontaneously produce the very writing which God designed, and which thus possesses the attributes of infallibility and authority as above defined.

This inspiration differs, therefore, from revelation—(1.) In that it was a constant experience of the sacred writers in all they wrote, and it affects the equal infallibility of all the elements of the writings they produced. While, as before said, revelation was supernaturally vouchsafed only when it was needed. (2.) In that revelation communicated objectively to the mind of the writer truth otherwise unknown. While Inspiration was a divine influence flowing into the sacred writer subjectively, communicating nothing, but guiding their faculties in their natural exercise to the producing an infallible record of the matters of history, doctrine, prophecy, etc., which God designed to send through them to his Church.

It differs from spiritual illumination, in that spiritual illumination is an essential element in the sanctifying work of the Holy Spirit common to all true Christians. It never leads to the knowledge of new truth, but only to the personal discernment of the spiritual beauty and power of truth already revealed in the Scriptures.

Inspiration is a special influence of the Holy Spirit peculiar to the prophets and apostles, and attending them only in the exercise of their functions as accredited teachers. Most of them were the subjects both of inspiration and spiritual illumination. Some, as Balaam, being unregenerate were inspired, though destitute of spiritual illumination.

The Bible's Witness to Jesus Christ

In his *Church Dogmatics*, Karl Barth developed an interpretation of the authority of the Bible that differed significantly from that of the Westminster Confession of Faith and the Princeton school of theology. Barth rejected the notion that the Bible is authoritative because of what it is or what it contains. "The Bible is not a book of oracles," according to Barth; rather, it is "genuine witness."

SOURCE

Barth, *Church Dogmatics*, I/2: 506–8.

FOR FURTHER STUDY

David H. Kelsey, *The Uses of Scripture in Recent Theology* (Philadelphia: Fortress, 1975), 39–50.

In the statement: we believe that the Bible is the Word of God, we must first emphasise and consider the word "believe." Believing does, of course, involve recognising and knowing. Believing is not an obscure and indeterminate feeling. It is a clear hearing, apperceiving, thinking and then speaking and doing. Believing is also a free human act, i.e., one which is not destroyed or disturbed by any magic; but, of course, a free act which as such is conditioned and determined by an encounter, a challenge, an act of lordship which confronts man, which man cannot bring about himself, which exists either as an event or not at all. Therefore believing is not something arbitrary. It does not control its object. It is a recognising, knowing, hearing, apperceiving, thinking, speaking and doing which is over-mastered by its object. Belief that the Bible is the Word of God presupposes, therefore, that this over-mastering has already taken place, that the Bible has already proved itself to be the Word of God, so that we can and must recognise it to be such. But when and where there is this proof, it must be a matter of the Word of God itself. We must say at once, that of itself the mere presence of the Bible and our own presence with our capacities for knowing an object does not mean and never will mean the reality or even the possibility of the proof that the Bible is the Word of God. On the contrary, we have to recognise that this situation as such, i.e., apart from faith, only means the impossibility of this proof. We have to recognise that faith as an irruption into this reality and possibility means the removing of a barrier in which we can only see and again and again see a miracle. And it is a miracle which we cannot explain apart from faith, or rather apart from the Word of God in which faith believes. Therefore the reality and possibility of it cannot be maintained or defended at all apart from faith and the Word. Nor can there be any assurances of it apart from faith and the Word. It is not only that we cannot attribute to ourselves any capacity or instrument for recognising the Word of God either in the Bible or elsewhere. It is also that if we are serious about the true humanity of the Bible, we obviously cannot attribute to the Bible as such the capacity—and in this it is distinguished, as we have seen, from the exalted and glorified humanity of Jesus Christ—in such a way to reveal God to us that by its very presence, by the fact that we can read it, it gives us a hearty faith in the Word of God spoken in it. It is there and always there as a sign, as a human and temporal word—and therefore also as a word which is conditioned and limited. It witnesses to God's revelation, but that does not mean that God's revelation is now before us in any kind of divine revealedness. The Bible is not a book of oracles; it is not an instrument of direct impartation. It is genuine witness. And how can it be witness of divine revelation, if the actual purpose, act and decision of God in His only-begotten Son, as seen and heard by the prophets and apostles in that Son, is dissolved in the Bible into a sum total of truths abstracted from that decision—and those truths are then propounded to us as truths of faith, salvation and revelation? If it tries to be more than witness, to be direct impartation, will it not keep from us the best, the one real thing, which God intends to tell and give us and which we ourselves need? But if it does not try to do this, if it is really witness, we must understand clearly what it means and involves that in itself it is only witness. It means the existence of those barriers which can be broken down only by miracle. The men whom we hear as witnesses speak as fallible, erring men like ourselves. What they say, and what we read as their word, can of itself lay claim to be the Word of God, but never sustain that claim. We can read and try to assess their word as a purely human word. It can be subjected to all kinds of immanent criticism, not only in respect of its philosophical, historical and ethical content, but even of its religious and theological. We can establish lacunae, inconsistencies and over-emphases. We may be alienated by a figure like that of Moses. We may quarrel with James or with Paul. We may have to admit that we can make little or nothing of large tracts of the Bible, as is often the case with the records of other men. We can take offence at the Bible. And in the light of the claim or the assertion that the Bible is the Word of God—granting that the miracle of faith and the Word does not intervene—we are bound to take offence at it. But this is a miracle which we cannot presuppose. We can remember it. We can wait for it. But we cannot set it up like one chessman with others, which we can "move" at the right moment. Therefore we are bound to take offence at the Bible in the light of that claim. If we do not, we have not yet realised the importance of that claim. Only the miracle of faith and the Word can genuinely and seriously prevent us from taking offence at the Bible. But the *theopneustia* of the Bible, the attitude of obedience in which it is written, the compelling fact that in it true men speak to us in the name of the true God: this—and here is the miracle of it—is not simply before us because the Bible is before us and we read the Bible. The *theopneustia* is the act of revelation in which the prophets and apostles in their humanity became what they were, and in which alone in their humanity they can become to us what they are.

The Bible as Witness to Jesus Christ in Twentieth-Century Reformed Confessions

Karl Barth's interpretation of the authority of the Bible is reflected in numerous twentieth-century Reformed confessional documents: "The Theological Declaration of Barmen" (1934), which Barth wrote, "The Confession of 1967" of the United Presbyterian Church in the United States of America, and *A Declaration of Faith*, written for but not adopted by the Presbyterian Church in the United States in 1977.

SOURCE

"The Theological Declaration of Barmen," in *Book of Confessions*, 8.10–12.

1. "I am the way, and the truth, and the life; no one comes to the Father, but by me." (John 14:6). "Truly, truly, I say to you, he who does not enter the sheepfold by the door but climbs in by another way, that man is a thief and a robber. . . . I am the door; if anyone enters by me, he will be saved." (John 10:1, 9.)

Jesus Christ, as he is attested for us in Holy Scripture, is the one Word of God which we have to hear and which we have to trust and obey in life and in death.

We reject the false doctrine, as though the Church could and would have to acknowledge as a source of its proclamation, apart from and besides this one Word of God, still other events and powers, figures and truths, as God's revelation.

SOURCE

"The Confession of 1967," in *Book of Confessions*, 9.27–30.

THE BIBLE

The one sufficient revelation of God is Jesus Christ, the Word of God incarnate, to whom the Holy Spirit bears unique and authoritative witness through the Holy Scriptures, which are received and obeyed as the word of God written. The Scriptures are not a witness among others, but the witness without parallel. The church has received the books of the Old and New Testaments as prophetic and apostolic testimony in which it hears the word of God and by which its faith and obedience are nourished and regulated.

The New Testament is the recorded testimony of apostles to the coming of the Messiah, Jesus of Nazareth, and the sending of the Holy Spirit to the Church. The Old Testament bears witness to God's faithfulness in his covenant with Israel and points the way to the fulfillment of his purpose in Christ. The Old Testament is indispensable to understanding the New, and is not itself fully understood without the New.

The Bible is to be interpreted in the light of its witness to God's work of reconciliation in Christ. The Scriptures, given under the guidance of the Holy Spirit, are nevertheless the words of men, conditioned by the language, thought forms, and literary fashions of the places and times at which they were written. They reflect views of life, history, and the cosmos which were then current. The church, therefore, has an obligation to approach the Scriptures with literary and historical understanding. As God has spoken his word in diverse cultural situations, the church is confident that he will continue to speak through the Scriptures in a changing world and in every form of human culture.

God's word is spoken to his church today where the Scriptures are faithfully preached and attentively read in dependence on the illumination of the Holy Spirit and with readiness to receive their truth and direction.

SOURCE

Declaration of Faith, 13.

(3) THE BIBLE IS THE WRITTEN
WORD OF GOD

Led by the Spirit of God
    the people of Israel and of the early church
preserved and handed on the story
    of what God had said and done in their midst
    and how they had responded to him.
These traditions were often shaped and reshaped
    by the uses to which the community put them.
They were cherished, written down, and collected
    as the holy literature of the people of God.

Through the inward witness of the same Spirit
    we acknowledge the authority of the Bible.
We accept the Old and New Testaments as the canon,
    or authoritative standard of faith and life,
    to which no further writings need be added.
The Scriptures of the Old and New Testaments
    are necessary, sufficient, and reliable
    as witnesses to Jesus Christ, the living Word.
We must test any word that comes to us
    from church, world, or inner experience
    by the Word of God in Scripture.

We subject to its judgment
　　all our understanding of doctrine and practice,
　　including this Declaration of Faith.
We believe the Bible to be the Word of God
　　as no other word written by human beings.

Relying on the Holy Spirit,
　　who opens our eyes and hearts,
　　we affirm our freedom to interpret Scripture responsibly.
God has chosen to address his inspired Word to us
　　through diverse and varied human writings.
Therefore we use the best available methods
　　to understand them in their historical and cultural settings
　　and the literary forms in which they are cast.
When we encounter apparent tensions and conflicts
　　in what Scripture teaches us to believe and do,
　　the final appeal must be to the authority of Christ.
Acknowledging that authority,
　　comparing Scripture with Scripture,
　　listening with respect to fellow-believers past and present,
　　　we anticipate that the Holy Spirit
　　　will enable us to interpret faithfully
　　　God's Word for our time and place.

The Functional Interpretation of Biblical Authority

In the twentieth century, several Reformed theologians have argued that the authority of the Bible should be understood in terms of its function within the life of the Christian community. One of the clearest statements of this point of view is David Kelsey's in *The Uses of Scripture in Recent Theology*.

SOURCE

David H. Kelsey, *The Uses of Scripture in Recent Theology* (Philadelphia: Fortress, 1975), 207–9.

AUTHORITY IN CHURCH AND WHERE TO TALK ABOUT SCRIPTURE

Both "scripture" and "authority" are best understood in functional terms. Since scripture's authority specifically for theology is a function of its authority for the common life of the church, it is best to review *first* how scripture's "normativeness" for the *church's life* may be understood in functional terms. We noted that to call a set of writings the "church's scripture" is by definition to say that they are "authority" for the church. It is to say that they are the writings that, given certain views of "church," *ought* to be *used* in her common life to nurture and correct her forms of speech and action so that she remains faithful to her task. They are "normative" precisely in that they are to be used in the context of self-critical reflection in which the church tests the forms of her common life and seeks to correct them where the need for that is apparent. In this use scripture is taken as having some kind of "logical force." That is, it is taken as *doing* something that decisively shapes the community's identity, whether teaching doctrine, proposing concepts, rendering an agent, expressing and occasioning saving events, etc. However, each different imaginative construal of the *discrimen*, i.e., the conjunction of God's presence and certain uses of scripture in the church, brings an importantly different sense of "authority." We saw that the differences can be noted (i) by attending to the different sorts of response each solicits (*belief* of doctrines taught, personal *appropriation* of concepts proposed, existential *encounter* with a present agent, quasi-*aesthetic response* to imagistic or symbolic "expressions" of the occurrence of saving events), (ii) by noting the different ranges of phenomena in relation to which each claims to be authoritative (beliefs, concepts, an agent's identity, modes of subjectivity), and, (iii) by distinguishing the various kinds of proximate basis for authority each assumes (something in the ideational mode, or in the mode of a concrete actuality, or in the mode of an ideal possibility).

This functionalist analysis of "scriptural authority over the church" brings with it an important implication concerning the conceptual home of some doctrines of scripture in some theological positions. Scripture's authority specifically for theology, we said, is a function of its authority for the common life of the church. Its authority for the church's common life consists in its being used in certain rulish and normative ways so that it helps to nurture and reform the community's self-identity and the personal identities of her members. Moreover, "theology" is charged with critical examination of the forms of the church's speech and action to see that they remain faithful to her "task." Hence the "authority of scripture" has the status of a *postulate* assumed in the doing of theology in the context of the practice of the common life of a Christian community in which "church" is understood in a certain way. In short, the doctrine of "scripture and its authority" is a postulate of practical theology. Therefore, the least misleading conceptual home of this sort of theological discussion of scripture's authority, i.e., doctrines about biblical authority, would be as part of the elaboration of doctrines about the shaping of Christian existence, both communal and individual, i.e., a part of doctrines of "sanctification" and "ecclesiology."

This would involve a departure from the standard location of doctrines about scripture in theological positions developed in the neo-orthodox period. There doctrines about scripture were consistently developed as part of doctrines of "revelation," rather than as part of doctrines about the shaping of Christian existence. It was regularly suggested that scripture is "authority" because it preserves for us in one form a "content" that has been revealed in the past and must be restated in new forms by contemporary theology.

The Authority of Scripture and the
Challenge of Feminism

In the last third of the twentieth century, the emergence of feminist theology has raised several important issues for Reformed theology. Feminists point out that the Bible was written in the context of patriarchal societies, and thus the Word of God written is tainted in at least some of its texts by patriarchy. A significant issue for Christian feminists is whether the Bible simply reflects the culture in which it is written but proclaims a gospel that transcends patriarchy or whether both the Bible and its gospel are tainted to the core by patriarchy. Those who hold the first point of view can remain within the Christian community and argue for its reform by means of God's liberating Word. Those who hold the second point of view often find it difficult to remain within the church and seek a religion based on the distinctive experiences of women. Letty Russell is an example of a Christian feminist committed to the liberating word in the Bible but not to the oppressive social structures that have been created in the name of the Bible and Christian faith.

SOURCE

Letty M. Russell, "Authority and the Challenge of Feminist Interpretation," in Letty M. Russell, ed., *Feminist Interpretation of the Bible* (Philadelphia: Westminster, 1985), 138–39.

THE BIBLICAL BASIS OF
MY THEOLOGY

In spite of the patriarchal nature of the biblical texts, I myself have no intention of giving up the biblical basis of my theology. . . . The evidence for a biblical message of liberation for women, as for other marginalized groups, is not found just in particular stories about women or particular female images of God. It is found in God's intention for the mending of all creation. The Bible has authority in my life because it makes sense of my experience and speaks to me about the meaning and purpose of my humanity in Jesus Christ. In spite of its ancient and patriarchal worldviews, in spite of its inconsistencies and mixed messages, the story of God's love affair with the world leads me to a vision of New Creation that impels my life.

Scripture and Script

I am one of those for whom the Bible continues to be a liberating word as I hear it together with others and struggle to live out its story. For me the Bible is "scripture," or sacred writing, because it functions as "script," or prompting for life. Its authority in my life stems from its story of God's invitation to participation in the restoration of wholeness, peace, and justice in the world. Responding to this invitation has made it my own story, or script, through the power of the Spirit at work in communities of struggle and faith. . . .

My particular story is one shaped by seventeen years with a poor, racially mixed community of struggle and witness in the East Harlem Protestant Parish in New York City. In such a context the Bible did not have all the answers, but it provided a source of meaning and hope for our lives. Somehow the texts we really lived with, and struggled with, seemed to speak in ever new ways on our road toward freedom. In East Harlem the story of God's concern for humanity showed us that "nobodies" in the eyes of the dominant society could be "somebodies." I still believe this, believe that in God's sight I am not marginal but that, like my Black and Hispanic sisters and brothers in East Harlem, I came created by God and called by the biblical word of promise to become what God intends me to become: a partner in the mending of creation.

Mending Creation

The particular interpretive key that assists me in continuing to give assent is the witness of scripture to God's promise (for the mending of creation) on its way to fulfillment. That which denies this intention of God for the liberation of groaning creation in all its parts does not compel or evoke my assent (i.e., it is not authoritative).

HERMENEUTICS

Prior to the nineteenth century, hermeneutics was understood to be the application of a series of grammatical rules to the text. In the nineteenth century, however, hermeneutics came to be understood in terms of the much broader process of *Verstehen*, or "understanding." With the development of different forms of historical criticism in the nineteenth and twentieth centuries, theologians became acutely aware of the enormous chasm that separated their world from that of the biblical text. First, in the work of David Friedrich Strauss in the nineteenth century, and, later, in the work of Rudolf Bultmann in the first half of the twentieth century, biblical scholars and theologians became aware of the variety of literary genres in the Bible, including myth. The hermeneutical challenge became how to interpret biblical myth in categories congruent with the text but also intelligible to the modern world. "Demythologization" meant not doing away with biblical myth but interpreting it so that the gospel proclaimed in the Bible could be heard by modern people.

In the twentieth-century debate over hermeneutics, some theologians have argued that the problem with most forms of demythologization is that they uncritically assume that "reality" is the world of the reader and that the hermeneutical task is to interpret the text by means of the reader's "reality." Another possibility, they suggest, one raised by the Bible itself, is that the reader is self-deceived and the world of the Bible is true. The hermeneutical challenge, therefore, is not how best to fit the Bible into the reader's world, but whether the reader can enter the world of the text and be transformed by it.

Another version of this hermeneutical debate is the argument between those who believe that a general philosophical theory of understanding can illumine what is involved in the interpretation of biblical texts and those who believe that the Bible demands its own reading, or special hermeneutics, which can be discovered only from within the text.

FOR FURTHER STUDY

Barth, *Church Dogmatics*, I/2: 457–740. Garrett Green, ed., *Scriptural Authority and Narrative Interpretation* (Philadelphia: Fortress, 1987). Werner G. Jeanrond, *Theological Hermeneutics: Development and Significance* (New York: Crossroad, 1991). David E. Klemm, *Hermeneutical Inquiry*, 2 vols., Vol. 1: The Interpretation of Texts, Vol. II: The Interpretation of Existence (Atlanta: Scholars Press, 1986). Frank McConnell, ed., *The Bible and the Narrative Tradition* (New York and Oxford: Oxford University Press, 1986). Richard E. Palmer, *Hermeneutics: Interpretation Theory in Schleiermacher, Dilthey, Heidegger, and Gadamer* (Evanston: Northwestern University Press, 1969). Paul Ricoeur, *Essays on Biblical Interpretation*, ed. Lewis S. Mudge (Philadelphia: Fortress, 1980). David Tracy, *Plurality and Ambiguity: Hermeneutics, Religion, Hope* (San Francisco: Harper & Row, 1987).

Schleiermacher and the Task of Interpretation

One of the first attempts at what modern theology recognizes as hermeneutics was Schleiermacher's lectures at the University of Berlin. He argued that understanding involves two "moments": (1) understanding what is said within the linguistic context, and (2) understanding what is said in terms of the intentions of the speaker. The first Schleiermacher describes as grammatical interpretation and the second as psychological interpretation.

SOURCE

Friedrich Schleiermacher, *Hermeneutics: The Handwritten Manuscripts*, ed. Heinz Kimmerle, trans. James Duke and Jack Forstman (Missoula, Mont.: Scholars Press, 1977), 100–101.

FOR FURTHER STUDY

Richard E. Palmer, *Hermeneutics: Interpretation Theory in Schleiermacher, Dilthey, Heidegger, and Gadamer*, 84–97.

Interpretation is an art.

1. Each side is itself an art. For each side constructs something finite and definite from something infinite and indefinite. Language is infinite because every element is determinable in a special way by the other elements.

This statement also applies to psychological interpretation, for every intuition of a person is itself infinite. Moreover, external influences on a person will have ramifications which trail off into infinity. Such a construction, however, cannot be made by means of rules which may be applied with self-evident certainty.

2. In order to complete the grammatical side of interpretation it would be necessary to have a complete knowledge of the language. In order to complete the psychological side it would be necessary to have a complete knowledge of the person. Since in both cases such complete knowledge is impossible, it is necessary to move back and forth between the grammatical and psychological sides, and no rules can stipulate exactly how to do this.

The success of the art of interpretation depends on one's linguistic competence and on one's ability for knowing people.

1. By "linguistic competence" I am not referring to a facility for learning foreign languages. The distinction between one's mother tongue and a foreign language is not at issue here. Rather, I refer to one's command of language, one's sensitivity to its similarities and differences, etc.—It could be claimed that in this respect rhetoric and hermeneutics must always belong together. But hermeneutics requires one kind of

competence, rhetoric requires another, and the two are not the same. To be sure, both hermeneutics and rhetoric require linguistic competence, but hermeneutics makes use of that competence in a different way.

2. One's ability to know people refers especially to a knowledge of the subjective element determining the composition of thoughts. Thus, just as with hermeneutics and rhetoric, so with hermeneutics and the artful description of persons, there is no permanent connection. Nonetheless, many errors in hermeneutics are due to a lack of this talent or to a flaw in its application.

3. Insofar as these abilities are universal gifts of nature, hermeneutics is everybody's concern. To the extent that a person is deficient in one of these talents, he is hampered, and the other gift can do no more than help him choose wisely from the suggestions made by others.

Karl Barth and the Realistic Reading of the Bible

Karl Barth was one of the few modern theologians to reject the notion of a general or philosophical theory of hermeneutics and to insist that the interpretation of the Bible is governed by the name the Bible proclaims, that is, Jesus Christ.

SOURCE
Barth, *Church Dogmatics*, I/2:719–20.

The decisive basis of this fundamental rule of all scriptural exegesis can be inferred, of course, only from the content of Scripture, and only from there can it become really intelligible. Why must we subordinate the testimony of our own spirit to the testimony of the spirit of Scripture? Why do we have this peculiar assumption which is so obviously out of accord with the technique of interpretation generally? Why is it that in this case interpretation is not a conversation *inter pares*, but *inter impares*, although here, too, we have one man confronting another man, and one human intellectual world another? We will leave aside for the moment what we have already established earlier in another connexion—that perhaps the technique of interpretation generally, in so far as it does not seem to go beyond that conversation *inter pares*, has every cause to learn from the special biblical science of interpretation which in the last resort is perhaps the only possible one. There will be reasons for the fact that it does not desire, and is not able, to do this. But it is certain that biblical hermeneutics must be controlled by this special fundamental principle because the content of the Bible imperatively requires it. The content of the Bible, and the object of its witness, is Jesus Christ as the name of the God who deals graciously with man the sinner. To heed and understand its witness is to realise the fact that the relation between God and man is such that God is gracious to man: to man who needs Him, who as a sinner is thrown wholly upon God's grace, who cannot earn God's grace, and for whom it is indissolubly connected with God's gracious action towards him, for whom therefore it is decisively one with the name of Jesus Christ as the name of the God who acts graciously towards him. To hear this is to hear the Bible—both as a whole and in each one of its separate parts. Not to hear this means *eo ipso* not to hear the Bible, neither as a whole, nor therefore in its parts. The Bible says all sorts of things, certainly; but in all this multiplicity and variety, it says in truth only one thing—just this: the name of Jesus Christ, concealed under the name Israel in the Old Testament, revealed under His own name in the New Testament, which therefore can be understood only as it has understood itself, as a commentary on the Old Testament. The Bible becomes clear when it is clear that it says this one thing: that it proclaims the name Jesus Christ and therefore proclaims God in His richness and mercy, and man in his need and helplessness, yet living on what God's mercy has given and will give him. The Bible remains dark to us if we do not hear in it this sovereign name, and if, therefore, we think we perceive God and man in some other relation than the one determined once for all by this name. Interpretation stands in the service of the clarity which the Bible as God's Word makes for itself; and we can properly interpret the Bible, in whole or part, only when we perceive and show that what it says is said from the point of view of that concealed and revealed name of Jesus Christ, and therefore in testimony to the grace of which we as men stand in need, of which as men we are incapable and of which we are made participants by God.

Paul Ricoeur and Religious Language as Redescription

Paul Ricoeur (b. 1913) describes himself as a philosopher, not a theologian, but his investigations of the nature of symbol, myth, metaphor, and narrative have been of great importance for many contemporary theologians. Ricoeur describes religious language as a "limit-expression" which redescribes human experience.

SOURCE

Paul Ricoeur, "Biblical Hermeneutics," in *Paul Ricoeur on Biblical Hermeneutics*, ed. John Dominic Crossan, *Semeia* 4 (Missoula, Mont.: Scholars Press, 1975), 127–28.

The *eruption of the unheard in* our discourse and *in* our experience constitutes precisely one dimension *of* our discourse and *of* our experience. To speak of a limit-experience is to speak of our experience. This expression in no way says that there is nothing in our common human experience and in our common language which corresponds to speech about the extreme. If this were not so, the claim of the Scriptures that Christian self-understanding in fact is the understanding of authentic human existence would fail entirely. It is precisely as extreme that religious language is appropriated. And it is this appropriateness of limit-expressions to limit-experiences which is signified by our affirmation that religious language, like all poetic language, in the strongest sense of the word, redescribes human experience.

In this expression—"redescribes human experience"—we must emphasize both halves: what religious language does is *to redescribe*; what it redescribes is *human experience*. In this sense we must say that the ultimate referent of the parables, proverbs, and eschatological sayings is not the Kingdom of God, but human reality in its wholeness, as this is indicated by numerous expressions in the works of Norman Perrin. This is where the unshakeable truth of the existential interpretation of the New Testament lies. Religious language discloses the religious dimension of *common* human experience.

Hans Frei and the Loss of Narrative Interpretation

One of the most provocative interpretations of biblical narrative in the last half of the twentieth century was Hans Frei's claim that realistic narrative in the Bible demands that the reader submit to the claims of the text rather than that the texts be submitted to the reader's criteria concerning truth and meaning. The eighteenth and nineteenth centuries marked the eclipse of the realistic reading of the Bible.

SOURCE

Hans W. Frei, *The Eclipse of Biblical Narrative: A Study in Eighteenth and Nineteenth Century Hermeneutics* (New Haven and London: Yale University Press, 1974), 149–50.

Much of the Bible consists of realistic narration, so much so that there is no surprise in its being subjected again and again, in this era of burgeoning realism, to inquiry as to whether it was *really* true to reality. How probable were the things that were told? Unlike other story traditions of the ancient world (the comparison with Homer becoming increasingly common among scholars as the century wore on), *this* story tradition appeared to be true and have the marks of verisimilitude and of probable factuality. This was the case most especially if one left out of account all miracle stories. But even they seemed to have the marks of realism about them. It was often asked what other explanation than the genuine resurrection of Jesus would account for the startling but seemingly genuine and believable change of outlook among the disciples who, on their own admission, had been so cowardly and discouraged at the time of Jesus' trial and death.

But the new tradition of a *literary* realism was never applied to the technical task of biblical interpretation, so that speculation about the possible fruits of such a procedure at the time are as useless as they are fascinating. For reasons already mentioned it was not to be: the debate over the factuality of the biblical reports was far too central and crucial. On apologetic as well as historical grounds the question of the factuality of biblical reports, and the cognate debate over whether its putative factuality or the recognition of some central ideational themes was really the important thing about the Bible, prevented any serious attention to narrative shape in its own right.

In both cases what the biblical narratives are all about is something other than their character as cumulatively or accretively articulated stories whose themes emerge into full shape only through the narrative rendering and deployment itself. The curious, unmarked frontier between history and realistic fiction allows easy transition if one's interest is the rendering and exploration of a temporal framework through their logically similar narrative structure, perhaps most of all in the case of the biblical stories where the question of fact or fiction is so problematical. But when prime interest is concentrated on the fact issue—and it could hardly be otherwise in eighteenth-century examination of the Bible—the unmarked frontier is no longer merely real. Now it becomes impenetrable; one is either on one side of it or the other, and the decision between them is the crucial issue.

Rules for the Interpretation of Scripture

In 1982, The United Presbyterian Church in the United States of America published a resource document on biblical authority and interpretation that summarized some of the basic principles of Reformed hermeneutics.

SOURCE

Biblical Authority and Interpretation (New York: Advisory Council on Discipleship and Worship, The United Presbyterian Church in the United States of America, 1982), 10–11.

Six basic rules for the interpretation of Scripture found in the confessions.

First, Jesus Christ, as our Redeemer, is the central focus of Scripture.

Second, our appeal should be to the plain text of Scripture, to the grammatical and historical context, rather than to allegory or subjective fantasy.

Third, the Holy Spirit aids us in interpreting and applying God's message.

Fourth, doctrinal consensus of the early church as summarized in the Apostles' Creed, the Nicene Creed, and the Definition of Chalcedon is the "rule of faith" that guides us.

Fifth, all interpretations must accord with the "rule of love," the two-fold commandment to love God and to love our neighbor.

Sixth, interpretation of the Bible requires human scholarship in order to establish the best text, to understand the original languages, and to interpret the influence of the historical and cultural context in which the divine message has come.

REVELATION

As modern theology searched for high ground in the aftermath of the flood of criticism let loose by the Enlightenment, some theologians turned to the concept of revelation. Many of those theologians who were often lumped together under the rubric of neo-orthodoxy made some interpretation of revelation the basis of their theological proposals. There was not, however, common agreement among neo-orthodox theologians about the meaning of revelation. In fact, one of the most heated and bitter theological exchanges in the twentieth century took place between Emil Brunner and Karl Barth, who were in substantial agreement about many theological issues.

Revelation was an attractive category to many neo-orthodox theologians for several reasons. First, contrary to some liberal proposals that Christian faith was amenable to rational explanation, revelation was a reminder that Christian faith and theology are rooted finally in holy mystery. Second, while much of modern theology had the look of a religious philosophy, revelation was a reminder that theology is not so much a human construction as it is a reflection on the prior reality of God's grace. Finally, revelation was a reminder that theology is not finally about historical facts or moral values; it refers to the self-revelation of a personal God in the figure of Jesus Christ.

FOR FURTHER STUDY

John Baillie, *The Idea of Revelation in Recent Thought* (New York: Columbia University Press, 1956). G. C. Berkouwer, *General Revelation* (Grand Rapids: Wm. B. Eerdmans, 1955). Emil Brunner, *Revelation and Reason*, trans. Olive Wyon (Philadelphia: Westminster, 1946). H. D. McDonald, *Ideas of Revelation: An Historical Study* A.D. *1700 to* A.D. *1860* (London: Macmillan, 1959).

Revelation and Religious Emotions

In *The Christian Faith*, Schleiermacher rejected the notion that revelation should be understood as a form of cognition which manifests itself in doctrine. Instead, he proposed that revelation refers to the originality of that fact which conditions human affections as religious emotions.

SOURCE

Schleiermacher, *Christian Faith*, 49–50.

The words *"reveal," "revealed," "revelation,"* present still further difficulties, since even originally they sometimes signify the illumination of what was obscure, confused, unobserved, and sometimes rather the disclosing and unveiling of what was hitherto concealed and kept secret, and still further confusion has been introduced by the distinction between mediate and immediate (direct and indirect) revelation. To begin with, all will at once agree that the word "revealed" is never applied either to what is discovered in the realm of experience by one man and handed on to others, or to what is excogitated in thought by one man and so learned by others; and further, that the word presupposes a divine communication and declaration. And in this sense we find the word very generally applied to the origin of religious communions. For of what religious mysteries and varieties of worship, either among the Greeks or among the Egyptians and Indians, would it not be asserted that they originally came from heaven or were proclaimed by Deity in some way which fell outside the human and natural order? Not seldom, indeed, we find even the beginning of civic communities (just as from the beginning we often find the moral and the religious unseparated) traced to a divine sending of the man who first gathered the tribe together into a civic union, and so the new organization of life is based on a revelation. Accordingly we might say that the idea of revelation signifies the *originality* of the fact which lies at the foundation of a religious communion, in the sense that this fact, as conditioning the individual content of the religious emotions which are found in the communion, cannot itself in turn be explained by the historical chain which precedes it.

Now the fact that in this original element there is a divine causality requires no further discussion; nor does the fact that it is an activity which aims at and furthers the salvation of man. But I am unwilling to accept the further definition that it operates upon man as a cognitive being. For that would make the revelation to be originally and essentially *doctrine*; and I do not believe that we can adopt that position, whether we consider the whole field covered by the idea, or seek to define it in advance with special reference to Christianity. If a system of propositions can be understood from their connexion with others, then nothing supernatural was required for their production. But if they cannot, then they can, in the first instance, only be apprehended (we need only appeal for confirmation to the first principles of Hermeneutics) as parts of another whole, as a moment of the life of a thinking being who works upon us directly as a distinctive existence by means of his total impression on us; and this working is always a working upon the self-consciousness. Thus the original fact will always be the appearing of such a being, and the original working will always be upon the self-consciousness of those into whose circle he enters.

Karl Barth and Revelation as "God with Us"

In his *Church Dogmatics*, Karl Barth describes the threefold form of revelation. In its first and immediate sense, revelation is Jesus Christ, "the Word made flesh," "God with us." The second and third forms of revelation are the Bible and proclamation, but these forms are human words which by means of God's grace may mediate the one Word of God, Jesus Christ.

SOURCE

Barth, *Church Dogmatics*, I/1:119–20.

All revelation, then, must be thought of as revealing, i.e., as conditioned by the act of revelation. The event in which revelation occurs must be seen in connexion with what has happened once and for all in this act. All fulfilled time must be seen as filled with the fulness of this time. Revelation itself, however, is not referred to anything other, higher, or earlier. Revelation as such is not relative. Revelation in fact does not differ from the person of Jesus Christ nor from the reconciliation accomplished in Him. To say revelation is to say "The Word became flesh." To be sure, one can say something quite different by revelation, something purely formal, and relative as such. But to say this is not to say what the Bible means by the word or what Church proclamation is referring to when it refers to the Bible or what must be called revelation in Christian dogmatics if this is to take itself seriously as such. When in the word revelation we say "The Word was made flesh and dwelt among us," then we are saying something which can have only an intertrinitarian basis in the will of the Father and the sending of the Son and the Holy Spirit, in the eternal decree of the triune God, so that it can be established only as knowledge of God from God, of light in light. The same applies if instead of Jesus Christ we say concretely "God with us." It is true that in the term revelation we might have something relative rather than this absolute in view, but the Bible is thinking only of this absolute, and in the knowledge of this absolute the Church with the help of the Bible recalls past revelation, and a dogmatics that works in the sphere of the Church and not in a vacuum has also to cling to it. But to say "God with us" is to say something which has no basis or possibility outside itself, which can in no sense be explained in terms of man and man's situation, but only as knowledge of God from God, as free and unmerited grace. As the Bible bears witness to God's revelation and as Church proclamation takes up this witness in obedience, both renounce any foundation apart from that which God has given once and for all by speaking. The Bible and proclamation both appeal to this fact that has been given here and now. They cannot reproduce it as a given fact. They cannot bring it on the scene themselves. They can only attest and proclaim it. To bring it about that the *Deus dixit* is present with the Church in its various times and situations is not in the power of the Bible or proclamation. The *Deus dixit* is true—now the *ubi et quando* must come into force again—where it *is* true, i.e., where and when God, in speaking once and for all, wills according to His eternal counsel that it be true, where and when God by His activating, ratifying and fulfilling of the word of the Bible and preaching lets it become true. This being and becoming true of revelation consists, then, in the fact that the Church really recollects past revelation, and in faith receives, grasps and really proclaims the biblical witness of it as the real promise of future revelation, future revelation here being simply that which has taken place once and for all but is now directed to us too, just as the Christ who comes again is no other than the Christ who has come, but this Christ as the One who now comes also to us. The "God with us" becomes actual for us *hic et nunc* as the promise received and grasped in faith because it is *illic et tunc* a divine act. It is thus that which is true in and for itself, and it becomes true for us as recollection and also as promise, as recollection of Christ come in the flesh and as hope of Christ coming again in glory. It is Jesus Christ Himself who here speaks for Himself and needs no witness apart from His Holy Spirit and the faith that rejoices in His promise received and grasped. This independent and unsurpassable origin of the Word of God that comes to us is what we have in view when we speak of its third form, or materially we should rather say its first form, i.e., its form as the Word of God revealed.

Revelation as the Confession of the Heart

In *The Meaning of Revelation*, H. Richard Niebuhr (1894–1962) described revelation as intensely personal knowledge. Consequently, revelation is best understood not as propositions or creeds, but as that moment in which we know ourselves to be known by one who can be trusted and who deserves our commitment and loyalty.

SOURCE
H. Richard Niebuhr, *The Meaning of Revelation* (New York: Macmillan, 1962), 111–13.

Revelation means the moment in our history through which we know ourselves to be known from beginning to end, in which we are apprehended by the knower; it means the self-disclosing of that eternal knower. Revelation means the moment in which we are surprised by the knowledge of someone there in the darkness and the void of human life; it means the self-disclosure of light in our darkness. Revelation is the moment in which we find our judging selves to be judged not by ourselves or our neighbors but by one who knows the final secrets of the heart; revelation means the self-disclosure of the judge. Revelation means that we find ourselves to be valued rather than valuing and that all our values are transvaluated by the activity of a universal valuer. When a price is put upon our heads, which is not our price, when the unfairness of all the fair prices we have placed on things is shown up; when the great riches of God reduce our wealth to poverty, that is revelation. When we find out that we are no longer thinking him, but that he first thought us, that is revelation. Revelation is the emergence of the person on whose external garments and body we had looked as objects of our masterful and curious understanding. Revelation means that in our common history the fate which lowers over us as persons in our communities reveals itself to be a person in community with us. What this means for us cannot be expressed in the impersonal ways of creeds or other propositions but only in responsive acts of a personal character. We acknowledge revelation by no third-person proposition, such as that there is a God, but only in the direct confession of the heart, "Thou art my God." We can state the convincement given in the revelatory moment only in a prayer saying, "Our Father." Revelation as the self-disclosure of the infinite person is realized in us only through the faith which is a personal act of commitment, of confidence and trust, not a belief about the nature of things. When we speak of revelation we mean that moment when we are given a new faith, to cleave to and to betray, and a new standard, to follow and deny. Now when we fail in faith, we fail in this faith; and when we transgress, it is this person we transgress against; when we reason falsely it is in violation of the first principle given in this event. All this, since it is in our history, is part of what we are and does not belong to a serial past. It is our past in our present. From this point forward we must listen for the remembered voice in all the sounds that assail our ears, and look for the remembered activity in all the actions of the world upon us. The God who reveals himself in Jesus Christ is now trusted and known as the contemporary God, revealing himself in every event; but we do not understand how we could trace his working in these happenings if he did not make himself known to us through the memory of Jesus Christ; nor do we know how we should be able to interpret all the words we read as words of God save by the aid of this Rosetta stone.

The Eschatology of Revelation

In the 1960s, Jürgen Moltmann reminded the theological world of one aspect of Christian faith and theology that had been overlooked by many theologians in the twentieth century—eschatology, the doctrine of "the last things," Christian hope in what God has promised to do. All of theology, including revelation, must be understood eschatologically.

SOURCE
Moltmann, *Theology of Hope*, 85–86.

It is ultimately always a result of the influence of Greek methods of thought and enquiry when the revelation of God which is witnessed in the biblical scriptures is understood as "epiphany of the eternal present." That describes the God of Parmenides rather than the God of the exodus and the resurrection. The revelation of the risen Christ is not a form of this epiphany of the eternal present, but necessitates a view of revelation as apocalypse of the promised future of the truth. In the light of this future of the truth, manifest in the promise, man experiences reality as history in all its possibilities and dangers, and is broken of that fixed view of reality in which it becomes an image of the deity.

Christian theology speaks of "revelation," when on the ground of the Easter appearances of the risen Lord it perceives and proclaims the identity of the risen one with the crucified one. Jesus is recognized in the Easter appearances as what he really *was*. That is the ground of faith's "historical" remembrance of the life and work, claims and sufferings of Jesus of Nazareth. But the messianic titles, in which this identity of Jesus in cross and resurrection is claimed and described, all anticipate at the same time the not yet apparent future of the risen Lord. This means that the Easter appearances and revelations of the risen Lord are manifestly understood as foretaste and promise of his still future glory and lordship. Jesus is recognized in the Easter appearances as what he really *will be*. The "vital point" for a Christian view of revelation accordingly lies neither in "that which came to expression in the man Jesus" (Ebeling) nor in the "destiny of Jesus" (Pannenberg) but—combining both of these—in the fact that in all the qualitative difference of cross and resurrection Jesus is the same. This identity in infinite contradiction is theologically understood as an event of identification, an act of the faithfulness of God. It is this that forms the ground of the promise of the still outstanding future of Jesus Christ. It is this that is the ground of the hope which carries faith through the trials of the god-forsaken world and of death.

"Revelation" in this event has not the character of *logos*-determined illumination of the existing reality of man and the world, but has here constitutively and basically the character of promise and is therefore of an eschatological kind. "Promise" is a fundamentally different thing from a "word-event" which brings truth and harmony between man and the reality that concerns him. "Promise" is in the first instance also a different thing from an eschatologically oriented view of reality as universal history. Promise announces the coming of a not yet existing reality from the future of the truth. Its relation to the existing and given reality is that of a specific *inadaequatio rei et intellectus*. On the other hand, it does not merely anticipate and clarify the realm of coming history and the realistic possibilities it contains. Rather, "the possible," and therewith "the future," arises entirely from God's word of promise and therefore goes beyond what is possible and impossible in the realistic sense. It does not illuminate a future which is always somehow already inherent in reality. Rather, "future" is that reality which fulfills and satisfies the promise because it completely corresponds to it and accords with it. It is only in that event which is spoken of as "new creation out of nothing," as "resurrection of the dead," as "kingdom" and "righteousness" of God, that the promise contained in the resurrection of Christ finds a reality which accords with it and completely corresponds to it. The revealing of the divinity of God therefore depends entirely on the real fulfillment of the promise, as *vice versa* the fulfillment of the promise has the ground of its possibility and of its reality in the faithfulness and the divinity of God. To that extent "promise" does not in the first instance have the function of illuminating the existing reality of the world or of human nature, interpreting it, bringing out its truth and using a proper understanding of it to secure man's agreement with it. Rather, it contradicts existing reality and discloses its own process concerning the future of Christ for man and the world. Revelation, recognized as promise and embraced in hope, thus sets an open stage for history, and fills it with missionary enterprise and the responsible exercise of hope, accepting the suffering that is involved in the contradiction of reality, and setting out towards the promised future.

FAITH AND OTHER SOURCES OF KNOWLEDGE

Although many theologians in the twentieth century made some form of revelation the center of their theologies, the question of what was once referred to as "natural theology" or "general revelation" continued to be fiercely debated. Is there knowledge of God only in Jesus Christ? Are there not some truths about God which can be inferred from the natural order, general human experience, and non-Christian religions? As theologians, along with the rest of Western culture, became more aware of the reality of religious and other forms of pluralism, could Christians claim that they alone knew the sole truth about God? Is Christian knowledge of God in Jesus Christ all there is to know about God? Is God's Spirit loose in the world, working among Christians and non-Christians alike? These kinds of questions formed much of the debate in twentieth-century theology, and Reformed theologians found themselves on different sides of the issues.

FOR FURTHER STUDY

Donald G. Dawe and John B. Carmen, eds., *Christian Faith in a Religiously Plural World* (Maryknoll, N.Y.: Orbis, 1978). John Hick, *God and the Universe of Faiths* (New York: St. Martin's Press, 1973). John Hick and Brian Hebblethwaite, eds., *Christianity and Other Religions* (Philadelphia: Fortress, 1980). Hendrik Kraemer, *Religion and the Christian Faith* (Philadelphia: Westminster, 1956). Lesslie Newbigin, *The Gospel in a Pluralist Society* (Grand Rapids: Wm. B. Eerdmans, 1989). H. Martin Rumscheidt, *Revelation and Theology: An Analysis of the Barth-Harnack Correspondence of 1923* (Cambridge: Cambridge University Press, 1972). Ernst Troeltsch, *The Absoluteness of Christianity and the History of Religions*, trans. David Reid (Richmond: John Knox Press, 1971).

Revelation versus Natural Theology

In 1934 Karl Barth and Emil Brunner engaged in a vigorous debate about the nature of revelation and the viability of natural theology. In the following section, Barth explains what he means by natural theology and why he rejects it.

SOURCE

Natural Theology: Comprising "Nature and Grace" by Professor Dr. Emil Brunner and the Reply "NO!" by Dr. Karl Barth, trans. Peter Fraenkel (London: Geoffrey Bles: Centenary Press, 1946), 74–76.

By "natural theology" I mean every (positive *or* negative) *formulation of a system* which claims to be theological, *i.e.* to interpret divine revelation, whose *subject*, however, differs fundamentally from the revelation in Jesus Christ and whose *method* therefore differs equally from the exposition of Holy Scripture. Such a system is contained not only in Brunner's counter-theses but also in the theses ascribed by him to me. Their wording may here and there recall my thoughts and my writings. But this does not mean that I am prepared to accept paternity and responsibility. For they represent—even though negatively—an abstract speculation concerning a something that is not identical with the revelation of God in Jesus Christ. Brunner failed to see that he made a fatal mistake in his initial definitions of my position by treating me as one of his kind. This has made debate difficult, for my first step has to consist in emphasising the distance between us. Or did he want to set me a trap by inviting me to expose myself that way to his counter-theses and thus to make my position as fundamentally questionable as his? However that may be, I do not think of exposing myself like that. For "natural theology" does not exist as an entity capable of becoming a separate subject within what I consider to be real theology—not even for the sake of being rejected. If one occupies oneself with real theology one can pass by so-called natural theology only as one would pass by an abyss into which it is inadvisable to step if one does not want to fall. All one can do is to turn one's back upon it as upon the great temptation and source of error, by having nothing to do with it and by making it clear to oneself and to others from time to time why one acts that way. A real rejection of natural theology does not differ from its acceptance merely in the way in which No differs from Yes. Rather are Yes and No said, as it were, on different levels. Really to reject natural theology means to refuse to admit it as a separate problem. Hence the rejection of natural theology can only be a side issue, arising when serious questions of real theology are being discussed. Real rejection of natural theology does not form part of the creed. Nor does it wish to be an exposition of the creed and of revelation. It is merely an hermeneutical rule, forced upon the exegete by the creed (e.g., by the clause *natus ex virgine*) and by revelation. It is not possible to expand and compound it into a system of special tenets explicating and defending it. Rather does it appear necessarily, but with the same dependence as that of shade upon light, at the edge of theology as its necessary limit. If you really reject natural theology you do not stare at the serpent, with the result that it stares back at you, hypnotises you, and is ultimately certain to bite you, but you hit it and kill it as soon as you see it! In all these matters rejection of natural theology differs from its acceptance even before the rejection takes place. Real rejection of natural theology can come about only in the fear of God and hence only be a complete *lack* of interest in this matter. If *this* matter is allowed to become of interest, though but in order to be rejected, then interest is no longer centred upon *theology*. For this rejection cannot within theology be made for its own sake. For it is not by this rejection that truth is known, the Gospel is expounded, God is praised and the Church is built.

Salvation by the Logos or by Jesus?

In the 1970s an important theological debate took place between a group of theologians who raised critical questions about some of the exclusive claims of Christian faith and those who defended the finality of Jesus Christ. At issue was whether there was saving knowledge of God in non-Christian religions. John Hick argued that in order to enter into genuine dialogue with other religious traditions Christians must give up the traditional doctrine of the incarnation and admit that saving knowledge of God is present in other religious communities.

SOURCE

John Hick, ed., *The Myth of God Incarnate* (Philadelphia: Westminster, 1977), 180–81.

Transposed into theological terms, the problem which has come to the surface in the encounter of Christianity with the other world religions is this: If Jesus was literally God incarnate, and if it is by his death alone that men can be saved, and by their response to him alone that they can appropriate that salvation, then the only doorway to eternal life is Christian faith. It would follow from this that the large majority of the human race so far have not been saved. But is it credible that the loving God and Father of all men has decreed that only those born within one particular thread of human history shall be saved? Is not such an idea excessively parochial, presenting God in effect as the tribal deity of the predominantly Christian West? And so theologians have recently been developing a mass of small print to the old theology, providing that devout men of other faiths may be Christians without knowing it, or may be anonymous Christians, or may belong to the invisible church, or may have implicit faith and receive baptism by desire, and so on. These rather artificial theories are all attempts to square an inadequate theology with the facts of God's world. They are thoroughly well-intentioned and are to be welcomed as such. But in the end they are an anachronistic clinging to the husk of the old doctrine after its substance has crumbled.

It seems clear that we are being called today to attain a global religious vision which is aware of the unity of all mankind before God and which at the same time makes sense of the diversity of God's ways within the various streams of human life. On the one hand, we must affirm God's equal love for all men and not only for Christians and their Old Testament spiritual ancestors. And on the other hand we must acknowledge that a single revelation to the whole earth has never in the past been possible, given the facts of geography and technology, and that the self-disclosure of the divine, working through human freedom within the actual conditions of world history, was bound to take varying forms. We must thus be willing to see God at work within the total religious life of mankind, challenging men in their state of "natural religion," with all its crudities and cruelties, by the tremendous revelatory moments which lie at the basis of the great world faiths; and we must come to see Christianity within this pluralistic setting. There is no space here to develop a theology of religions along these lines, taking account of the many problems which arise for such an approach; but I have attempted to do this in *God and the Universe of Faiths* and can refer the reader to that attempt. I suggest that we have in the end to say something like this: All salvation—that is, all creating of human animals into children of God— is the work of God. The different religions have their different names for God acting savingly towards mankind. Christianity has several overlapping names for this—the eternal Logos, the cosmic Christ, the Second Person of the Trinity, God the Son, the Spirit. If, selecting from our Christian language, we call God-acting-towards-mankind the Logos, then we must say that *all* salvation, within all religions, is the work of the Logos and that under their various images and symbols men in different cultures and faiths may encounter the Logos and find salvation. But what we cannot say is that all who are saved are saved by Jesus of Nazareth. The life of Jesus was one point at which the Logos—that is, God-in-relation-to-man—has acted; and it is the only point that savingly concerns the Christian; but we are not called upon nor are we entitled to make the negative assertion that the Logos has not acted and is not acting anywhere else in human life. On the contrary, we should gladly acknowledge that Ultimate Reality has affected human consciousness for its liberation or "salvation" in various ways within the Indian, the semitic, the Chinese, the African . . . forms of life.

Finally, should *our* revelation of the Logos, namely in the life of Jesus, be made available to all mankind? Yes, of course; and so also should other particular revelations of the Logos at work in human life—in the Hebrew prophets, in the Buddha, in the *Upanishads* and the *Bhagavad Gīta*, in the *Koran*, and so on. The specifically Christian gift to the world is that men should come to know Jesus and take him into their religious life—not to displace but to deepen and enlarge the relationship with God to which they have already come within their own tradition. And we too, in turn, can be spiritually enriched by God's gifts mediated through other faiths.

Christian Faith in a Global Context

In the last half of the twentieth century, theologians in Third World and non-Western countries began to ask what the gospel might mean if it were stripped of its Western cultural trappings and allowed to speak to new social-cultural contexts. One example of this development is the work of Korean theologian

Chung Hyun Kyung. She attempts to understand Christian faith in the context of the oppression of Korean women and the liberation of the gospel.

SOURCE

Chung Hyun Kyung, *Struggle to Be the Sun Again: Introducing Asian Women's Theology* (Maryknoll, N.Y.: Orbis, 1990), 103–4.

Asian women's approach to the creation of theology, like all other forms of liberation theology in the Third World, is *inductive*, drawn from experience and commitment. It is also *collective* in its approach and *inclusive* in its perspective and goal.

This inductive, collective, and inclusive methodology creates a distinctive *Asian women* flavor in their theology. During the last decade women in several Asian countries conducted many Asian women's theological consultations. Many of these consultations followed the method proposed by the Women's Committee of EATWOT. The EATWOT method has its circular steps: listening to individual's situations, social analysis, and then theological analysis.

It starts with women's *storytelling*. Women from various backgrounds gather and listen to one another's stories of victimization and liberation. Educated middle-class women theologians are committed to inviting or visiting poor farmers, factory workers, slum-dwellers, dowry victims, and prostitutes and listening to their life stories. Storytelling has been women's way of inheriting truth in many Asian countries because the written, literary world has belonged to privileged males. Until the turn of the century many Asian families did not teach girls how to read and write. Women sustained their truth, which was distorted by the definitions of the male literary world, by telling stories mouth to mouth. The power of storytelling lies in its *embodied truth*. Women talked about their concrete, historical life experience and not about abstract, metaphysical concepts. Women's truth was generated by their *epistemology from the broken body*. Women's bodies are the most sensitive receiver for historical reality. Their bodies record what has happened in their lives. Their bodies remember what it is like to be a *no-body* and what it is like to be a *some-body*.

Korean minjung theologian Kim Young Bok, who as a male minjung theologian feels deep solidarity with women's struggle in Korea, proposes a theological methodology based on storytelling for *han*-ridden Korean women and other oppressed people. He and Korean women theologians want to form bridges between minjung theology and Korean

47

women's theology. Kim calls this storytelling methodology *socio-biography*. According to Kim, women's socio-biography shows an under-standing of history which cannot be perceived by so-called objective social analysis. Women's socio-biography brings out the "hidden reality" behind official sociological and historical documents. Listeners of socio-biography hear not cold data but actual people's suffering, crying, and longing. This encounter with foremothers and contemporary sisters in struggle through their storytelling touches Asian women's hearts. It motivates Asian women to participate in the people's struggle for libera-tion because the people in the stories are real people who tremble with fear and yearn for the touch of their beloved.

2

THE DOCTRINE
OF GOD

During the twentieth century, theologians rediscovered some traditional affirmations about the God of Christian faith, such as the claim that God is triune, which had not been given much attention in the eighteenth and nineteenth centuries. At the same time the Trinity was being rediscovered, some theologians also raised significant critical questions about the interpretation of God in classical theology. They began to suspect that the classical model for interpreting the reality of God was more a reflection of Greek metaphysics than of the God of the Bible.

As scientific knowledge about the world and the cosmos exploded, theologians found themselves having to rethink their understanding of the reality of God, and what they meant by claims such as "God acts" and "God is a person." Various new models for interpreting the reality of God appeared in response to rapidly changing developments in politics, the social sciences, and the natural sciences. At the beginning of the twentieth century, neo-orthodoxy had emphasized the transcendence of God in response to the emphasis on God's immanence in Protestant liberalism. But by the middle of the century, new interpretations of God, such as that of process theology, challenged the basic convictions of neo-orthodoxy. Process theology, following the philosophical work of A. N. Whitehead and Charles Hartshorne, described God as a "dipolar" reality who is primordial and as such "transcends" the world, but at the same time is internally related to the world so that God is changed by what happens in the world. This second, "consequent" pole to God's nature seemed to some Reformed theologians to go beyond an affirmation of God's immanence and to undercut the sovereignty of God.

From yet another perspective, that of emerging feminist theology, the interpretation of God by classical theology, including Reformed theology, seemed to reflect male self-interest and male experience to the exclusion of female experiences of God. In much Christian feminist theology, as it has emerged in the latter third of the twentieth century, God is not so much sovereign Lord as partner, lover, and friend. God's relation to the world is not one of domination and coercion. Rather, God lures and persuades.

In the liberation theology that has emerged in Central and Latin America and in much of the Third World, attention has been given to a theme long neglected in classical, Western theology—God's preferential option for the poor. In liberation theology, the God of the Bible is in solidarity with the victims of oppression and poverty.

Perhaps the most significant development in the interpretation of God in twentieth-century theology was the shift in metaphors and paradigms used to describe God. While much of classical theology emphasized God's sovereign will, many contemporary theologians describe God not so much in terms of sovereign will as in terms of sovereign love.

FOR FURTHER STUDY

Herman Bavinck, *The Doctrine of God*, trans. William Henderson (Edinburgh: Banner of Truth Trust, 1951). Helmut Gollwitzer, *The Existence of God as Confessed by Faith*, trans. James W. Leitch (Philadelphia: Westminster, 1965). H. R. Mackintosh, *The Christian Apprehension of God* (London: Student Christian Movement, 1934). John S. Mbiti, *Concepts of God in Africa* (London: SPCK, 1970). Heinrich Ott, *God*, trans. Iain and Ute Nicol (Richmond: John Knox, 1974).

THE REALITY, MAJESTY, AND GLORY OF GOD

The difference between Charles Hodge and Karl Barth, who were only a generation apart, regarding the reality of God is perhaps greater than that between Hodge and any number of theologians in the medieval period. Hodge described God in categories compatible with the Protestant scholasticism of the seventeenth century, while Barth turned from abstract categories to a more biblical and christological interpretation of God. These two theologians—Hodge and Barth—represent some of the major differences between Reformed theology in the nineteenth and twentieth centuries.

The Being of God

Charles Hodge described the being of God in language reminiscent of that used two hundred years earlier by the Westminster divines.

SOURCE

Hodge, *Systematic Theology*, 1:367–68.

BEING OF GOD

By *being* is here meant that which has a real, substantive existence. It is equivalent to substance, or essence. It is opposed to what is merely thought, and to a mere force or power. We get this idea, in the first place, from consciousness. We are conscious of self as the subject of the thoughts, feelings, and volitions, which are its varying states and acts. This consciousness of substance is involved in that of personal identity. In the second place, a law of our reason constrains us to believe that there is something which underlies the phenomena of matter and mind, of which those phenomena are the manifestation. It is impossible for us to think of thought and feeling, unless there be something that thinks and feels. It is no less impossible to think of action, unless there be something that acts; or of motion, unless there be something that moves. To assume, therefore, that mind is only a series of acts and states, and that matter is nothing but force, is to assume that nothing (nonentity) can produce effects.

God, therefore, is in his nature a substance, or essence, which is infinite, eternal, and unchangeable; the common subject of all divine perfections, and the common agent of all divine acts. This is as far as we can go, or need to go. We have no definite idea of substance, whether of matter or mind, as distinct from its attributes. The two are inseparable. In knowing the one we know the other. We cannot know hardness except as we know something hard. We have, therefore, the same knowledge of the essence of God, as we have of the substance of the soul. All we have to do in reference to the divine essence, as a Spirit, is to deny it, as we do of our own spiritual essence, what belongs to material substances; and to affirm of it, that in itself and its attributes it is infinite, eternal, and unchangeable. When, therefore, we say there is a God, we do not assert merely that there is in our minds the idea of an infinite Spirit; but that, entirely independent of our idea of Him, such a Being really exists.

God's Being in Act

In the second volume of his *Church Dogmatics*, Karl Barth rejects the category of essence as appropriate for the description of the God revealed in Jesus Christ. The being of God is not some static, abstract essence. Rather, God's being is to be found in what God does, in God's acts; and God's acts are a self-revelation of God's being.

SOURCE

Barth, *Church Dogmatics* II/1:260–62.

Although we cannot allow as such the objection to the possibility of a special doctrine of God, there is something to be learned from it. When we ask questions about God's being, we cannot in fact leave the sphere of His action and working as it is revealed to us in His Word. God is who He is in His works. He is the same even in Himself, even before and after and over His works, and without them. They are bound to Him, but He is not bound to them. They are nothing without Him. But He is who He is without them. He is not, therefore, who He is only in His works. Yet in Himself He is not another than He is in His works. In the light of what He is in His works it is no longer an open question what He is in Himself. In Himself He cannot, perhaps, be someone or something quite other, or perhaps nothing at all. But in His works He is Himself revealed as the One He is. It is, therefore, right that in the development and explanation of the statement that God is we have always to keep exclusively to His works (as they come to pass, or become visible as such in the act of revelation)—not only because we cannot elsewhere understand God and who God is, but also because, even if we could understand Him elsewhere, we should understand Him only as the One He is in His works, because He is this One and no other. We can and must ask about the being of God because as the Subject of His works God is so decisively characteristic for their nature and understanding that without this Subject they would be something quite different from what they are in accordance with God's Word, and on the basis of the Word of God we can necessarily recognise and understand them only together with this their Subject. . . .

At the same time we must be quite clear on the other side, that our subject is God and not being, or being only as the being of God. In connexion with the being of God that is here in question, we are not concerned with a concept of being that is common, neutral and free to choose, but with one which is from the first filled out in a quite definite way. And this concretion cannot take place arbitrarily, but only from the Word of God, as it has already occurred and has been given to us in the Word of God. This means that we cannot discern the being of God in any other way than by looking where God Himself gives us Himself to see, and therefore by looking at His works, at this relation and attitude—in the confidence that in these His works we do not have to do with any others, but with His works and therefore with God Himself, with His being as God.

What does it mean to say that "God is"? What or who "is" God? If we want to answer this question legitimately and thoughtfully, we cannot for a moment turn our thoughts anywhere else than to God's act in His revelation. We cannot for a moment start from anywhere else than from there. . . .

What God is as God, the divine individuality and characteristics, the *essentia* or "essence" of God, is something which we shall encounter either at the place where God deals with us as Lord and Saviour, or not at all. The act of revelation as such carries with it the fact that God has not withheld Himself from men as true being, but that He has given no less than Himself to men as the overcoming of their need, and light in their darkness—Himself as the Father in His own Son by the Holy Spirit. The act of God's revelation also carries with it the fact that man, as a sinner who of himself can only take wrong roads, is called back from all his own attempts to answer the question of true being, and is bound to the answer to the question given by God Himself. And finally the act of God's revelation carries with it the fact that by the Word of God in the Holy Spirit, with no other confidence but this unconquerable confidence, man allows being to the One in whom true being itself seeks and finds, and who meets him here as the source of his life, as comfort and command, as the power over him and over all things.

The Death of the God of European Consciousness

In his *Foundations of Dogmatics*, Otto Weber (1902–66), like Karl Barth, distinguishes between Christian faith and religion, and argues that the task of modern theology is to separate the Christian understanding of God from its cultural and philosophical trappings.

SOURCE

Weber, *Foundations*, 1:397–98.

The Traditional Doctrine of God. We are discussing the question, "What is God like," after our presentation of the Doctrine of the Trinity, for the reasons already given. Indeed, we discuss this question in the context of the Doctrine of the Triune God itself. If it is correct that we are speaking of God himself when we speak of him as the Three in One, then it is impossible to develop the doctrine of God's "essence," his "reality," and his "attributes" on the basis of some kind of God per se, a genus "God" or even of the Father alone.

There is a broadly held view that in the whole "problem of God as such" there is agreement both within the Christian Church and between it and European thought. To put it simply, there is more or less a consensus in regard to "God," but the special feature of "Christianity" is that Jesus Christ and the Holy Spirit, in addition, so to speak, have been ascribed divine dignity. Or even more crudely: The problems are not related to the "First Article," about whose essential contents even non-Christians (say, post-Christian Judaism or Islam or even religious philosophy) would make statements similar to those of the Church's theology. The problem areas, the sources of controversy, are to be found in the Second and Third Articles. Theology has tended to encourage this view by developing its "general doctrine of God" to a great extent out of a general concept of God.

The doctrine of God in the early Church, in the Middle Ages, and in Orthodoxy is a curious mixture of Greek, especially Neo-Platonic, and biblical ideas. Since the Reformation showed little interest in the traditional doctrine of God, it survived the fiery ordeal of the Reformation's reworking of all tradition far more unscathed than was really good. For this reason, Protestant Orthodoxy on the whole maintained the traditional mixture of non-Christian and biblical statements. Or, to put it better, the European world-consciousness, which found in a certain understanding of the essence *(essentia)* of God its ultimate point, was more or less taken over by Orthodoxy too. The result of this was that the profound change of this world-consciousness and of the world view which was introduced in the modern age of necessity involved the concept of God which was a part of it. As far back as Rationalism and from another point of departure as Schleiermacher, dogmatics has endeavored to harmonize its own understanding of God with the constant change of world-consciousness and world views. Only seldom has it simply given up the traditional composite concept in favor of the new world view. Normally it has remained in its traditional duplicity (or dichotomy), except that both components have received new illumination. This whole endeavor has intended to move in the direction of modern man, but in point of fact it has made little impression upon him. The sole result was that some kind of God idea remains as the ultimate point of the world-consciousness in general, and the objections of both Feuerbach and Nietzsche, who perceived that in this concept of God man was only expressing himself, were only grasped by smaller groups of people. Today, this world-consciousness itself has been shaken, and the world view is involved in a process of change whose conclusion cannot be predicted. In accordance with that, the traditional idea of God is beginning to dissolve into nothingness. In regard to the "God" of European consciousness, Nietzsche was right: "All gods are dead." For faith, this means that a clarification of the situation has occurred, and contemporary theology is presently occupied with the separation of the original Christian statement about God from all of the general religious ideas which have clustered about it.

God as the Ultimate Object of Loyalty and Ordering

In his *Ethics from a Theocentric Perspective*, James Gustafson expresses a "preference" for the Reformed tradition. Three elements are stressed in the Reformed tradition, the last of which is that all of human life should be ordered in relation to the purposes of God.

SOURCE
Gustafson, *Ethics*, I:163–64.

When the Reformed tradition in theology is mentioned there is but one decisive generating source for its identity, the work of John Calvin. Within the proportions required for the development of this book it is not possible to engage in all of the exposition that seems to be promised by my identification with this tradition. I shall not offer an interpretation of Calvin's theology, or of the theologies of the Synod of Dort, the Dutch Calvinists, the Puritans, Jonathan Edwards, Schleiermacher, Barth, H. Richard Niebuhr, or others I consider to be within the perimeters of that tradition. Nor is a historical account of that tradition in order here, not even a brief one that would indicate the prominent lines both of continuity and of change within it. I also have in mind authors from whose works Calvin learned deeply, principally Augustine, and various aspects of the biblical materials. As I noted in the introduction to this chapter, to indicate a preference for the Reformed tradition is not to suggest that it is the only historic tradition that informs the present work.

Of course there are great differences in theologians who would be placed under the heading of the Reformed tradition. Again, it is not my intention to assess which representatives are, in my judgment, more or less satisfactory, or even to isolate the issues that are under debate among them. Indeed, in the end readers who most consciously and loyally adhere to the Reformed tradition in theology might well take great umbrage at my claims to develop my thought in continuity with it.

There are three elements in this theological tradition which I believe to be properly stressed, and which I affirm not because they can be authorized by a particular historical strand of Christian thought but because I believe they can be justified on grounds that are being gradually exposed in this book. These are (1) a sense of a powerful Other, written about in the post-Calvin developments as the sovereignty of God. (2) The centrality of piety or the religious affections in religious and moral life. By piety I mean not Pietism as that developed in Protestantism in many forms, nor do I mean piousness, that pretentious display of religion which offends me as much as it does anyone. I mean an attitude of reverence, awe, and respect which implies a sense of devotion and of duties and responsibilities as well. (3) An understanding of human life in relation to the powerful Other which requires that all of human activity be ordered properly in relation to what can be discerned about the purposes of God. These three elements are reciprocally interrelated; it is the powerful God who evokes piety; it is the powerful God who is the ultimate condition of possibility for human action and the ordering of life: individual, interpersonal, social, historical, and in relation to nature. Without piety it is relatively meaningless to make a case for the existence or presence of God. Without piety it is relatively meaningless to bring into the centrality of moral life the "senses" that are the hinges on which religious belief and moral obligations and opportunities turn. Without a disciplined ordering of human activities piety can become those instrumental, self-regarding practices which I criticized above; without God as the ultimate object of loyalty and ordering, moral concerns readily become limited to the anthropocentric concerns also criticized above.

The Supremely Personal God of
Biblical Religion

Donald G. Bloesch, an evangelical Presbyterian, argues that an authentic evangelical theology is the God of the Bible and not the God described in various forms of speculative philosophy.

SOURCE

Donald G. Bloesch, *Essentials of Evangelical Theology,* 2 vols., Vol. 1: *God, Authority, and Salvation* (San Francisco: Harper & Row, 1978), 45–46.

Process philosophy, presently in vogue especially in America, posits a God who is bound to the world, at least in his concrete nature (as in Whitehead and Hartshorne). Teilhard de Chardin is also a major influence in this school of thought. A common axiom is that God is the soul of the world just as the world is the body of God. God is fulfilled or completed in the pleroma of the universe (Teilhard de Chardin). For Whitehead it is as true to say that the world creates God as that God creates the world. God does not call the world into being (as in the biblical view), but he saves it by presenting it with persuasive ideals. In process thought both God and the world are in the grip of creativity. Hartshorne remarks: "What is not to be decided, even by God, is that progress . . . there shall be." What we are left with is a God who, though infinite in some of his aspects, is essentially finite and at the mercy of the creature.

In opposition to process philosophy and theology I contend that the true God is essentially independent of the world though he makes himself dependent in his relationship to his children. God needs man only in relation to the realization of his plan for the world, not because there is any deficiency in himself.

Especially noticeable is the wide gulf between the God of biblical faith and the God of modern culture-religion (in both its conservative and liberal modes). The God of folk religion is a God of sentimental love, not holy love. He is the One who forgives no matter what we do. He is the "Man Upstairs" who is approached as an indulgent father, not as a Sovereign King. This is the God who is a means to man's own happiness, who enables man to attain self-fulfillment.

Modern evangelicalism opposes this kind of God, but it too is sometimes inclined to place a limit on the sovereignty of God. It is said that God only offers man salvation but does not effect salvation. Salvation is made dependent on man's own free will rather than divine election. In popular evangelicalism God is portrayed as powerful, but not invincible. His loving mercy is exalted but not his universal Lordship. God, it is thought, desires our worship, but little recognition is given to his kingship over all areas of life including politics and economics.

In some strands of evangelicalism, especially in fundamentalism, God's revelation is depicted as a static deposit of truth that is directly accessible to man's reason. But this subverts the idea that God is sovereign even in his revelation, that God remains hidden until he gives himself to be known. The knowledge and grace of God are not simply available to man even in the Bible, and this means that God remains the Master and man the servant even in the area of the knowledge of God.

An authentically evangelical theology will uphold the supremely personal God of biblical religion over the suprapersonal God of speculative philosophy on the one hand and the crudely personal God of culture-religion on the other. It will side with the transcendent God of the prophets over the immanent God of the mystics. It will proclaim the infinite God of the historic catholic faith over the finite God of modernistic theology. It will appeal to the concrete Absolute, as seen in Jesus Christ, over the metaphysical principle of pure abstraction. The God of the Scriptures is a supremely moral deity who demands our obedience, not an infinite abyss beyond good and evil wholly detached from the creature; nor is he the tolerant, benign deity of the folk tradition who merely desires our friendship. This God is jealous of his rights and solicitous for the welfare of his children (cf. Exod. 20:5, 6; Deut. 6:14–19). He is neither an unfeeling Primal Source nor "the fellow-sufferer who understands" (Whitehead), the one who needs us just as we need him. He is not to be equated with "the personality-producing forces of the cosmos" (Shailer Mathews), but he is the sovereign king who rules the cosmos. The true God is the holy, majestic Lord who gives himself in love but who demands our faith and love in return. He creates not because the Good must necessarily be productive or creative (as in Plato and Plotinus), but because he chooses to do so in his sovereign freedom.

"Like a mother . . . like a father"

A Brief Statement of Faith (1991) of the Presbyterian Church (U.S.A.) reflects many of the themes related to God that were developed in the last half of the twentieth century. The sovereignty of God is not God's will, but God's love. And God is described in biblical imagery that reflects both female and male experience.

SOURCE

"A Brief Statement of Faith," in *Book of Confessions,* 10.3.

We trust in God,
    whom Jesus called Abba, Father.
  In sovereign love God created the world good
    and makes everyone equally in God's image,
      male and female, of every race and people,
    to live as one community.
  But we rebel against God; we hide from our Creator.

Ignoring God's commandments,
we violate the image of God in others and ourselves,
accept lies as truth,
exploit neighbor and nature,
and threaten death to the planet entrusted to our care.
We deserve God's condemnation.
Yet God acts with justice and mercy to redeem creation.
In everlasting love,
the God of Abraham and Sarah chose a covenant people
to bless all families of the earth.
Hearing their cry,
God delivered the children of Israel
from the house of bondage.
Loving us still,
God makes us heirs with Christ of the covenant.
Like a mother who will not forsake her nursing child,
like a father who runs to welcome the prodigal home,
God is faithful still.

THE NAMING OF GOD

Classical theology has always been interested in the name of God. For example, in Anselm of Canterbury's *Proslogion* (1077), the name of God as "that than which none greater can be conceived" is understood by many theologians to be a proof for the existence of God. However, in the last half of the twentieth century the question of God's name also bears on the question of God's reality, but no longer in regard to God's existence. In the contemporary discussion, the issue is whether the reality of God can be freed from the patriarchal imagery of the Christian tradition. The issue becomes especially complex in regard to the doctrine of the Trinity and the traditional formula of "Father, Son, and Holy Spirit." Is there other language that can be used to "name" God that does not regress to one of the ancient heresies by collapsing the distinctions within the three persons into different functions of one God or does not subordinate the second and third persons of the Trinity to the first? At the end of the twentieth century, most Christian communities are still searching for answers to those questions.

FOR FURTHER STUDY

Ruth C. Duck, *Gender and the Name of God: The Trinitarian Baptismal Formula* (New York: Pilgrim, 1971). Elisabeth Moltmann-Wendel and Jürgen Moltmann, *God—His and Hers* (New York: Crossroad, 1991). Diane Tennis, *Is God the Only Reliable Father?* (Philadelphia: Westminster, 1985).

God Is Our Primary Thou

In the first volume of his *Dogmatics*, Emil Brunner argues that God makes God's self known by revealing God's name.

SOURCE

Brunner, *Dogmatics*, 1:120–22.

(1) God is known only where He Himself makes His Name known. Apart from this self-manifestation He is unknowable; from our point of view He is remote, inaccessible. The "Name" is that which is peculiar to Himself, it is that which distinguishes Him from all else, that which cannot be expressed by any general conception; which is not an object of human knowledge of any kind; we cannot discover it by the exercise of our own faculty of reason; it is a knowledge which—in the strict sense of the word—can only be *given*.

The Greek Fathers made a great mistake (and this error bore disastrous fruit) in turning the Name of Yahweh (and especially the Name as described by the Elohist writer in the narrative of the revelation of the Divine Name on Horeb) into an ontological definition. The words "I AM THAT I AM" ought not to be translated in the language of speculative thought, as a definition: "I AM HE WHO IS." To do this not only misses the meaning of this statement, but it turns the Biblical idea of revelation into its opposite. The "Name" which cannot be defined is turned into a definition. The meaning of the Sacred Name is precisely this: I am the Mysterious One, and I will to remain so; I AM THAT I AM. I AM the Incomparable, therefore I cannot be defined nor named. This description is similar to that in the Book of Judges, which is intended to warn man off "holy ground": "Why askest thou thus after My Name?" God is the Unknown God, until He makes Himself known.

This does not mean that pagans have no knowledge of God at all; such a foolish statement, and one which is utterly contrary to experience, does not occur anywhere in the Bible. But it does mean that those who do not possess the historical revelation, those to whom God has not made known His Name, do not know Him truly, do not know Him in such a way that they are in communion with Him. The pagan—or what comes to the same thing in the end—philosophical knowledge of God, does not create communion with God, because it is not knowledge of the God who—since He makes Himself known—creates communion with Himself.

Even the man to whom God has not made His Name known is not without a certain knowledge of God; for a knowledge of the Creator forms part of the creaturely existence of man. But this possibility of knowing God is not sufficient to remove the sinful blindness of man. It extends to the point of making man "without excuse," but it does not suffice to bring him to glorify God and to enter into communion with Him. In sinful man this natural knowledge of God becomes necessarily the delusion of idolatry, or—what amounts to the same thing in principle—the abstract, impersonal idea of God. Man who is left alone with Nature and with himself does not know the true God, because he does not know the God of revelation, the God whose Nature it is to be the Revealer, the one who communicates Himself. God in His Self-communication—that is *the Name of God;* hence where God does not make His Name known, He cannot be known aright.

(2) Secondly, the concept, the "Name" of God, suggests further that God is Person: He is not an "IT"; He is our primary "Thou." That which we can think and know by our own efforts is always an object of thought and knowledge, some *thing* which has been thought, some *thing* which has been known, therefore it is never "Person." Even the human person is never truly "person" to us so long as we merely "think" it; the human being only becomes "person" to us when he speaks to us himself, when he manifests the mystery of his being as a "thou," in the very act of addressing us.

The "Thou" is something other than the "Not-I"; the "Not-I" is the world, the sum-total of objects. But the "Thou" is that "Not-I" which is an "I" (or a Self) as I am myself, of which I only become aware when it is not thought by my own efforts, or perceived as an object, but when it makes itself known to me as self-active, self-speaking, as "I-over-against me."

It is true, of course, that to a certain extent we can know the human "thou" by our own efforts, because, and in so far as it is "also an I," a fellow-human being. The mystery of human personality is not absolute; it is only relative, because it is not only "other than I" but "the same as I." It can be placed under the same general heading "Man" along with me; it is not an unconditioned "Thou" because it is at the same time a "co-I." There is no general heading for God. God in particular has no "I" alongside of Himself. He is the "Thou" which is absolutely over against everything else, the "Thou" who cannot at the same time be on the same level with "me," "over-against" whom He stands.

Therefore I cannot myself unconditionally think God as this unconditioned "Thou," but I can only know Him in so far as He Himself, by His own action, makes Himself known to me.

The Limits of God's Name

In comparison to Emil Brunner, the Dutch theologian Herman Bavinck (1854–1921) takes a different point of view of the relation between God's name and God's being. Bavinck denies that God's name in the Bible describes God as God exists in God's self. God's names simply describe the way in which God has chosen to relate to humanity.

SOURCE

Herman Bavinck, *The Doctrine of God*, trans. William Hendriksen (Edinburgh: The Banner of Truth Trust, 1977), 85–86.

C. God's names as we find them in Scripture are not the revelation of his being as such but make God known unto us in his relation to creatures. Of course, God's revelation is true to his being. Because his names are a revelation of his relation to his creatures, particularly to man, it follows that Scripture is anthropomorphic. If God spake to us in Divine language, we would not be able to understand him. Hence, human attributes, organs, emotions, actions, etc., are ascribed to God.

The *name* of God in Scripture does not designate him as he exists in himself, but in his manifold revelation and relation to the creature. Nevertheless, this name is not arbitrary, but God reveals himself as he *is*. Hence, God's name stands for his honor, glory, excellencies, revelation, and divine essence. Hence, whosoever receives a revelation of that name receives a special privilege, and is, therefore, under special obligations. Whereas God reveals himself by means of his name, he requires his creatures to call him in accordance with that name. The "name by which God reveals himself" becomes the "name by which we address him." In Scripture "to be" and "to be called" indicate the same thing viewed from different angles: God *is* that which he *calls* himself, and he *calls* himself that which he *is*. Whatever God reveals of himself is expressed in certain definite names. To his creatures he grants the privilege to name him and to speak to him on the ground of and in conformity with his revelation. The *one* name of God, as inclusive of his entire revelation both in nature and in grace, is for us resolved into many, very many names. Only in that way do we obtain a view of the riches of his revelation and of the deep significance of his name. We are indeed *privileged* to address him in accordance with all that is revealed of his being in creation and redemption. Nevertheless, whereas all these names which we use to address him are names of *God*, we are obliged to sanctify and extol them. It is the *one* name, the full revelation, and in so far, it is the very being of God with which the names have to do. By means of his name God places himself in a very definite relation to us. Our relation to him ought to be in conformity with this relation which he assumes to us.

Hence, the names which we use in mentioning and addressing God are not arbitrary: they are not the mere inventions of our mind. Rather, it is God himself who in nature and in grace reveals himself consciously and freely, who gives us the right to name him on the ground of this revelation, and who has even made known to us in his Word the names which are based on that revelation. God's names, therefore, have this in common: they are all derived from God's revelation: there is not one name which is expressive of the being of God "in itself." The "revealed name" is the basis of all the "names by which we address God." Moreover, whereas God's revelation in nature and Scripture is definitely directed to man, God uses human language to reveal himself and manifests himself in human forms. It follows that Scripture does not merely contain a few anthropomorphisms; on the contrary, *all* Scripture is anthropomorphic. From beginning to end Scripture testifies a condescending approach of God to man. The entire revelation of God becomes concentrated in the Logos, who became "flesh." It is as it were *one* humanization, *one* incarnation of God. If God were to speak to us in divine language, no one would be able to understand him; but ever since creation, he, in condescending grace, speaks to us and manifests himself to us in human fashion. Hence, all the names with which God names himself and by means of which he allows us to address him are derived from earthly and human relations.

The Issue of Inclusive Language

In the late 1970s the Presbyterian Church in the United States, the so-called Southern church, commissioned a study paper on the issue of language about God. Published in 1980, the paper acknowledged the deep divisions within the church over issues of inclusive language, especially language used to describe God. But the paper also insisted that the language and imagery of the Bible in regard to God is richer than is the church's language.

SOURCE

Language About God (Atlanta: The Presbyterian Church in the United States, 1980), lines 378–410.

On the basis of this study at least five conclusions have emerged:

1) Language is too important to be used uncritically. The meaning of terms may change in the course of time. Thus, clear communication requires careful consideration of the language we choose to use.

2) The Bible is the primary source for language about God and the proper norm for evaluating that language. In our search for appropriate language for our time the Bible remains our only sure guide.

3) The imagery of the Bible in reference to God is much more rich and varied than the liturgy of the Church in recent centuries has reflected. The Bible offers numerous ways of talking about God which can expand our understanding of God and enhance our efforts to communicate our faith within our culture.

4) Our liturgical use of language about God needs enrichment. In the recent past only a few biblical images of God have been employed along with an over-dependence upon the masculine pronoun. The Bible offers many more ways to speak about God. We need to make strenuous efforts in incorporating this wide range of imagery. Terms which unmask old stereotypes wait to be used. Addressing God as Sustainer, Redeemer, Helper, Fortress, Savior, Leader, Guide, Guardian, Shield, Creator, Alpha and Omega, Light, Vindicator, Ancient of Days, Foundation, Refuge, etc., may provide immediate assistance. New hymns, new prayers, new affirmations of faith, and liturgical-creedal elements can be written and should be an order of high priority in view of the fact that language significantly influences the perceptions of those who use it.

5) There is no short, simple answer to the situation that has prompted this study. This study is but the first step. The Church will need to turn repeated and careful attention to this subject in the years ahead. Ongoing reflection and discussion will be needed.

Language is a powerful force in the life of people. The Church has been created by the Word of God and continues to be reformed, revitalized, redefined as it struggles to understand and respond to the living God. The development of new alternatives which can nourish and sustain the Church will take time, struggle, careful reflection, and commitment.

A Nonpatriarchal God

In the context of discussing Jesus' use of the word *Abba* to address God, Elisabeth Moltmann-Wendel argues that Jesus' use of that name points to a nonpatriarchal God. Jesus' God, she contends, reflects a matriarchal Sophia tradition.

SOURCE

Elisabeth Moltmann-Wendel, *A Land Flowing with Milk and Honey: Perspectives on Feminist Theology,* trans. John Bowden (New York: Crossroad, 1986), 100–102.

So Abba is an intimate word and thus an affront to any patriarchal structure. It shows no respect and makes God familiar and near. However, only Mark has preserved this direct familiarity between father and child; in the later Gospels the relationship between the two is already characterized by obedience. "To do the will of God" in Mark is still a matter of being in tune with the community of God, something which also comes about through communion with sisters and brothers. This traumatic word "obedience" is only developed fully in Pauline theology. In Mark we can detect nothing of this structure of obedience which was later to have a fatal effect, and which entered Christianity with hierarchical and patriarchal thought. Thus from the perspective of the psychology of religion, Christa Mulack can say of this original, non-patriarchal use by Jesus of the term Abba: "The Father has become one with the Great Mother: he realizes her, she has entered into him and realizes herself through him, so that the two can no longer be distinguished."

Gerhard Lohfink's comment on Jesus' understanding of the Father shows a similar break with the current image of Jesus. Jesus calls people out of family ties, himself violates family duties, in a way which according to Old Testament law calls for the death penalty. "He who does the will of God is my mother, my brother, my sister." These are the words he uses to describe the new community. Those who follow him and have left all family ties—father, mother, children—behind them will rediscover in the new community everything that they have left behind: "house and brothers and sisters and mothers and children and fields . . ." However, remarkably there is no mention of fathers that they will rediscover (Mark 10:29, 30). The new community is a community of wives and mothers, but it is free from paternal structures, even if it came into being in the environs of the man Jesus. According to Elisabeth Schüssler-Fiorenza, "Call no one father, for you have one Father" must therefore have been what Jesus originally said (Matt. 23:9). Here is a challenge to today's churches with their fathers in the faith, fathers in orders, church fathers and Holy Father. As Elisabeth Schüssler-Fiorenza puts it, "The Father God of Jesus makes possible the sisterliness of men by challenging the right of all fathers and all patriarchy to exist." Underneath the upper stratum of the New Testament, which seems to us to be so male, with its conflict between Father and Son, and the twelve male disciples, we can see a stratum in which a non-patriarchal community is given the right to exist by a non-patriarchal God. But church history shows that this breakthrough was not maintained and that is already evident from the New Testament. It is important today to uncover the roots again and see behind the patriarchal language and structure of the tradition the non-patriarchal heritage which has become obscured.

However, what remain in the centre of theological interest are not the hidden conceptions of Jesus about Sophia God, but the ideas he expressed about God the Father. They shaped the fate of church and theology. Here the theologians began with their basic interest in male models. These conceptions found their way into the Bible. The conflict between Father and Son was reflected in the doctrine of the Trinity and ethics. Faith in God the Father was significantly and usefully turned into the formation of personality in a patriarchal society.

But the God whom Jesus proclaimed is rooted in the matriarchal Sophia tradition. Jesus' way of addressing God as Abba and the sisterly, non-patriarchal social order which he depicts are in accord with this picture of God. However, these matriarchal beginnings were absorbed by patriarchal society and remained a living potential only in marginal Christian traditions, which offered self-awareness, wisdom and survival above all to women.

The images of God in the Bible have more possibilities for female identification than is generally assumed. They were and are capable of being interpreted in non-patriarchal ways. They were and are open for theophantasy. This is above all evident, however, in the conceptions of the sub-culture.

THE TRIUNE GOD

Some of the most significant theologians in the twentieth century have made the recovery of the Trinity the centerpiece of their reinterpretations of Christian faith. Karl Barth and Jürgen Moltmann have given the Trinity a prominence it had not received in many post-Enlightenment theologies. Barth argued that God revealed God's self to be triune. In the 1980s Moltmann argued that even Barth's theology was insufficiently trinitarian, and that a properly trinitarian interpretation of God would be one in which the three persons of the Trinity would be understood not just as different "modes of the one God's being" (as Barth suggested), but three centers of self-consciousness.

To some readers, Moltmann's position seems to come perilously close to tritheism. For his part, Moltmann argued that only a fully trinitarian interpretation of God could do full justice to the stories of the Bible. The trinitarian

God of the Bible stands in sharp contrast to the speculative, philosophical god of Greek metaphysics, who, as "first mover," is immutable and unchanging. The problem with this Greek god, Moltmann insists, is that a god who is immutable is a god without pathos and a god who cannot love.

FOR FURTHER STUDY

Colin Gunton, *The Promise of Trinitarian Theology* (Edinburgh: T. & T. Clark, 1991). Eberhard Jüngel, *The Doctrine of the Trinity: God's Being Is in Becoming* (Grand Rapids: Wm. B. Eerdmans, 1976). Eberhard Jüngel, *God as the Mystery of the World: On the Foundation of the Theology of the Crucified One in the Dispute Between Theism and Atheism,* trans. Darrell L. Guder (Grand Rapids: Wm. B. Eerdmans, 1983). Lesslie Newbigen, *Trinitarian Faith and Today's Mission* (Richmond: John Knox, 1963). Claude Welch, *In This Name: The Doctrine of the Trinity in Contemporary Theology* (New York: Charles Scribner's Sons, 1952).

Schleiermacher on the Trinity

One of the interesting puzzles about Schleiermacher's magnum opus, *The Christian Faith,* is why he waited until the final pages to discuss the doctrine of the Trinity. One interpretation is that Schleiermacher wanted his remarks on the Trinity to be the last and most important thing he said about Christian faith. Another, quite different interpretation is that he considered the Trinity unimportant and relegated it to an appendix.

SOURCE

Schleiermacher, *Christian Faith,* 738–39.

THE DIVINE TRINITY

§170. *All that is essential in this Second Aspect of the Second Part of our exposition is also posited in what is essential in the doctrine of the Trinity; but this doctrine itself, as ecclesiastically framed, is not an immediate utterance concerning the Christian self-consciousness, but only a combination of several such utterances.*

I. An essential element of our exposition in this Part has been the doctrine of the union of the Divine Essence with human nature, both in the personality of Christ and in the common Spirit of the Church; therewith the whole view of Christianity set forth in our Church teaching stands and falls. For unless the being of God in Christ is assumed, the idea of redemption could not be thus concentrated in His Person. And unless there were such a union also in the common Spirit of the

67

Church, the Church could not thus be the Bearer and Perpetuator of the redemption through Christ. Now these exactly are the essential elements in the doctrine of the Trinity, which, it is clear, only established itself in defence of the position that in Christ there was present nothing less than the Divine Essence, which also indwells the Christian Church as its common Spirit, and that we take these expressions in no reduced or sheerly artificial sense, and know nothing of any special higher essences, subordinate deities (as it were) present in Christ and the Holy Spirit. The doctrine of the Trinity has no origin but this; and at first it had no other aim than to equate as definitely as possible the Divine Essence considered as thus united to human nature with the Divine Essence in itself. This is the less doubtful that those Christian sects which interpret the doctrine of redemption differently are also necessarily without the doctrine of the Trinity—they have no point of belief to which it could be attached—which could not possibly be the case if even in Catholic doctrine there existed at least some other points than this to which the attachment could be made. It is equally clear from this why those divergent sects which are chiefly distinguishable by their denial of the Trinity are not thereby forced into still other divergences in the doctrine of God and the divine attributes, as must have been the case if the doctrine of the Trinity were rooted in a special view of the nature of the Supreme Being as such. But on the other hand, they *are* forced to set up a different theory of the Person of Christ, and hence also of man's need for redemption and of the value of redemption. In virtue of this connexion, we rightly regard the doctrine of the Trinity, in so far as it is a deposit of these elements, as the coping-stone of Christian doctrine, and this equating with each other of the divine in each of these two unions, as also of both with the Divine Essence in itself, as what is essential in the doctrine of the Trinity.

God's Self-Revelation as Trinity

While it may be questionable to what extent the Trinity is central to Schleiermacher's theology, Karl Barth made it very clear in the first volume of his *Church Dogmatics* that what God reveals is that God is triune.

SOURCE
Barth, *Church Dogmatics*, I/1:295–96.

If in order to clarify how Church proclamation is to be measured by Holy Scripture we first enquire into the prior concept of revelation, already in this enquiry itself we must keep to Holy Scripture as the witness of revelation. Perhaps more important than anything dogmatics can say with reference to the pre-eminent place of Scripture in the Church and over against the Church is the example which dogmatics itself must give in its own fundamental statements. It must try to do what is undoubtedly required of the Church in general, namely, to pay heed to Scripture, not to allow itself to take its problems from anything else but Scripture. The basic problem with which Scripture faces us in respect of revelation is that the revelation attested in it refuses to be understood as any sort of revelation alongside which there are or may be others. It insists absolutely on being understood in its uniqueness. But this means that it insists absolutely on being understood in terms of its object, God. It is the revelation of Him who is called Yahweh in the Old Testament and Θεός or, concretely, κύριος in the New Testament. The question of the self-revealing God which thus forces itself upon us as the first question cannot, if we follow the witness of Scripture, be separated in any way from the second question: How does it come about, how is it actual, that this God reveals Himself? Nor can it be separated from the third question: What is the result? What does this event do to the man to whom it happens? Conversely the second and third questions cannot possibly be separated from the first. So impossible is any separation here that the answer to any one of the questions, for all the autonomy and distinctiveness it has and must continue to have as the answer to a particular question, is essentially identical with the answer to the other two. *God* reveals Himself. He reveals himself *through Himself*. He reveals *Himself*. If we really want to understand revelation in terms of its subject, i.e., God, then the first thing we have to realise is that this subject, God, the Revealer, is identical with His act in revelation and also identical with its effect. It is from this fact, which in the first instance we are merely indicating, that we learn we must begin the doctrine of revelation with the doctrine of the triune God.

The Three Unitarianisms

One of the many contributions of H. Richard Niebuhr to Reformed theology was his ability to clarify diverse theological positions by means of typologies and models. In an article on the Trinity, Niebuhr demonstrated how different theological positions can be shown to result from an emphasis (and in some cases an overemphasis) on one of the three persons of the Trinity.

SOURCE

H. Richard Niebuhr, "The Doctrine of the Trinity and the Unity of the Church," *Theology Today* 3, no. 3 (October 1946), 372–84 (selections).

THE THREE UNITARIANISMS
IN CHRISTIANITY

Christianity has often been accused of being a polytheism with three gods and, indeed, the tendency toward such tritheism is probably always present in Christendom. Yet it seems nearer the truth to say that Christianity as a whole is more likely to be an association, loosely held together, of three Unitarian religions. Though we are accustomed to think of Unitarianism as being the doctrine that there is only one God and that this God is the Father, the Creator referred to in the first article of the Creed, a fresh approach to Christian history and to contemporary Christian thinking suggests the hypothesis that there are two other positions comparable to the first. It has often been maintained in effect that the one God on whom men must rely for salvation is Jesus Christ; hence there is a kind of Unitarianism of the Son. And it has often been held in theory and practice that the one God is the Spirit, rather than the Creator known in Nature or the Son known in Scriptures. The common monotheism of Christian faith asserts itself in the first part of each of these statements—there is but one God and God is one. The divergences in Christianity enter with the definition of the nature of the one God and of the place where he is to be found.

The Unitarianism of the Creator seems to be easily identifiable. Its first interest has always been monotheistic. It is a protest against polytheistic and idolatrous tendencies in the Churches. But it has seemed self-evident to this monotheism that the one God whom it is man's duty to worship and on whom he depends for significance and salvation is the reality which accounts for the presence and the pattern and the dynamic of the natural world. He is the Almighty Maker of heaven and earth, the first cause and the great designer. God is the being with whom a philosophy that proceeds from nature to super-nature is concerned and this is the same One of whom Hebrew religion and Jesus Christ spoke. This Unitarianism must always have a large interest in natural theology as presenting the primary approach to the problem of the existence and nature of the super-natural, while historical theology or Biblical theology and the theoretical examination of inner experience tend to take secondary places. . . .

In modern Protestantism the Unitarianism of Jesus Christ appears in many forms. Among them is the Jesus-cult of pietism with its practice of the mystic sense of Jesus' presence, its hymns of adoration, and its prayers addressed to him. For such pietism it is not the Father who "so loved the world that he gave his only begotten Son" or who commends his love to men in Christ, but Jesus is the source and center of love, so that no reference to the Creator is necessary. The love of Jesus for men is the divine reality on which men depend and which they adore. Another form of this modern Unitarianism of the Son is ethical rather than mystic in character, though the ethical and mystical forms are often closely related. For it the significance of Jesus lies in the fact that he is the Son of Man, the ideal Man, who not only set before men the ideal of a perfect society but undertook by means of his life and death to inaugurate it. This ethical Unitarianism of the Son is often regarded as atheistic since it makes no references to a super-historical or super-natural reality. But in its magnifying of Jesus Christ as the leader and martyr of a new humanity it assumes a definitely religious form. It is at least a sort of hero-cult for which Christ is not only an historical figure but a source of present strength and a real object of adoration. . . .

The third sort of Unitarianism for which the Spirit is the one and only God, or which absorbs the Creator and the Son into the Spirit, may be the most prevalent of all. Certainly it is so in modern Christianity. All Christian spiritualism tends in this direction. It looks to the reality found in the inner life rather than to the Being beyond nature or to the Redeemer in history for the fundamental principle of reality and value. It does not only say that God is spirit but converts the proposition and usually affirms that spirit is God. The reality with which men come into touch when they turn to reasoning itself, to awareness as subjective, to conscience and self-consciousness—this is the reality on which they are absolutely dependent and from which alone they can expect illumination, purification, perfection. Neither the Creator of nature nor the Jesus Christ of history can redeem men from death, but in the inner life the immortal power which cannot be held by death is manifest. No laws of nature and no counsels of the Sermon on the Mount but only the conscience within can lead to repentance and moral renewal. An objective God, a "Thou" corresponding to an "I," is not to be found amidst the mediations of sensation nor in the historic documents but only in the direct spiritual awareness of religious experience. The way to God, to the one Spirit, cannot be found by means of natural philosophy nor of historic revelation but only through spiritual awareness, through inner knowledge of inner truth and good. . . .

In every case it appears true that none of the positions can stand alone but must borrow something from the other positions, that the three Unitarianisms are interdependent. If this is the case, then apart from any other considerations which may lead the Church to the formulation of a Trinitarian doctrine, it must endeavor to do so because it must set forth the faith which is not the realized conviction of any of its parts but rather the common faith. The Trinitarianism of the whole Church must undertake to state what is implicit in the faith and knowledge of all of its parts though it is not explicit in any one of them. It must undertake to correct the over-emphases and partialities of the members of the whole not by means of a new over-emphasis but by means of a synthesized formula in which all the partial insights and convictions are combined. A doctrine of the Trinity, so formulated, will never please any one part of the Church but it will be an ecumenical doctrine providing not for the exclusion of heretics but for their inclusion in the body on which they are actually dependent. Truth, after all, is not the possession of any individual or of any party or school, but is represented, insofar as it can be humanly represented, only by the whole dynamic and complementary work of the company of knowers and believers.

A Social Doctrine of the Trinity

Twentieth-century theology has included several significant proposals for the reinterpretation of the doctrine of the Trinity. Several Western theologians have questioned the traditional claim that the Spirit proceeds from the Father through the Son (the *filioque*). Important objections have been raised to ontological categories of "substance" and "hypostasis" in the classical doctrine of the Trinity. Jürgen Moltmann, among others, has attempted to develop a social doctrine of the Trinity in place of the classical doctrine.

SOURCE

Moltmann, *The Trinity and the Kingdom*, 18–20.

FOR FURTHER STUDY

Jürgen Moltmann, *History and the Triune God: Contributions to Trinitarian Theology*, trans. John Bowden (New York: Crossroad, 1992).

A new treatment of the doctrine of the Trinity today has to come to terms critically with these philosophical and theological traditions. A return to the earlier Trinity of substance is practically impossible, if only because the return to the cosmology of the old way of thinking about being has become impossible too, ever since the beginning of modern times. To carry on with the more modern "subject" Trinity is not in fact very fruitful either, because modern thinking in terms of "subject" is increasingly losing force and significance. Anthropological thinking is giving way to the new, relativistic theories about the world, and anthropocentric behaviour is being absorbed into social patterns. The belief that the most important thing about experience is the experiencing of it, and about deeds the doing of them, is beginning to strike most people as naïve. The world of growing interdependencies can no longer be understood in terms of "my private world." Today the appeal to pure subjectivity is viewed as an inclination towards escapism.

The present book is an attempt to start with the special Christian tradition of the history of Jesus the Son, and from that to develop a historical doctrine of the Trinity. Here we shall presuppose the unity of God neither as homogenous substance nor as identical subject. Here we shall enquire about that unity in the light of this trinitarian history and shall therefore develop it too in trinitarian terms. The Western tradition began with God's unity and then went on to ask about the trinity. We are beginning with the trinity of the Persons and shall then go on to ask about the unity. What then emerges is a concept of the divine unity as the union of the tri-unity, a concept which is differentiated and is therefore capable of being thought first of all.

In distinction to the trinity of substance and to the trinity of subject we shall be attempting to develop a social doctrine of the Trinity. We understand the scriptures as the testimony to the history of the Trinity's relations of fellowship, which are open to men and women, and open to the world. This trinitarian hermeneutics leads us to think in terms of relationships and communities; it supersedes the subjective thinking which cannot work without the separation and isolation of its objects.

Here, thinking in relationships and communities is developed out of the doctrine of the Trinity, and is brought to bear on the relation of men and women to God, to other people and to mankind as a whole, as well as on their fellowship with the whole of creation. By taking up panentheistic ideas from the Jewish and the Christian traditions, we shall try to think *ecologically* about God, man and the world in their relationships and indwellings. In this way it is not merely the Christian *doctrine* of the Trinity that we are trying to work out anew; our aim is to develop and practise trinitarian *thinking* as well.

The Trinity and Contemporary Culture

While it might seem that the doctrine of the Trinity would be irrelevant to the complexities and varied movements of contemporary culture, Dutch Reformed theologian Arnold A. van Ruler (1908–70) argued that it is precisely the Trinity and only the Trinity that can encompass what van Ruler referred to as "worldly reality."

SOURCE

Arnold A. van Ruler, *Calvinist Trinitarianism and Theocentric Politics: Essays Toward a Public Theology*, trans. John Bolt, Toronto Studies in Theology 38 (Lewiston/Queenston/Lampeter: Edwin Mellen, 1989), 13–14.

Naturally the church cannot become modern. It is orthodox. That is precisely its essence. But let it then be an orthodoxy of the church and not an orthodoxy of one part in it. This means that this orthodoxy must be truly catholic in its dimensions by integrating within itself many of the new insights and struggles of the last centuries.

The real difficulty here undoubtedly lies in the historical rootedness of the Christian faith. This faith claims that eternal salvation rests in an historical fact, namely, that Jesus is the Christ. To lighten the problem one could add that the people of Israel are God's chosen people. The situation becomes even more joyful when one adds that the church with its tradition and apostolic, missionary activity *(apostolische arbeid)* in the world is the body of Christ. But one is always busy with historical realities in their—from the point of view of reason—complete contingency. That is not merely a burden; it is also the glory of the Christian faith. It takes the world, in its historicity, the entire historical process in its reality, with utmost seriousness, namely, from out of God and before his face. This brings with it the necessity of a philosophy of history as an inevitable development from the Christian faith. It is here, in such a philosophy of history, that one perhaps finds the most significant link between the Christian faith and the modern world. Or do we remain then in a too one-sided pneumatological framework? Does a fully developed trinitarian theology not compel us toward the mystical unity of history and reality before the face of the triune God, and in that mystical unity to seek the point of contact between the Chrsitian faith and culture, also modern culture? In every age, from the time of Origen and Augustine on, that has been the case. Trinitarian mysticism has always been the deepest and most attractive as well as the most encompassing and far-reaching. In a trinitarian framework, so to speak, everything finds its place.

But then it is no longer possible to say that everything is already given in Jesus Christ. For example, is complete truth already given in him? Are the communists completely wrong when they claim that material reality is the truth? Is the whole world not in a representative and thus soteriological way gathered together for a time in Jesus Christ? It is *this* truth that is preached! But does this mean that there is no truth to be found in a science such as geology? Or must such a science in a simple fashion become a Christian science, science which proceeds from Christ? That Jesus Christ, and thus Christian dogma, has a significance for science and culture, I would scarcely deny. On the contrary! It is my conviction that only the church can maintain the great vision of a culture authoritatively bound together by dogmas. It is in this sense that complete truth and existence in its entirety are integrated in Christ. It is in this way that Jesus Christ takes form *(gestalte)* in us. It is in this way that reality in its entirety is experienced as proceeding from Christ. But Jesus Christ is not all that there is and the preaching of the gospel is not all that there is. We humans and worldly reality also exist; culture and historical processes exist as well. And each of these has its own independence and its own significance. But, in the Christian faith, this cannot be understood christologically but only in a trinitarian way.

GOD'S NATURE AND ATTRIBUTES

Many Reformed theologians in the nineteenth century, such as R. L. Dabney of the Presbyterian Church in the United States, continued to affirm the doctrine of God as described in the second chapter of the Westminster Confession of Faith. In the twentieth century, however, increasing numbers of Reformed theologians sought a different understanding of God, one that would be faithful to the witness of the Bible but that would also enable them to converse with a culture that understood reality no longer as fixed and unchanging but as dynamic, developmental, and relational.

Furthermore, the horror of twentieth-century history—two world wars, the Holocaust and Hiroshima—left many theologians struggling simply to make sense out of what it might mean to affirm God's presence and love in the world. While classical Reformed theology had stressed the sovereignty of God's will, contemporary theology emphasized the cross and stressed the suffering love of God.

FOR FURTHER STUDY

Paul S. Fiddes, *The Creative Suffering of God* (New York: Oxford University Press, 1988). Alexander J. McKelway, *The Freedom of God and Human Liberation* (London: SCM, and Philadelphia: Trinity, 1990). Daniel L. Migliore, *The Power of God* (Philadelphia: Westminster, 1983).

The Immutability of God

In his lectures on systematic theology at Union Theological Seminary in Richmond, Virginia, Robert Lewis Dabney (1820–98) affirmed a classical understanding of the immutability of God. Particularly interesting is Dabney's attempt to reconcile God's immutability with the Bible's description of God's anger and love.

SOURCE

Robert L. Dabney, *Systematic Theology*, 2d ed. (Edinburgh: The Banner of Truth Trust, 1985), 152–54.

That God is immutable in His essence, thoughts, volitions, and all His perfections, has been already argued from His perfection itself, from His independence and sovereignty, from His simplicity and from His blessedness. This unchangeableness not only means that He is devoid of all change, decay, or increase of substance: but that His knowledge, His thoughts and plans, and His moral principles and volitions remain forever the same. This immutability of His knowledge and thoughts flows from their infinitude. For, being complete from eternity, there is nothing new to be added to His knowledge. His nature remaining the same, and the objects present to His mind remaining forever unchanged, it is clear that His active principles and purposes must remain forever in the same state; because there is nothing new to Him to awaken or provoke new feelings or purposes.

Our Confession says that God hath neither parts nor passions. That He has something analogous to what are called in man active principles, is manifest, for He wills and acts; therefore He must feel. But these active principles must not be conceived of as emotions, in the sense of ebbing and flowing accesses of feeling. In other words, they lack that agitation and rush, that change from cold to hot, and hot to cold, which constitute the characteristics of passion in us. They are, in God, an ineffable, fixed, peaceful, unchangeable calm, although the springs of volition. That such principles may be, although incomprehensible to us, we may learn from this fact: That in the wisest and most sanctified creatures, the active principles have least of passion and agitation, and yet they by no means become inefficacious as springs of action—e.g., moral indignation in the holy and wise parent or ruler. That the above conception of the calm immutability of God's active principles is necessary, appears from the following: The agitations of literal passions are incompatible with His blessedness. The objects of those feelings are as fully present to the Divine Mind at one time as another; so that there is nothing to cause ebb or flow. And that ebb would constitute a change in Him. When, therefore, the Scriptures speak of God as becoming wroth, as repenting, as indulging His fury against His adversaries, in connection with some particular event occurring in time, we must understand them anthropopathically. What is meant is, that the outward manifestations of His active principles were as though these feelings then arose.

God's immutability, as thus defined is abundantly asserted in Scriptures (Numb. xxiii:19; Ps. cii:26; xxxiii:11; cx:4; Is. xlvi:10; Mal. iii:6; Jas. 1:17; Heb. vi:17; xiii:8.)

Objections Answered.

This attribute has been supposed to be inconsistent with the incarnation of the Godhead in Christ; with God's work done in time, and especially His creation; and with His reconciliation with sinners upon their repentance. To the first, it is enough to reply, that neither was God's substance changed by the incarnation; for there was no confusion of natures in the person of Christ, nor was His plan modified; for He always intended and foresaw it. To the second, the purpose to create precisely all that is created, was from eternity to God, and to do it just at the time He did. Had He not executed that purpose when the set time arrived, there would have been the change. To the third, I reply, the change is not in God: but in the sinner. For God to change His treatment as the sinner's character changes, this is precisely what His immutability dictates.

God as the One Who Loves in Freedom

In his *Church Dogmatics*, Karl Barth rejected the term "attributes" in favor of the term "perfections." Furthermore, Barth insisted that God's being cannot be understood apart from God's "works," or acts. When the biblical story of God's acts is studied closely, Barth believed it would be clear that the two primary "perfections" of God are love and freedom and that these are dialectically related. God is the being who freely loves and who loves in freedom.

SOURCE
Barth, *Church Dogmatics*, II/1:322.

God lives His perfect life in the abundance of many individual and distinct perfections. Each of these is perfect in itself and in combination with all the others. For whether it is a form of love in which God is free, or a form of freedom in which God loves, it is nothing else but God Himself, His one, simple, distinctive being.

God's being consists in the fact that He is the One who loves in freedom. In this He is the perfect being: the being which is itself perfection and so the standard of all perfection; the being, that is, which is self-sufficient and thus adequate to meet every real need; the being which suffers no lack in itself and by its very essence fills every real lack. Such a being is God. He is this being because He lives as such. It is as we return to life as the fundamental element in the divine being that we also move forward to God's perfections. The one perfection of God, His loving in freedom, is lived out by Him, and therefore identical with a multitude of various and distinct types of perfection. There is no possibility of knowing the perfect God without knowing His perfections. The converse is also true: knowledge of the divine perfections is possible only in knowledge of the perfect God, of His loving in freedom. But because God lives His perfect being the knowledge of His perfections is also a way—the way which in the presence of the living God we must tread. In other words, even in the knowledge of the one perfect God we are confronted by His richness. The real God is the one God who loves in freedom, and as such is eternally rich. To know Him means to know Him again and again, in ever new ways—to know only Him, but to know Him as the perfect God, in the abundance, distinctness and variety of His perfections.

The Passion of God

Jürgen Moltmann argues eloquently that Christian theology has its proper beginning in the history of Christ's passion and in particular at the foot of the cross. A theology that begins and ends with the cross cannot help but affirm that the passion of the Christ is also the suffering of the triune God.

SOURCE

Moltmann, *The Trinity and the Kingdom*, 21–23.

GOD'S "APATHY" OR HIS PASSION?

If, in the manner of Greek philosophy, we ask what characteristics are "appropriate" to the deity, then we have to exclude difference, diversity, movement and suffering from the divine nature. The divine substance is incapable of suffering; otherwise it would not be divine. The absolute subject of nominalist and Idealist philosophy is also incapable of suffering; otherwise it would not be absolute. Impassible, immovable, united and self-sufficient, the deity confronts a moved, suffering and divided world that is never sufficient for itself. For the divine substance is the founder and sustainer of this world of transient phenomena; it abides eternally, and so cannot be subjected to this world's destiny.

But if we turn instead to the theological proclamation of the Christian tradition, we find at its very centre the history of Christ's passion. The gospel tells us about the sufferings and death of Christ. The delivering up of God's Son for the reconciliation of the world is communicated to us in the eucharist in the form of bread and wine. When the passion of Christ becomes present to us through word and sacrament, faith is wakened in us—the Christian faith in God. The person who believes owes his freedom to Christ's representation. He believes in God for Christ's sake. God himself is involved in the history of Christ's passion. If this were not so, no redeeming activity could radiate from Christ's death. But how is God himself involved in the history of Christ's passion? How can Christian faith understand Christ's passion as being the revelation of God, if the deity cannot suffer? Does God simply allow Christ to suffer for us? Or does God himself suffer in Christ on our behalf?

Christian theology acquired Greek philosophy's ways of thinking in the Hellenistic world; and since that time most theologians have simultaneously maintained the passion of Christ, God's Son, and the deity's essential incapacity for suffering—even though it was at the price of having to talk paradoxically about "the sufferings of the God who cannot suffer." But in doing this they have simply added together Greek philosophy's "apathy" axiom and the central statements of the gospel. The contradiction remains—and remains unsatisfactory.

Right down to the present day the "apathy" axiom has left a deeper impress on the basic concept of the doctrine of God than has the history of Christ's passion. Incapacity for suffering apparently counts as being the irrelinquishable attribute of divine perfection and blessedness. But does this not mean that down to the present day Christian theology has failed to develop a consistent Christian concept of God? And that instead—for reasons which still have to be investigated—it has rather adopted the metaphysical tradition of Greek philosophy, which it understood as "natural theology" and saw as its own foundation.

The ability to identify God with Christ's passion becomes feeble in proportion to the weight that is given to the "apathetic" axiom in the doctrine of God. If God is incapable of suffering, then—if we are to be consistent—Christ's passion can only be viewed as a human tragedy. For the person who can only see Christ's passion as the suffering of the good man from Nazareth, God is inevitably bound to become the cold, silent and unloved heavenly power. But that would be the end of the Christian faith.

This means that Christian theology is essentially compelled to perceive God himself in the passion of Christ, and to discover the passion of Christ in God. Numerous attempts have been made to mediate between apathy and passion in a christological sense, in order to preserve the apathetic axiom; but—if we are to understand the suffering of Christ as *the suffering of the passionate God*—it would seem more consistent if we ceased to make the axiom of God's apathy our starting point, and started instead from the axiom of God's passion. The word "passion," in the double sense in which we use it, is well suited to express the central truth of Christian faith. Christian faith lives from the suffering of a great passion and is itself the passion for life which is prepared for suffering.

A Straight-Line God

Asian Reformed theologian C. S. Song questions whether the concept of salvation history *(Heilsgeschichte),* with its emphasis on continuity, can do justice to much of human experience. In addition, this "straight-line" concept of history presupposes a straight-line God who is far more orderly than the God of the Bible. Love, Song insists, is not straight but round.

SOURCE

C. S. Song, *The Compassionate God* (Maryknoll, N.Y.: Orbis, 1982), 25–27.

I seriously doubt that a straight line can express the immense complexity of God's saving activity in the world. A straight line simplifies. It cuts off irregularities. It straightens out knotty problems. It geometrizes everything it touches, even God and what God does. It is such a handy tool for theologians to have. We have to concede that a straight line is one of the most basic and essential units for science and technology. Without it skyscrapers would collapse and human adventures into space would be forced to stop.

Modern culture of science and technology is a straight-line culture. Should a straight line refuse to cooperate and begin to bend, turn or wiggle, horrible consequences would surely follow. A metropolis might turn into a heap of ruins. Human habitats would change their shape out of recognition. If we had to single out the important items that make life not only livable but enjoyable, the straight line would have to be high on our list. We are all children of this straight-line culture, for better or for worse.

But when it comes to a quite complex matter such as God's dealings with humankind, we begin to wonder if the straight-line concept can still work. In fact, to turn God into a straight-line God is to caricature God. Love, for example, is a most simple and yet most powerful thing. It brings lives into being, sustains them, nourishes and enriches them. Love is the Word through which God comes to us and we to God. "God is love," says 1 John 4:8.

It is plain to everyone that love is not a geometrical concept. It cannot be measured by a ruler. It cannot be weighed on a balance. It cannot be straightened out by a line. And least of all is it a straight line. Love is round, not straight. It does not penetrate space like a straight line, but fills it and saturates it. It is not a linear but a concentrical movement. It is not analytical but synthetic. It is not judgmental but embracing. A straight line judges, punishes, eliminates, but love forgives, caresses, embraces, and includes. God is not a straight line but love. The straight-line God of *Heilsgeschichte* is a hard, stern God who has predetermined who are to be saved and who are to be condemned.

Furthermore, the straight-line God must be a monotonous and unamusing God. The God of traditional theology wears a long face, sitting grimly on the theological throne. Even saints and angels surrounding the divine throne are caught in this grim and pensive mood of the straight-line God. It is seldom that one comes across a laughing God, a laughing Christ, a laughing saint, or a laughing angel in the Christian church—Catholic, Orthodox, or Protestant.

Laughter has long departed from the church and theology. Once stepping into the church, we Christians leave our laughter behind. We forget to laugh in the church. We think it not proper to laugh during worship service. Even when singing: "Hosanna, in the highest!" we are straight-faced and solemn. We are too conscious of the straight-line God staring at us from a pedestal high above. He seems ready to catch any sign of mischievousness in us. But a religion that has done away with laughter can be a dangerous thing. It can stir up witch-hunting. It can resort to burning heretics at the stake. It can start a religious war, exterminating unbelievers and infidels. Should we not then pray: O God, give us back our laughter!

God's Sovereign Love

In "The Confession of 1967" of the Presbyterian Church (U.S.A.), God is described in terms of sovereign love, and the power of that love is interpreted by means of Jesus' cross.

SOURCE
"The Confession of 1967," in *Book of Confessions*, 9.15.

God's sovereign love is a mystery beyond the reach of man's mind. Human thought ascribes to God superlatives of power, wisdom, and goodness. But God reveals his love in Jesus Christ by showing power in the form of a servant, wisdom in the folly of the cross, and goodness in receiving sinful men. The power of God's love in Christ to transform the world discloses that the Redeemer is the Lord and Creator who made all things to serve the purpose of his love.

The Abba of Sovereign Love

"A Brief Statement of Faith" (1991), like "The Confession of 1967" of the Presbyterian Church (U.S.A.), makes sovereign love the primary attribute of God.

SOURCE
"A Brief Statement of Faith," in *Book of Confessions*, 10.3.

We trust in God,
    whom Jesus called Abba, Father.
In sovereign love God created the world good
    and makes everyone equally in God's image,
        male and female, of every race and people,
    to live as one community.

PREDESTINATION

One of the ways in which classical Reformed theology emphasized the sovereignty of God was by means of a doctrine of predestination, or election. Chapters 20–24 of Book 3 of John Calvin's *Institutes of the Christian Religion* and chapter 3 of the Westminster Confession of Faith ("Of God's Eternal Decrees") are perhaps the best-known statements of predestination in classical Reformed theology: From the sinful mass of humanity God chooses some for eternal blessedness and communion and others, in the words of Westminster, for "everlasting death."

Nineteenth- and twentieth-century Reformed theology has been characterized by a serious reappraisal of predestination. The doctrine of "double election" as taught by Calvin and Westminster has been reinterpreted christologically. The result has been that predestation is understood to lean in the direction of universalism or to imply a greater modesty or even agnosticism about what can be known about the scope of God's salvation.

A surprising number of confessional documents of twentieth-century Reformed churches say little or nothing about predestation. The deemphasis on predestation may also be the result of the shift in metaphors for interpreting the sovereignty of God from "will" to "love." Anything resembling predestination would seem to presuppose the active agency of God in human affairs and history, and that conviction apparently is no longer shared by all Reformed theologians.

FOR FURTHER STUDY

G. C. Berkouwer, *Divine Election,* trans. Hugo Bekker (Grand Rapids: Wm. B. Eerdmans, 1960). Loraine Boettner, *The Reformed Doctrine of Predestination* (Grand Rapids: Wm. B. Eerdmans, 1932). James Daane, *The Freedom of God: A Study of Election and Pulpit* (Grand Rapids: Wm. B. Eerdmans, 1973). Paul K. Jewett, *Election and Predestination* (Grand Rapids: Wm. B. Eerdmans, 1985). Jürgen Moltmann, *Prädestination und Perseveranz: Geschichte und Bedeutung der reformierten Lehre "de perseverantia sanctorum"* (Neukirchen: Neukirchener Verlag, 1961).

The Mercy of a Freely Electing God

Benjamin Breckinridge Warfield (1851–1921) was one of the distinguished members of the Princeton school of theology. Like other members of the Princeton school, Warfield fiercely defended what he believed to be classical Calvinism, a significant part of which was the doctrine of double election.

SOURCE

Benjamin Breckinridge Warfield, *Biblical Doctrines* (New York: Oxford University Press, 1929), 64–66.

The Biblical writers are as far as possible from obscuring the doctrine of election because of any seemingly unpleasant corollaries that flow from it. On the contrary, they expressly draw the corollaries which have often been so designated, and make them a part of their explicit teaching. Their doctrine of election, they are free to tell us, for example, does certainly involve a corresponding *doctrine of preterition.* The very term adopted in the New Testament to express it—ἐκλέγομαι, which, as Meyer justly says (Eph. i. 4), *"always* has, and must *of logical necessity* have, a reference to *others* to whom the chosen would, without the ἐκλογή, still belong"—embodies a declaration of the fact that in their election others are passed by and left without the gift of salvation; the whole presentation of the doctrine is such as either to imply or openly to assert, on its every emergence, the removal of the elect by the pure grace of God, not merely from a state of condemnation, but out of the company of the condemned—a company on whom the grace of God has no saving effect, and who are therefore left without hope in their sins; and the positive just reprobation of the impenitent for their sins is repeatedly explicitly taught in sharp contrast with the gratuitous salvation of the elect despite their sins. But, on the other hand, it is ever taught that, as the body out of which believers are chosen by God's unsearchable grace is the mass of justly condemned sinners, so the destruction to which those that are passed by are left is the righteous recompense of their guilt. Thus the discrimination between men in the matter of eternal destiny is distinctly set forth as taking place in the interests of mercy and for the sake of salvation: from the fate which justly hangs over all, God is represented as in His infinite compassion rescuing those chosen to this end in His inscrutable counsels of mercy to the praise of the glory of His grace; while those that are left in their sins perish most deservedly, as the justice of God demands. And as the broader lines of God's gracious dealings with the world lying in its iniquity are more and more fully drawn for us, we are enabled ultimately to perceive that the Father of spirits has not distributed His elective grace with niggard hand, but from the beginning has had in view the restoration to Himself of the whole world; and through whatever slow approaches (as men count slowness) He has made thereto—first in the segregation of the Jews for the keeping of the service of God alive in the midst of an evil world, and then in their rejection in order that the fulness of the Gentiles might be gathered in, and finally through them Israel in turn may all be saved— has ever been conducting the world in His loving wisdom and His wise love to its destined goal of salvation,—now and again, indeed, shutting up this or that element of it unto disobedience, but never merely in order that it might fall, but that in the end He might have mercy upon all. Thus the Biblical writers bid us raise our eyes, not only from the justly condemned lost, that we may with deeper feeling contemplate the marvels of the Divine love in the saving of sinners not better than they and with no greater claims on the Divine mercy; but from the relatively insignificant body of the lost, as but the prunings gathered beneath the branches of the olive-tree planted by the Lord's own hand, to fix them on the thrifty stock itself and the crown of luxuriant leafage and ever more richly ripening fruit, as under the loving pruning and grafting of the great Husbandman it grows and flourishes and puts forth its boughs until it shall shade the whole earth. This, according to the Biblical writers, is the end of election; and this is nothing other than the salvation of the world. Though in the process of the ages the goal is not attained without prunings and fires of burning,—though all the wild-olive twigs are not throughout the centuries grafted in,—yet the goal of a saved world shall at the end be gloriously realized. Meanwhile, the hope of the world, the hope of the Church, and the hope of the individual alike, is cast solely on the mercy of a freely electing God, in whose hands are all things, and not least the care of the advance of His saving grace in the world. And it is undeniable that whenever, as the years have passed by, the currents of religious feeling have run deep, and the higher ascents of religious thinking have been scaled, it has ever been on the free might of Divine grace that Christians have been found to cast their hopes for the salvation alike of the world, the Church, and the individual; and whenever they have thus turned in trust to the pure grace of God, they have spontaneously given expression to their faith in terms of the Divine election.

Jesus Christ—Electing God and Elected Human

Karl Barth believed that the classical doctrine of election, double predestination, does not have sufficient biblical warrant. The interpretation of predestination in Calvin and Westminster, Barth argued, says more and is clearer than the Bible. Barth thought, furthermore, that the classical doctrine was too speculative and was insufficiently focused on the Bible's witness to Jesus Christ.

Barth believed that there is only person who is "elect," and that is Jesus Christ, who, following the two-natures logic of Chalcedon, is both the electing God and the elect human. Does God's grace in Jesus Christ mean that all people are predestined for salvation? Barth insisted that the answer to that question, either yes or no, is beyond the reach of faith and is known only to God.

SOURCE
Barth, *Church Dogmatics*, II/2:94–95, 417–19.

THE ELECTION OF JESUS CHRIST

The election of grace is the eternal beginning of all the ways and works of God in Jesus Christ. In Jesus Christ God in His free grace determines Himself for sinful man and sinful man for Himself. He therefore takes upon Himself the rejection of man with all its consequences, and elects man to participation in His own glory.

I. Jesus Christ, Electing and Elected

Between God and man there stands the person of Jesus Christ, Himself God and Himself man, and so mediating between the two. In Him God reveals Himself to man. In Him man sees and knows God. In Him God stands before man and man stands before God, as is the eternal will of God, and the eternal ordination of man in accordance with this will. In Him God's plan for man is disclosed, God's judgment on man fulfilled, God's deliverance of man accomplished, God's gift to man present in fulness, God's claim and promise to man declared. In Him God has joined Himself to man. And so man exists for His sake. It is by Him, Jesus Christ, and for Him and to Him, that the universe is created as a theatre for God's dealings with man and man's dealings with God. The being of God is His being, and similarly the being of man is originally His being. And there is nothing that is not from Him and by Him and to Him. He is the Word of God in whose truth everything is disclosed and whose truth cannot be over-reached or conditioned by any other word. He is the decree of God behind and above which there can be no earlier or higher decree and beside which there can be no other, since all others serve only the fulfillment of this decree. He is the beginning of God before which there is no other beginning apart from that of God within Himself. Except, then, for God Himself, nothing can derive from any other source or look back to any other starting-point. He is the election of God before which and without which and beside which God cannot make any other choices. Before Him and without Him and beside Him God does not, then, elect or will anything. And He is the election (and on that account the beginning and the decree and the Word) of the free grace of God. For it is God's free grace that in Him He elects to be man and to have dealings with man and to join Himself to man. He, Jesus Christ, is the free grace of God as not content simply to remain identical with the inward and eternal being of God, but operating *ad extra* in the ways and works of God. And for this reason, before Him and above Him and beside Him and apart from Him there is no election, no beginning, no decree, no Word of God. Free grace is the only basis and meaning of all God's ways and works *ad extra*. For what *extra* is there that the ways and works could serve, or necessitate, or evoke? There is no *extra* except that which is first willed and posited by God in the presupposing of all His ways and works. There is no *extra* except that which has its basis and meaning as such in the divine election of grace. But Jesus Christ is Himself the divine election of grace. For this reason He is God's Word, God's decree and God's beginning. He is so all-inclusively, comprehending absolutely within Himself all things and everything, enclosing within Himself the autonomy of all other words, decrees and beginnings. . . .

And now, if we may venture a final word, the determination of the elect consists in the fact that in and with his election and calling, in and with the service for which he is intended and which he has to perform, the ongoing of the reconciling work of the living God in the world is included and takes place. The election of each individual involves, and his calling completes, an opening up and enlargement of the (in itself) closed circle of the election of Jesus Christ and His community in relation to the world—or (from the standpoint of the world) an invasion of the dark kingdom of the lies which rule in the world, a retreat and shrinkage of its godless self-glorification. The existence of each elect means a hidden but real crossing of frontiers, to the gain of the kingdom of God as the kingdom of grace. It is the concern of God that there should be these frontier-crossings. It is also His concern how and when they should take place. Again, it is His concern what should be the end of these frontier-crossings, which are many (in relation to the unworthiness of all men), or few (in relation to the great numbers of mankind). It is His concern what is to be the final extent of the circle. If we are to respect the freedom of divine grace, we cannot venture the statement that it must and will finally be coincident with the world of man as such (as in the doctrine of the so-called *apokatastasis*). No such right or necessity can legitimately be deduced. Just as the gracious God does not need to elect or call any single man, so He does not need to elect or call all mankind. His election and calling do not give rise to any historical metaphysics, but only to the necessity of attesting them on the ground that they have taken place in Jesus Christ and His community. But, again, in grateful recognition of the grace of the divine freedom we cannot venture the opposite statement that there cannot and will not be this final opening up and enlargement of the circle of election and calling. Neither as the election of Jesus Christ, the election of His community, nor the election of the individual do we know the divine election of grace as anything other than a decision of His loving-kindness. We would be developing an opposing historical metaphysics if we were to try to attribute any limits—and therefore an end of these frontier-crossings—to the loving-kindness of God. We avoid both these statements, for they are both abstract and therefore cannot be any part of the message of Christ, but only formal conclusions without any actual substance. We keep rather to the clear recognition that whenever an individual is elected and called, a new man is created out of the old, the reconciled world is fashioned out of the unreconciled, and to that extent, in secret, it becomes the kingdom of God and at the same time a new witness and messenger of the truth of the divine election of grace. This is the determination of every elect individual in salvation-history, and it cannot be treasured too highly. Independently of all that it means for himself, a victorious step is taken. For although (like the whole community of God, and even the man Jesus Christ Himself) he belonged and still belongs to the world of men, elected now in Jesus Christ he is taken from it and put in that service and commission. In this way the truth is repeated and confirmed, and a new sign erected in face of the whole world of men. This sign points unambiguously in one direction, that the gracious God is in the right and the man who denies Him is in the wrong. The free decision of God alone can lead further, but this step is one which gives us every reason and confidence to believe and hope that there will be further steps of the same kind, further confirmations and repetitions of the same truth, further signs pointing in the same direction. It gives us every reason and confidence to suppose that the people of God concealed in this world of men, which does not yet recognise the love of God for men, and its Lord Jesus Christ, and therefore its own true self, may be greater than was previously visible. It gives us every reason and confidence to go after this concealed and dormant people of God in the world. Clearly, his part in its awakening is the determination of every elect person. He is called in order that he himself may be one who calls within the world. It is not for him to know or to decide the result of his call. The actual opening up and enlargement of that circle will always take place exactly in the area which corresponds to the eternal free will of God. There will always be those who hear the proclamation of their election, always those who believe it, whom God has chosen in Jesus Christ and therefore determined for this faith and hearing. Those who are really this people by the grace of God will always recognise and confess Jesus Christ, emerging, therefore, as His people, as the communion of saints, recognising and confessing Him. That will always happen by the power and grace of God (of Jesus Christ and the Holy Spirit). It will always happen at His time (the time determined by Him). He Himself directs His own affairs. That is what makes those two statements impossible. But one thing is sure. The elect man is chosen in order that the circle of election—that is, the circle of those who recognise and confess Jesus Christ in the world—should not remain stationary or fixed, but open up and enlarge itself, and therefore grow and expand and extend. What is given him in his election and calling is undoubtedly the task not to shut but to open, not to exclude but to include, not to say No but Yes to the surrounding world; just as he himself is undoubtedly one to whom it was opened, who was included, to whom Yes was said—the Yes of the unmerited, free and eternal grace and love of God. It is by and in this Yes that he must live with others. He represents and reflects the gracious God, and Jesus Christ and His people, as he causes them to hear this Yes. If he says No he also says Yes; even when he closes he opens; even when he excludes he includes. He will face others wrathfully but never contemptuously, with indignation but never with malice, angered but never embittered, a guest and a stranger but never an enemy. He will never renounce the recognition of their (and his own) lost condition. But he will also never renounce the obligation by which he is bound to them, as a lost soul to whom the grace of God has been revealed and come. Nor will he renounce the confidence that the same grace is addressed to them too. He will not weary in his service towards them, nor will he ever be disloyal to it, because of any self-made judgments of his own concerning them. It belongs to God Himself to determine and to know what it means that God was reconciling the world unto Himself (2 Cor. 5). The concern of the elect is always the "ministry of reconciliation" (2 Cor. 5), and no other. This is the determination under which he has to live.

The Responsibility of the Elect

In the last half of the twentieth century, neo-orthodoxy slowly pervaded the life of the Presbyterian church in the United States. One of the most influential books written during that period was Shirley C. Guthrie's *Christian Doctrine*. Steeped in the theology of Barth, Guthrie was able to make neo-orthodoxy intelligible and compelling for the layperson.

SOURCE

Shirley C. Guthrie, Jr., *Christian Doctrine: Teachings of the Christian Church* (Atlanta: John Knox, 1968), 145–46.

To be one of the elect is a high honor and privilege. Predestination is the gift of what matters most in all the world: freedom to live both now and forever the genuinely human life God wills for us. But it is the honor and privilege and gift of being the *servant* of God and fellowmen. Christ, *the* "Chosen One" of God (Luke 9:35), God's "beloved Son" (Matthew

3:17), was chosen to be the Suffering Servant of God. Life for him meant the sacrifice of his life in obedience to God and in love for other men. Freedom meant freedom from the temptation to make himself a great political ruler, freedom to fulfill his destiny to be the Savior of the world by dying a criminal's death.

For us too, then, to be chosen "insiders" who receive God's gift of life does not mean the occasion for a feeling of pride or superiority in being God's elite. It is no occasion for us insiders to look at outsiders with contempt or pity or indifference. That was precisely the mistake by which Israel misunderstood her election: "God is for us and against them, and therefore we will have nothing to do with all those sinful outsiders." It was the mistake of the disciples who wanted the first place for themselves in the Kingdom. We never will understand the meaning of predestination so long as we think of it only as getting and enjoying something others do not have, perhaps even being thankful that we are "not like other men" (Luke 18:11).

Or to put it positively: If we interpret our election in the light of Christ, we will know that it means not only a gift but a command, not only life passively received from God but life actively lived in obedience to God. God chooses us not so we can sit around and enjoy our election, but get to work. And the work he gives us is the work of participating in his plan and will to give life and freedom to *all* men—outsiders as well as insiders, our enemies as well as our friends, social outcasts as well as respectable solid citizens, black as well as white, immoral as well as moral.

That means trouble, of course. It is dangerous and costly to be loved and chosen by God. It means to become a follower of Jesus in caring for the "wrong" people, upsetting the political and social and maybe even the religious status quo—and suffering the consequences. That is the warning that goes with the good news of being predestinated to belong to the people of God. Be careful if you want to be an insider! It does not mean escape from the dirty, guilty, painful world; it means you will be sent into the very middle of its life. For you have been given the gift of freedom—freedom to obey the God who loved the world and gave his own Son for it; freedom to follow the one who said, "The Son of man also came not to be served but to serve, and give his life as a ransom for many" (Mark 10:45).

But those who are willing to accept their election on these terms will also learn the promise that goes with it and the secret of the deepest meaning of the doctrine of predestination: "'For whoever would save his life will lose it, and whoever loses his life for my sake will find it'" (Matthew 16:25).

THE COVENANTS

Although the concept of covenant has often been given a prominent place in classical Reformed theology, especially in the so-called federal theology of the seventeenth century, it has not been given the same visibility in modern Reformed theology. Classical theology often drew an important distinction between the covenant of works and the covenant of grace. Modern Reformed theology, however, appeals to the concept of covenant in order to clarify the nature of God's relation to the world and to humanity.

FOR FURTHER STUDY

Barth, *Church Dogmatics*, IV/1:3–78. L. Berkhof, *Systematic Theology* (Grand Rapids: Wm. B. Eerdmans, 1941), 211–18, 262–301. Arthur C. Cochrane, "Karl Barth's Doctrine of the Covenant," in *Major Themes in Reformed Tradition*, ed., Donald K. McKim (Grand Rapids: Wm. B. Eerdmans, 1992), 108–16. Weber, *Foundations*, 1:293–308.

Creation and Covenant

In his *Church Dogmatics*, Karl Barth developed the thesis that creation is the external basis of the covenant and the covenant is the inner basis of creation.

SOURCE

Barth, *Church Dogmatics*, III/1:97.

We have to make a self-evident restriction. Creation is not itself the covenant. The existence and being of the one loved are not identical with the fact that it is loved. This can be said only in respect of the love with which God loves Himself—the Father the Son and the Son the Father in the Holy Spirit. It cannot be said of God's relationship to the creature posited in distinction from Himself. The existence and being of the creature willed and constituted by God are the object and to that extent the presupposition of His love. Thus the covenant is the goal of creation and creation the way to the covenant. Nor is creation the inner basis of the covenant. (At a later point we shall have to state conversely that the covenant is the inner basis of creation; but this relationship is not reversible.) The inner basis of the covenant is simply the free love of God, or more precisely the eternal covenant which God has decreed in Himself as the covenant of the Father with His Son as the Lord and Bearer of human nature, and to that extent the Representative of all creation. Creation is the external—and only the external—basis of the covenant. It can be said that it makes it technically possible; that it prepares and establishes the sphere in which the institution and history of the covenant take place; that it makes possible the subject which is to be God's partner in this history, in short the nature which the grace of God is to adopt and to which it is to turn in this history. As the love of God could not be satisfied with the eternal covenant as such; as it willed to execute it and give it form outside the divine sphere, it made itself this external ground of the covenant, i.e., it made necessary the existence and being of the creature and therefore of creation. It is, however, only its external basis. If it has taken place for its sake and may be called grace in view of this goal, it is so only as it points to grace itself and prepares for it. But what does "only" signify in this connexion? As that which genuinely points to grace, as its necessary preparation, it is itself already grace, but only in this sense and context and not without it.

The Human Being as the Purpose of God

Dutch theologian Hendrikus Berkhof (b. 1914) uses the category of covenant to describe the nature of the relationship between God and the human creature.

SOURCE

Berkhof, *Christian Faith*, 427, 429.

The golden thread which runs through all the preceding, linking the deeds, events, developments, structures, and institutions discussed there, is God's intention to adopt people as his children, to make them his covenant partners. This intention can be individualistically misunderstood (as is often done) as if God's concern is persons as pure individuals. For God there are no pure individuals; nor, however, is there an abstract "mankind." For God sees people as they interact with others in the extensive fabric of space and time, of society and history, of structures, tradition, culture, and nature. We are persons, people meant for fellowship with God and humans because of and in all the structures in which we have been placed. This is such a fundamental fact that before we could speak about the renewal of man we had to deal with the church. But now, at last, the way is clear to do full justice to the fact that God has pleasure in *man*. In all these structures his concern is mankind, people, each as he is, unique, human. In that respect, what we have broadly called the "structures" are secondary or, more accurately, instrumental in significance. Their significance is often neglected in the study of the faith. In the next chapter we shall specifically deal with that significance. But here we must note that their importance lies exactly in their instrumentality. About nature we need to be more reserved. We have no right to say that it exists only for the sake of man. Rather, it is partly our servant, partly our companion. As a creation of God which is different from man, it is largely unfathomable to us and as such a pointer to the unfathomableness of its creator; and that is cause for us to be humble (cf. Job 38–41). In calling man the purpose of God, we do not thereby exclude the possibility that God may have other, entirely different purposes in mind with and for his creation. Yet the course of his acts in history, a course in which we participate by faith and which we probe in the study of the faith, discloses him to us as a God of people whose goal is to enter into an eternal covenant with them. On the basis of our knowledge of that covenantal path we may say that apparently in that unique event man is God's purpose. . . .

The expression "man the purpose of God" has an unusual, even provocative ring in the tradition of theology. It gives the impression that we are misunderstanding the Christian faith and giving it an anthropocentric twist. Should we not say the opposite, namely that God is the purpose of man? That is, however, not the opposite of the first statement, only its reverse. For a covenant implies the orientation of the one party to the other. For the creature, man, a covenant with his God can mean nothing less than a radical orientation to him who in this covenant radically orients himself to us. But it does imply for man who is alienated from God a radical reorientation and about-face. God wants a covenant relationship with man as he is; yet for the sake of that relationship he cannot possibly leave him as he is. God's gracious turning to man is correlated from man's side by his turning to God. In this turning man bows before him who intends his salvation. Hence that about-face is not man's alienation from himself, but rather his home-coming, his reaching his destiny.

THE CALLING OF ISRAEL

Unfortunately, Reformed theology prior to the middle of the twentieth century, like most other forms of Christian theology, contains numerous instances of anti-Semitism. Although Reformed theology has usually insisted that the Old Testament is an indispensable portion of the one written Word of God, some Reformed confessions include comments about Israel and Judaism that can only be described as anti-Semitic.

In the latter half of the twentieth century, in the aftermath of World War II and the Holocaust, many theologians discerned that Christian theology must (1) confess its complicity in the anti-Semitism that produced the slaughter of the Holocaust, and (2) reappraise its understanding of the relation between the church and Judaism. Although there were many Christian martyrs in World War II, on both sides of the conflict, it is still regrettable that The Theological Declaration of Barmen, written in 1934, made no mention of what was already beginning to happen to Jews in Germany.

The reappraisal of the relationship between Christianity and Judaism in the second half of the twentieth century is most evident in the emphasis on the Judaism of Jesus (for example, the Confession of 1967 of the Presbyterian Church (U.S.A.) describes Jesus as a "Palestinian Jew") and in the reinterpretation of providence.

FOR FURTHER STUDY

Hendrikus Berkhof, "Israel as a Theological Problem," in *Journal of Ecumenical Studies* 6:34 (Summer, 1969), 329–47. Bertold Klappert, *Israel und die Kirche: Erwagungen zur Israellehre Karl Barths*, "Theologische Heute," 207 (Munich: Kaiser, 1980). Friedrich-Wilhelm Marquardt, *Die Entdeckung des Judentums für die Christliche Theologie: Israel im Denkens Karl Barths*. Abhandlung zum Christlich-Judischen Dialog, Vol. 1, ed. Helmut Gollwitzer (Munich: Kaiser, 1967). Jürgen Moltmann and Pinchas Lapide, *Israel und Kirche: Ein Gemeinsamer Weg?: Ein Gespräch* (Munich: Kaiser, 1980). Jürgen Moltmann and Pinchas Lapide, *Jewish Monotheism and Christian Trinitarian Doctrine*, trans. Leonard Swidler (Philadelphia: Fortress, 1981). Alan P. F. Sell, ed., *Reformed Theology and the Jewish People* (Geneva: World Alliance of Reformed Churches, 1986). Paul van Buren, *A Theology of the Jewish Christian Reality*, 3 parts, Part One: Discerning the Way, Part Two: A Christian Theology of the People Israel; Part Three: Christ in Context (San Francisco: Harper & Row, 1980–88).

The One Way of the One God

In comparison to most other Reformed theologians, Hendrikus Berkhof gives significant attention to Israel in his one-volume systematic theology, *Christian Faith*. Berkhof stresses that unless Christians understand Jesus as a child of Israel they will misunderstand him.

SOURCE
Berkhof, *Christian Faith*, 225–26.

What is called Israel here is by and large discussed as the Old Testament in the Christian church. It contains the first and by far the largest part of the Bible. Therefore, it is self-evident that everywhere in the Christian churches it should have an important role. In this chapter we shall constantly speak about the Old Testament. But deviating from usual practice, we make this name subordinate to the name Israel. For here we are not concerned with the book as such, but with the faith and the history of the people of Israel to which this book bears witness. By recognizing this book as a source of revelation, the Christian church professes its belief that God pursues a unique course through history, and that the appearance of Jesus Christ was not an isolated epiphany but a decisive phase on a way which had begun ages ago, a way which took the shape of an electing, guiding, judging, and saving concern with one special people.

The Christian church has off and on, sufficiently or insufficiently, been aware of that. Sometimes she has regularly related the New Testament to the Old, but at other times (unfortunately, more often) she has read the New separate from the Old. In some respects she is intensely concerned with the Old Testament; think of the important place Israel has in her instruction or the Psalms in her liturgy. In other respects she seems to forget Israel almost completely and not need her at all. The latter is especially the case in the creedal statements and systematic theology handbooks. An example is the structure of the Apostles' Creed: the confession jumps directly from the Creator to Christ. This happens especially with an unhistorically vertical trinitarian mode of thinking; beginning with the Father who is the creator, one continues with the Son who is the redeemer. In the study of the faith this can never be consistently maintained, for in between creation and redemption one must assume the fact of sin. But usually one proceeds then directly from the doctrine of sin to Christology. There is hardly room and interest for God's history with Israel. The impression is given that after a long period of divine inactivity, Jesus drops out of heaven. There are, however, not only vertical incursions from eternity, but there is also a horizontal course of God with us through time. From the second perspective, God's centuries-long association with Israel as the Old Testament describes it assumes great theological significance.

Of course, this importance has hardly or never been denied in the study of the faith. Yet often this has been regarded as a purely historical circumstance in the sense that Jesus Christ happened to be born from the people of Israel and thus can be understood only against the background of its history and holy books, just as a knowledge of the antecedent evolvement of Greek culture is necessary to understand Plato. But in the case of Jesus the historical setting points to a much deeper connection: in the Old Testament he found the God whom he began to call "Father" in a special sense and whose way with his people Israel he wanted obediently to walk to the end. Therefore one cannot be a Christian without accepting in one way or another *with* the authority of Christ also that of the Old Testament. We say "in one way or another," because it is clear that is is impossible to put Christ's relation to the preceding way of Israel on a common denominator. We have to do justice to at least two fundamental realities: (1) that Jesus knew that he had been sent by Israel's God and wanted to be obedient to the Old Testament; (2) that Jesus was rejected by leaders of the people of Israel because they regarded his claims and actions as being in conflict with the Old Testament. This duality recurs in Paul's speaking about the Old Testament as on the one hand the book which prophesies of Christ and his grace and on the other as the law that kills and the "ministry that brought death." Whether and how these two approaches can be brought together will have to become clear in later paragraphs. But both presuppose that there is an intrinsic connection between Christ and the Old Testament, and that we cannot understand Christ unless we understand God's way with Israel, regardless whether Christ is the continuation or the radical turning of that way. The assumption of the entire New Testament is that Israel's way and the way of Jesus Christ are together the *one* way of the *one* God. Furthermore, if one calls Christ the fulfillment or the end of Israel's way, this is based on the presupposition that his significance depends on the experiences and results of that preceding way. Unless the Christian church in her faith and reflection regularly experiences that way, she cannot understand the import of Jesus' work and lot; then, as we see happen all the time, she interprets him in categories imported from elsewhere, and so misunderstands him.

Christology and Messianism

Jürgen Moltmann has been an active participant in Jewish-Christian theological conversations. In his Christology he argues that although Christians and Jews may disagree as to whether Jesus is the Messiah, they share far more common ground than either may have realized. This common ground is their shared conviction that hope is rooted in a coming Messiah. Christians, of course, believe that this Messiah has already come and will come again; Jews insist that the Messiah is yet to come because the world remains unredeemed.

SOURCE

Jürgen Moltmann, *The Way of Jesus Christ: Christology in Messianic Dimensions*, trans. Margaret Kohl (San Francisco: HarperCollins, 1990), 147–48.

JESUS AND ISRAEL

Jesus' life and the way he acted was related to community, and it was therefore always a receiving and an acting on behalf of other people, and in their stead. According to the gospels, it was just as much related to Israel as was the life and ministry of John the Baptist. For the early Jewish-Christian community, the unity between Jesus and Israel was especially important. Mark 3:14 tells us that "he appointed twelve, to be with him, and to be sent out to preach. . . ." According to this passage, Jesus called *twelve* to be special disciples out of the wider circle of those who followed him, passing on to them his own messianic mission (Matt. 10:5ff.). The number twelve represents the twelve tribes of the people of Israel, for the messianic hope was aligned towards the restoration of this people in the era of salvation. According to Ezekiel, this was also to be linked with the reoccupation of the land of Israel. Jesus' choice of twelve disciples is a messianic act: with them the end-time gathering of Israel, as the renewed people of God, is to begin. Consequently, the twelve are also sent to "the whole of Israel," but not to the Gentiles (Matt. 10:5). If the kingdom of God "is near," the gathering of God's people for this kingdom must begin. Then Israel will become the messianic light of the Gentile nations, and the nations will come to Zion to receive God's righteousness and justice (Isa. 2:1–3). In this order of things, salvation comes "first to the Jews and then to the Gentiles."

Although Jesus turns first of all to Israel, this is not meant exclusively, for in his concern for Israel God is concerned about the Gentile nations and the earth. The appointment of the twelve disciples for Israel's revival is not the same thing as the call to follow Jesus, or identical with the community of women and men who followed him. It has a symbolic meaning for Israel alone. In choosing the twelve, Jesus was not founding any church. He was thinking solely of Israel. Only one person was evidently "co-opted" to this group later on: Matthias took the place of Judas. After that the group did not perpetuate itself. It probably broke up when Christianity spread beyond the bounds of what was open to it among the Jews. For that reason, to trace the church back historically and dogmatically to the calling of the twelve, and the special call to Peter, is untenable, and also pernicious, because it allows the church to push Israel out of salvation history. The church "of Jews and Gentiles" only came into being after the resurrection, and through the experience of the Spirit, and with the rejection of the gospel by "all Israel."

At the same time this early Jewish-Christian hope for the revival of the nation of the twelve tribes binds Jesus into a unity with his people which Gentile Christians must not destroy. The synoptics tell the life-history of Jesus in the pattern of the collective remembrance of the history of Israel. The future hope of the people is summed up in their expectation of the messiah. In the gospel to the Gentile nations, the presence of Jesus Christ makes Israel present also, just as, conversely, Gentile Christians through their faith participate in the remembrance, the hope and also the sufferings of Israel, the people of God.

Jews and Christians: Partners in Waiting

In 1987, the General Assembly of the Presbyterian Church (U.S.A.) approved a paper entitled "A Theological Understanding of the Relationship Between Christians and Jews." The paper's theological position is formulated by means of seven theses.

SOURCE

"A Theological Understanding of the Relationship Between Christians and Jews," in *Minutes; 199th General Assembly; Part I: Journal* (New York and Atlanta: Office of the General Assembly, 1987), 419–23 (27.051–27.089).

1. We affirm that the living God whom Chrisitians worship is the same God who is worshiped and served by Jews. We bear witness that the God revealed in Jesus, a Jew, to be the Triune Lord of all, is the same one disclosed in the life and worship of Israel. . . .

2. We affirm that the church, elected in Jesus Christ, has been engrafted into the people of God established by the covenant with Abraham, Isaac, and Jacob. Therefore, Christians have not replaced Jews. . . .

3. We affirm that both the church and the Jewish people are elected by God for witness to the world and that the relationship of the church to contemporary Jews is based on that gracious and irrevocable election of both. . . .

4. We affirm that the reign of God is attested both by the continuing existence of the Jewish people and by the church's proclamation of the gospel of Jesus Christ. Hence, when speaking with Jews about matters of faith, we must always acknowledge that Jews are already in a covenantal relationship with God. . . .

5. We acknowledge in repentance the church's long and deep complicity in the proliferation of anti-Jewish attitudes and actions through its "teaching of contempt" for the Jews. Such teaching we now repudiate, together with the acts and attitudes which it generates. . . .

6. We affirm the continuity of God's promise of land along with the obligations of that promise to the people Israel. . . .

7. We affirm that Jews and Christians are partners in waiting. Christians see in Christ the redemption not yet fully visible in the world, and Jews await the messianic redemption. Christians and Jews together await the final manifestation of God's promise of the peaceable kingdom.

Jesus and Israel

The Confession of 1967 of the United Presbyterian Church in the U.S.A. affirmed that Jesus was "a Palestinian Jew" and that God raised Jesus up out of Israel.

SOURCE

"The Confession of 1967" in *Book of Confessions*, 9.18–9.19.

God expressed his love for all mankind through Israel, whom he chose to be his covenant people to serve him in love and faithfulness. When Israel was unfaithful, he disciplined the nation with his judgments and maintained his cause through prophets, priests, teachers, and true believers. These witnesses called all Israelites to a destiny in which they would serve God faithfully and become a light to the nations. The same witnesses proclaimed the coming of a new age, and a true servant of God in whom God's purpose for Israel and for mankind would be realized.

Out of Israel God in due time raised up Jesus. His faith and obedience were the response of the perfect child of God. He was the fulfillment of God's promise to Israel, the beginning of the new creation, and the pioneer of the new humanity. He gave history its meaning and direction and called the church to be his servant for the reconciliation of the world.

God and the People of Israel

"A Declaration of Faith" of the Presbyterian Church in the United States, like "The Confession of 1967" of the Presbyterian Church (U.S.A.), differs strikingly from classical Reformed confessions in the prominence it gives to Israel.

SOURCE

Declaration of Faith, 4–6.

GOD AND THE PEOPLE OF ISRAEL

(1) God chose one people for the sake of all.

To the world in its rebellion and alienation
    God promised blessing and restoration.
The Lord chose Abraham and his descendants
    as bearers of that promise for all peoples.
They had done nothing more than others
    to deserve the Lord's favor,
    but God loved them and made them his own.

We acknowledge God's freedom and grace.
Though we are unworthy,
    the Lord has made us his own in Christ.
God has chosen us as his servants for the sake of the world
    and destined us to be his daughters and sons,
    giving us love and life,
    calling us to worship and honor him.

(2) God delivered his people.

When Abraham's descendants were slaves in Egypt,
    God heard their cries and prayers.
God remembered his promise
    and sent Moses to free them from bondage.

We declare God's steadfast love and sovereign power.
The Lord can be trusted to keep promises.
The Lord still acts in the affairs of individuals and nations
    to set oppressed and persecuted people free.

(3) God bound his people to himself in covenant.

Freed slaves became the people of God
    when they accepted the Lord's covenant.
God charged them to respond to his rescuing love
    by obeying his commandments.
Their life together was to express
    the justice and compassion of their holy God.

Since we, too, are the Lord's covenant people,
    we know we must be holy as the Lord is holy.

We must keep God's commandments,
> not in order to earn or compel the Lord's favor,
> but to reflect the character of God
> and to be his grateful and loving people.

(4) God blessed and judged his people.

The Lord's care sustained the people of Israel.
God gave them a land where they could celebrate his goodness.
The Lord established their kingdom and
> promised a ruler from the line of David
> to reign in justice and peace.

When God's people worshipped the gods of the land,
> when they put their trust in military alliances,
> when they failed to do justice and oppressed the poor,
> God sent the prophets to condemn their sins
> and to call the people back to obedience.

There were times of repentance and reform,
> but in the end their kingdoms fell.

We declare God's goodness and justice.
God has blessed us beyond our deserving.
When we forget the Lord and worship our possessions,
> when we fail to deal justly with the poor,
> when we seek security no matter what it costs others,
> we can expect God's judgment upon us.

(5) God did not forsake his people.

God restored some of the people to their land
> and left others scattered over the earth.

In a time of exile and alien rule,
> the Jews survived and multiplied.

They enriched the whole world:
> they compiled the Scriptures, preserving God's Word to them;
> they sang their songs of praise and lamentation;
> they sought wisdom, examining God's ways in the world;
> they searched the mysteries of rising and falling kingdoms
> and set their hope on the kingdom of God.

We testify that God is faithful.
Even when we are faithless, God remains faithful.

The Lord still brings from oppressed and uprooted peoples
    riches of insight and daring visions
    that can judge and bless the world.
We can have confidence in God's coming kingdom
    even in the darkest times.

3

MAKER OF
HEAVEN AND EARTH

In the last half of the twentieth century, as the world slowly came to terms with the environmental crisis, Reformed theologians began to examine the charge that Christian theology is anthropocentric and has not given sufficient attention to the natural world. There is considerable evidence to substantiate this indictment in the classical statements of Reformed theology, which say very little about the natural world.

In addition, in at least two respects theologians interpreted God's relation to the world very differently than had their classical predecessors. First, while classical Reformed theology interpreted providence as God's preservation, concurrence, and rule or government (*conservatio, concursus, gubernatio*) of creation, twentieth-century theologians, working in the shadows of two world wars, Hiroshima, and the Holocaust, were often only able to affirm God's presence, not God's rule in human events.

Second, because of the magnitude of the social crises facing humanity in the second half of the twentieth century, some theologians insisted that human beings had to assume more autonomy and responsibility for the course of history. In some quarters that meant that theologians began to describe humanity as God's "partner" and, in some cases, as God's "co-creator." Although many Reformed theologians were no longer able to affirm God's rule of the events of human history, their commitment to some version of the sovereignty of God made it difficult for them to accept the notion that human beings can or should be placed on equal footing with God, "the maker of heaven and earth."

CREATION

Although one of the features of contemporary theology has been its search for a new paradigm for interpreting the reality of God after the collapse of classical metaphysics, there are several important themes in the classical depiction of God, such as the claim that God creates *ex nihilo*, out of nothing, that many contemporary Reformed theologians continued to affirm. Perhaps in the twentieth century, more than in any previous century, the claim that God creates *ex nihilo* was important because it reminded Christians of the contingency of the created order.

FOR FURTHER STUDY

Barth, *Church Dogmatics*, III/1–4. Brunner, *Dogmatics*, 2: 3–45. Langdon Gilkey, *Maker of Heaven and Earth: The Christian Doctrine of Creation in the Light of Modern Knowledge* (Lanham, Md.: University Press of America, 1959). Zachary Hayes, *What Are They Saying About Creation?* (New York: Paulist Press, 1980). George S. Hendry, *Theology of Nature* (Philadelphia: Westminster, 1980).

The Historicity of Genesis

At the beginning of the nineteenth century, Friedrich Schleiermacher, in his book *The Christian Faith*, took a bold step that foreshadowed a debate that would continue for the rest of the century. Schleiermacher suggested that the biblical texts that are the basis of the doctrine of creation—the first two chapters of Genesis—are not historical.

SOURCE

Schleiermacher, *Christian Faith*, 150–52.

ACTS 17:24, ROM. 1:19, 20, HEB. 11:3

1. The New Testament passages quoted above lead us to reject any more definite conception of the Creation. The expression ῥ ή μ α τ ι is merely the negative of any closer definition, so as to exclude all idea of instrument or means. It is quite consistent with it and equally correct to say that the world itself, since it came into existence through the spoken word, is the word of God. Thus we may be satisfied to put forward this negative character as a standard of criticism for that which has, as it seems to us, wrongly intruded itself as a more exact definition of this conception in Dogmatics. For as our immediate self-consciousness represents finite being only in the identity of origination and continuance, we find in that self-consciousness neither motive nor guidance for a treatment of origination taken by itself, and therefore we can take no particular interest in it.

The further elaboration of the doctrine of Creation in Dogmatics comes down to us from times when material even for natural science was taken from the Scriptures and when the elements of all higher knowledge lay hidden in Theology. Hence the complete separation of these two involves our handing over this subject to natural science, which, carrying its researches backward into time, may lead us back to the forces and masses that formed the world, or even further still. On this assumption we may patiently await the result, since every scientific endeavour which works with the ideas "God" and "world" must, without being dependent on Christian doctrine or becoming so, be limited by the very same determinations, if these two ideas are not to cease to be two.

2. As the New Testament passages give no material for a further development of the doctrine of Creation, and dogmaticians have always referred back to the Scriptures even when confusing their problem with that of philosophy, we must, in the first place, pass in review the Mosaic narrative and the Old Testament passages, which really in a sense are wholly dependent on it.

The Mosaic account was undeniably received by the Reformers as a genuinely historical narrative. Luther's statements, however, are chiefly directed against the allegorical interpretation, and Calvin's view really excludes any use of the narrative for the development of a genuine theory. It is an advantage in every way that nothing on the subject has become a part of Confessions of Faith, especially as (if we do not force ourselves to look upon the second account in Genesis as a recapitulating continuation of the first) the difference between the two is of such importance that we can hardly attribute to them a genuine historical character. If we further take into consideration that in the Old Testament passages referring to the Creation sometimes the same simplicity prevails as in the New Testament, and that sometimes the Mosaic statements, although made fundamental, are very freely handled: also that nowhere is a purely didactic use made of this account, and that Philo, who absolutely rejects the "six days" in the literal sense, must certainly have had predecessors who did the same—in view of all this we may conclude pretty certainly that in that age the literal interpretation was never universally prevalent, but that there always survived a somewhat obscure but healthy feeling that the old record must not be treated as historical in our sense of the word. We have therefore no reason to maintain a stricter historical interpretation than the Hebrews themselves did in their best days.

Supposing, however, we were right in assuming that the Mosaic description was an historical account communicated in an extraordinary way, it would only follow that in this way we had attained to a scientific insight we could not otherwise have acquired. But the particular pieces of information would never be articles of faith in our sense of the phrase, for our feeling of absolute dependence does not gain thereby either a new content, a new form, or clearer definition. That is why it cannot be the task of Dogmatics to give an explanatory commentary or a criticism of such comments.

3. As regards the stated definitions themselves, it is quite clear that our feeling of absolute dependence could not refer to the universal condition of all finite being if anything in it (i.e., that being) were independent of God or ever had been. It is just as certain that if there could be anything in the whole of finite existence as such which entered into it at its origin independently of God, then because it must exist in us too, the feeling of absolute dependence could have no truth even in relation to ourselves. But if, on the other hand, we think of God the Creator in any way as limited, and thus in His activity resembling that which should be absolutely dependent on Him, then the feeling expressing this dependence likewise could not be true (since equality and dependence neutralize each other), and thus the finite in that it resembled God could not be absolutely dependent upon Him. But except in one of these two forms, a contradiction between any theory of creation and the universal basis of our religious self-consciousness is not conceivable. With the Christian form of religious self-consciousness, which presupposes an experience, the doctrine of mere creation cannot be in contradiction, because it disregards continuity. Christian piety can, then, have no other interest in these researches than to avoid both these dangers. Whether this is easy, or if in avoiding one we only too easily fall into the other, must be seen from a closer consideration of the corollaries accepted by Dogmatics.

Creation Out of Nothing

Like many other twentieth-century theologians, Karl Barth affirmed the claim of classical theology that God creates *ex nihilo* while, at the same time, emphasizing the importance of God's relatedness to the world. Barth differs from some of the theologians who followed him by insisting that God's relatedness (or love) must be understood as dialectically related to God's freedom (or holiness).

SOURCE

Karl Barth, *Credo* (New York: Charles Scribner's Sons, 1962), 30–33.

The statement: "God is the Creator of the World" has in the main a double content: it speaks of the *freedom* of God (one could also say: of His *holiness*) over against the world, and of His *relationship* (one could also say: of His love) to the world.

I. With the proposition: God is the Creator! we acknowledge that the relationship of God and world is fundamentally and in all its implications not one of equilibrium or of parity, but that in this relationship God has the absolute *primacy*. This is no mere matter of course, but rather a mystery, which all along the line determines the meaning and the form of this relationship: that there is a reality at all differentiated from the reality of God, a being beside the divine Being. There is that. There are heaven and earth, and between the two, between angel and animal, man. But quite apart from the explicit proposition about Creation, for Scripturally based thinking there follows from the fact that their being is so closely related to the Being of God, this: that their being can only be one that is radically dependent on the Being of God, therefore one that is radically relative and without independence, dust, a drop in the bucket, clay in the hand of the potter—mere figures of speech which far from saying too much, say decidedly much too little. Heaven and earth are what they are *through* God and *only* through God. This brings us to the true thought of creation.

Heaven and earth are *not themselves God*, are not anything in the nature of a divine generation or emanation, are not, as the Gnostics or mystics would again and again have it, in some direct or indirect way, identical with the Son or Word of God. In opposition to what even Christian theologians have on occasion taught, the world must not be understood as eternal. It has, and with it time and space have, a *beginning*. Their infinity is not only limited by the finite as such. Rather, their infinity is, *along with* everything finite, limited and encompassed by God's eternity and omnipotence, i.e., by God's lordship over time and space, in which it itself does not share. Therefore the creation of the world is not a movement of God in Himself, but a free *opus ad extra*, finding its necessity only in His love, but again not casting any doubt on His self-sufficiency: the world cannot exist without God, but if God were not love (as such inconceivable!), He could exist very well without the world. "And all this out of pure paternal, divine goodness and mercy, without any merit or worthiness of mine," as again Luther says, speaking not yet of our salvation, but of our creation.

Again heaven and earth are not God's work in the sense that God created them according to some *ideas* in themselves given and true, or out of some *material* already existing, or by means of some *instrument* apt in itself for that purpose. Creation in the Bible sense means: Creation solely on the basis of God's own wisdom. It means, *creatio ex nihilo* (Rom. iv.17). It means, creation by the word, which is indeed the eternal Son and therefore God Himself. If that is so, if there is no question of an identity of the created world with God, no question of its existing under any circumstances as a legitimate possibility (i.e., apart from sin) in formal or material independence over against God, then it necessarily follows that the *meaning* and the *end* of the world of His creation is not to be sought in itself, that the purpose and the destiny of this world could only be to serve God as the world's Creator and indeed to serve as "theatre of His glory" (Calvin). From God's creating the world it follows that He created it for *this* purpose and with this destiny and therefore created it in accordance with this purpose and this destiny and therefore *good*. Here we must of course acknowledge anew the primacy of God and must therefore in *our* estimate of the "goodness" of this world hold to the judgment of *God*. He knows what serves His glory. We must believe that the world as He created it is appointed to serve His glory, and we must not allow ourselves to be misled here by our feelings and reflections over good and evil, however justified. No doubt it is scriptural to say that the world was created for man's sake. But yet only because man was in a pre-eminent sense created for the service of God, created to be the "image of God," not only as theatre, but as active and passive bearer of that glory. It is the concrete content of faith in God the Creator that the world is "good" for man in and for this service of God. How should man have to decide and decree what is "good"? He has just got to *believe* that God has created the world and him himself really *good*.

Continuous Creation by the Word Out of Nothing

George S. Hendry (b. 1904), a Presbyterian from Scotland, taught theology in the mid-twentieth century at Princeton Theological Seminary and played a significant role in the North American appropriation of Karl Barth's theology. In his study of creation, Hendry identified three important themes.

SOURCE

George S. Hendry, *God the Creator* (London: Hodder & Stoughton, 1937), 178–81.

Traditional theology has incorporated the distinctive notes of the Christian doctrine of God the Creator in three formulas, the intention of which is not to provide a rational account of it but to emphasise its uniqueness and to differentiate it clearly from philosophical cosmology.

1. *Creatio ex nihilo*, creation out of nothing, distinguishes creation definitely from causation. The idea of a cause requires that of a material on which it operates in order to produce an effect. Creation takes place "in the beginning"; the postulate of a pre-existent material is incompatible with the notion of creation as the absolute beginning and the absolute sovereignty of the Creator over all creatures.

2. *Creatio per verbum*, creation by the word, enforces the distinction between creation and causality. Creation is not a process. All human "creation," including that of the artist, is processional or discursive; it involves first an act of volition and then, as a second thing, the practical realisation of it. But the activity of the Creator is not of this order; in Him the volition and the practical realisation of it are not only inseparable but they are identical: "God said, Let there be light: and there was light" (Gen. i.3); "He spake, and it was done; he commanded, and it stood fast" (Ps. xxxiii.9). The created world does not proceed or emanate from the Creator, but it is set in existence by the sole act of His will.

The formula, creation by the word, or by the will, serves further to emphasise that the meaning and purpose of the created world are not to be found within itself but are determined by the will of its Creator. Faith recognises this will, but it does not presume to comprehend the mind which informs it, and thus it does not make of it a principle by which the world can be interpreted as a unity. Nevertheless, by its factual acknowledgment of the will of God the Creator faith holds to the conviction that the created world has a purpose and a destination; and in this way faith in the Creator is possible only as the acknowledgment of our own absolute responsibility to Him.

3. *Creatio continua*, continuous creation, is the endeavour to indicate that the world not only came into existence but it actually exists by the creative will of God. Creation is not a single event in the past, but at every moment the world is called out of nothingness into being by the will of the Creator; it is sustained by His will and is absolutely dependent upon it: "If he gather unto himself his spirit and his breath, all flesh shall perish together, and man shall return again unto dust" (Job xxxiv.14f.). This is the meaning of the divine immanence. It does not imply—as it would seem sometimes to be understood—any diminution of the transcendence of God, any slurring over of the distinction between the Creator and the creature, any attribution of a divine quality to any part or aspect of the creation. It means that while the Creator is "wholly other" than the creature and is not continuous with it, yet no indepen-

dent material and no interval of time separates Him from it. At every moment and everywhere God is immediately present in His creation.

The intention of these formulæ is not to provide a rational account of the nature of creation, but rather to show that no such account can be given. Creation is *sui generis* and without analogy. It is well that we should be reminded that the Christian doctrine of creation is not properly a doctrine of creation but a doctrine of God the Creator. The Apostles' Creed speaks neither of the creation of heaven and earth nor of the world created by God but of "God the Father almighty, Creator of heaven and earth." The faith in God the Creator is not a *Weltanschauung*; it is the deliberate renunciation of it. There are problems to which faith provides no solution. We walk by faith and not by sight. And now we see through a glass darkly, but then—*then*, when the new creation of God is finished—we shall know even as we are known.

Creatio Ex Nihilo and the Forgiveness of Sins

In *God in Creation*, which he describes as "a pneumatological doctrine of creation," Jürgen Moltmann links creation with Christology and redemption by insisting that it is the triune God who both creates and redeems.

SOURCE

Jürgen Moltmann, *God in Creation: A New Theology of Creation and the Spirit of God*, trans. Margaret Kohl (San Francisco: Harper & Row, 1985), 90–91.

If God's creativity goes back to a creative resolve, this already implies the Creator's openness for redeeming suffering and his readiness for his own self-humiliation. Because of the self-isolation of his creatures through sin and the consequence of sin, death, God's adherence to his resolve *to create* also means a resolve *to save*. *Creatio ex nihilo* in the beginning is the preparation and promise of the redeeming *annihilatio nihili*, from which the eternal being of creation proceeds. The creation of the world is itself a promise of resurrection, and the overcoming of death in the victory of eternal life (1 Cor. 15:26, 55–57). So the resurrection and the kingdom of glory are the fulfillment of the promise which creation itself represents.

This brings us to a final interpretation of the statement about the *creatio ex nihilo*, from the standpoint of the cross of Christ. If God creates his creation out of nothing, if he affirms it and is faithful to it in spite of sin, and if he desires its salvation, then in the sending and surrender of his own Son he exposes himself to the annihilating Nothingness, so that he may overcome it in himself and through himself, and in that way give his creation existence, salvation and liberty. In this sense, by yielding up the Son to death in God-forsakenness on the cross, and by surrendering him to hell, the eternal God enters the Nothingness out of which he created the world. God enters that "primordial space" which he himself conceded through his initial self-limitation. He pervades the space of God-forsakenness with his presence. It is the presence of his self-humiliating, suffering love for his creation, in which he experiences death itself. That is why God's presence in the crucified Christ gives creation eternal life, and does not annihilate it. In the path of the Son into self-emptying and bondage, to the point of the death he died, and in the path of his exaltation and glorification by the whole creation, God becomes omnipresent. By entering into the God-forsakenness of sin and death (which is Nothingness), God overcomes it and makes it part of his eternal life: "If I make my bed in hell, thou art there" (Ps. 139:8).

In the light of the cross of Christ, *creatio ex nihilo* means forgiveness of sins through Christ's suffering, justification of the godless through Christ's death, and the resurrection of the dead and eternal life through the lordship of the Lamb.

In the light of creation, the cross of Christ means the true consolidation of the universe. Because from the very beginning the Creator is prepared to suffer in this way for his creation, his creation endures to eternity. The cross is the mystery of creation and the promise of its future.

THE HUMAN CONDITION

Theological descriptions of human beings have always reflected the historical and cultural settings in which they were formulated. It is not surprising, therefore, that one of the distinctive features of theology in the nineteenth and twentieth centuries has been a marked shift in the construction of theological anthropology. Two developments are especially important for understanding why contemporary theologians describe human beings differently than do classical theologians. First, contemporary theological anthropology has been deeply influenced by the emergence and development of the so-called social sciences: psychology, anthropology, and sociology. That influence is clearly evident in the shift in categories used in theological anthropology. Whereas classical theology usually described human beings in ontological categories derived from Plato and Aristotle—categories, for example, such as nature, being, and substance—theologians in the nineteenth and twentieth centuries have used categories borrowed from the social sciences that emphasize the dynamic, developmental, and social character of human identity. Indeed, contemporary theologians, like their counterparts in the social sciences, find the category of "human nature" highly suspect and in its place tend to speak of "human identity."

Second, contemporary theological anthropology has been significantly shaped by the growing awareness of historical and cultural relativity. How one understands human beings is very much a question of the vantage point from which one views them. How one interprets human identity—what constitutes it and what, if anything, is "normative" about it—is inseparable from the gender, race, economic condition, and social class of the interpreter.

FOR FURTHER STUDY

Barth, *Church Dogmatics*, III/2. G. C. Berkouwer, *Man: The Image of God*, trans. Dirk W. Jellema (Grand Rapids: Wm. B. Eerdmans, 1962). Brunner, *Dogmatics*, 2:46–88. Edward Farley, *Ecclesial Man: A Social Phenomenology of Faith and Reality* (Philadelphia: Fortress, 1975). Douglas John Hall, *Imaging God: Dominion as Stewardship* (Grand Rapids: Wm. B. Eerdmans, 1986). Jürgen Moltmann, *Man: Christian Anthropology in the Conflicts of the Present*, trans. John Sturdy (London: SPCK, 1974). Paul Ricoeur, *Fallible Man*, trans. Charles Kelbley (Chicago: Henry Regnery Company, 1965). Letty M. Russell, *Becoming Human* (Philadelphia: Westminster, 1982).

The Predisposition to God-Consciousness

One of the reasons Friedrich Schleiermacher has sometimes been described as the "first parent" of contemporary theology is that he marks the watershed between classical descriptions of God, humanity, and the world and new idioms that began to emerge in the nineteenth century. For Schleiermacher what is constitutive of human being are states of self-consciousness, one of which manifests itself as "the feeling of absolute dependence" and which Schleiermacher describes as "God-consciousness."

SOURCE

Schleiermacher, *Christian Faith*, 244–46.

§ 60. *The predisposition to God-consciousness, as an inner impulse, includes the consciousness of a faculty of attaining, by means of the human organism, to those states of self-consciousness in which the God-consciousness can realize itself; and the impulse inseparable therefrom to express the God-consciousness includes in like manner the connexion of the race-consciousness with the personal consciousness; and both together form man's original perfection.*

I. If the God-consciousness in the form of the feeling of absolute dependence can only become actual in connexion with a sensible determination of self-consciousness, the tendency towards God-consciousness would be altogether nugatory if the condition necessary for it in human life could not be evoked; and we should be no more able to think of it as actual than in the case of the beasts, because the confused state of man's consciousness would not exhibit the conditions under which alone that feeling could emerge. Religious experience, however, consists precisely in this, that we are aware of this tendency to God-consciousness as a living impulse; but such an impulse can only proceed from the true inner nature of the being which it goes to constitute. Hence, at least in so far as we are religious men, we reckon the whole range of those states with which the God-consciousness can unite as belonging to this true inner nature. And as it would be an absolute imperfection of human nature—that is to say, a complete absence of inner coherence—if the tendency were indeed present latently, but could not emerge, so it is an essential element in the perfection of human nature that those states which condition the appearance of the God-consciousness are able to fill the clear and waking life of man onwards from the time when the spiritual functions are developed. And as we consider it an imperfect state of religious life in the individual if many moments of clear sensibly determined self-consciousness occur without the God-consciousness being combined with them, so we account it part of the original perfection of man that in our clear and waking life a continuous God-consciousness as such is possible; and on the contrary, we should have to regard it as an essential imperfection if the emergence of the feeling of absolute dependence, though not abrogating any feeling of partial dependence or freedom, were confined as such to separate and scattered moments.

The God-consciousness, moreover, combines not only with those sensible excitations of self-consciousness which express life-enhancements or life-hindrances immediately arising out of the impression of the world, but also with those which accompany the cognitive activities, and finally with those which are connected with every kind of outwardly directed action. Hence all these mental life-functions and the relative disposition of the organism belong together to the original perfection of man, though only in so far as the demand which we make for God-consciousness is conditioned by them, and in such a way that the first place always belongs to it. Thus, first of all, there is the physical basis of spiritual life, i.e., the fact that the spirit, become soul in the human body, acts also on the rest of the world in innumerable ways, and asserts its nature, just as the other living forces assert their nature relatively to it, so that life-feeling in general takes shape as the consciousness of interaction; from which it follows that to the original perfection of man this also belongs, that opposite life-moments, hindrances and furtherances, have one and the same bearing on the excitation of the God-consciousness. Next, there is the intellectual basis of spiritual life, i.e., the fact that the spirit by means of sense-impressions can obtain that knowledge of existence which is one element in its own nature, as also knowledge of what we ourselves by our activity can produce in and from existence, and can express this knowledge with actual consciousness in the most varied degrees of general and particular ideas, and that thereby it arrives at the accompanying consciousness of a natural order in connexion with which the God-consciousness develops. Upon the agreement of these ideas and judgments with the being and relations of things depends all the influence of man on external nature which is more than simply instinctive, and also the connexion between knowledge and practical life. But though the knowledge of God, in this sphere, is bound up pre-eminently and fundamentally with the idea of a natural order, the excitation of the God-consciousness is not at all imperilled though certain ideas should not agree with the actual being of the object presented; as indeed the comprehensive interconnexion of all being would not be mirrored in our idea if we did not assume that so long as the whole of existence is not reflected in our thought every act of thought contains an element of error.

Human Self-transcendence

In his Gifford Lectures of 1939, Reinhold Niebuhr identified the human capacity for self-transcendence as the unique feature of human beings, what classical theologians had described as the "image of God" (*imago dei*) in humanity.

SOURCE
Niebuhr, *Nature and Destiny*, 1:150, 163–64.

The Christian view of man is sharply distinguished from all alternative views by the manner in which it interprets and relates three aspects of human existence to each other: (1) It emphasizes the height of self-transcendence in man's spiritual stature in its doctrine of "image of God." (2) It insists on man's weakness, dependence, and finiteness, on his involvement in the necessities and contingencies of the natural world, without, however, regarding this finiteness as, of itself, a source of evil in man. In its purest form the Christian view of man regards man as a unity of God-likeness and creatureliness in which he remains a creature even in the highest spiritual dimensions of his existence and may reveal elements of the image of God even in the lowliest aspects of his natural life. (3) It affirms that the evil in man is a consequence of his inevitable though not necessary unwillingness to acknowledge his dependence, to accept his finiteness and to admit his insecurity, an unwillingness which involves him in the vicious circle of accentuating the insecurity from which he seeks escape. . . .

In Christian faith the place of Christ as both the revelation of the character of God and of the essential nature of man (the "second Adam") does justice to the fact that man can find his true norm only in the character of God but is nevertheless a creature who cannot and must not aspire to be God. The God who is his norm is God as He is revealed in a character of human history, that is, in Christ. Christ is at once an historical character and more than an historical character. His life transcends the possibilities of history but it remains relevant to all historical striving, for all historical goals can be expressed only in supra-historical terms. If stated in purely historical terms they will embody some contingency of nature and history and set a false limit for the human spirit. This aspect of Christian Christology is not understood by naturalistic versions of the Christian faith in which the "Jesus of history" becomes the norm of life. These versions do not understand the total stature of freedom in which human life stands and are therefore not able to appreciate the necessity of a trans-historical norm of historical life.

The perfect love of the life of Christ ends on the Cross, after having existed in history. It is therefore supra-historical, not in the sense of setting up a non-historical eternity as the goal of human life; but in the sense that the love which it embodies is the point where history culminates and ends.

Implicit in the human situation of freedom and in man's capacity to transcend himself and his world is his inability to construct a world of meaning without finding a source and key to the structure of meaning which transcends the world beyond his own capacity to transcend it. The problem of meaning, which is the basic problem of religion, transcends the ordinary rational problem of tracing the relation of things to each other as the freedom of man's spirit transcends his rational faculties.

The True Human

A major issue in theological anthropology is what criterion or norm to use to determine what is truly human. In his *Church Dogmatics*, Karl Barth argues that our focus should be not on other people or on humanity as an abstraction but on the man Jesus, "that one man among all others."

SOURCE

Barth, *Church Dogmatics*, III/2:132–34.

Turning now from the critical to the constructive part of our task, we must try to give a positive answer to the question of the being which within the cosmos constitutes human being, i.e., the question of real man.

The ontological determination of humanity is grounded in the fact that one man among all others is the man Jesus. So long as we select any other starting point for our study, we shall reach only the phenomena of the human. We are condemned to abstractions so long as our attention is riveted as it were on other men, or rather on man in general, as if we could learn about real man from a study of man in general, and in abstraction from the fact that one man among all others is the man Jesus. In this case we miss the one Archimedean point given us beyond humanity, and therefore the one possibility of discovering the ontological determination of man. Theological anthropology has no choice in this matter. It is not yet or no longer theological anthropology if it tries to pose and answer the question of the true being of man from any other angle.

We remember who and what the man Jesus is. As we have seen, He is the one creaturely being in whose existence we have to do immediately and directly with the being of God also. Again, He is the creaturely being in whose existence God's act of deliverance has taken place for all other men. He is the creaturely being in whom God as the Saviour of all men also reveals and affirms His own glory as the Creator. He is the creaturely being who as such embodies the sovereignty of God, or conversely the sovereignty of God which as such actualises this creaturely being. He is the creaturely being whose existence consists in His fulfillment of the will of God. And finally He is the creaturely being who as such not only exists from God and in God but absolutely for God instead of for Himself.

From this knowledge of the man Jesus we have derived the criteria which indicate the limits within which the attempt to attain knowledge of human existence must always move. We have thus been warned against confusing the reality of man with mere phenomena of man. We have been unable to accept those determinations of man in which his relationship to God, his participation in the history inaugurated between him and God, and the glory, lordship, purpose and service of God, are not brought out as the meaning of human life. We have also had to be critical even where the concept of God seemed to play a certainly not unimportant role, but where it remained empty to the extent that there did not emerge anything of His saving action and the related actuality of the being of man. We have now to show the fact and extent that the ontological determination of man results from the fact that one man among all others is this creaturely being, the man Jesus.

Our first point is that the message of the Bible about this one man has amongst other things this ontological significance. Speaking of this one man, it says of all other men—those who were before Him and those who were after Him, those who knew Him and those who did not know Him or did so only indirectly, those who accepted Him and those who rejected Him—at least that they were and are creaturely beings whom this man is like for all His unlikeness, and in whose sphere and fellow-ship and history this one man also existed in likeness with them. This means that a decision has been made concerning the being and nature of every man by the mere fact that with him and among all other men He too has been a man. No matter who or what or where he may be, he cannot alter the fact that this One is also man. And because this One is also man, every man in his place and time is changed, i.e., he is some-thing other than what he would have been if this One had not been man too. It belongs to his human essence that Jesus too is man, and that in Him he has a human Neighbour, Companion and Brother. Hence he has no choice in the matter. The question whether and to what extent he knows this Neighbour, and what attitude he adopts to Him, is no doubt important, but it is secondary to that which has already been decided, namely, whether he can be a man at all without this Neighbour. Once for all this question has been decided in the negative for every man. We cannot break free from this Neighbour. He is definitively our Neighbour. And we as men are those among whom Jesus is also a man, like us for all His unlikeness.

The Responsible Person

H. Richard Niebuhr described human beings by means of the category of "responsibility." A human being is a responding and, therefore, responsible self.

SOURCE

H. Richard Niebuhr, *The Responsible Self: An Essay in Christian Moral Responsibility* (New York: Harper & Row, 1963), 65–67.

The idea or pattern of responsibility, then, may summarily and abstractly be defined as the idea of an agent's action as response to an action upon him in accordance with his interpretation of the latter action and with his expectation of response to his response; and all of this is in a continuing community of agents.

The idea of the moral life as the responsible life in this sense not only has affinities with much modern thinking but it also offers us, I believe, a key—not *the* key—to the understanding of that Biblical ethos which represents the historic norm of the Christian life. In the past many efforts have been made to understand the ethos of the Old and New Testaments with the aid of the teleological theory and its image of man-the-maker. Thus the thinking of the lawgivers and prophets, of Jesus Christ and the apostles, has been set before us in the terms of a great idealism. Sometimes the ideal has been described as that of the vision of God, sometimes as perfection, sometimes as eternal happiness, sometimes as a harmony of all beings, or at least of all men, in a kingdom of God. Each of these interpretations has been buttressed by collections of proof texts, and doubtless much that is valid about the Bible and about the Christian life which continues the Scriptural ethos has been said within the limits of this interpretation. But much that is in Scriptures has been omitted by the interpreters who followed this method, and much material of another sort—the eschatological, for instance—has had to be rather violently wrenched out of its context or laid aside as irrelevant in order to make the Scriptures speak in this fashion about the self. At all times, moreover, but particularly among the German interpreters in whom the Kantian symbolism holds sway, the deontological interpretation of man the obedient legislator has been used not only as the key to Biblical interpretation but for the definition of the true Christian life. For Barth and Bultmann alike in our times, not to speak of most interpreters of the Old Testament, the ethics of the Bible, and

Christian ethics too, is the ethics of obedience. How to interpret Christian freedom and what to make of eschatology within this framework has taxed the ingenuity of the interpreters severely. Bultmann has transformed eschatology into existentialism in order to maintain an ethics of radical obedience; Barth has had to transform the law into a form of the gospel and the commandment into permission in order to reconcile the peculiarity of gospel ethos with deontological thinking. There is doubtless much about law, commandment, and obedience in the Scriptures. But the use of this pattern of interpretation does violence to what we find there.

If now we approach the Scriptures with the idea of responsibility we shall find, I think, that the particular character of this ethics can be more fully if not wholly adequately interpreted. At the critical junctures in the history of Israel and of the early Christian community the decisive question men raised was not "What is the goal?" nor yet "What is the law?" but "What is happening?" and then "What is the fitting response to what is happening?" When an Isaiah counsels his people, he does not remind them of the law they are required to obey nor yet of the goal toward which they are directed but calls to their attention the intentions of God present in hiddenness in the actions of Israel's enemies. The question he and his peers raise in every critical moment is about the interpretation of what is going on, whether what is happening be, immediately considered, a drought or the invasion of a foreign army, or the fall of a great empire. Israel is the people that is to see and understand the action of God in everything that happens and to make a fitting reply. So it is in the New Testament also. The God to whom Jesus points is not the commander who gives laws but the doer of small and of mighty deeds, the creator of sparrows and clother of lilies, the ultimate giver of blindness and of sight, the ruler whose rule is hidden in the manifold activities of plural agencies but is yet in a way visible to those who know how to interpret the signs of the times.

It will not do to say that the analysis of all our moral life in general and of Biblical ethics in particular by means of the idea of responsibility offers us an absolutely new way of understanding man's ethical life or of constructing a system of Christian ethics. Actuality always extends beyond the patterns of ideas into which we want to force it. But the approach to our moral existence as selves, and to our existence as Christians in particular, with the aid of this idea makes some aspects of our life as agents intelligible in a way that the teleology and deontology of traditional thought cannot do.

The Center of God's Interest

In its "Confession of Faith," written in 1977, the Reformed-Presbyterian Church of Cuba affirmed that God places supreme value on the human creature. Furthermore, the confession insists that God's valuation of all things centered in the human being is a "divine necessity." This confession is of particular interest because it is a statement of faith by a Reformed community living in the midst of the state socialism of Fidel Castro's Cuba.

SOURCE

"Confession of Faith" (1977) of the Reformed-Presbyterian Church of Cuba, in *Reformed Witness Today*, 170–73.

B. The Human Being: The Center of God's Interest

The Scriptures witness to the fact that the human being is the center of all God's interest. All through the pages of the Bible, God's love for the creature is not only made evident, but it is also presented as a divine necessity. God's loving interest in the human creature is identified in the Scriptures with God's very essence.

The Church finds in this Love, and only in it, all the theological material with which to formulate its doctrinal truth. The doctrinal development of the Church and all the doctrines it has elaborated in its theological undertakings through the centuries, are valid to the extent that they explain in a better way God's loving purpose for the human being.

When the Church emphasizes the doctrines of Incarnation and Atonement, it witnesses to God's love for the human being, since it proclaims the magnitude of his sacrificial and solidary nature.

In this way, the Church raises God's interest and concern and his valuation of all things centered in the human being, to the level of a divine necessity, interpreting correctly what the Scriptures teach us about his "Nature" and "Attributes."

C. The Human Being: The Center of the Church's Interest in Jesus Christ

The Church on being interested in Jesus Christ and only in Jesus Christ and him crucified and risen from the dead, centers its interest in the human being.

The Church's faithfulness to Jesus Christ ties it to its Lord's historic commitment, a commitment of human Redemption through sacrificial, solidary and unconditional Love for the human being.

When the Church proclaims that Jesus Christ is the "Incarnate Son of God," and Our "Risen Older Brother," it witnesses to the fact that sacrificial and solidary Love is not only a divine necessity, but also a human necessity, "signs" of the "mystery of God" and of the "mystery of man."

When the Church teaches that the Scriptures witness to the supreme value God places on the human creature, becoming his Creator, Reconciler and Redeemer, it recognizes the fact that sacrificial, and solidary and unconditional Love for the human being constitutes its own and only necessity.

The Church recognizes that sacrificial, solidary and unconditional Love is necessary for it to be the Church of Jesus Christ; and, espousing the cause of human dignity and decorum in every moment and in whatever place, as its only reason for being—without placing any condition on its commitment, and without having it matter what the circumstances are in which it lives or the risk it runs—it participates fully in human Redemption.

When the Church lives this way, it is living in God, by God and for God. To serve and love God in Jesus Christ is for the Church to center its interest, its concern and its valuation of all things in the human being, appropriating the Christological form of being as the only way for God to make himself accessible to the Creature and the only way for the Church to make itself acceptable to God and to other human beings.

If the Church should cease existing for, by and in the human being, it would cease being the Church of Jesus Christ, the Son of God and Our Older Brother.

When the Church lives its historical reality placing the human being in the very center of its interest in Jesus Christ, it does not lose its identity as the "Body of Christ" or as "Christ's bride," but all the contrary; even in its greatest degree of secularization, the Church achieves the realization of its irrenunciable commitment of serving and loving Jesus Christ, since in Him, at His own expense, God is secularized radically and unconditionally in his redemptive task of working for the fullness of the decorum and dignity of all human beings.

SECTION II:
THE HUMAN BEING: AN "ECONOME"

The Scriptures teach us that the human being is characterized by being an "econome" of all things, God's "steward." All goods, material and spiritual, that we obtain as persons or as nations, cannot be considered in the final analysis as "individual" or "national" property in an exclusive way, be it individualistic, classist, elitist or nationalistic. Much less can they have a transcendent value which, by reason of the "natural law" or "divine law," has been given goods as private ownership of the means of production.

To make human spiritual essentiality depend on the exercising of the so-called "right to private property," constitutes one of the most tragic aberrations—because of its consequences—that human spirituality has suffered to this day.

The Scriptures teach us that the human being will be whatever he is able to do and become as an "econome." The word "econome" (*oikónomos*) is the one most used in the New Testament when it is a matter of judging the achievements of human life. In the Old Testament the term "econome" (*menshala*) is given equal importance.

When the Marxists insist on the "economical" as the basic element, fundamental for interpreting the significance of human life as it is developed in History, they make the Church—one of those ironies of History—reconsider the Biblical criterion of the human being as an "econome."

The Church proclaims that the human vocation is that of being a "good econome." The "house" that the human creature administers is the whole world of Creation; and each person is responsible for it to his fellow creatures and to God.

The responsibility of creating goods and administrating them is the first right of every human being, the essential principle of his spirituality. The Church teaches that each and every human being should share responsibility in the mutual exercise of that right. To violate that right is the first criminal act against human dignity and decorum.

The most perfect social system will be the one that guarantees the responsible participation of all citizens in the matters of "public administration." The effective respect for that right is necessary in order for the society to be made up of persons and not infrahuman individuals. Such is the real principle of true "demo-cracy."

The Church teaches that the committed participation of its members in public life, in the administration of its economy, is not something one can choose to add or not to add to his condition of believer; on the contrary, the responsible exercise of this right is an integral and inseparable part of the loving practice of the Christian faith.

Therefore the Church teaches that it is an integral part of the life of the Christian believer to exercise his rights and to fulfill his duties as a citizen, especially in our case, where democracy is made effective through the constitution of the Popular Power and the participation in labor unions in the different places of work.

The aberrations of a "faith" which calls itself "a-political," are of such consequence for the falsification of human spirituality and the meaning of the social nature of life, that the Church, indignant, rejects them and combats them as "heretical." Only an interested distortion of the faith—against all argumentation grounded on scriptural truth—can make the simple Christian believer renounce the struggle and effort to find, together with his fellow countrymen, the most adequate solutions to the problems patent in the neighborhood, in the city or in the nation, and keep him from enriching the life of all and making it more decorously human through a better "economy" of his time, his abilities, his knowledge and the goods he produces.

SIN

The interpretation of sin by Reformed theologians in the nineteenth and twentieth centuries has been directly influenced by historical events. One of the features of theological liberalism in the nineteenth century was an optimism about what human beings could achieve individually and collectively. This optimism often went hand-in-hand with a minimal statement about the reality and the consequences of sin.

In the twentieth century, in the aftermath of massive human slaughter in two world wars, innumerable regional conflicts, the Holocaust, and Hiroshima, theologians were forced to reexamine and reappropriate the classical doctrine of the total depravity of human beings as well as the sense in which sin is paradoxically a description of both a universal human condition and a particular individual act. This recovery of "original sin" led theologians to recognize sin as both an individual human reality and a collective reality in institutions and social structures.

Recent feminist theology has raised the question whether the classical interpretation of pride as the primary form of sin is not largely a reflection of male experience and, as such, an inadequate interpretation of the experience of women.

FOR FURTHER STUDY

G. C. Berkouwer, Sin, trans. Philip C. Holtrop (Grand Rapids: Wm. B. Eerdmans, 1971). Emil Brunner, Man in Revolt: A Christian Anthropology, trans. Olive Wyon (Philadelphia: Westminster, 1947). Hodge, Systematic Theology, 2:123–277. Paul Ricoeur, The Symbolism of Evil, trans. Emerson Buchanan (New York: Harper & Row, 1967), esp. pp. 47–99.

Sin as Arrested God-Consciousness

Having described human beings in terms of self-consciousness and religion as God-consciousness, it is not surprising that Friedrich Schleiermacher also described sin as that which arrests the development of God-consciousness.

SOURCE

Schleiermacher, *Christian Faith*, 271–72.

Without running counter to our method we cannot at the outset give an objective elucidation of sin, but must revert to the personal self-consciousness which attests an inner state as sin—a procedure all the less open to objection because sin cannot emerge in the life of the Christian apart from such a consciousness. To lack this consciousness would simply be an additional sin, of which, as such, we could not fail subsequently to become conscious. If, then, it is our primary object to ascertain the characteristic element in the consciousness of sinfulness, we ought not, within the sphere of Christian piety, to look for it except in relationship to the God-consciousness, and accordingly the only course open to us is to reckon everything as sin that has arrested the free development of the God-consciousness. Now, if in any particular moment under examination God has formed part of our self-consciousness, but this God-consciousness has not been able to permeate the other active elements therein, thus determining the moment, then sin and the consciousness of sin are simultaneous, and the sensuous self-consciousness by reason of its having been gratified is affected with pleasure, but the higher, owing to the impotence of the God-consciousness, with pain. If, on the other hand, God has not formed part of the moment at all, if, that is to say, the occurrence of the moment excludes the God-consciousness, showing that the God-consciousness cannot make the moment its own, which also means that it cannot be supposed to accord and acquiesce in it, then the consciousness of sin follows on the sin itself. Supposing, however, that the God-consciousness has determined the moment, and that pleasure is present in the higher self-consciousness, still every attendant feeling of effort implies a consciousness of sin—in some degree, consequently, annulling that pleasure—since we thereby are made aware that if the sensuous elements which have been overcome had been reinforced from without, the God-consciousness would have been unable to determine the moment. In this sense, therefore—but only because there exists a living seed of sin ever ready to burst forth—there is such a thing as an abiding consciousness of sin, now preceding the sin itself as a warning presentiment, now accompanying it as an inward reproof, or following it as penitence. That no God-consciousness, however, should ever be directed at all upon a moment such as that described could only happen if in the person acting there were no relationship between the moment and the class of actions under discussion (in which case he would be in a state of innocence), or if the God-consciousness were no longer active within him (which would be the state of hardening).

Moral Man and Immoral Society

In the introduction to his book *Moral Man and Immoral Society*, written in 1932, Reinhold Niebuhr argued that the immorality of groups and societies is always more than the sum of the immorality of the individuals within them. It was this conviction about social immorality that led Niebuhr to reject religious and secular views about moral progress.

SOURCE

Reinhold Niebuhr, *Moral Man and Immoral Society* (New York: Charles Scribner's Sons, 1960), xi–xii.

The thesis to be elaborated in these pages is that a sharp distinction must be drawn between the moral and social behavior of individuals and of social groups, national, racial, and economic; and that this distinction justifies and necessitates political policies which a purely individualistic ethic must always find embarrassing. The title "Moral Man and Immoral Society" suggests the intended distinction too unqualifiedly, but it is nevertheless a fair indication of the argument to which the following pages are devoted. Individual men may be moral in the sense that they are able to consider interests other than their own in determining problems of conduct, and are capable, on occasion, of preferring the advantages of others to their own. They are endowed by nature with a measure of sympathy and consideration for their kind, the breadth of which may be extended by an astute social pedagogy. Their rational faculty prompts them to a sense of justice which educational discipline may refine and purge of egoistic elements until they are able to view a social situation, in which their own interests are involved, with a fair measure of objectivity. But all these achievements are more difficult, if not impossible, for human societies and social groups. In every human group there is less reason to guide and to check impulse, less capacity for self-transcendence, less ability to comprehend the needs of others and therefore more unrestrained egoism than the individuals, who compose the group, reveal in their personal relationships.

The inferiority of the morality of groups to that of individuals is due in part to the difficulty of establishing a rational social force which is powerful enough to cope with the natural impulses by which society achieves its cohesion; but in part it is merely the revelation of a collective egoism, compounded of the egoistic impulses of individuals, which achieve a more vivid expression and a more cumulative effect when they are united in a common impulse than when they express themselves separately and discreetly.

Inasfar as this treatise has a polemic interest it is directed against the moralists, both religious and secular, who imagine that the egoism of individuals is being progressively checked by the development of rationality or the growth of a religiously inspired goodwill and that nothing but the continuance of this process is necessary to establish social harmony between all the human societies and collectives. Social analyses and prophecies made by moralists, sociologists and educators upon the basis of these assumptions lead to a very considerable moral and political confusion in our day. They completely disregard the political necessities in the struggle for justice in human society by failing to recognise those elements in man's collective behavior which belong to the order of nature and can never be brought completely under the dominion of reason or conscience. They do not recognise that when collective power, whether in the form of imperialism or class domination, exploits weakness, it can never be dislodged unless power is raised against it.

Anxiety as the Temptation to Sin

One of the most important works of twentieth-century Reformed theology was Reinhold Niebuhr's *The Nature and Destiny of Man*. Niebuhr argued that sin has its origin in the way human beings deal with the reality of their finitude.

SOURCE

Niebuhr, *Nature and Destiny* 1: 185–86.

Anxiety about perfection and about insecurity are thus inexorably bound together in human actions and the errors which are made in the search for perfection are never due merely to the ignorance of not knowing the limits of conditioned values. They always exhibit some tendency of the agent to hide his own limits, which he knows only too well. Obviously the basic source of temptation is, therefore, not the inertia of "matter" or "nature" against the larger and more inclusive ends which reason envisages. It resides in the inclination of man, either to deny the contingent character of his existence (in pride and self-love) or to escape from his freedom (in sensuality). Sensuality represents an effort to escape from the freedom and the infinite possibilities of spirit by becoming lost in the detailed processes, activities and interests of existence, an effort which results inevitably in unlimited devotion to limited values. Sensuality is man "turning inordinately to mutable good" (Aquinas).

Anxiety, as a permanent concomitant of freedom, is thus both the source of creativity and a temptation to sin. It is the condition of the sailor, climbing the mast (to use a simile), with the abyss of the waves beneath him and the "crow's nest" above him. He is anxious about both the end toward which he strives and the abyss of nothingness into which he may fall. The ambition of man to be something is always partly prompted by the fear of meaninglessness which threatens him by reason of the contingent character of his existence. His creativity is therefore always corrupted by some effort to overcome contingency by raising precisely what is contingent to absolute and unlimited dimensions. This effort, though universal, cannot be regarded as normative. It is always destructive. Yet obviously the destructive aspect of anxiety is so intimately involved in the creative aspects that there is no possibility of making a simple separation between them. The two are inextricably bound together by reason of man being anxious both to realize his unlimited possibilities and to overcome and to hide the dependent and contingent character of his existence.

When anxiety has conceived it brings forth both pride and sensuality. Man falls into pride, when he seeks to raise his contingent existence to unconditioned significance; he falls into sensuality, when he seeks to escape from his unlimited possibilities of freedom, from the perils and responsibilities of self-determination, by immersing himself into a "mutable good," by losing himself in some natural vitality.

The Ultimate Mystery of Sin

Paul Ricoeur (b. 1913), a French Reformed philosopher, argued that original sin must be understood as a symbol and, consequently, cannot be the basis for speculation or explanation. As a symbol, original sin expresses what can be confessed but cannot be explained. Theologians continually get themselves in serious difficulty when they forget that original sin is a symbol and try to turn confession into explanation.

SOURCE

Paul Ricoeur, "'Original Sin': A Study in Meaning," in *The Conflict of Interpretations*, ed. Don Ihde (Evanston, Ill.: Northwestern University Press, 1974), 286.

I will conclude with these three warnings. (1) We never have the right to speculate about the concept of original sin—which, taken in itself, is only a rationalized myth—as if it had a proper consistency. It makes explicit the Adamic myth, just as this myth makes explicit the penitential experience of Israel. One must always come back to the Church's confession of sins. (2) We never have the right to speculate on *the evil already there*, outside the evil that we do. Here, doubtless, is the ultimate mystery of sin. We *inaugurate* evil. It is through us that evil comes into the world. But we inaugurate evil only on the basis of an evil already there, of which our birth is the impenetrable symbol. (3) We never have the right to speculate on either the evil that we inaugurate, or on the evil that we find, without reference to the history of salvation. Original sin is only an antitype. But type and antitype are not only parallel ("just as . . . so too"), but there is a movement from one to the other, a "how much more," an "all the more": "where sin abounded, grace did much more abound" (Romans 5:20).

Sin as Lack of Self-esteem

In the last half of the twentieth century many feminist theologians have argued that pride is a better description of male sinfulness than it is of the experience of women, many of whom suffer more a lack of self-esteem than they do individualism and domination.

SOURCE

Letty M. Russell, *Becoming Human* (Philadelphia: Westminster, 1982), 82–83.

One way of regaining a more wholistic understanding of sin is to try to move beyond the stereotypes that project our responsibilities onto others. The divisions between body and soul, person and society, or any other such dualisms prevent us from seeing the whole picture of sin.

They give us a false picture of human reality in which one whole interrelated life/body is related to all other parts of creation. All of us, both body and spirit, both person and society, both male and female, are included in broken relationships with God and with others, and not just part of us.

Dualistic stereotypes mask the actual differences in the way women and men experience sin in their lives. For men frequently experience sin at the point of their strength (independence, assertion of rights, domination over others). Women in turn then experience it at their point of strength (interdependence, assertion of responsibilities, subordination to others). To overcome these particular forms of broken relationship, attention needs to be given to the way men and women develop and to their particular ways of relating to the world so that each may receive the help that she or he needs (Carol Gilligan). Without this attention, stereotypes of the meaning of sin may lead to reinforcement of the actual problems being faced. For instance, Valerie Saiving has pointed out that women's greatest temptation is not so much the pride and will to power that besets many men, but rather lack of self-esteem and a willingness to remain weak. Failure to recognize this is a form of collective social sin that results in such dehumanization as that of the battered woman.

EVIL

One of the perennial puzzles of theology is the problem posed by evil. What is evil? And how can its reality be reconciled with the Christian confession that God is both good and omnipotent? In the twentieth century, evil became not so much an intellectual puzzle as an existential reality which threatened the intelligibility of Christian faith. Contemporary theologians, more than their classical predecessors, drew a distinction between sin and evil and often did not attempt to explain evil as the result, in any causal sense, of human sin. The challenge for many theologians was how to acknowledge the reality of evil, refuse to attribute it to human sin, and yet avoid the implication of a cosmic dualism, a struggle between good and evil, which would deny the sovereignty of God.

FOR FURTHER STUDY

Edward Farley, *Good and Evil: Interpreting A Human Condition* (Minneapolis: Fortess, 1990). Douglas John Hall, *God and Human Suffering: An Exercise in the Theology of the Cross* (Minneapolis: Augsburg, 1986).

Evil as "Nothingness"

One of the most interesting attempts to describe evil by a twentieth-century theologian is Karl Barth's depiction of evil as *das Nichtige*, or "nothingness." Evil, Barth argued, is not nothing; rather, it is nothingness. By "nothingness" Barth meant that "which opposes and resists God." Hence it is not a positive but a negative reality, somewhat similar to Augustine's description of evil as the absence or privation of good.

SOURCE

Barth, *Church Dogmatics*, III/3:305.

What is nothingness, the real nothingness which is not to be confounded with the negative side of God's good creation behind which it seeks to shelter for greater strength? What is nothingness unmasked and deprived of that camouflage by which it seeks to deceive us, and we ourselves? In plain and precise terms, the answer is that nothingness is the "reality" on whose account (i.e., against which) God Himself willed to become a creature in the creaturely world, yielding and subjecting Himself to it in Jesus Christ in order to overcome it. Nothingness is thus the "reality" which opposes and resists God, which is itself subjected to and overcome by His opposition and resistance, and which in this two-fold determination as the reality that negates and is negated by Him, is totally distinct from Him. The true nothingness is that which brought Jesus Christ to the cross, and that which He defeated there. Only from the standpoint of Jesus Christ, His birth, death and resurrection, do we see it in reality and truth, without the temptation to treat it as something inclusive or relative, or to conceive it dialectically and thus render it innocuous. From this standpoint we see it with fear and trembling as the adversary with whom God and God alone can cope. But it is to be noted that in this we see it where our one real hope against it is grounded and established. If there is confusion concerning it, we obviously do not see it from the standpoint of Jesus Christ.

From Image to Likeness

John Hick identifies in Western Christianity two different traditions of interpreting evil. The first, which he describes as "the majority report," is the interpretation of evil in the Augustinian tradition. Here evil is the absence of being, is an intruder, and does not belong in God's good world. The second

interpretation, "the minority report," Hick associates with Irenaeus. In this interpretation, human beings are created in the image, but not the likeness, of God;
and life, which includes the possibility of evil, is the process whereby human
beings grow into the likeness of God.

SOURCE

John Hick, *Evil and the God of Love* (London: Collins, 1974), 289–91.

THE "VALE OF
SOUL-MAKING" THEODICY

Fortunately there is another and better way. As well as the "majority
report" of the Augustinian tradition, which has dominated Western
Christendom, both Catholic and Protestant, since the time of Augustine
himself, there is the "minority report" of the Irenaean tradition. This
latter is both older and newer than the other, for it goes back to St.
Irenaeus and others of the early Hellenistic Fathers of the Church in the
two centuries prior to St. Augustine, and it has flourished again in more
developed forms during the last hundred years.

Instead of regarding man as having been created by God in a finished
state, as a finitely perfect being fulfilling the divine intention for our
human level of existence, and then falling disastrously away from this,
the minority report sees man as still in process of creation. Irenaeus
himself expressed the point in terms of the (exegetically dubious) distinction between the "image" and the "likeness" of God referred to in
Genesis i. 26: "Then God said, Let us make man in our image, after
our likeness." His view was that man as a personal and moral being
already exists in the image, but has not yet been formed into the finite
likeness of God. By this "likeness" Irenaeus means something more than
personal existence as such; he means a certain valuable quality of personal life which reflects finitely the divine life. This represents the
perfecting of man, the fulfillment of God's purpose for humanity,
the "bringing of many sons to glory," the creating of "children of God"
who are "fellow heirs with Christ" of his glory.

And so man, created as a personal being in the image of God, is only
the raw material for a further and more difficult stage of God's creative
work. This is the leading of men as relatively free and autonomous
persons, through their own dealings with life in the world in which He
has placed them, towards that quality of personal existence that is the
finite likeness of God. The features of this likeness are revealed in

the person of Christ, and the process of man's creation into it is the work of the Holy Spirit. In St. Paul's words, "And we all, with unveiled faces, beholding the glory of the Lord, are being changed into his likeness (ε ι κ ώ ν) from one degree of glory to another; for this comes from the Lord who is the Spirit"; or again, "For God knew his own before ever they were, and also ordained that they should be shaped to the likeness (ε ι κ ώ ν) of his Son." In Johannine terms, the movement from the image to the likeness is a transition from one level of existence, that of animal life (*Bios*), to another and higher level, that of eternal life (*Zoe*), which includes but transcends the first. And the fall of man was seen by Irenaeus as a failure within the second phase of this creative process, a failure that has multiplied the perils and complicated the route of the journey in which God is seeking to lead mankind.

In the light of modern anthropological knowledge some form of two-stage conception of the creation of man has become an almost unavoidable Christian tenet. At the very least we must acknowledge as two distinguishable stages the fashioning of *homo sapiens* as a product of the long evolutionary process, and his sudden or gradual spiritualization as a child of God. But we may well extend the first stage to include the development of man as a rational and responsible person capable of personal relationship with the personal Infinite who has created him. This first stage of the creative process was, to our anthropomorphic imaginations, easy for divine omnipotence. By an exercise of creative power God caused the physical universe to exist, and in the course of countless ages to bring forth within it organic life, and finally to produce out of organic life personal life; and when man had thus emerged out of the evolution of the forms of organic life, a creature had been made who has the possibility of existing in conscious fellowship with God. But the second stage of the creative process is of a different kind altogether. It cannot be performed by omnipotent power as such. For personal life is essentially free and self-directing. It cannot be perfected by divine fiat, but only through the uncompelled responses and willing co-operation of human individuals in their actions and reactions in the world in which God has placed them. Men may eventually become the perfected persons whom the New Testament calls "children of God," but they cannot be created ready-made as this.

The value-judgment that is implicitly being invoked here is that one who has attained to goodness by meeting and eventually mastering temptations, and thus by rightly making responsible choices in concrete situations, is good in a richer and more valuable sense than would be one created *ab initio* in a state either of innocence or of virtue.

PROVIDENCE

While many classical Reformed theologians boldly declared that God not only creates and sustains the world but also governs and rules the events of human history, contemporary theologians have found it difficult, in light of the events of the twentieth century, to affirm that God governs events. Insofar as contemporary Reformed theology affirms some form of God's providence, it is not a providence of the rule and government of human events but a providence of presence. At best, contemporary theologians struggle to find some basis for affirming that God is present in the world.

FOR FURTHER STUDY

Benjamin Wirt Farley, *The Providence of God* (Grand Rapids: Baker, 1988). Langdon Gilkey, *Reaping the Whirlwind: A Christian Interpretation of History* (New York: Seabury, 1976).

God's Presence in the Midst of Dread

G. C. Berkouwer acknowledges that Christian interpretations of providence have been challenged by catastrophic events in the twentieth century. Much of humanity looks upon the world with dread. The Bible, however, reveals that the human problem is still what it always has been—estrangement between humanity and God.

SOURCE

G. C. Berkouwer, *The Providence of God*, trans. Lewis Smedes (Grand Rapids: Wm. B. Eerdmans, 1952), 12–16.

These are times in which the Church of Christ must ask herself whether she still has the courage, in profound and unshakable faith, in boundless confidence, to proclaim the Providence of God. Or is she possessed of secret doubts fed by daily events? Can she still speak of God's rule over *all* things, of His holy presence in *this* world? Can she yet proclaim confidently His unlimited control over the world and life—war and peace, East and West, pagans . . . and Jews? Dare she still, with eyes open to the facts of life—no less than those who *from the facts* conclude an imperative atheism—still confess her old confession?

It is necessary to pause over this question, the more since God's Providence seems to be one of the most self-evident articles of the Church's confession. The confessions of the churches contain a common witness to the Providence of God over "all things," those of the Roman Catholic as well as those of the Lutheran and Reformed churches. In Protestant confessions there is a remarkably uniform definition. In the handbooks of theology, too, the definitions and distinctions appear in striking consensus. We read in all of them of sustenance and rule, and of God's embracing in His prescient government all that occurs in the universe.

Many of the treatises give little if any attention to crisis phenomena. The doctrine of Providence is discussed usually in general and timeless terms. We receive the impression that a finished definition has been reached, that we may now content ourselves with a repetition of the many lucid declarations of the Church. Thus, this article of faith for a long period failed to arouse the same kind of opposition as did, for instance, the doctrines of substitution and satisfaction. When the person and work of Christ was in the center of dispute, the Providence doctrine had not yet become a serious stumbling block. Providence seemed to be a "truth" which could rely upon universal assent—in distinction from other truths like the virgin birth, the resurrection, and the ascension, which were the *scandalon* of the nineteenth century. Anyone who accepted the existence of God usually believed as well that He sustained and ruled the world. The Providence doctrine was often used as another way of stating man's belief in progressive evolution. God was discernibly leading the world to His own benevolent end. Not only the maintenance of the world, but the sequence of historical events appeared to confirm the confession of the Church. Of course, the Church did not speak of evolution. But it did speak of fulfillment and purpose; and was not *purpose* a catchword in the optimism of the last century—and, for that matter, in the preaching of the kingdom of God?

All this in our century is radically altered. The friendliness of God, which man thought he saw reflected in the stream of history, has become increasingly disputable. In truth, has it not been disproven by historical reality? Do not the researches of such men as Spengler, Lessing, and Toynbee underscore it? In all this, the reality of God, His guidance and purposeful management, has today become a profound problem—*the* problem for persons who have never even considered it before. Many feel themselves forced into agnosticism or atheism. The facts of experience which used to be the most striking illustrations of God's Providence have become an even more convincing counter-argument. Everywhere profound doubts have risen as to the reality of God; men not only deny Providence over *all things*, but ridicule the idea by pointing to the reality around us. True, the confessions of the Church also speak of human suffering and grievous distress. They avoid adversity no more than prosperity, and embrace barren with fruitful years, sickness with health, and "all that can yet come over us." They even include the evil that God in His *pity* sends. But the proportion of this evil has become so great and frightful that the word *pity* must, it seems, be forced to take on a new meaning.

We can perhaps thus frame the contradiction which life poses: the comfort of the old confession of God's Providence versus the *dread* that rises from the events of our century. Dread has now become the essence and intensification of the unrest and concern latently present in all times. "In a period in which the problem of man is anew considered and argued, with the authority of the traditional constructions rejected, dread—a dread which invades the essence of man—arises anew in all her nakedness and primitive strength." Dread may be considered the result of man's being more or less ruthlessly snatched out of an old and trusted order and forced into a strange, hostile world. We may say that the trusted order out of which man is plucked is the order of Providence. But the causes of man's radical displacement and estrangement are complex. . . .

In this situation the confession of God's Providence over all things seems the last thing which could justly pretend to answer the basic question of human existence. The confession of God's Providence has become, now more than ever, a stone of stumbling.

The conflict between the confession of God's Providence and the modern mind poses a threat which the Church should understand. And the Church will understand it so long as she truly lives out of the Word of God. For it is the Word which points most clearly to the deep distress which rises from life's displacement into a hostile order. It shows us how seriously the influence of sin and enmity against God and man alienates and displaces man from the fellowship of God, the fellowship which casts out dread.

This is the light that the Scriptures cast on dread. They do not isolate one or more aspects of the phenomenon, but reveal the radical estrangement which is the cause of dread. The Scriptures diagnose the sickness unto death at its source, and thus explain its effect on the whole complicated human situation. That is why the believer knows that the problem of estrangement is the problem of his own relationship to God. He is shown how in man's estrangement empirical reality seems to speak with final authority and brings on a crisis of belief in God's Providence. Thus, this belief can never be the consequence of empirical considerations and reasoned conclusions. It is, rather, that the displacement and disperse-ment are overcome from above. The Church knows that this victory is not the crown of autonomous thinking, but a gift of God's grace. In this victory the Church must, in humility and courage, go *through* the world and through the crisis of our time. She knows from Scripture and experience how often her faith has been tried by the riddles of history, by the terrifying enigmas of experience. She knows, too, that in her own past the timid question provoked by a failure to understand has often crescendoed into a revolt of doubt and faithlessness. The Bible does not hide from us the fact that questions born in fear and uncertainty can whelm up with remarkable force in the hearts of believers. Recall the illustrations in Scripture: in the Psalms, the Book of Job, and Ecclesi-astes—illustrations which contradict all rational self-evidence.

Providence and Omnicausality

Otto Weber, following Karl Barth, interprets providence christologically rather than speculatively. To interpret providence christologically is to interpret it soteriologically and confessionally. God's activity cannot be explained by means of philosophical principles but only by means of what God has done and will do in Jesus Christ.

SOURCE

Weber, *Foundations*, 2:505.

The Difference Between Creation and Providence. Creation and conser-vation, or creation and providence cannot be identified as one, although certainly the Creator is the Conserver and Ruler. The most illuminating reason for this is the simple fact that God's conserving and ruling activity, his providence, by no means takes place "out of nothingness," but con-serves created existence as something already extant and active and thus presupposes it. Both Scholasticism and Orthodoxy were acutely aware of this. They attempted to respect it by distinguishing between God as the "first cause" and the "second causes" within created reality. Regard-less of the way one proceeds terminologically, the distinction between creation and providence should be quite clearly obvious. Christian theol-ogy in general has never fallen prey to the temptation of assuming the Creator's omnicausality so that the reality of the creature's activity was severely restricted. Conversely, it has never assigned such importance to the creature's own causality that the effectiveness and reality of the

Creator were made into nothing more than the initiative past. It has avoided both Pantheism and Deism. In doing so, however, it has confronted in the creature's own capacity to work effectively in the world one of the two great problems of the doctrine of providence. The other great problem is raised by the fact of evil. How is God, in his preserving, accompanying, and ruling the creature (to use K. Barth's expression), to be seen in relationship to the evil which is also the evil in the creature? God's providence must cope not with something neutral, nor with something created good, but with the creature who is resisting God's will. The fact of sin makes our thinking about God's providence fraught with profound tension. If faith states that God's will happens, then it cannot avoid the riddle that God's will does not in fact take place in our lives, and so it can then only speak of God's providence in the petition which is confident of its own fulfillment, "Thy will be done."

e. The Concrete Import of the Doctrine of Providence. Under these circumstances, the doctrine of providence is not dealing with a problem which is only found in the realm of intellectual reflection. We stated that our confession of God as the Creator is both a comfort and a declaration of battle, because it amounts to the rejection of the creature's own autonomous powers and denies both the trust of the creature and the fear of it. In the same way, our confession of God in his providence is our rejection of the omnipotence of sin and our testimony to the certainty that God does accomplish his will in spite of myself and the power of all evil, and that he will accomplish it. It is our certainty that God for the sake of Jesus Christ has taken sides for me as his creature against all the assembled powers, including the powers which attack and enslave me. Speculation about God's "providence" (*pronoia*) holding sway in all things does not "cost" anything. But faith in God and in his providence does "cost" something, for it cannot exist at all without the practical knowledge that I am not intended to do the will of the Evil One but rather to do God's will and to pray that his will be done.

f. The Faith in Providence and the Idea of Divine Omnicausality. Accordingly, the doctrine of providence like the doctrine of the creation is to be seen in clear relationship to soteriology. Faith in providence is' not "a kind of forecourt, or common foundation, on which the belief of the Christian Church may meet with other concepts of the relationship of what is called 'God' with what is called 'world.'" It is faith in the Creator who does not let himself be dethroned as Creator by all of the creature's own work and by all of sin, nor as the Lord of the Covenant. It is faith in Christ.

137

It cannot be said that the dogmatic tradition has in every instance dealt properly and adequately with the fact that belief in providence is Christian belief. The main reason for this is that Christian theology from very early was involved in contact and disputation with the Stoic doctrine of providence, the doctrine of "fate" (ananke). In addition, the ontological conception, chiefly derived from Aristotle but also to a degree from Neo-Platonism, renders its influence; it asserts that God is the "first cause" of all things that happen. The common and fundamental thought, which was not without its effect on the Church's theology, was that everything happens according to an inviolable law and that God was its cause or epitome. It is immediately clear that God in such a thought is not free. At the most, he could have been free when he set the worlds in motion. But now everything must proceed as he has established it, that is, as he has ordained it to function causally. God is in any event in this deterministic view the ultimate component part of the world structure, but certainly not its Creator. He is what is beyond it, but he is not opposite to it. When Christian theology absorbs such thinking, and when it believes that it can combine it with the ontologically applied concept of God's omnipotence (omnicausality), it becomes enmired in a road leading nowhere. It can certainly never successfully show what such a God is supposed to have to do with the God who discloses himself to us in Jesus Christ.

g. *The Creature's Own Reality.* The difference between the Christian discussion of God's providence and the idea of omnicausality is seen even more clearly when we bear in mind that the Christian doctrine of providence includes the creature's own activity and acknowledges the reality of evil in the realm of the creation.

The creature's own activity can only be dealt with mediately in the context of an ontologically determined doctrine of providence. It then belongs to the circle of "second causes" which all result from the "first cause." But if God's providence consists of his making the creature's own activity mediate, then we have in fact the conditionedness, but never the responsibility of man. In other words, it is man's createdness which is at stake here.

What is the place of evil in the context of a reality which is determined by divine omnicausality? It is quite clear that evil then belongs to caused reality. If it really happens, then God willed it to happen. And if that is true, then evil loses its character as evil or evil is acknowledged as such in the specific instance and in regard to the specific person, but in the process of speculative thought it is built into the total process of the event as a positive element. The "theodicy" idea, which we have thus approached, when it is built upon the presupposition of divine omnicausality, always results in depriving evil of its actual wickedness by explaining it and building it into a conceptual whole. It can only appear to be evil, or be relatively evil, since it is also integrated as the evil in the good, in the purposeful course of the totality of reality.

Reformed Confessions

We Are Not Alone

"A Creed (1980)" of the United Church of Canada implies that the major religious issue is not whether God rules the world God has created but whether there is any sense that God is present in it.

SOURCE

"A Creed (1980)" of the United Church of Canada, in *Reformed Witness Today*, 196.

We are not alone, we live in God's world.
We believe in God:
    Who has created and is creating,
    Who has come in Jesus, the Word made flesh,
    to reconcile and make new,
    Who works in us and others
    By the Spirit.

We trust in God.

We are called to be the Church:
    To celebrate God's presence,
    To love and serve others,
    To seek justice and resist evil,
    To proclaim Jesus, crucified and risen,
    Our Judge and our Hope.

In life, in death, in life beyond death,
    God is with us.

We are not alone.

Thanks be to God.

God's Presence and Rule

"A Declaration of Faith" of the Presbyterian Church in the United States does affirm that the God who creates the world continues to rule it. It also speaks to the distinctive religious needs of people in the last half of the twentieth century by affirming that there is "no event from which God is absent."

SOURCE

Declaration of Faith, 2.

God created and rules in love.
 God created all the worlds that are
  and upholds and rules everything.

 We affirm that the universe exists
  by the power of God's Word and Spirit.
 God has chosen to give it reality
  out of the love we have come to know in Christ.

 God still works
  through the processes that shape and change the earth
  and the living things upon it.
 We acknowledge God's care and control
  in the regularity of the universe
  as well as in apparently random happenings.
 There is no event from which God is absent
  and his ultimate purpose in all events is just and loving.
 That purpose embraces our choices
  and will surely be accomplished.
 The Creator works in all things
  toward the new creation that is promised in Christ.

4

JESUS CHRIST

When the claims of Christian faith are subjected to serious criticism and attack, the church and its theologians often return to the central convictions of the gospel. One consequence of Enlightenment criticisms of classical Christian theology was that theologians in the nineteenth and twentieth centuries returned to what they believed to be the central focus of Christian faith—the man Jesus and God's presence and activity in him.

Modern theologians attempted to construct a basis for Christian faith in the Jesus of history. They assumed that dogmas and doctrines about Jesus as the Christ would be more secure if they could be shown to be rooted in what the historical Jesus said and did.

The attack by major figures of the Enlightenment on concepts such as superstition, tradition, special revelation, original sin, and miracle meant that theologians in the modern period were increasingly critical of the metaphysical language used by theologians in the fourth and fifth centuries to articulate faith in Jesus as the Christ. So too many of the same theologians considered the interpretations of the doctrine of the atonement to be increasingly irrelevant to the modern world.

Reformed theology, like most other Christian traditions in the modern period, found itself returning to the figure of Jesus of Nazareth in order to rethink its understanding of the gospel, but at the same time discovering that it had to find a new language and a new paradigm by which to say what it believed when it confessed with the apostle Paul that "God was in Christ reconciling the world to himself."

FOR FURTHER STUDY

John Baillie, *The Place of Jesus Christ in Modern Christianity* (Edinburgh: T. & T. Clark, 1929). J. M. Creed, *The Divinity of Jesus Christ: A Study in the History of Christian Doctrine Since Kant* (London: Collins, 1964). Colin E. Gunton, *Yesterday & Today: A*

Study of Continuities in Christology (Grand Rapids: Wm. B. Eerdmans, 1983). John Macquarrie, *Jesus Christ in Modern Thought* (London: SCM and Philadelphia: Trinity, 1990). Alister McGrath, *The Making of Modern German Christology* (Oxford: Basil Blackwell, 1986). Priscilla Pope-Levison and John R. Levison, *Jesus in Global Contexts* (Louisville: Westminster/John Knox, 1992). Jon Sobrino, *Jesus in Latin America* (Maryknoll: Orbis, 1987). Claude Welch, ed., *God and Incarnation in Mid-Nineteenth Century German Theology: G. Thomasius, I. A. Dorner, and A. E. Biedermann* (New York: Oxford University Press, 1965).

THE PERSON OF JESUS CHRIST

During the last two centuries, a growing number of theologians have come to the conclusion that the language and paradigm of classical Christology (i.e., that Jesus Christ is one person in two natures, truly human and truly God) were no longer intelligible to contemporary Christians. Much of nineteenth- and twentieth-century Christology could be described as a search for a new idiom and paradigm. In their quest for a new language, many theologians emphasized the particularity of Jesus, his Judaism, and the social context of the first century. Furthermore, some theologians concluded that understanding what it means to confess that Jesus is the Christ is something that comes only with the practice of discipleship and the praxis of "following Jesus."

FOR FURTHER STUDY

G. C. Berkouwer, *The Person of Christ*, Studies in Dogmatics, trans. John Vriend (Grand Rapids: Wm. B. Eerdmans, 1954). Emil Brunner, *The Mediator: A Study of the Central Doctrine of the Christian Faith*, trans. Olive Wyon (Philadelphia: Westminster, 1947). P. T. Forsyth, *The Person and Place of Jesus Christ* (London: Independent Press, 1955).

Jesus' Perfect God-Consciousness

Just as Friedrich Schleiermacher argued that human beings are constituted by the feeling of utter dependence, so too he saw in the man Jesus "an absolutely powerful God-consciousness" which was "a veritable existence of God in Him."

SOURCE

Schleiermacher, *Christian Faith*, 385–87.

§ 94. *The Redeemer, then, is like all men in virtue of the identity of human nature, but distinguished from them all by the constant potency of His God-consciousness, which was a veritable existence of God in Him.*

1. That the Redeemer should be entirely free from all sinfulness is no objection at all to the complete identity of human nature in Him and others, for we have already laid down that sin is so little an essential part of the being of man that we can never regard it as anything else than a disturbance of nature. It follows that the possibility of a sinless development is in itself not incongruous with the idea of human nature; indeed, this possibility is involved, and recognized, in the consciousness of sin as guilt, as that is universally understood. This likeness, however, is to be understood in such a general sense that even the first man before the first sin stood no nearer the Redeemer, and was like Him in no higher sense, than all other men. For if even in the life of the first man we must assume a time when sin had not yet appeared, yet every first appearance of sin leads back to a sinful preparation. But the Redeemer too shared in the same vicissitudes of life, without which we can hardly imagine the entrance of sin at a definite moment even in Adam, for they are essential to human nature. Furthermore, the first man was originally free from all the contagious influences of a sinful society, while the Redeemer had to enter into the corporate life when it had already advanced far in deterioration, so that it would hardly be possible to attribute His sinlessness to external protection—which we certainly must somehow admit in the case of the first man, if we would not involve ourselves in contradictions. Of the Redeemer, on the contrary, we must hold that the ground of His sinlessness was not external to Himself, but that it was a sinlessness essentially grounded in Himself, if He was to take away, through what He was in Himself, the sinfulness of the corporate life. Therefore, so far as sin is concerned, Christ differs no less from the first man than from all others.

The identity of human nature further involves this, that the manner in which Christ differs from all others also has its place in this identity. This would not be the case if it were not involved in human nature that individuals, so far as the measure of the different functions is concerned, are originally different from each other, so that to every separate corporate life (regarded in space as well as in time) there belong those who are more and less gifted; and we only arrive at the truth of life when we thus correlate those who differ from each other. In the same way, therefore, all those who in any respect give character to an age or a district are bound up with those over whom (as being defective in that particular respect) they extend an educative influence, even as Christ is bound up with those whom His preponderatingly powerful God-consciousness links to the corporate life thus indicated. The greater the difference, and the more specific the activity, the more must these also have established themselves against the hindering influences of a worthless environment, and they can be understood only by reference to this self-differentiating quality of human nature, not by reference to the group in which they stand; although by divine right they belong to it, as the Redeemer does to the whole race.

2. But in admitting that what is peculiar in the Redeemer's kind of activity belongs to a general aspect of human nature, we by no means wish to reduce this activity, and the personal dignity by which it is conditioned, to the same measure as that of others. The simple fact that faith in Christ postulates a relation on His part to the whole race, while everything analogous is valid only for definite individual times and places, is sufficient to prove this. For no one has yet succeeded, in any sphere of science or art, and no one will ever succeed, in establishing himself as head, universally animating and sufficient for the whole human race.

For this peculiar dignity of Christ, however, in the sense in which we have already referred back the ideality of His person to this spiritual function of the God-consciousness implanted in the self-consciousness, the terms of our proposition alone are adequate; for to ascribe to Christ an absolutely powerful God-consciousness, and to attribute to Him an existence of God in Him, are exactly the same thing.

The Absolutely Unique Character of Jesus

Swiss theologian Philip Schaff (1819–93) taught at the German Reformed Seminary in Mercersburg, Pennsylvania (now Lancaster Theological Seminary), and was one of the founders of the American Society of Church History. In his book *The Person of Christ: The Miracle of History*, Schaff depicted Jesus in a manner common to much of nineteenth-century Christology; what is significant about Jesus is not what Jesus says and does—his proclamation of the coming kingdom of God—but his strength of character.

SOURCE

Philip Schaff, *The Person of Christ: The Miracle of History* (Boston: The American Tract Society, 1865), 104–6, 109–12.

CHRIST'S CHARACTER THE GREATEST
MORAL MIRACLE OF HISTORY

Such was Jesus of Nazareth,—a true man in body, soul, and spirit, yet differing from all men; a character absolutely unique and original from tender childhood to ripe manhood, moving in unbroken union with God, overflowing with the purest love to man, free from every sin and error, innocent and holy, teaching and practicing all virtues in perfect harmony, devoted solely and uniformly to the noblest ends, sealing the purest life with the sublimest death, and ever acknowledged since as the one and only perfect model of goodness and holiness! All human greatness loses on closer inspection; but Christ's character grows more pure, sacred, and lovely, the better we know him. The whole range of history and fiction furnishes no parallel to it. There never was any thing even approaching to it, before or since, except in faint imitation of his example.

No biographer, moralist, or artist can be satisfied with any attempt of his to set forth the beauty of holiness which shines from the face of Jesus of Nazareth. It is felt to be infinitely greater than any conception or representation of it by the mind, the tongue, or the pencil of man or angel. We might as well attempt to empty the waters of the boundless sea into a narrow well, or to portray the splendor of the risen sun and the starry heavens with ink. No picture of the Saviour, though drawn by the master hand of a Raphael or Dürer or Rubens; no epic, though conceived by the genius of a Dante or Milton or Klopstock,—can improve on the artless narrative of the Gospels, whose only but all-powerful charm is truth. In this case, certainly, truth is stranger than fiction, and speaks best for itself without comment, explanation, or eulogy. Here, and here alone, the highest perfection of art falls short of the historical fact, and fancy finds no room for idealizing the real; for here we have the absolute ideal itself in living reality. It seems to me that this consideration alone should satisfy any reflecting mind that Christ's character, though truly natural and human, rises far above the ordinary proportions of humanity, and can not be classified with the purest and greatest of our race. . . .

Yes: Christ's person is, indeed, a great but blessed mystery. It can not be explained on purely humanitarian principles, nor derived from any intellectual and moral forces of the age in which he lived. On the contrary, it stands in marked contrast to the whole surrounding world of Judaism and Heathenism, which presents to us the dreary picture of internal decay, and which actually crumbled into ruin before the new moral creation of the crucified Jesus of Nazareth. He is the one absolute and unaccountable exception to the universal experience of mankind. He is the great central miracle of the whole gospel-history. All his miracles are but the natural and necessary manifestations of his miraculous person, and hence they were performed with the same ease with which we perform our ordinary daily works. In the Gospel of St. John, they are simply and justly called his "works." It would be the greatest miracle indeed, if He, who is a miracle himself, should have performed no miracles.

Here is just the logical inconsistency, contradiction, and absurdity of those unbelievers who admit the extraordinary character of Christ's person, and yet deny his extraordinary works. They admit a cause without a corresponding effect, and involve the person in conflict with his works, or the works with the person. You may as well expect the sun to send forth darkness as to expect ordinary works from such an extraordinary being. The person of Christ accounts for all the wonderful phenomena in his history, as a sufficient cause for the effect. Such a power over the soul as he possessed, and still exercises from day to day throughout Christendom,—why should it not extend also over the lesser sphere of the body? What was it for him, who is spiritually the Resurrection and the Life of the race, to call forth a corpse from the grave? Could such a heavenly life and heavenly death as his end in any other way than in absolute triumph over death, and in ascension to heaven, its proper origin and home?

The supernatural and miraculous in Christ, let it be borne in mind, was not a borrowed gift or an occasional manifestation, as we find it among the prophets and apostles, but an inherent power in constant silent or public exercise. An inward virtue dwelt in his person, and went forth from him, so that even the fringe of his garment was healing to the touch through the medium of faith which is the bond of union between him and the soul. He was the true Shekinah, and shone in all his glory, not before the multitude or the unbelieving Pharisees and scribes, but when he was alone with his Father, or walked in the dark night over the waves of the sea, calming the storm of nature and strengthening the faith of his timid disciples, or when he stood between Moses and Elijah before his favorite three on the mount of transfiguration.

Thus from every direction we arrive at the conclusion, that Christ, though truly natural and human, was at the same time truly supernatural and divine. The wonderful character of his person forces upon us the inevitable admission of the indwelling of the Divinity in him, as the only rational and satisfactory explanation of this mysterious fact; and this is the explanation which he gives himself.

The Unity of God and Man in Christ

One of the important features of Karl Barth's theology is its christocentrism. We are able to know God through God's self-revelation in the person of Jesus

Christ. Barth's christological emphasis was so great that some commentators have accused him of going beyond christocentrism to a christomonism, a theology in which the first and third persons of the trinity are collapsed into christology. A careful reading of the *Church Dogmatics*, however, discloses that Barth believed that what is revealed through Jesus Christ is God's triune identity.

In interpreting the incarnation, Barth argues that the unity of God and the human in Jesus Christ does not mean either that the Word ceases to be the Word or that the union of God and the human creates some kind of third creature which is neither God nor human. For Barth, Jesus Christ lives not only through and with God. "He is Himself God."

SOURCE

Barth, *Church Dogmatics*, I/2, 160–62.

FOR FURTHER STUDY

Bruce Marshall, *Christology in Conflict: The Identity of a Saviour in Rahner and Barth* (Oxford: Basil Blackwell, 1987). John Thompson, *Christ in Perspective: Christological Perspectives in the Theology of Karl Barth* (Grand Rapids: Wm. B. Eerdmans, 1978). Charles T. Waldrop, *Karl Barth's Christology: Its Basic Alexandrian Character* (Berlin: Mouton, 1984).

If we paraphrase the statement "the Word became flesh" by "the Word assumed flesh," we guard against the misinterpretation already mentioned, that in the incarnation the Word ceases to be entirely Himself and equal to Himself, i.e., in the full sense of Word of God. God cannot cease to be God. The incarnation is inconceivable, but it is not absurd, and it must not be explained as an absurdity. The inconceivable fact in it is that without ceasing to be God the Word of God is among us in such a way that He takes over human being, which is His creature, into His own being and to that extent makes it His own being. As His own predicate along with His original predicate of divinity, He takes over human being into unity with Himself. And it is by the paraphrase "the Word assumed flesh" that the second misunderstanding is also guarded against, that in the incarnation, by means of a union of divine and human being and nature, a third is supposed to arise. Jesus Christ as the Mediator between God and man is not a third, midway between the two. In that case God has at once ceased to be God and likewise He is not a man like us. But Jesus is the Mediator, the God-Man, in such a way that He is God and Man. This "and" is the inconceivable act of the "becoming" in the incarnation. It is not the act of the human being and nature.

How can it be capable of such an act? Nor is it the act either of the divine being and nature as such. It is not the divine nature that acts where God acts. But it is the triune God in His divine nature, One in the three modes of existence of Father, Son and Holy Spirit. So, too, in this assumption of human being by the eternal Word. He, the eternal Word, in virtue of His own will and power as well as in virtue of the will and power of Father and Holy Spirit, becomes flesh. The unity into which the human nature is assumed is thus unity with the Word, and only to that extent—because this Word is the eternal Word—the union of the human with the divine nature. But the eternal Word is with the Father and the Holy Spirit the unchangeable God Himself and so incapable of any change or admixture. Unity with Him, the "becoming" of the Word, cannot therefore mean the origination of a third between Word and flesh, but only the assumption of the flesh by the Word. . . .

The unity of God and man in Christ is, then, the act of the Logos in assuming human being. His becoming, and therefore the thing that human being encounters in this becoming of the Logos, is an act of God in the person of the Word. Therefore God and man, Creator and creature cannot be related to each other in this unity as in other men or in creation generally. We can and must, indeed, speak of a presence, even of a personal presence of God in all created being, and to that extent of a unity also of God with all created being. But then this created being has an independent existence in relation to God. It is real only in virtue of creation and preservation, through God, and to that extent only in unity with God. But it is real in this unity, not as though it were itself God, but in such a way that, being in God, it is different from God, in such a way that through God it possesses an existence of its own different from the existence of God. It is the same with God's gracious presence in the word preached and in the sacrament (so far as by that is meant the outward creaturely sign of word and elements), and with God's gracious presence in the hearts of those chosen and called by faith. Unity with God in the former case means that man's speech, that water, bread and wine, are real not only through God, but as inseparably bound to God, and similarly in the latter case, that believing man may live not only through God but inseparably bound to God. But unity with God cannot mean in the former case that man's speech, that water, bread and wine, or in the latter case that believing man, is identical with God. What is proclaimed by the unity of God and man in Jesus Christ the God-Man is as follows. This Man Jesus Christ is identical with God because the Word became flesh in the sense just explained. Therefore He does not only live through God and with God. He is Himself God. Nor is He autonomous and self-existent. His reality, existence and being is wholly and absolutely that of God Himself, the God who acts in His Word. His manhood is only the predicate of His Godhead, or better and more concretely, it is only the predicate, assumed in inconceivable condescension, of the Word acting upon us, the Word who is the Lord.

The Paradox of the Incarnation

Donald M. Baillie (1887–1954) taught systematic theology at St. Andrews University in Scotland from 1934 until his death. In *God Was in Christ*, Baillie attempted to interpret the meaning of the incarnation not by means of the classical formula of two natures in one person but by means of the category of paradox.

SOURCE

Donald M. Baillie, *God Was in Christ: An Essay on Incarnation and Atonement* (New York: Charles Scribner's Sons, 1948), 117–18.

This is the deepest paradox of our whole Christian experience, and it runs right through it, woven into its very texture. It is, moreover, virtually peculiar to Christianity. More than all the other paradoxes, it is a distinctive product of the religion of the Incarnation.

What I wish to suggest is that this paradox of grace points the way more clearly and makes a better approach than anything else in our experience to the mystery of the Incarnation itself; that this paradox in its fragmentary form in our own Christian lives is a reflection of that perfect union of God and man in the Incarnation on which our whole Christian life depends, and may therefore be our best clue to the understanding of it. In the New Testament we see the man in whom God was incarnate surpassing all other men in refusing to claim anything for Himself independently and ascribing all the goodness to God. We see Him also desiring to take up other men into His own close union with God, that they might be as He was. And if these men, entering in some small measure through Him into that union, experience the paradox of grace for themselves in fragmentary ways, and are constrained to say, "It was not I but God," may not this be a clue to the understanding of that perfect life in which the paradox is complete and absolute, that life of Jesus which, being the perfection of humanity, is also, and even in a deeper and prior sense, the very life of God Himself? If the paradox is a reality in our poor imperfect lives at all, so far as there is any good in them, does not the same or a similar paradox, taken at the perfect and absolute pitch, appear as the mystery of the Incarnation?

Models of Christology

In *The Shape of Christology*, the Scottish theologian John McIntyre described several models for doing Christology but argued that no particular model is "compulsive" in the sense that it is mandated by the Bible. Rather, models are usually an answer to the situation and the circumstances of the theologian.

SOURCE

John McIntyre, *The Shape of Christology* (Philadelphia: Westminster, 1966), 172–73.

It will be useful perhaps in conclusion to draw together one or two points which seem to be emerging from this examination of models and to make one general reflection upon the character of christological method and study. Concerning the models it must by this time be fairly obvious that it would be wrong to attach a compulsive character to any one of the models (or to try to offer some brand new model to lord it over those we have examined). Models seem to vary according to the circumstance in the christological situation which their exponents wish to emphasize or which they regard as specially important. It would be more difficult now than it was in our first chapter to argue for the specific given-ness of one model over any of the others. Someone might be tempted to call our bluff here and to argue that some pre-eminence should be given to the biblical models—Son of God, Son of Man, Logos or Messiah. But the very interesting fact is that there has not been in the history of christology proper—as distinct from biblical christological word-studies which one cannot regard as serious christology—any sustained attempt to elevate any one of those concepts into a thoroughgoing christological model. The Word of God model which we have not here considered has established itself and would merit detailed consideration on its own but it cannot be regarded as derived from the Logos concept, or yet as an extension of it into systematic christology. These biblical models had they been used in christological systematization might have had some claim to given-ness, some compulsive character. But their non-appearance in christology as models has eliminated even them from consideration. What has to be recognized, however, is that once we do adopt a model, it tends to become compulsive for us. It prescribes the kind of system we construct. It determines the method that we follow in such systematic construction. It sharpens and defines the presentation we give of the person Jesus Christ.

The God Who Is Free to Make Himself Poor

Scottish theologian Thomas F. Torrance (b. 1913) attempts to bring Christian theology into conversation with modern scientific thought. The incarnation, he argues, has implications for our understanding of space and time, which theologians have failed to explore.

SOURCE

Thomas F. Torrance, *Space, Time, and Incarnation* (Oxford: Oxford University Press, 1969), 74–75.

The world, then, is made open to God through its intersection in the axis of Creation-Incarnation. Its space-time structures are so organized in relation to God that we who are set within them may think in and through them to their transcendent ground in God Himself. Jesus Christ constitutes the actual centre in space and time where that may be done. But what of the same relationship the other way round, in the *openness of God* for the world that He has made? Does the intersection of His reality with our this-worldly reality in Jesus Christ mean anything for God? We have noted already that it means that space and time are affirmed as real for God in the actuality of His relations with us, which binds us to space and time, so that neither we nor God can contract out of them. Does this not mean that God has so opened Himself to our world that our this-worldly experiences have import for Him in such a way, for example, that we must think of Him as taking our hurt and pain into Himself? This is what we cannot do from the approach of deistic dualism—why, for example, Schleiermacher could not hold that God is merciful and why Bultmann cannot allow that the love of God is a fact within the cosmos. Thus it would appear that the question as to the impassibility of God is the question as to the actuality of the intersection of God's reality with worldly reality, and as to the depth of its penetration into our creaturely being. If God is merely impassible He has not made room for Himself in our agonied existence, and if He is merely immutable He has neither place nor time for frail evanescent creatures in His unchanging existence. But the God who has revealed Himself in Jesus Christ as sharing our lot is the God who is really free to make Himself poor, that we through His poverty might be made rich, the God invariant in love but not impassible, constant in faithfulness but not immutable.

The Human "I" and the "I" of God

In his systematic theology, Hendrikus Berkhof rejects any interpretation of Jesus as the Christ that suggests that he is "a dual being." He argues that there are not two subjects in the one man Jesus; rather, Jesus' human "I" is completely "permeated by the 'I' of God."

SOURCE

Berkhof, *Christian Faith*, 291.

Is Jesus the Son thus not really a man, but God? If he were not a man, his way within humanity would be an isolated spectacle, of no concern to us. In the New Testament, nothing is proclaimed about him which would be nonhuman or extra-human. But also very little that is simply empirically-human. Everything is related to human existence as it was intended and promised by God in the covenant. Jesus is man, the perfected covenant man, *the* new man, the eschatological man.

The question is now, however, what these far-reaching words imply. Furthermore, how they fit in with the emphasis with which in the New Testament, Jesus, as the Son, is put on the side of God over against men. Are there then two subjects in him? No, he is not a dual being; "For there is . . . one mediator between God and men, the man Christ Jesus" (1 Timothy 2:5). But that he is able to be the mediator in our alienation from God is based thereon that he is a new start from God, "conceived by the Holy Spirit." So through him God's purpose can land in the world. There are thus not two subjects in Jesus, but his human "I" is, out of free will, fully and exhaustively permeated by the "I" of God; and in virtue of this permeation he becomes the perfect instrument of the Father. This completed covenant relationship signifies a new union of God and man, far beyond our experience and imagination.

Reformed Confessions

Contemporary Reformed confessions typically emphasize the ministry of Jesus far more than did the classical confessions. They attempt to do so, however, without compromising the Christian confession that Jesus Christ is truly human and truly God. Furthermore, they acknowledge that Jesus was Jewish and that Jesus' identity cannot be separated from God's promises to Israel.

Jesus' Limited Knowledge

In *A Declaration of Faith* of the Presbyterian Church in the United States, the most controversial line was that which acknowledged that Jesus' humanity meant that his knowledge was limited by his time and place in history.

SOURCE

Declaration of Faith, 6–7.

GOD IN CHRIST

(1) God sent the promised Deliverer to his people.
Jesus, the long expected Savior,
   came into the world as a child,
      descended from David,
      conceived by the Holy Spirit,
      born of Mary, a virgin.
He lived as a Jew among Jews.
He announced to his people
   the coming of God's kingdom of justice and peace on earth.

We affirm that Jesus was born of woman
   as is every child,
   yet born of God's power
   as was no other child.
In the person and work of Jesus,
   God himself and a human life
   are united but not confused,
   distinguished but not separated.
The coming of Jesus was itself
   the coming of God's promised rule.
Through his birth, life, death, and resurrection,
   he brings about the relationship between God and humanity
   that God always intended.

(2) Jesus lived a truly human life.
Jesus was what we are.
He grew up in a family and a society
   troubled by the common problems of the world.

His knowledge was limited
  by his time and place in history.
He felt deeply the joy of friendship
  and the hurt of being rejected.
Jesus prayed,
    struggled with temptation,
    knew anger,
    and was subject to suffering and death.
He was like us in every way except sin.

Jesus was what we should be.
He served his Father with complete trust
  and unwavering obedience.
He loved all kinds of people
  and accepted their love.
In constant dependence upon the Holy Spirit,
    Jesus allowed no temptation or threat to keep him
    from loving God with his whole being
    and his neighbor as himself.
We recognize in Jesus what God created us to be.
He exposes our failure to live as he lived.
He demonstrates the new humanity
  God promises to give us through him.

(3) Jesus was God in the flesh.

Jesus Christ overthrew evil powers
    that enslaved and degraded people,
    yet he made no use of power to protect himself.
He healed those who were sick in body and mind,
    yet he did not avoid pain and suffering for himself.
He commanded his followers to place loyalty to him
    above loyalty to family and country,
    yet he lived among them as a servant.
Jesus taught with authority,
    challenging many time-honored customs and ideas,
    yet he submitted to humiliation and death
    without a word on his own behalf.
He forgave sinners,
    yet he was counted among sinners.

We recognize the work of God in Jesus' power and authority.
He did what only God can do.
We also recognize the work of God in Jesus' lowliness.
When he lived as a servant
    and went humbly to his death
    the greatness that belongs only to God was manifest.
In both his majesty and lowliness
    Jesus is the eternal Son of God,
    God himself with us.

Jesus, a Palestinian Jew

"The Confession of 1967" of the Presbyterian Church (U.S.A.) based its Christology on 2 Corinthians 5:18-19, and made reconciliation its central theme. This document is important because it is one of the first confessions to refer explicitly to the fact that Jesus was Jewish and to emphasize his humanity and his ministry to all kinds of sinful people.

SOURCE

"The Confession of 1967," in *Book of Confessions*, 9.07–8.

THE CONFESSION

In Jesus Christ God was reconciling the world to himself. Jesus Christ is God with man. He is the eternal Son of the Father, who became man and lived among us to fulfill the work of reconciliation. He is present in the church by the power of the Holy Spirit to continue and complete his mission. This work of God, the Father, Son, and Holy Spirit, is the foundation of all confessional statements about God, man, and the world. Therefore the church calls men to be reconciled to God and to one another.

PART I
GOD'S WORK OF RECONCILIATION

Section A. The Grace of Our Lord Jesus Christ

1. Jesus Christ

In Jesus of Nazareth true humanity was realized once for all. Jesus, a Palestinian Jew, lived among his own people and shared their needs, temptations, joys, and sorrows. He expressed the love of God in word and deed and became a brother to all kinds of sinful men. But his complete obedience led him into conflict with his people. His life and teaching judged their goodness, religious aspirations, and national hopes. Many rejected him and demanded his death. In giving himself freely for them he took upon himself the judgment under which all men stand convicted. God raised him from the dead, vindicating him as Messiah and Lord. The victim of sin became victor, and won the victory over sin and death for all men.

THE WORK OF CHRIST

Contemporary theologians recognize that the distinction between the person and the work of Jesus Christ is artificial. That is, the identity of any person cannot be understood apart from what that person says and does. And the same is true of Jesus of Nazareth. Who Jesus is cannot be understood apart from what Jesus says and does, and what Jesus says and does is a manifestation of his identity as the Christ.

In their depiction of the "work" of Christ, theologians in the nineteenth and twentieth centuries have given much greater emphasis to the description of Jesus in the Synoptic Gospels than did their classical predecessors. Instead of following the classical pattern of incarnation, crucifixion, and resurrection, some contemporary theologians have argued that apart from Jesus' ministry his death and resurrection will be misunderstood.

In the last half of the twentieth century, Reformed theologians also have been influenced by the emphasis of liberation theology on the significance of Jesus' ministry for understanding both the identity of Jesus and the mission to which Jesus calls his disciples.

FOR FURTHER STUDY

G. C. Berkouwer, *The Work of Christ*, trans. Cornelius Lambregtse (Grand Rapids: Wm. B. Eerdmans, 1965). P. T. Forsyth, *The Work of Christ* (London: Independent Press, 1938). R. S. Franks, *The Work of Christ* (London: Thomas Nelson & Sons, 1962).

The Threefold Office

In classical Reformed theology, Jesus Christ is described as "mediator," which is, in turn, explicated by means of the *munus triplex*, the threefold office of prophet, priest, and king. Although not all Reformed theologians continue to use the *munus triplex*, those who do have significantly reinterpreted it in light of new discoveries in biblical scholarship. What contemporary theologians mean by Christ's prophetic office, for example, is quite different from the way

John Calvin understood it. The abiding strength of the *munus triplex*, however, is what theologians have seen from their first use of it—its identification of Jesus in light of the faith, history, and scriptures of Israel.

FOR FURTHER STUDY

John Frederick Jansen, *Calvin's Doctrine of the Work of Christ* (London: James Clarke & Co., 1956).

The Unity of the Threefold Office

Emil Brunner argues that as a description of Jesus Christ the *munus triplex* is both similar to and different from the Old Testament understanding of prophet, priest, and king. In Jesus Christ the three offices refer to the work of one person, not three different individuals.

SOURCE

Brunner, *Dogmatics*, 2: 273–74.

It is no accident that it was Reformed theology which, in its doctrine of the "offices" of Christ, re-emphasized this original Biblical stress on *saving history*, which, in the period of medieval scholasticism, had been lost. The work of Jesus is the fulfillment of the Old Covenant. In the doctrine of the Three "Offices" of Christ we are again reminded of the truth that we know Jesus through God's action in Him; this had already been suggested in the various titles given to Jesus in the Primitive Church, all of which have a "functional" character and suggest His Work rather than His Person.

The fact that the Reformed theologians speak of the threefold "office" or "work" of Christ, is due to the fact that under the Old Covenant there were three theocratic figures: the Prophet, the Priest, and the King; in Jesus all that these three represented was fulfilled since they all merged into a complete unity in His Person. Whereas in the Old Testament these three functions were divided among three different persons, which accounts both for their limitations, and for their provisional character—in Jesus Christ they are blended into a unity; only then is their full and real significance perceived. In the Old Testament indeed, there is an evident tension, if not an absolute contrast, between these three. The Prophet, at least in the days of the great Prophets, is deliberately and consciously on the defensive against the priesthood and the Temple; more than once this attitude developed into fierce hostility. The Priestly element, from the Prophetic point of view, is something which, at its best, can barely be tolerated, and often seems an utter impossibility. It is indeed that element in which the religion of the Old Testament is least differentiated from the pagan religion of the surrounding nations; therefore it is also the point from which paganism continually penetrated into the life of Israel or Judah.

But from the point of view of the theocratic idea, the King is also a very ambiguous phenomenon. On the one hand, from the time of David the Monarchy was always closely connected with the Messianic Hope of the future, so that the Messiah is expected to issue from the House of David, and to be a powerful and righteous King. On the other hand, from the time of Moses and the Judges, from the classical period of Yahwist religion, there was a very critical attitude towards the Monarchy, because it seemed to interfere with the direct divine guidance of the nation. Israel, in contrast to the surrounding Eastern nations, was not originally a monarchy nor a hierocracy, but a *pneumatocracy.*" The ruler of Israel is to be a leader called and empowered by God, not an hereditary sovereign. Saul, as the first King, as an elected King and as a "Nabi," is evidently a transitional phenomenon. Thus the monarchy exists in a kind of twilight between God's highest will for His people, and that which is in direct opposition to His Will, owing to the blurring of the distinction between Israel and the surrounding nations, reducing it to the merely human level.

Both tensions: that between Prophet and Priest, and that between Prophet and King, could not be overcome under the old dispensation. It is only Jesus the Messiah, whose Kingship is totally different in kind from that of the Davidic dynasty, and whose Priesthood is so entirely different from that of the Jerusalem priesthood, and, still more, who was not a Prophet of the Old Testament kind at all, who can eliminate these tensions and contradictions because He gathers up these three "offices" in His own Person. In His Word He is both Reconciler and King; in His sovereignty, He is both Revealer and the Sacrificial Lamb; in His Priesthood, He is both the One who proclaims the Name of God, and asserts God's glory and God's Sovereignty.

The Danger of One-Sided Approaches

Otto Weber argues that one reason for interpreting the work of Christ by means of the *munus triplex* is that its diversity means that Christ's work cannot be easily reduced to a single dimension. The three aspects of the one office complement and enhance each other.

SOURCE

Weber, *Foundations*, 2:174–76.

The doctrine of the "threefold office" of Christ is a dogmatic conception. At the same time, and in this we go beyond Calvin, it is an ethical conception. For this "for us" always means that the Community itself participates in what Christ has done for it and is for it. It cannot be a speechless Community when the One on whom it is dependent is and was the Proclaimer. It cannot pass man's misery by when it knows the One who as a priest took upon himself all the perversion and distress of man. It cannot be complacent about the arbitrary rule of the mighty when it knows the One who is the King. It does not prolong his work. But it follows him. Because he has done everything, it does its part.

At the same time, the Community is protected by the doctrine of the "threefold office" from seeing Jesus Christ's activity for us in too one-sided a way.

1) This activity could be seen one-sidedly as declarative (the "prophetic office"). Jesus would then be the last and perhaps most sublime herald of the mysteries of God. This could even be understood Gnostically. It could also mean that we are supposed to uphold the "teaching of Christ" in the Enlightenment sense. It could mean as well that he had disclosed to us a new self-understanding. However it were done, we would have to be the ones who appropriated what he brought to us. We ourselves would be dependent on our applying what he declared. Perhaps his declaration would confirm us, perhaps it would demolish us. But we would have the word! The "prophetic office" would make us dependent on ourselves as such.

2) The work of Jesus Christ could be seen one-sidedly in terms of the priestly office, as the work of forgiveness granted to us, redemption provided to us, the work Jesus completed in his death and resurrection. Obviously this is a correct and necessary statement. But when it stands alone, it is very easy for a passive inwardness to develop. The individual is then satisfied that "he is blessed." The Community becomes the institution which offers the means for us to reach our "blessedness." But it really has no task at all in the world. Eschatology then becomes one-sidedly the realm of "eternal blessedness," and there is then scarcely any mention of a renewed world.

3) The work of Jesus Christ could also be understood one-sidedly as lordship. This is especially suggested by the Christ-title. Jesus' activity

would then consist solely of his becoming the Ruler of man who is ultimately without a lord, the Governor of disoriented man, the Shepherd who restores the wandering sheep to the right path ("shepherd" is a kingly title). The task then given to us would be one of subordination, obedience, following. The Community then would be supposed to announce or spread the Kingdom in the world. We scarcely need to say that here, as well as in regard to the work of Jesus as declaration, necessary and correct things are being said, things which have often and wrongly been forgotten, particularly in Germany. The Dutch "Theology of the Kingdom," the idea of the Kingdom of Christ in John Frederick Denison Maurice (1805–72) and, not unconnected to him, in English Socialism and in the American Social Gospel, the strong emphasis on the Kingdom in both the older and younger Blumhardt (1805–80, 1842–1919) and in the Swiss Religious-Social movement—none of these is a misunderstanding by any means. But we must remember what Calvin emphasized so strongly, that the "reign of Christ" is an enduring Kingdom because it is "not earthly or carnal." We dare not forget that Christ's kingship consists in the fact that he "governs us by his Word and Spirit, and defends and preserves us in the redemption obtained for us." Wherever this is not acknowledged, talk about the kingship of Christ rapidly is transformed into the lordly claims of "Christianity" to which Christians are supposed to commit themselves, and it is not very far from there to the view that we are the ones who must establish the lordship of "Christianity." What results would be an autonomous secular Messianism, which must necessarily fail just as the worldly Messianism of late Jewish groupings failed.

There have always been one-sided approaches like these. The first one leads quite logically to the idea of Jesus as the "divine teacher," which was so influential during the Enlightenment. The second one, influential in Lutheran Orthodoxy, easily leads to a special form of religious egoism. The third, which emerged primarily in the sphere of Reformed theology and was already anticipated in Bucer, leads logically to a new legalism.

In contrast, the doctrine of the "threefold office" is an appropriate tool for the prevention of every one-sidedness and for the full interpretation of the oneness and totality of the work of this one person in all its fullness. God's activity in Jesus Christ sets an end to our lie and our confusion, to our complacency and our autonomous busyness, to our perversion and our lostness. It makes men witnesses of the One who testifies of himself to man, obedient disciples of the One who confronts us as the rightful ruler and, in all of that, liberated creatures who belong confidently and gratefully to their Creator. No single element can be wrenched out of this unity. And in that fashion, this "dogmatic" view, which it certainly is, shows itself to be correct.

The Munus Triplex and Christian Ethics

Paul Lehmann (b. 1906) argued that the recovery of the *munus triplex* was important for Christian ethics because (1) it gives the Christian a clear sense of what he or she is called to do in the world; (2) it unites the church and the world in one story of salvation; and (3) it unites believer and unbeliever in Christ.

SOURCE

Lehmann, *Ethics*, 115–17.

It has been pointed out that the Reformers were more reserved in their teaching concerning the kingship of Christ than they were about his other offices. This hesitation was due partly to their struggle against the anarchistic political implications of sectarian teaching and influence and partly to the fact that the Reformers were especially concerned with the basis and origin of salvation rather than with its fruit and goal. Consequently, Protestant theology has never sufficiently regarded the world in the light of the victory of Christ. A theological analysis of ethics in the tradition of the Reformation would, therefore, seek not only to correct the Reformers at this point but to make the fullest possible use of the resources which they have placed at the disposal of a theological ethic. "This does not mean that we can afford to forget the prophetic and priestly Christ, but it does mean that we seek to rediscover the royal nature of our prophetic and priestly Lord."

The bearing of such a recovery of the doctrine of the threefold office of Christ upon Christian thinking about ethics is at least threefold. In the first place, the political character of what God is doing in the world expressed in the trinitarian statement of the divine economy is brought directly to bear upon the life of the believer by means of a functional, christological context and connection. This is not only a reversal of the general tendency of Protestantism, according to which "Christianity becomes more and more introspective and the Church knows less and less what to do with the world-embracing and world-shaking affirmations of the Bible." It is also a way of giving to the believer a clear understanding of the environment and direction of what he is to do and thus a firm ethical foundation for behavior. In the second place, the recovery of the doctrine of the threefold office of Christ creatively unites the church and the world in the ongoing story of salvation. This does not mean that the church and the world are identical. But also and no less importantly, it does not mean that the church manifests itself chiefly as church by speaking against the world. The kingship of Christ means that Christ is important not only for those who recognize him but for the whole world. As Dr. Visser 't Hooft has put it, "history deals not only with the fate of individual souls and the destiny of the people of God. God thinks and plans in terms of humanity and of the universe . . . church and world have, therefore, a great deal in common. Both have the same Lord. Both live in the light of the same victory of Christ over the powers of sin and death. . . . The church is the inner circle, the world the outer circle, but both together are the realm over which Christ is king." In the third place and as a corollary of the point just made, the recovery of the doctrine of the threefold office of Christ safeguards a *koinonia* ethic against the peril of a double standard. The christological focus and foundation of behavior mean that believer and unbeliever are both alike in the same ethical situation. Both believer and unbeliever belong to Christ. Both believer and unbeliever are promised in him the secret and the power of maturity. Both believer and unbeliever are being confronted, in the environment being shaped by Christ's royal and redemptive activity, by the decision to accept or to reject the conditions of a new humanity on Christ's terms, not their own. The difference is that for believers, as members of the *koinonia*, the kingship of Christ "is revealed; in the world (that is, among unbelievers) it is hidden. The church lives as the people who know that the victory has been won. The world lives on as if nothing had happened. The church realizes that the powers which militate against God's plan are under control. The world lives on as if these powers were still able to shape the ultimate destiny of men." The difference between believers and unbelievers is not defined by church membership, or even, in the last analysis, by baptism. The difference is defined by imaginative and behavioral sensitivity to what God is doing in the world to make and to keep human life human, to achieve the maturity of men, that is, the new humanity.

The Prophetic Office

Contemporary theologians have reinterpreted the prophetic office of Christ in two ways that differ significantly from that of earlier theologians. First, while Calvin and the classical tradition understood Christ's prophetic work to be his teaching of pure doctrine, contemporary theologians, instructed by what modern biblical scholarship has demonstrated concerning the centrality of the kingdom of God to what Jesus says and does, have emphasized Jesus' embodiment of God's Word. Jesus not only teaches the truth; he is the truth in both what he says and what he does. Second, liberation theology has demonstrated that the prophetic ministry of Jesus has unavoidable political consequences for all those who call him Lord.

Teaching, Prophesying, and Working Miracles

For Friedrich Schleiermacher, Christ's prophetic office could not be reduced simply to the teaching of true doctrine but also referred to Christ's prophesying and miracles.

SOURCE
Schleiermacher, *Christian Faith*, 441–42.

§ 103. *First Theorem.—The prophetic office of Christ consists in teaching, prophesying, and working miracles.*

1. These three activities also constituted the dignity of the Old Testament prophets. Certainly the essential thing was always stimulus by means of teaching and admonition; but in all important instances, where the teaching had some definite occasion, it at once became prophecy (since the idea of the divine retribution was dominant), now threatening, now promising, in agreement with the original type created when the law was given. But since the prophets never appeared except in connexion with crimes or public misfortunes, which might be supposed always to involve the guilt of those to whom they had to speak, they required, in default of an outward vocation to which they might have appealed, some special proof of their authority. Hence miracles were expected or assumed as a token of their divine mission. It was only the absence of this third mark of a prophet that made it possible for the Baptist to say that he was no prophet, in spite of his very definite divine vocation. For he certainly had taught and prophesied but the gift of miracles had not been granted him, and hence he would not be troubled with a useless question about it.

In Christ these three signs of a prophet did not follow one from the other; all three were one from the very outset. For the preaching of the Kingdom of God was both teaching and prophecy, and the Kingdom of God itself is properly the miracle accomplished by Christ; but since its fulfillment began simultaneously with the preaching, all three elements were present in one and the same germ, and we can differentiate them only as this germ develops further.

Jesus—The Incomparable Revolutionary

Long before liberation theology, Karl Barth recognized that Jesus Christ and his kingdom cannot be identified with any political or social program. Hence, Jesus is free of every human ideology. But in his freedom from every human program and agenda, Jesus remains the partisan of the poor.

SOURCE

Barth, *Church Dogmatics*, IV/2:179–80.

But we have not yet mentioned the decisive point at which the man Jesus is the image and reflection of God Himself. In all the matters that we have emphasised so far we have been protecting this point against any attempt to render it innocuous or trivial. We have been forestalling the opinion that what we have to call the decisive point is something that can be attained and conceived and controlled by men, and incorporated into the scale of known relationships of magnitude and value. That is why we have first had to set Jesus against man and his cosmos as the poor man who if He blessed and befriended any blessed and befriended the poor and not the rich, the incomparable revolutionary who laid the axe at the root of the trees, who pitilessly exposed the darkness of human order in the cosmos, questioning it in a way which is quite beyond our capacity to answer. We do not know God at all if we do not know Him as the One who is absolutely opposed to our whole world which has fallen away from Him and is therefore self-estranged; as the Judge of our world; as the One whose will is that it should be totally changed and renewed. If we think we know Him in any other way, what we really know (in a mild or wild transcendence) is only the world itself, ourselves, the old Adam. In the man Jesus, God has separated Himself from this misinterpretation. And we have had to copy this divine separation in all that we have said so far. But again, we do not really know Jesus (the Jesus of the New Testament) if we do not know Him as this poor man, as this (if we may risk the dangerous word) partisan of the poor, and finally as this revolutionary. We have to be warned, therefore, against every attempt to interpret and use Him as a further and perhaps supreme self-manifestation and self-actualisation of the old Adam. But this certainly cannot be our last word. Indeed, it cannot really be our first word except didactically—a truth which is often overlooked in the justifiable reaction against every attempted softening and trivialisation of the Gospel.

The Priestly Office

A major challenge for contemporary theology has been interpreting the meaning of salvation in general and the significance of Jesus Christ's cross in particular for Christians living in the modern world. In the history of Christian thought, Jesus' cross has been interpreted in ways that were both meaningful to the church and that reflected the particular historical context in which the church found itself. For example, Christ's cross represented the defeat of evil, those principalities and powers that were locked in a cosmic conflict with the almighty God. Or it represented the overcoming of the problem created by human sin, the satisfaction of a righteous, feudal Lord whose honor was offended by subjects so sinful they could not make things right between themselves and their master. Both these models reflect a cosmology and a worldview difficult for modern people to understand. If that is the case, however, how should salvation and Christ's cross be understood? Contemporary Reformed theologians have sought to interpret the cross and Jesus' death in ways which are faithful to what the gospel says about salvation and also speak to the experience of modern people.

FOR FURTHER STUDY

Horace Bushnell, *The Vicarious Sacrifice* (London: Richard D. Dickinson, 1880). Paul S. Fiddes, *Past Event and Present Salvation: The Christian Idea of Atonement* (Louisville: Westminster/John Knox, 1989). P. T. Forsyth, *The Cruciality of the Cross* (London: Independent Press, 1955). Colin E. Gunton, *The Actuality of the Atonement: A Study of Metaphor, Rationality and the Christian Tradition* (Grand Rapids: Wm. B. Eerdmans, 1989). H. D. McDonald, *Forgiveness and Atonement* (Grand Rapids: Baker Book House, 1984).

Christ's Atonement for All People

In the middle of the nineteenth century, an important debate about the nature of Christ's atonement took place in the Church of Scotland. John McLeod Campbell (1800–1872) argued against the classical Reformed concept of a limited atonement and instead advocated a universal atonement. Because of his position on the atonement, Campbell was deposed from the established church. Campbell's reference to "President Edwards" is to Jonathan Edwards, the eighteenth-century New England minister and theologian.

SOURCE

John McLeod Campbell, *The Nature of the Atonement and Its Relation to Remission of Sins and Eternal Life* (London: Macmillan, 1915), 108–9.

FOR FURTHER STUDY

Eugene Garrett Bewkes, *Legacy of a Christian Mind* (Philadelphia: Judson, 1937). B. A. Gerrish, *Tradition and the Modern World: Reformed Theology in the Nineteenth Century* (Chicago and London: University of Chicago Press, 1978), 71–98.

It will simplify our task in considering Christ's doing of the will of God, if we remember the relation of the second commandment to the first, as being "like it"; that is to say, that the spirit of sonship in which consists the perfect fulfilment of the first commandment, is one with the spirit of brotherhood which is the fulfilment of the second. Loving the Father with all His heart and mind and soul and strength, the Saviour loved His brethren as Himself. He, the perfect elder brother, unlike the elder brother in the parable, sympathized in all the yearnings of the Father's heart over His prodigal brethren; and the love which in the Father desired to be able to say of each of them, My son was dead, and is alive again; he was lost, and is found; in Him equally desired to be able to say, My brother was dead, and is alive again; he was lost, and is found. Present Edwards, in tracing out the fitness and suitableness of the mediation of our Lord, dwells upon His interest in the glory of God with whom He was to intercede, and because of which He could propose nothing derogatory to it; and His love to those for whom He was to intercede, because of which He felt so identified with them that what touched them touched Him. There is something which surely commends itself to us in this recognition of love as that which identifies the Saviour with those to whom He is a Saviour, and this, as Edwards traces it out, both in His own consciousness and in the Father's thoughts of Him as the Mediator. May we not go further and say, that as love was thus a fitness for the office, so it necessitated the undertaking of the office, moving to the exercise of this high function, as well as qualifying for it? And seeing love *to all men* as that law of love under which Christ was, must we not both wonder and regret, that his deeply interesting thoughts in this region did not lead Edwards to see, that by the very law of the spirit of the life that was in Christ Jesus He must needs come under the burden of the sins of all men—become the Saviour of all men, and, loving them as He loved Himself, seek for them that they should partake in His own life in the Father's favour,—that eternal life which He had with the Father before the world was?

When God sent His own Son in the likeness of sinful flesh to accomplish our redemption, the Apostle says He sent Him as "a sacrifice for sin." (Romans viii. 3, margin.) To send Him in the likeness of sinful flesh was to make Him a sacrifice for sin, for it was to lay the burden of our sins upon Him. Thus related to us, while by love identified with us, the Son of God necessarily came under all our burdens, and especially our great burden—sin. And this not merely as President Edwards represents our sins as being laid upon Christ, in that a vivid sense of their evil oppressed His Holy Spirit, nor even in that through love to us (as he speaks with reference to the elect) the realisation of the misery to which we were exposed would give Him pain; but that living the life of love in humanity He must needs care for all humanity, for all partaking in humanity even as for Himself: so being affected by the evil of the life of self, and enmity in humanity according to His own consciousness of the life of love,—and at once condemning that life of self, desiring its destruction, and feeling Himself by love devoted to the work of delivering man from it, at whatever cost to Himself. Thus moved by love, and in the strength of love, must we conceive of the Saviour as taking upon Him all our burden, undertaking our cause to do and suffer all that was implied in obtaining for us redemption. The love that came into humanity had manifested its own nature even in coming into humanity—its self-sacrificing nature; though this we can less understand or measure.

The Cross as the Center of Gravity in the Gospel

Typical of many twentieth-century theologians, P. T. Forsyth interprets Jesus' cross by means of the Pauline category of reconciliation. Forsyth argues eloquently that the cross and reconciliation are the basis of Christian faith.

SOURCE

P. T. Forsyth, *The Work of Christ* (London: Independent Press, 1910), 51–53.

The doctrine of Christ's reconciliation, or His Atonement, is not a piece of medieval dogma like transubstantiation, not a piece of ecclesiastical dogma or Aristotelian subtlety which it might be the Bible's business to destroy. If you look at the Gospels you will see that from the Transfiguration onward this matter of the Cross is the great centre of concern; it is where the centre of gravity lies. I met a man the other day who had come under some poor and mischievous pulpit influence, and he said, "It is time we got rid of hearing so much about the Cross of

Christ; there should be preached to the world a humanitarian Christ, the kind of Christ that occupies the Gospels." There was nothing for it but to tell that man he was the victim of smatterers, and that he must go back to his Gospels and read and study for a year or two. It is the flimsiest religiosity, and the most superficial reading of the Gospel, that could talk like that. What does it mean that an enormous proportion of the Gospel story is occupied with the passion of Christ? The centre of gravity, even in the Gospels, falls upon the Cross of Christ and what was done there, and not simply upon a humanitarian Christ. You cannot set the Gospels against Paul. Why, the first three Gospels were much later than Paul's Epistles. They were written for Churches that were made by the apostolic preaching. But how, then, do the first three Gospels *seem* so different from the Epistles? Of course, there is a superficial difference. Christ was a very living and real character for the people of His own time, and His grand business was to rouse his audiences' faith in His Person and in His mission. But in His Person and in His mission the Cross lay latent all the time. It emerged only in the fullness of time—that valuable phrase— just when the historic crisis, the organic situation, produced it. Jesus was not a professor theology. He did not lecture the people. He did not come with a theology of the Cross. He did not come to force events to comply with that theology. He did not force His own people to work out a theological scheme. He did force an issue, but it was not to illustrate a theology. It was to establish the Kingdom of God, which could be established in no other wise than as He established it—upon the Cross. And He could only teach the Cross when it had happened—which He did through the Evangelists with the space they gave it, and through the Apostles and the exposition they gave it.

To come back to this work of Christ described by Paul as reconciliation. On this interpretation of the work of Christ the whole Church rests. If you move faith from that centre you have driven *the* nail into the Church's coffin. The Church is then doomed to death, and it is only a matter of time when she shall expire. The Apostle, I say, described the work of Christ as above all things reconciliation.

The Cross as the Suffering of God

Jürgen Moltmann interprets Jesus' cross as an event within the life of the triune God. The cross represents the Father's loss of the Son. Hence God cannot be said to be immutable, because the God of the cross is a God of suffering love.

SOURCE

Moltmann, *Crucified God*, 242–43.

Paul introduces a radical change in the sense of "deliver up" when he recognizes and proclaims the godforsakenness of Jesus in the eschatological context of his resurrection rather than in the historical context of his life. In Rom. 8.31f., we read: "If God is for us, who is against us? He who did not spare his own Son but gave him up for us all, will he not also give us all things with him?" According to this God gave up his own Son, abandoned him, cast him out and delivered him up to an accursed death. Paul says in even stronger terms: "He made him sin for us" (2 Cor. 5:21) and "He became a curse for us" (Gal. 3:13). Thus in the total, inextricable abandonment of Jesus by his God and Father, Paul sees the delivering up of the Son by the Father for godless and godforsaken man. Because God "does not spare" his Son, all the godless are spared. Though they are godless, they are not godforsaken, precisely because God has abandoned his own Son and has delivered him up for them. Thus the delivering up of the Son to godforsakenness is the ground for the justification of the godless and the acceptance of enemity by God. It may therefore be said that the Father delivers up his Son on the cross in order to be the Father of those who are delivered up. The Son is delivered up to this death in order to become the Lord of both dead and living. And if Paul speaks emphatically of God's "own Son," the not-sparing and abandoning also involves the Father himself. In the forsakenness of the Son the Father also forsakes himself. In the surrender of the Son the Father also surrenders himself, though not in the same way. For Jesus suffers dying in forsakenness, but not death itself; for men can no longer "suffer" death, because suffering presupposes life. But the Father who abandons him and delivers him up suffers the death of the Son in the infinite grief of love. We cannot therefore say here in patri-passian terms that the Father also suffered and died. The suffering and dying of the Son, forsaken by the Father, is a different kind of suffering from the suffering of the Father in the death of the Son. Nor can the death of Jesus be understood in theopaschite terms as the "death of God." To understand what happened between Jesus and his God and Father on the cross, it is necessary to talk in trinitarian terms. The Son suffers dying, the Father suffers the death of the Son. The grief of the Father here is just as important as the death of the Son. The Fatherlessness of the Son is matched by the Sonlessness of the Father, and if God has constituted himself as the Father of Jesus Christ, then he also suffers the death of his Fatherhood in the death of the Son. Unless this were so, the doctrine of the Trinity would still have a monotheistic background.

Reformed Confessions

Contemporary Reformed confessions differ from their classical predecessors in that they do not usually attempt to explain in what sense the cross is salvific for humanity. At the same time, they insist on the confession that Jesus' cross is the reconciliation of God and the world.

Hatred Absorbed in Suffering

In "A Declaration of Faith" (1967) of the Congregational Church in England and Wales, the cross is described as "a mystery of holy love" in which hatred was absorbed in suffering and humanity was given new birth.

SOURCE

"A Declaration of Faith" (1967) of the Congregational Church in England and Wales in *Reformed Witness Today*, 123–24.

8. . . . and in the death of Jesus . . .

Jesus died on the cross. He accepted this death, and the path which inexorably led towards it, with perfect grace. At that moment of history three things met in decisive encounter: the love of God, focused for the work of redeeming mankind; the true love and obedience of man towards God; sinfulness among men, taken to the point of hardened and active hatred. Here, in a mystery of holy love and anguish which men do not and cannot fathom, this third element failed, and failed decisively, to divide the acts of man from the life of God. On the cross hatred was absorbed in suffering endured to the depths of spiritual dereliction and the giving up of life itself, but the love at work at this meeting point of God's life and man's was not deflected and not frustrated. Sin and all creatures corrupted by sin were fully exposed for judgement by God; but the judgement he carried out was grounded in the love which prevailed at the cross and it secured to his creatures a future in which they are to declare the love and judgement of God. Under these conditions we can take up life for the future as from a new birth. We can live as new creatures whose sole and sufficient security comes, in forgiveness, from the grace accomplished in the death of Jesus.

A Diversity of Images

The Confession of 1967 of the United Presbyterian Church in the United States of America acknowledges the importance of the many different images used in the New Testament to interpret the meaning of Christ's death.

SOURCE

"The Confession of 1967" in *Book of Confessions*, 9.09–11.

God's reconciling act in Jesus Christ is a mystery which the Scriptures describe in various ways. It is called the sacrifice of a lamb, a shepherd's life given for his sheep, atonement by a priest; again it is ransom of a slave, payment of debt, vicarious satisfaction of a legal penalty, and victory over the powers of evil. These are expressions of a truth which remains beyond the reach of all theory in the depths of God's love for man. They reveal the gravity, cost, and sure achievement of God's reconciling work.

The risen Christ is the savior for all men. Those joined to him by faith are set right with God and commissioned to serve as his reconciling community. Christ is head of this community, the church, which began with the apostles and continues through all generations.

The same Jesus Christ is the judge of all men. His judgment discloses the ultimate seriousness of life and gives promise of God's final victory over the power of sin and death. To receive life from the risen Lord is to have life eternal; to refuse life from him is to choose the death which is separation from God. All who put their trust in Christ face divine judgment without fear, for the judge is their redeemer.

The Reconciler Between God and the World

A Declaration of Faith of the Presbyterian Church in the United States, like many other contemporary Reformed confessions, uses the category of reconciliation to describe the meaning of Christ's cross. It does not attempt to explain how Christ's cross is salvific but modestly confesses that Jesus was "the Savior who died in our place."

SOURCE

Declaration of Faith, 8.

(4) Jesus died for sinners.

Religious leaders hated Jesus
    because he criticized their hypocrisy
    and reproved their neglect of justice and mercy.
They charged him with blasphemy and sedition
    when he claimed to speak and act with God's authority.
One of Jesus' followers betrayed him.
Others abandoned and denied him
    because they were afraid to stand with him.
Civil authorities condemned him
    because he provoked unrest among the people.
He was sentenced, mocked, beaten,
    and crucified as a common criminal.

We confess that in the execution of Jesus
    the sin of the human race reached its depths.
The only innocent One was condemned and put to death,
    not by the sinfulness of one nation,
    but by the sinfulness of us all.
In the presence of Jesus,
    who lived out what God wants us all to be,
    we were threatened beyond endurance.
Blinded by our rebellion against our Creator,
    we killed his Son when we met him face to face.

We believe that in the death of Jesus on the cross
    God achieved and demonstrated once for all
    the costly forgiveness of our sins.
Jesus Christ is the Reconciler between God and the world.
He acted on behalf of sinners as one of us,
    fulfilling the obedience God demands of us,
    accepting God's condemnation of our sinfulness.
In his lonely agony on the cross
    Jesus felt forsaken by God
    and thus experienced hell itself for us.
Yet the Son was never more in accord with the Father's will.
He was acting on behalf of God,
    manifesting the Father's love that takes on itself
    the loneliness, pain, and death
    that result from our waywardness.

In Christ, God was reconciling the world to himself,
   not holding our sins against us.
Each of us beholds on the cross
   the Savior who died in our place,
     so that we may no longer live for ourselves,
     but for him.
In him is our only hope of salvation

The Royal Office

Twentieth-century theology has discussed the resurrection of Jesus Christ in terms of two major issues—historicity and eschatology. In regard to the first, contemporary theologians have debated the extent to which New Testament claims about Jesus' resurrection can be said to refer to an event in history. Some of the issues debated here have to do with whether there can be a unique or anomalous event in history and whether an "event" such as the resurrection is in principle open to verification and/or falsification.

The second issue is the result of recent work by contemporary biblical scholars who have pointed out that, for at least the apostle Paul, Jesus' resurrection cannot be separated from the eschatological horizon in which Paul interprets it in texts such as 1 Corinthians 15. If the resurrection is necessarily an eschatological event, then how should contemporary theologians interpret eschatology in order to be faithful both to the biblical text (and the claims of Christian faith) and to the human experience of the modern world?

FOR FURTHER STUDY

Karl Barth, *The Epistle to the Romans*, 6th ed., trans. Edwyn C. Hoskyns (London: Oxford University Press, 1933), 188–207. Moltmann, *Theology of Hope*, 139–229. Richard R. Niebuhr, *Resurrection and Historical Reason: A Study of Theological Method* (New York: Charles Scribner's Sons, 1957).

Resurrection without an Empty Tomb

Emil Brunner insisted that faith in Jesus Christ is not based primarily on apostolic testimony and does not entail faith in a "physical resurrection." Rather, because Christians know Jesus to be a living, present Lord, they believe him to be the risen Lord.

SOURCE

Brunner, *Dogmatics*, 2: 370–72.

We believe in the Resurrection of Jesus because through the whole witness of the Scriptures He attests Himself to us as the Christ and as the Living Lord. The Apostles' account of their meetings with the Risen Lord are not the basis of, but an element in, the testimony of revelation, which is the basis of our faith in Christ, and therefore of our faith in His Resurrection. He who manifests Himself to us as the Christ through the testimony of the Scriptures as the Son of the Living God, as the God-Man, is no other than the Risen Lord. The question whether we could believe in Him as the Risen Lord if there were no special testimonies to His resurrection is an idle one, since these testimonies do, in fact, exist. It has at least this justification, however, that it draws our attention to the fact that our belief in the Resurrection of Jesus is not only, and not primarily, based upon the Apostles' testimony to the Resurrection. The Christ, whom we know through their witness; cannot be other than the Risen Lord Himself.

The significance of the Apostles' experiences of the Resurrection is not the same for the Apostles, and for ourselves. The Apostles needed these appearances in order to restore their faith in Him, the Christ, which had been shattered by the catastrophe of Good Friday, and to bring them to full certainty of faith. Through these appearances, of which they alone, and not we, are witnesses, they were enabled to know Him, and to be sure who, and what, He is. These Resurrection experiences alone ensure our knowledge of their witness to Christ, and through this witness of theirs, we also, on our part, can know Him to be who and what He is. Through their witness as a whole He authenticates Himself to us as the Living and Present Lord; through their witness He has become living and present to us too. Through the faith which He creates by means of the witness of the Apostles—by means of that witness, which contains both the story of His life and the doctrine of His Person—He is "with us all the days, even unto the end of the world." We are thus ourselves enabled, from our own knowledge, to be His witnesses, although we have not experienced those appearances of the Risen Lord. He *had* to attest Himself thus to the Apostles by those appearances as the Risen Lord, in order that they should believe in Him, see Him again, and really see Him as He is. He does not make Himself known to us in the same way. He makes Himself known to us through the collective witness of the Apostles, through the story of His life (in the Gospels), and the explanation of this story which the Apostles give us, through which we see Himself, and can ourselves learn to know Him as they saw Him and knew Him.

Hence our faith is not based upon the record of their experiences of the Resurrection. Every believing Christian knows this. He believes in the Risen Lord not because the Resurrection is told as a narrative of something that happened, but because he knows Christ as the living present Lord. Indeed, we might say: we would believe in Him as the Risen Lord, even if there were no narratives of the Resurrection at all; we must only add it is not an accident that there *are* accounts of the Resurrection given us by the Apostles. Only because they met the Risen Lord, as Paul and others tell us, is there an apostolic witness to Jesus, the Christ, and only because there is this apostolic witness, can we ourselves know Him.

Hence all questions of "how" and "where" the Resurrection took place, including the question of the Empty Tomb and the physical Resurrection understood in this sense, are secondary. This is so because we who, in view of our own resurrection, are called "His brethren," among whom He is the First-born, do not believe in our physical resurrection in the sense of an empty tomb. Here again we see the significance of the original Pauline account of the Resurrection. Just as Paul lays no stress upon the Empty Tomb, so, on the other hand, he lays decisive emphasis upon the parallels between the Resurrection of Jesus and our own, on the fact that "He is the first-born among many brethren." Even if Paul (which we simply do not know) did know anything about the Empty Tomb, it was not for him a fact of central importance, because for *us* there will not be an empty grave.

The Resurrection as Eschatological Event

In the context of commenting on the Apostles' Creed, Czechoslovakian theologian Jan Lochman describes the Pauline interpretation of the resurrection in 1 Corinthians 15 as an eschatological event that alters the meaning of life lived here and now.

SOURCE
Lochman, *The Faith We Confess*, 235–36.

In its uniqueness, this Easter event certainly is past history. Hence the question quite naturally arises: How is the nasty ditch between that past event and our future bridged? How is what happened then communicated to us now so as to become a present reality? The New Testament is not at a loss for an answer to these questions. Engaged as we now are in an exposition of the Third Article of the Creed, we cannot fail to be impressed by the number of important New Testament passages in which this answer is given in pneumatological terms, in terms of the work of the Holy Spirit. In Paul's letter to the Romans, for example, we read: "If the Spirit of him who raised Jesus from the dead dwells in you, he who raised Christ Jesus from the dead will give life to your mortal bodies also through his Spirit which dwells in you" (Rom. 8:11). There is no room for doubt: the Spirit is the bridge! In the power and presence of the Holy Spirit, Christ's past is firmly connected with our future. The eschatological event of Jesus' resurrection is communicated and made operative in the experience of the Spirit. It is for this reason, this good and valid reason, that the Creed continues its Third-Article affirmation of faith in the Holy Spirit with the words: "I believe in the resurrection of the flesh."

The clearest account of the apostles' experience of the resurrection and its detonating character and universal "follow-through" is found in 1 Corinthians 15, the key New Testament passage on the resurrection. Paul begins very concretely and precisely with the Easter event, then goes on to narrate experiences of the risen Christ and to cite witnesses. The resurrection is not a general notion, a universal idea, but a concrete event with a quite specific beginning. There is no room for any doubt on that score. Yet, precisely as such it is also an eschatological event; no isolated episode in a purely individual destiny, but an incursion into the whole realm of death, a breakthrough for the many. Paul calls the risen Jesus Christ "the first fruits of those who have fallen asleep" (v. 20). In Rom. 8:29 Paul speaks of him even more vividly as "the first-born among many." Biblically, this can only mean that Christ's history becomes human history, Christ's destiny *our* destiny. "For as in Adam all die, so also in Christ shall all be made alive" (1 Cor. 15:22).

This "in Christ" becomes for Paul the decisive sign outside the brackets of our human life. The brackets are still there: we still live and die as mortal and sinful human beings. But outside the brackets there now stands this key signature that qualifies (and changes) everything within the brackets. According to the New Testament this "in Christ" shifts our human life out of the blind necessity and fatalism of fortuitous circumstances and inexorable processes into the wider horizon of eschatological hope, a horizon that immediately, here and now, upholds us and transforms our human condition. Thus at the end of this resurrection chapter the message that had its original setting in the Easter event is now extended to us all: "Death is swallowed up in victory. O death, where is thy victory? O death, where is thy sting? The sting of death is sin, and the power of sin is the law. But thanks be to God, who gives us the victory through our Lord Jesus Christ!" (vv. 54ff.). In the Easter event *our* future has already begun!

Reformed Confessions

God's Vindication of Jesus

"A Declaration of Faith" (1967) of the Congregational Church in England and Wales echoes a typical theme in contemporary theology: Jesus' resurrection is God's vindication of not only Jesus' death but also his ministry and teaching.

SOURCE

"A Declaration of Faith" (1967) of the Congregational Church in England and Wales in *Reformed Witness Today*, 124.

9. . . . and in his resurrection . . .

By the resurrection of Jesus we understand God's vindication of him, and we affirm that God delivered him completely from the death into which he had fully entered. We acknowledge that no exact description can possibly be given either of the resurrection event or of the way in which death's effects were overcome. We share with the original witnesses to his resurrection their faith in God who wrought it and in Jesus whom it vindicated. Jesus, given back to them as their living friend, was given to them anew as their Lord and so too he is given to us. His ministry and teaching awaken belief that a new way of hope and trust and fulfillment is being opened for mankind. In death on the cross his opposition to sin and his fidelity to love were completed in the obscurity of dereliction. In his resurrection it is disclosed that sinfulness and death have been and henceforth will be robbed of their seemingly inevitable and lasting hold upon human life. From this point of disclosure, the triumph of grace comes into our lives and undermines both sin and the fear of sin, death and the fear of death. We echo and prolong the confident praise of God which rings throughout the New Testament and could not conceivably be sustained had Jesus not been raised from the dead.

Lord from the Beginning, Now, and at the End

A Declaration of Faith of the Presbyterian Church in the United States confesses that the resurrection of Jesus Christ means that he is a living lord in the present and that finally his lordship will no longer be hidden but will set free humanity from all powers that now appear to dominate human life.

SOURCE

Declaration of Faith, 8–9.

(5) Jesus is our living Lord.

Jesus was dead and buried,
> but God raised him from the dead.

The risen Lord appeared to his followers.
They recognized him as their Master
> who had been crucified.

Before Jesus left them,
> he commissioned them to proclaim to all people
> the good news of his victory over death,
> and promised to be with them always.

We are certain that Jesus lives.
He lives as God with us,
> touching all of human life with the presence of God.

He lives as one of us with God.
Because he shares our humanity
> and has bound us to himself in love,
> we have an advocate in the innermost life of God.

We declare that Jesus is Lord.
His resurrection is a decisive victory
> over the powers that deform and destroy human life.

His lordship is hidden.
The world appears to be dominated by people and systems
> that do not acknowledge his rule.

But his lordship is real.
It demands our loyalty and sets us free
> from the fear of all lesser lords who threaten us.

We maintain that ultimate sovereignty
> now belongs to Jesus Christs
> in every sphere of life.

Jesus is Lord!
He has been Lord from the beginning.
He will be Lord at the end.
Even now he is Lord.

5

THE HOLY SPIRIT
AND THE CHRISTIAN LIFE

In classical Reformed theology, the Holy Spirit has not received the same attention as have the first two persons of the Trinity. This "slighting" of the Holy Spirit is not the result of anti-trinitarian tendencies in Reformed theology. Rather, the Reformed tradition has been characterized by a keen awareness of the depth and pervasiveness of sin and, consequently, a distrust of religious "enthusiasm," social disorder, and an undue emphasis on personal experience that leads to preoccupation with self instead of service to God and neighbor. It is not surprising, therefore, that Reformed theology, like many other forms of mainline Protestantism, has adhered to the *filioque*, the interpretation of the Trinity in Western Christianity in which the Spirit proceeds from the Father and the Son. The Eastern Orthodox church rejected this interpretation because it feared it subordinated the Holy Spirit to the first two persons of the Trinity. Reformed theology has insisted that the Spirit is always the Spirit of Jesus Christ and that the principal work of the Spirit is to give Christians faith by binding them to Jesus Christ. Book 3 of Calvin's *Institutes* and the last two-thirds of the Westminster Confession of Faith represent slightly different interpretations of the theological "order" or structure (what is sometimes referred to as the *ordo salutis*) of the work of the Holy Spirit in transforming individuals and communities, a process sometimes described as "the Christian life."

In the nineteenth century, many Reformed theologians were influenced by revival movements, by the emphasis given to piety in Schleiermacher's theology, and by the dominant role given to Spirit in Hegel's thought. In the first half of the twentieth century, neo-orthodoxy, typified by Karl Barth, insisted that God's self-revelation in Jesus Christ should be the central focus of Christian faith and theology, and, for that reason, distrusted theologies that made human experience the norm for theological reflection. The objective reality of God's self-revelation in Jesus Christ should take precedence over revelation's subjective reality (the human experience and appropriation of revelation). The objective reality of what God has done in Jesus Christ—and not personal experience—should be the good news the church proclaims to the world.

This neo-orthodox position is reflected in The Confession of 1967 of the Presbyterian Church (U.S.A.). Part I is entitled "God's Work of Reconciliation" and part II is "The Ministry of Reconciliation." One brief section in part I discusses "the new life" which the Holy Spirit creates. The issue of how "God's work" is appropriated by individuals and communities in order that they may engage in "the ministry of reconciliation" is discussed only briefly. This failure to attend to the theological reality of the dynamics of the Christian life has been a major factor in the decline of Reformed churches in the United States and Western Europe.

In the last half of the twentieth century, Reformed theologians have given greater attention to the Holy Spirit and the Christian life. One reason for this turn of events has been a widespread concern in Protestant congregations about the demise of traditional forms of piety, the apparent triumph of material secularism, and a renewed interest in Christian spirituality. Although not a great deal of attention has been given to prayer by Reformed theologians in the nineteenth and twentieth centuries, increasing numbers of Christians have found that the emphasis of many denominations on social witness and ministry cannot be sustained unless it is grounded in a vital, ongoing spirituality.

FOR FURTHER STUDY

Karl Barth, *The Christian Life: Church Dogmatics Volume IV, Part 4, Lecture Fragments,* trans. Geoffrey W. Bromiley (Grand Rapids: Wm. B. Eerdmans, 1981). Karl Barth, *The Holy Ghost and the Christian Life,* trans. R. Birch Hoyle (London: F. Muller, 1938). Abraham Kuyper, *The Practice of Godliness* (Grand Rapids: Wm. B. Eerdmans, 1948). Jürgen Moltmann, *The Passion for Life: A Messianic Lifestyle,* trans. M. Douglas Meeks (Philadelphia: Fortress, 1978). Lesslie Newbigin, *Journey into Joy* (Grand Rapids: Wm. B. Eerdmans, 1972).

THE PERSON AND WORK OF THE HOLY SPIRIT

Just as Christology has often been described by means of the analytic categories of "person" and "work," so too the same categories have been used to describe the Holy Spirit, although in practice theologians have had more to say about what the Spirit *does* than who the Spirit *is.* The Spirit is wind or breath, and as such it is the Spirit, according to the Bible, who gives life; and it is the Holy Spirit who recreates, transforms, and renews life.

Because Reformed theology has affirmed the *filioque,* it has insisted that the Spirit is always the Spirit of Jesus Christ. It is the Spirit who inspires and illumines individuals and communities in order that they may hear the Word, and it is the same Spirit who makes Christ present in the world. Without the activity of the Spirit, Christian faith and theology would be empty, lifeless, and sterile.

FOR FURTHER STUDY

Hendrikus Berkhof, *The Doctrine of the Holy Spirit* (Atlanta: John Knox, 1964). George S. Hendry, *The Holy Spirit in Christian Theology* (Philadelphia: Westminster, 1956). Alasdair I. C. Heron, *The Holy Spirit* (Philadelphia: Westminster, 1983). Abraham Kuyper, *The Work of the Holy Spirit*, trans. Henri De Vales (New York & London: Funk & Wagnalls, 1900). Jürgen Moltmann, *The Spirit of Life: A Universal Affirmation* (Minneapolis: Fortress, 1992).

Church, Spirit, and Christ

Although Friedrich Schleiermacher was responsible for many innovations in the interpretation of theology, his understanding of the relationship among "the fellowship of believers," the Holy Spirit, and Jesus Christ places him squarely in the mainstream of the Reformed tradition.

SOURCE

Schleiermacher, *Christian Faith*, 574–75.

Up to this point the question as to how redemption is realized in the human soul has been answered by saying that it happens through being taken up into living fellowship with Christ. Now the demand is made that everyone must partake of the Holy Spirit. This, however, is not at all to be understood as meaning that the experience is actually in two parts, and that some new and special thing happens to a regenerate person when he becomes a partaker in the Holy Spirit. Neither in fact nor in point of time are the two things to be distinguished, but in strictness we must say that everyone, as regenerate, also receives a share in the Holy Spirit. For being taken up into living fellowship with Christ includes at the same time being conscious both of our sonship with God and of the Lordship of Christ; and both in Scripture are ascribed to the indwelling of the Holy Spirit. We therefore cannot imagine how one could exist were the other absent. If, to indulge in a flight of fancy, we suppose that we could find ourselves placed in a similar common life representative of the Kingdom of God, and led by the Holy Spirit as its common spirit, with only this difference that we knew nothing of any such Founder as

Christ is; yet we should not, when contrasting that condition and the sinful common life, be able to derive the first from the second; and at the same time, since in all the members of that common life sin, while not willed, is yet present, we should have to hold that the sinful common life is not something grounded within itself (that is to say, something such as it was in its first origin), for otherwise it must have been capable of originating in the same way also at other points. This, we remark in passing, is also the reason why those who start from so imperfect and partial a divine revelation always so easily recognize one another, even in their hostility. So long, therefore, as we do not admit that other similar kingdoms of God may arise independently of the Christian Church at other times or places, we are compelled to accept for it a single origin outside of the common life of sin, from which the divine communication found within it is derived. Membership in this common life therefore means at the same time being set within the sphere of operation of the sole Founder. Thus we find expressed the belief that such an outpouring of the Spirit would only have been possible after the appearance of the Son of God, and on the basis of His personal influence; and this carries with it the implication that our participation in that Spirit and our own bond with the living influence of Christ are one and the same thing.

On the other side, the same thing holds good. If we begin with Christ and hold to the proposition that the union of the Divine with His human personality was at the same time an enrichment of human nature as a whole, it follows not only in general that even after His departure this union must continue, but also (since this continuation is to proceed from the union itself) that wherever it exists there must be a bond with Christ, and *vice versa*. And since after the departure of Christ the enlarged range of connexion with Him can only proceed from the fellowship of believers, these three facts—being drawn by that union into the fellowship of believers, having a share in the Holy Spirit, and being drawn into living fellowship with Christ—must simply mean one and the same thing.

The Holy Spirit and Revelation

Revelation, as Karl Barth describes it, has an objective side and a subjective side. The two can be distinguished but not separated. The doctrine of the Holy Spirit has to do with the subjective reality of revelation. The "third article" refers to the third paragraph of the Apostles' Creed.

SOURCE

Karl Barth, *Credo* (New York: Charles Scriber's Sons, 1962), 129–33.

FOR FURTHER STUDY

Philip J. Rosato, *The Spirit as Lord: The Pneumatology of Karl Barth* (Edinburgh: T. & T. Clark, 1981).

The third article as doctrine of the Holy Spirit and of what man obtains through Him, obviously stands over against the *second* article as the doctrine of *Christ* and His work in a special direct relationship. There is such a thing as a Church, because Jesus Christ is our Lord, sitting at the right hand of God—forgiveness of sins, because Jesus Christ was crucified and died—resurrection of the flesh, because Jesus Christ rose from the dead—eternal life, because He comes again to judge the quick and the dead. Here nothing counts by itself, everything only in this relationship. We can say in advance that even the Holy Spirit Himself is in exactly the same position. He is the *Holy* Spirit because He is the Spirit of Jesus Christ. But clearly the reverse of this is also true. It is possible to speak rightly of Christ only if and while we are also speaking of the Holy Spirit and His work, and therefore of man, which means of Church, forgiveness of sins, resurrection of the dead and eternal life. From the fact of this connection we gather that what the Creed in conjunction with Holy Scripture wants to certify as God's revelation, does not on the one side confine itself to what happened once and for all, the fact of Christ in itself, but includes in this something that happens to many men at many times—and, on the other side, will not suffer itself to be limited by the human experiences of the various other times in which it is received and accepted as revelation. Nay, but the one actual, divine revelation has, as it were, an objective and a subjective side. It would not be the actual divine revelation if it were merely, so to speak, an objective divine performance, out of which men could then make what is possible and permissible according to some other prescription. But no less and nothing else than actual divine revelation is also the subjective side, i.e., the participation men get and take in it. With the reserve, which the philosophical overloading of these conceptions makes necessary, we can say: the doctrine of *Christ* points to the *objective*, the doctrine of the *Holy Spirit* to the *subjective* side of this reality. To which we add again that, while we have to distinguish the two, we have not for a moment or in any respect to separate them.

The clear Biblical fundamental doctrine of the work of the Holy Spirit which the symbol has in view with its *credo in Spiritum sanctum* is that the revelation of the Father in the Son is the revelation through the Holy Spirit. We say exactly the same thing when we say that the reconciliation of the world to God in Christ is the reconciliation through the Holy Spirit. By Holy Spirit is to be understood: God Who comes to man and indeed comes to him in such a way that He is *known* to him, that man lets himself be reconciled, in other words, that he *believes* in God's Word and Son Jesus Christ. As the πνεῦμα, i.e., as the wind, goes from here to there, as the breath of our mouth goes from one to the other, so God as Holy Spirit goes out from Himself to man, yes, right into man, in order to make him open, free, ready for, capable to receive, Himself, that is, His Son, His Word. Man *needs* to be made open and free for God's revelation and reconciliation. He is not already that in himself. The Holy Ghost by effecting revelation and reconciliation makes it impossible for us to cherish the thought that we are open for God, that we could prepare and get ourselves ready for this event. "I believe that I cannot by my own reason and strength believe in Jesus Christ my Lord or come to Him" (Luther). Accordingly, he who believes, knows that even this—the fact that he *believes*, is God's work and gift; knows that He cannot see the ground in himself of his faith, cannot understand it as his doing, but again can only—believe. In believing, a man lets himself be told that he not only *commits* sin but *is* a sinner, that is, a rebel against grace and as such incapable of the decision of faith. If it is nevertheless true that he believes, then that means that a miracle has taken place in him. That will be accomplished in the shape of all sorts of definite events and experiences; certainly he will acquire in the process all sorts of definite insights, will make all sorts of definite resolutions and no doubt carry them out. But it will not be from his experiences, from his insights and resolutions, it will not be in any way out of himself that he will explain to himself the fact that he really believes, that he is therefore one to whom God is manifest, one who is reconciled with God. On the contrary, for the very fact that the journey from death to life which Christ accomplished affects him personally, he will give the glory to God Himself, as amazed and as thankful as he was before the cradle at Bethlehem and before the Cross at Golgotha. He who has learned to reverence free grace in the miracle of the Virgin Birth and in the miracle of the Ascension will reverence it all the more in the miracle that he—he who does *not* know himself as other than God's enemy, other than as contemner of grace, other than as one who openly or secretly trusts in works!—may in faith have peace with God, be called God's child, do the works of a pardoned man, go to meet his Judge with uplifted head. It will never occur to him to seek to understand himself as one who, acting in freedom and on the basis of that freedom, has achieved all that. He will understand and glory in God's freedom, the freedom of *grace*, in which he has had all that bestowed upon him. "No man can say that Jesus is Lord but by the Holy Spirit" (1 Cor. xii.3). "If any man have not the Spirit of Christ, he is none of His" (Rom. viii.9). He, "the Holy Spirit, has called me through the Gospel, enlightened me by His gifts, and sanctified and preserved me in the true faith, just as He calls, gathers, enlightens and sanctifies the whole Christian Church on earth and pre-serves it in union with Jesus Christ in the one true faith" (Luther).

Holy Scripture *distinguishes* the *Spirit* of God from the *Word* of God; it distinguishes Him also from *Christ*. As in the one reality of revelation and reconciliation it is something *special* that God is not only veiled from us as the Father but is unveiled as the Son, so it is once more something *special* and new that on this road from concealment into the light of day God *imparts Himself to us, to us men*, takes us, so to speak, with Him on this way, which is at once the way from judgment to grace, from death to life, and so becomes manifest *to us*, so becomes *our* reconciler. Christ and His way from death to resurrection is the presup-position, is the objective in relation to which this subjective—certainly not as a matter of course, but as fulfilment of *special* promise after the significant pause between Ascension and Pentecost—becomes *event*, the "coming down" indeed the "falling down" of the Spirit upon those to whom the exalted Lord, sitting at the right hand of the Father, will "send" Him. It could well be asked whether the step which is once more made here in the revelation of the Spirit is not *still* greater, more aston-ishing, stranger than the step from Good Friday to Easter, from the revelation of the Father to the revelation of the Son. It is at least *equally* great. And so we understand the necessity for solemnly introducing the Holy Spirit in the symbol with *credo*, for expressly marking Him out also as object of faith. In believing that Christ is God's Son we must again and specially believe, must start out by believing, in the work of God that is visible in the *fact that* we believe!

Reinterpreting *Filioque*

In the last half of the twentieth century, several Reformed theologians, such as Jürgen Moltmann, Dietrich Ritschl, and Alasdair Heron, have argued that the time has come to reinterpret the relation between the Holy Spirit and the first two persons of the Trinity. Heron suggests that neither the traditional Western nor Eastern position is entirely satisfactory. He advocates "a double relation-ship between the Son and Spirit."

SOURCE

Alasdair I. C. Heron, *The Holy Spirit* (Philadelphia: Westminster, 1983), 176–78.

Just as in both East and West there was a certain tendency for the doctrine of the Trinity to become detached from its concrete reference to the history of Christ and the Spirit, and with it the danger of treating the divine persons as corresponding equivalents to each other, there also was at work an inclination to set up further parallels within the Trinity, arranging the three persons into a group of two and a third standing over against the others. The East depicted the Father as the sole source and origin of the Son and Spirit, each issuing from him in the appropri-ate, parallel but distinct modes of generation and procession. The West, by contrast, came to posit the Father and the Son together as the single source of the Spirit, their common love and gift. This is certainly not all there is to say about either Eastern or Western trinitarian theology, but it may serve to focus the difference in approach expressed on the one hand by the medieval Western defence of the *filioque* as stated in the Councils of Lyons and Florence, and on the other by Photius' insistence in the eighth century that the Spirit proceeds *ek monou tou patros*, "from the Father alone."

If we have been at all on the right track in the last pages, then neither of these positions can be regarded as entirely satisfactory. The Trinity cannot be thus subdivided into "two here" and "one there," or "two of this sort" and "one of that," without doing violence to the pattern and dynamic of God's being and movement as Father, Son and Holy Spirit. The Son and Spirit are not adequately depicted as two parallel productions "from the Father alone," nor can the Father and Son be effectively conflated in the breathing-forth of the Spirit. In the East the relation and distinction between the Son and Spirit, in the West those between the Father and the Son fall too far into the back-ground, whereas in each case the relation and distinction between these pairs and the remaining person is placed in the centre of atten-tion. Neither view is adequately trinitarian; both reflect a double rather than a triple pattern.

Consistently with this non-trinitarianism, neither approach is easily reconcilable with the history of Christ and the Spirit as presented in the

New Testament. A Spirit proceeding *from* (rather than *to*) the Son in eternity squares ill with a Spirit coming upon, being received by, and then given from the Son in history. Similarly, however, a Spirit that proceeds in eternity from the Father alone would seem to stand in a different eternal relation to the Son from that enacted and realised in the movement from incarnation to Pentecost. Must room not somehow be found to affirm a double relationship between the Son and Spirit which is as ultimate in the life of God as in the work of salvation? Otherwise must not the doctrine of the Trinity at its heart and centre remain detached from its roots, by which alone we have access to it? In one way it may be suggested that Augustine's arguments for the *filioque* did drive in the needed direction; for as we saw, he described the procession of the Spirit as *principally* from the Father, yet as opening up in the generation of the Son in such a fashion that the Spirit proceeds from both. And, to follow up the motif of the *vinculum caritatis*, it proceeds both from the Father to the Son and from the Son to the Father. This avenue was later closed by the medieval concentration on the other Augustinian theme of the *unity of being* of the Father and the Son; but it could offer a conception of the inner-trinitarian relations which would better correspond to the pattern of the economy of salvation than either the medieval Western or the Photian roads.

That is one side of the matter. The other, of course, is that the *filioque* combined with the *vinculum caritatis* model has the tendency to project a sense of the Spirit as being somehow less "real" or "personal" than the Father and the Son. This is justified to the extent that it recognises the distinct nature of the Spirit's "person," but it can be taken to the point where the Spirit effectively disappears from view as the living and present and working Spirit *of God*. As T. F. Torrance has pointedly observed, the *filioque* in the West has commonly been replaced by an *ecclesiaque* or an *homineque*, the Spirit *of Christ* displaced by the spirit of the church or of man himself.

The answer here is not, however, simply to restate in Photian fashion the distinct procession of the Spirit from the Father alone. While that might serve in part to reinforce awareness of the distinct divinity of the Spirit, it is all too exposed to Lampe's charge of an over-hasty transference to the Spirit of the scheme of theology first applied to christology, a transference which is insufficiently grounded in the relation of the Spirit to Christ and Christ to the Spirit. That connection, to which the *filioque* inadequately witnesses, remains crucial if the Spirit of God is truly the Spirit of the Son, in whom we too cry, "Abba! Father!," and may also say

Glory be to the Father,
   and to the Son,
   and to the Holy Spirit,
As it was in the beginning,
   is now,
   and ever shall be,
   world without end.

Amen.

Friend of the Weak and Fighter Against the Oppressors

The "New Confession" (1972) of the Presbyterian Church in the Republic of Korea contains many themes used by other confessions to describe the Holy Spirit. What is new is its claim that the person who is filled with the Spirit is "the friend of the weak and the fighter against the oppressors and their oppressive evil structures."

SOURCE

"New Confession" (1972) of the Presbyterian Church of Korea, in *Reformed Witness Today*, 80–81.

V. THE HOLY SPIRIT AND LIFE IN THE SPIRIT

1. The Holy Spirit

After the resurrection of Jesus Christ the Holy Spirit was sent by the Father and the Son in order to continue the redemptive work of Christ in history until the end of the world. Like the Father and the Son, he is our one Lord God, the Spirit of the Father, and he works among us as the Spirit of Christ.

2. The Work of the Holy Spirit

The Holy Spirit not only continues the redemptive work of Christ, but he is also at work preserving creation through the historical process taking place between man and nature (John 14:16; Rom. 8:9–17).

The Holy Spirit makes Jesus Christ known among men and makes the children of God into the "new humanity."

The Holy Spirit enables us to meet Jesus Christ, so that through this encounter we may see ourselves as sinners, confess Jesus as Christ, be justified by faith and live a Christian life by faith in God. The Holy Spirit allows us to experience justification by faith while we are conscious of our sins. The Holy Spirit sanctifies our lives and enables us to live humble lives through grace and through prayer.

The Holy Spirit brings together the believers and establishes the Church, initiates mission work proclaiming the Lord's favour and liberates people. He brings out hidden truth; he fights evil and is active to bring about world peace. The Holy Spirit does the same things as Christ, and at no time is he in conflict with Christ.

The confession that Jesus is Christ (1 John 4:3) is the criterion by which the work of the Holy Spirit is distinguished from that of the worldly spirits. The fruits of the Holy Spirit prove it.

3. The Life of Love

The Holy Spirit builds the image of God in us, enables us to resemble Christ in personality and life and to follow his steps with joy (1 Pet. 2:21). He creates among us a "new life," according to which we "present our bodies as a living sacrifice, holy and acceptable to God" (Rom. 12:1). Life in the Spirit—i.e., the life of sinners whose sins are forgiven, of those who were lost and are found again—is a Christlike life for others. The "new man" in the Spirit follows the example of Christ in becoming the friend of the weak and the fighter against the oppressors and their oppressive evil structures; he sacrifices himself for the sake of the oppressed and organizes forces who also wish to support the oppressed. Life in the Spirit means a life dedicated to sharing in the suffering and resurrection of Christ (2 Cor. 4:11–12). Such a life is one of gratitude and praise to God.

4. The Gifts of the Spirit

The Holy Spirit gives varieties of gifts for the common good of the community of believers (1 Cor. 12:8-11, 28). They are varieties of works and talents all of which are to be used under the guidance of the Holy Spirit and in the service of our Lord. They include wisdom, love, gifts of healing, knowledge, the creative arts and service. God wants us to use and develop these gifts for the service of the Church, of society and of all men. When we forget that the gifts of the Spirit come from God, we become haughty and selfish, thus falling out of grace. We must seek above all the utmost gift, love (1 Cor. 12:31). The fruit of the Spirit is love, joy, peace, patience, kindness, goodness, faithfulness, gentleness and self-control (Gal. 5:22–23).

JUSTIFICATION BY GRACE
THROUGH FAITH

Most Reformed theologians would agree with Calvin's claim that the doctrine of justification is "the main hinge on which religion turns." That judgment concerning the meaning of the gospel is no less true in the twentieth century than it was in the sixteenth century or the first century. It is also no less difficult for people today to accept that there is nothing they can do to deserve God's grace and mercy.

The doctrine of justification has an interesting history. A case could be made that many of the turning points in the history of Christian theology have involved a recovery and a reinterpretation of what Paul calls "the righteousness of faith" and what has come to be known as "the doctrine of justification by grace through faith." Some of the best known of these "turning points" are Augustine's debate with Pelagius, Luther's protest against medieval Catholicism, the controversy surrounding Arminius and the Synod of Dort, and the attack by neo-orthodox theologians on Protestant liberalism.

The challenge for theologians in the modern period, however, has been to construct language, metaphors, and paradigms that will enable contemporary Christians to hear and understand the central claims of the doctrine of justification. In classical theology, justification was formulated in juridical language that often presupposed a medieval cosmology. Contemporary theology has sought language with which to express the conviction that God's salvation in Jesus Christ is a gift of sheer grace, but which does not assume an unintelligible view of the nature of sin and of God's relation to the world.

FOR FURTHER STUDY

G. C. Berkouwer, *Faith and Justification*, trans. Lewis B. Smedes (Grand Rapids: Wm. B. Eerdmans, 1954). Alister E. McGrath, *Iustitia Dei: A History of the Christian Doctrine of Justification*, 2 vols., Vol. 1: Beginnings to 1500; Vol. 2: From 1500 to the Present Day (Cambridge: Cambridge University Press, 1986).

Justification as Connection with God

Writing in 1874, Congregationalist minister Horace Bushnell (1802–76) departed from the traditional language of debt, penal suffering, merit, and justice, and described justification as a restoration of the sinner's connection with God made possible by the sacrifice of Jesus Christ. Bushnell's rejection of classical idioms and his adoption of the language of connection is an early example of the shift in modern theology from ontology to the language of relationship.

SOURCE

Horace Bushnell, *Forgiveness and Law: Grounded in Principles Interpreted by Human Analogies* (Hicksville, N.Y.: Regina, 1975), 203–6.

Here then is the grand renewing office and aim of the gospel of Christ. He comes to men groping in a state of separation from God, consciously not even with their own standards of good, and, what is more, consciously not able to be—self-condemned when they are trying most to justify themselves, and despairing the more, the more they endeavor to make themselves righteous by their own works—to such Christ comes forth, out of the righteousness of God, and also in the righteousness of God, that he may be the righteousness of God upon all them that believe, and are so brought close enough to him in their faith, to receive his inspirations. And this is the state of justification, not because some debt is made even, by the penal suffering of Christ, but because that normal connection with God is restored by his sacrifice, which permits the righteousness of God to renew its everlasting flow.

When I speak thus of the connection with God as being restored by the sacrifice of Christ, let me not be understood as meaning by the sacrifice, only what is tenderly sympathetic and submissive in Christ's death. I include all that is energetic, strong, and piercing; his warnings, the pressure of his discipline, all that is done, by his powerful ministry and doctrine, to save us from the wrath to come. His sacrifice is no mere suit or plaint of weakness, for the righteousness of God is in it. When the metallic ring of principle, or everlasting right, is heard in the distress and wail of the cross, the sacrifice becomes itself a sword of conviction, piercing irresistibly through the sinner, and causing him to quiver on the point by which he is fastened. Mere sympathy, as we commonly speak, is no great power; it must be somehow a tremendous sympathy, to have the true divine efficacy. Hence the glorious justifying efficacy of Christ; because the righteousness of God is declared in his sacrifice.

Again, secondly, a more deliberate statement of the relations of faith to justification appears to be demanded. Though the righteousness of God is declared and made to shine with its true divine lustre and glory by Christ, still the justification is not conceived to be an accomplished fact, as indeed it never can be, prior to faith in the subject. It is justification by faith and not without—"and the justifier of him that believeth in Jesus." What is this faith, and why is it necessary?

It is not the belief that Christ has come to even our account with justice; neither is it the belief that he has obtained a surplus merit, which is offered, over and above, as a positive righteousness, and set to our credit, if we will have it. Neither of the two is a fact, or at all credible any way. Nor would both, if believed as mere facts, do any thing more for us than a belief in any other facts. Our sins do not fly away because we believe in a fact of any kind. We can even believe in all the historic facts of Christianity, as thousands do, without being any the more truly justified.

No, the real faith is this, and very little intelligence is required to see the necessity of it; viz., the trusting of one's self over, sinner to Saviour, to be in him, and of him, and new charactered by him; because it is only in that way that the power of Christ gets opportunity to work. So the sinner is justified, and the justification is a most vital affair; "the justification of life." The true account of it is that Jesus, coming into the world, with all God's righteousness upon him, declaring it to guilty souls in all the manifold evidences of his life and passion, wins their faith, and by that faith they are connected again with the life of God, and filled and overspread with his righteousness. And there springs up, in this reconnection of the soul with God's righteousness, a perfect liberty and confidence; for it is no more trying to climb up into a righteous consciousness and confidence by itself, but it has the righteousness by derivation; flowing down upon it, into it, and through it, by the eternal permeation of God's Spirit. And just here it is that Christianity wins its triumph. It shows man how to be free in good, and makes it possible. The best that all other religions and moralities can do, is to institute a practice of works, and a climbing up into perfection by our own righteous deeds; but the gospel of Jesus comes to our relief, in showing us how to find righteousness, and have it as an eternal inspiration; "even the righteousness of God that is by the faith of Jesus Christ unto all and upon all them that believe." In it we do not climb, but rest; we goad ourselves into no impossibilities, groan under no bondage that we can not lift; sink into no deep mires because we try to struggle out. We have a possible righteousness, because it is not ours but God's; Christ received by our faith, to be upon us and for us, all that we could wish to be for ourselves. This is the transcendent distinction, the practically sublime glory of our gospel, our great all-truth—Justification by Faith. Here is conquered the grandest of all problems, how to put confidence in the bosom of guilt, and settle a platform of virtue that shall make duty free and joyful under all conscious disabilities.

Justified by Grace Rather Than Faith

"Justification by faith," as Karl Barth describes it, does not mean that sinful human beings can claim to deserve God's mercy and forgiveness because of their faith or because of anything else they have said or done. God's grace, not human faith, is the sole basis for justification.

SOURCE

Barth, *Church Dogmatics* IV/1:615–17.

FOR FURTHER STUDY

Hans Küng, *Justification: The Doctrine of Karl Barth and a Catholic Reflection* (Philadelphia: Westminster, 1981).

"Justification by faith" cannot mean that instead of his customary evil works and in place of all kinds of supposed good works man chooses and accomplishes the work of faith, in this way pardoning and therefore justifying himself. As his action, the action of sinful man, faith cannot do this. Nor does it make any odds whether a man means by faith a mere knowledge and intellectual understanding of the divine work and judgment and revelation and pardon (*notitia*), or an assent of the mind and will to it, the acceptance as true of that which is proclaimed as the truth of this work of God (*assensus*), or finally a heart's trust in the significance of this work for him (*fiducia*). It is not in and with all this that a man justifies himself, that he pardons himself, that he sets himself in that transition from wrong to right, from death to life, that he makes himself the subject of that history, the history of redemption. There is always something wrong and misleading when the faith of a man is referred to as his way of salvation in contrast to his way in wicked works, or his true way of salvation in contrast to his way in the supposed good works of false faith and superstition. Faith is not an alternative to these other ways. It is not the way which—another Hercules at the crossroads—man can equally well choose and enter, which he can choose and enter by the same capacity by which he might go any other way. Even in the action of faith he is the sinful man who as such is not in a position to justify himself, who with every attempt to justify himself can only become the more deeply entangled in his sin. He is awakened and called to will and achieve this by the work of God (otherwise he certainly will not do it). But in so far as it is his own—as it must be—even in his faith he confirms and repeats himself. Even as a believer he can represent himself to God only as the one he is in virtue of his past, only with the request: "God be merciful to me, a sinner." If his faith is his justification, his pardon, if in faith he can recognise the man justified by God in his own person, if, because in his own person, he can see in the man justified by God the divine mystery of grace of the existence of all his fellow-men, he does not owe this in the very least to what he is and feels and thinks and says and does as a believing man. He is as little justified in faith as in his other good or evil works. He needs justification just as much in faith as anywhere else, as in the totality of his being. In relation to it, considering himself as a believer, he cannot see himself as justified, he cannot be certain of his own justification or of the justification of man in general and as such. In faith he will be no less aware of his transgression and need and shame than in his other states and achievements. The image of himself as a believer—in so far as he has time and the desire to concern himself with it—can only incite and impel him to that other request: "Lord, I believe; help thou mine unbelief" (Mk. 9:24). There is as little praise of man on the basis of his faith as on that of his works. For there is as little justification of man "by"—that is to say, by means of—the faith produced by him, by his treading the way of faith, by his achievement of the emotions and thoughts and acts of faith, by his whole consciousness of faith and life of faith, as there is a justification "by" any other works. Faith is not at all the supreme and true and finally successful form of self-justification. If it tried to be this, if man tried to believe with this purpose and intention and claim, then even if his faith was not a "dead" faith, even if it was a most "hearty" faith, even if it was a fiduciary faith most active in love, it would be the supreme and most proper form of his sin as the sin of pride. To play off a faith in which man thinks that he can and should pardon and justify himself against other attempts at self-justification in the form of fidelity to the Law and good works is not merely nonsensical. It is the enterprise and conduct of a Pharisaism which is the most evil Pharisaism of all: the Pharisaism of the publican. It may well happen that the most audacious man of works, the Christian or secular pietist or activist, will go back to his house justified rather than this man: not by his little works but because—who can tell?—there is perhaps behind his works in some hidden form a real faith which is completely lacking in the one who simply justifies himself in all his righteousness of faith. If it is in his real righteousness of faith that a Christian can and should boast, then he above all men must know better than this; he must not on any account regard it as his own; he must not on any account tread the way of self-righteousness as one who is justified by faith, but only the way of the real publican.

The Two Sides of Grace

According to Reinhold Niebuhr, Western Christianity has always struggled with the paradox that Christians are at one and the same time made righteous by Christ's death and still remain sinners. Those theologies that emphasize that Christians are sinners run the risk of minimizing the call of the gospel to discipleship and growth in the Christian life, while those theologies that emphasize the sense in which Christians are a "new creation" face the peril of turning the gospel into a thinly disguised moralism.

SOURCE

Niebuhr, *Nature and Destiny,* 2:124–26.

It is not easy to express both these two aspects of the life of grace, to which all history attests without seeming to offend the canons of logic. That is one reason why moralists have always found it rather easy to discount the doctrine of "justification by faith." But here, as in many cases, a seeming defiance of logic is merely the consequence of an effort to express complex facts of experience. It happens to be true to the facts of experience that in one sense the converted man is righteous and that in another sense he is not.

The complexity of the facts not only makes it difficult to comprehend them in a formula which does not seem to offend canons of consistency. It is also difficult to express both aspects of the experience of grace without unduly suppressing one or the other side of it. The theologies which have sought to do justice to the fact that saints nevertheless remain sinners have frequently, perhaps usually, obscured the indeterminate possibilities of realizations of good in both individual and collective life. The theologies which have sought to do justice to the positive aspects of regeneration have usually obscured the realities of sin which appear on every new level of virtue. This has been true particularly of modern versions of Christian perfectionism; because in them evolutionary and progressive interpretations of history have been compounded with illusions which have a more purely Christian source.

We must trace the course of this debate in detail presently; for it embraces the whole history of western Christendom and it involves all the issues which are crucial for an understanding, and a possible reorientation, of the spiritual life of our day.

At the moment it is important to emphasize that the two sides of the experience of grace are so related that they do not contradict, but support each other. To understand that the Christ in us is not a possession but a hope, that perfection is not a reality but an intention; that such peace as we know in this life is never purely the peace of achievement but the serenity of being "completely known and all forgiven"; all this does not destroy moral ardour or responsibility. On the contrary it is the only way of preventing premature completions of life, or arresting the new and more terrible pride which may find its roots in the soil of humility, and of saving the Christian life from the intolerable pretension of saints who have forgotten that they are sinners.

The simple moralists will always regard this final pinnacle of the religious experience with little or no comprehension. They will assert that it is merely a formula which allows us "to continue in sin that grace may abound." But if the "foolishness of God" has been truly incorporated into the wisdom of faith the simple answer to this charge can be: "God forbid. How shall we, that are dead to sin, live any longer therein?" (Romans 6:3).

The Justification of Creation

The whole of Christian faith and life, writes Jürgen Moltmann, has an eschatological horizon. Justification, like the rest of Christian faith, is based on the death and resurrection of Jesus Christ and looks forward to God's transformation of the world. As such, it is not simply the article of faith by which the church stands or falls, but the last, best hope of all humanity.

SOURCE

Jürgen Moltmann, "Justification and New Creation," in idem, *The Future of Creation: Collected Essays,* trans. Margaret Kohl (London: SCM, 1979), 171.

Creation is oppressed by Nothingness. In the justification of the godless and in faith we see the beginning of the transformation and the creation of the whole for the glorification of God.

The gospel becomes restorative in the notion of the restoration of the original creation, which was said to be good.

If it is only taken by itself as healing power for sinners and the miserable, without criticism of what is and what considers itself of importance, the gospel becomes the uncritical compensation for existing evil.

Its liberating power only becomes manifest when it is based on the resurrection of the crucified Jesus, and when it is directed critically towards the eschatological transformation of the unjust world, which has been reduced to misery and is sinking into Nothingness. Then what Albert Camus supposed would happen will be impossible: that Christianity will insist on letting the virtue of rebellion and protest against suffering be torn from it—the virtue that once belonged to it a long time ago. Then its faith and its hope for the divine righteousness "in heaven and on earth" will enter into dialogue with the movements for righteousness on earth, with the philosophy of the cross (Camus) and the philosophy of the resurrection (Bloch). Justifying faith will then belong entirely to the others, because it belongs entirely to the crucified liberator, Jesus Christ. The doctrine of the creative righteousness of God revealed in the resurrection of the crucified Jesus is the *articulus stantis et cadentis hominis.*

REGENERATION AND SANCTIFICATION

In Reformed theology the triune God not only justifies but also regenerates and sanctifies the sinner. Regeneration is inner renewal and new birth; sanctification is the transformation of the sinner. Justification and sanctification are two sides of one coin, a twofold grace, and both are the work of the Holy Spirit binding the Christian to Jesus Christ. Like most forms of Protestantism, classical Reformed theology was reluctant to use the language of "virtue" and "fruits of the Spirit" to describe sanctification, but some contemporary theologians have argued that these themes have a proper role in any interpretation of the Christian life. Contemporary interpretations of sanctification often reflect the influence of the social sciences and describe sanctification as a dynamic process.

FOR FURTHER STUDY

G. C. Berkouwer, *Faith and Sanctification*, trans. John Vriend (Grand Rapids: Wm. B. Eerdmans, 1952). Benjamin Breckinridge Warfield, *Perfectionism.* 2 vols. (New York: Oxford University Press, 1931).

Faith's Visible Fruit

Emil Brunner describes the paradox of sanctification. On the one hand, the New Testament claims that faith issues in visible fruit, but, on the other hand, this visible fruit is not the basis of faith's assurance. The latter is grounded solely in Jesus Christ.

SOURCE

Brunner, *Dogmatics*, 3:302–4.

There has therefore been much debate on the question whether the results of this sanctification, which the New Testament describes as "fruits of the Spirit," are observable and visible or invisible and purely interior. Here also we meet with the same misunderstandings on the right hand and on the left. On the one side it is said that the Christian never scrutinizes himself or indeed the fruits of faith, not even to test himself by this standard, but that he looks only to Christ. The other side maintains that our standing in faith can actually be assessed, as it were "proved," by the fruits. The New Testament can be adduced to support either view. "For your life is hidden with Christ in God" (Col. 3:3). Justifying faith means in fact that we should place our sole confidence in the Word of Christ, living entirely on the gift of grace, and making it the sole foundation of our life. On the other side it is just as clear that when scripture speaks of the fruits of the Spirit it means visible manifestations of the Spirit. There are no "invisible fruits" for it, any more than there are for the botanist. Thus it is expressly said, "Let your light so shine before men that they may see your good works and praise your Father which is in heaven" (Matt. 5:16).

Obviously we have here come to a point where the truth of the gospel can find expression only in paradox. And yet we are on dangerous ground when the Reformed doctrine of the *syllogismus practicus* which is mentioned in the Heidelberg Catechism maintains that we must "be assured of our *faith* by the fruits thereof." Yet statements of a quite similar tenor are to be found in Luther also. It is clear that faith must bear visible fruit, it must prove itself in action. But, on the other side, this verification can never be the *basis* of faith and faith's certainty. We must teach both things: the necessity of practical verification in love and the continually humbling fact that such love comes short of God's claim upon us. "For all our deeds are nothing worth, even in the best of lives." Both things must be said: the believer looks not on himself at all, but on Christ, and inasmuch as he looks on Christ he sees in Him One who summons him to discipleship.

But true discipleship consists above all in this, that we should dwell in Him, in being rather than in doing. It is not quietism to lay the accent on this new being, for what the world needs beyond anything else is not action, but new men. From this new being there arises ever and again a new action. The world, that is the unbelieving world, has no understanding of the new being. Its only standard of ethical measurement is action. Therefore Christ's command is "Let your light shine," the light that Christ alone can give, the light that shines forth only from those who *are* in Him.

This is what we Protestants have to learn from the saints. The saints prove themselves as such, not so much by their doing as by their being, as men who live from the love of Christ and in His love. What makes us true saints is not our action. It is equally the case that what the world needs is not action, and this is quite specially true of our so pragmatic modern technical world. What we are able to achieve—even the holiest of us—can be a manifestation only, a demonstration which does not heal the world. The new being, indeed, like our action, is something which comes far short of what is meant by that sonship of God which is identical with true humanity. But it can at least be a pointer thereto. True humanity, however, is never solitariness, but always a being-with. To be a true fellow man to men; that is the authentic meaning of sanctification.

Between Antinomianism and Legalism

Hendrikus Berkhof argues that a proper interpretation of sanctification must avoid the tendency toward complacency and quietism, on the one hand, and legalism and self-salvation, on the other.

SOURCE

Hendrikus Berkhof, *The Doctrine of the Holy Spirit* (Atlanta: John Knox, 1976), 74–75.

A declaration, an appointment, etc., are not mere words; they change relations, and therefore they also change the men involved in these relations. In God's case, that is not only a subsequent fact—it is his aim that men should be changed according to the image of his Son. We are engrafted in order that we may grow. We are appointed in order that we may follow a new calling. We are adopted as sons in order that we may behave as sons. The work *pro nobis* seeks a follow-up in the work *in nobis*. Even this way of expressing the togetherness of justification and sanctification is dangerous, however. It suggests two more or less connected successive acts; but we are dealing with one and the same movement. God's Word is always a creative act. In calling us his sons, he makes us behave as sons. In creating a new relation, he creates a new being. It is really one twofold grace. In that one grace, justification and sanctification are not two parts; in the one event they are related as fundament and goal, as root and fruit. Our regeneration is that we are engrafted into Christ in such a way that we become changed according to his image.

I assume that we all more or less agree about this unity of justification and sanctification. However, as soon as we try to formulate this connection more precisely, new differences arise. On the one hand, I think of a man like the great Reformed preacher Kohlbrugge (1803–1875), for whom the justification of the ungodly was the one and the all of the Word of God. He disliked exhortations to sanctification, because he was afraid that this would lead to self-salvation and Phariseeism. For him the main sin was man's pride, his rebellious inclination to take his salvation in his own hands. Man has nothing to do except to stick to his justification, to believe that Christ has done all for him and that the only thing we can do is to be grateful. It was Kohlbrugge's confidence that such an attitude of faith would be the most fertile soil for real good works.

On the other hand, I think of a man like John Wesley (1703–1791), to whom justification by faith alone was a living reality, but who made a sharp distinction between justification and sanctification and who saw as the goal to be pursued seriously by every Christian: to put on love as the bond of perfection. Continuous exhortation to holiness was at the center of his preaching. He believed in "inherent perfection," i.e., in the perfectability of the faithful in this life.

Kohlbrugge and Wesley would have abhorred one another's preaching. In my opinion dogmatical theology should not decide in favor of one or the other. It ought to remind us, instead, of three facts. First: Sin manifests itself in different forms. Sin can have the form of pride, Phariseeism, self-salvation. Sin can also have the form of slowness and quietism. These different forms demand different emphases. Second: We have to remind one another that the first emphasis brings us very near to antinomianism and quietism, and the second to legalism and self-salvation. Third: Both approaches have to be understood as complementary. Faith in Christ without love is dead, is a pseudo-faith. And a sanctification which is not rooted in gratitude for justification is but a kind of Christian personality-culture. We easily forget that the two words "justification" and "sanctification" do not describe different spiritual stages or situations, but are in their togetherness an attempt to point from two sides, from the basis and from the goal, to the movement in which the Holy Spirit involves us: the movement toward our Redeemer, in order to be changed according to his image. That is the movement of our rebirth.

The Eschatological Character of Rebirth

A persistent theme in Jürgen Moltmann's theology is the importance of eschatology for interpreting the whole of Christian faith. No less than the rest of the Christian life, regeneration is an eschatological orientation toward the new creation. Such an orientation means that the Christian cannot become preoccupied with self or live in isolation but must be open for community.

SOURCE
Moltmann, *The Church*, 278–80.

BORN AGAIN TO A LIVING HOPE

Before we consider the life which is stamped for freedom by the gospel, it may be helpful to look round for the theological concept which expresses this experience of faith. Here we shall take the concept of "rebirth." *Regeneratio, renovatio—"incipit vita nova"* seem to capture the sense of what is meant better than sanctification, with its many levels of meaning. The actual word "rebirth" is seldom used in the New Testament (Matt. 19:28; Titus 3:5). But the fact is often treated in the context of baptism. Like all related concepts, rebirth is to be understood eschatologically. Matthew 19:28 means by it the renewal and rebirth of the world in the future of the Son of man and his glory. Titus 3:5 talks about the rebirth (regeneration) of believers in the Holy Spirit according to the mercy of God through Jesus Christ, which makes them already heirs of eternal life "in hope." When the Johannine writings talk about new birth "from God" and "from the Spirit" they are talking about the new source of new life. Born again of the Spirit, believers acquire a share in the kingdom of God. The first epistle of Peter talks about being born again "to a living hope" (1:3) by the mercy of God through the resurrection of Jesus Christ from the dead. In the rebirth of life the new creation of the world into the kingdom of God in an individual life is already experienced and anticipated *here*. This has its foundation in the prevenient mercy of God; it is manifest in the resurrection of Christ from the dead; and it is efficacious in the Spirit, which moulds life in faith to the living hope. Theological tradition has seldom taken account of this eschatolog-ical character of rebirth. But it is just this that makes it clear that the rebirth of an individual means his orientation towards the new creation: "The one who is born again is, as it were, ahead of himself; he lives from the thing that is coming to him, not from what is already in him." The one who is born again cannot, therefore, be scrupulously and anxiously preoccupied with himself, although he lives in this experience. His life has become new because, being orientated towards the new creation, he lives in the presence of the Spirit and under his influence, the "earnest of glory." At the same time the eschatological orientation of the individual's rebirth opens him for the community and for the world. The experience is his own—irreplaceably so; but it sets him in the movement of hope and in the fellowship of the messianic community. Re-birth does not isolate a person, even though it affects the individual in his unrepeatable character. On the contrary, it links his life with the future, giving that life, limited as it is, a meaning that transcends it. Rebirth does not isolate the individual, even though it makes him a person, but sets him in the common movement of the Spirit which is poured out "on all flesh." Where the messianic gospel is heard and evokes faith, life is born again "to a living hope" and—in however fragmentary a form—the rebirth of the world is anticipated. The "new man," the heir of the future and citizen of the kingdom, takes form. As the concepts which are related to "rebirth" show, this means that the Messiah takes form in the individual and in the community, in the soul and in the body.

Qualities of the Sanctified Life

John Leith argues that there is growth and transformation in Christians' lives even when they do not recognize it. Although the nature of sanctification cannot be precisely defined, it does have identifiable features.

SOURCE

John H. Leith, *The Reformed Imperative: What the Church Has to Say That No One Else Can Say* (Philadelphia: Westminster, 1988), 96–97.

Our pessimism about the possibilities of transforming human life can be easily understood. The lives of many Christians do not significantly differ from the lives of non-Christians. The recalcitrance of human life to renewal and transformation once it has been set by many years of practice or become addicted to drugs is obvious. Yet human lives do change under the power of the Holy Spirit. In many churches, the witness to this transforming power occurs in dramatic conversions. In some church situations, the growth of character takes place below the level of observation. The human self grows under the unobserved influence of the Holy Spirit through the means of grace in the fellowship of the Christian church. More often than we know, hate is changed into love, doubt and fear into trust, deceit into integrity. Persons do grow, not simply in their capacity to love but in the power of imagining how love acts creatively in particular situations. Lives do grow in their capacity to detach themselves from things, to make use of this world's goods without becoming addicted to their necessity. Human beings do grow in their capacity to trust God as well as to love their neighbor, to commit all that they are and do into the keeping of God.

To boast of sanctification is to lose it. Hence there is a wholesome reticence about being holy. Yet modesty must not obscure the fact that we are called to holiness, and in remarkable degrees people achieve holiness under the power of the Holy Spirit in the fellowship of the church. In any case, in the life of the church we live not by the pessimism that may grow out of particular experiences but by the enthusiastic promises of the New Testament that those who are in Jesus Christ become new creatures.

The content of sanctification cannot be defined with precision because of the freedom of the Holy Spirit and the freedom of the human self. It has been understood as the imitation of Christ, as the freedom of a new person in Christ, as the vision of God, as obedience to the law of God. These images can both enlarge and restrict the meaning of sanctification. For example, those who conceive of the Christian life as obedience to the law of God may have the strength of a sure direction, but they may also become legalists who confuse God's laws with the laws of their culture and who lack the creativity to handle complex new moral crises. Others have understood the Christian life in less specific terms, which allow for the freedom of the self and the freedom of God as the obligated life, or the responsible life, or the answering life.

Certain qualities of the sanctified life, however, are clear. To be sanctified is first to trust God, living with the faith, serenity, and dignity of those who know this world as the creation of the God who made us and redeemed us. It is, second, a humane life, open to the neighbor and ready to forgive. It is, third, a life that knows its accountability, its answerability, not only to the self and neighbor but also to God. A fourth quality of the sanctified life is growth in the capacity to detach oneself from the things and enterprises of earth without denying their goodness. As Paul put it, whether we live or die we are the Lord's (Rom. 14:8). Being the Lord's gives a capacity to suffer deprivation without despair and affluence without arrogance.

VOCATION AND DISCIPLESHIP

A hallmark of the Reformed tradition has been its conviction that not only does God elect individuals to faith and salvation, but God also calls them to faithful service in their occupations in the world. Christians are called to glorify God and enjoy God forever not only in worship but also in their daily lives. Consequently, Christians in the Reformed tradition have believed that discipleship does not mean withdrawal and separation from a sinful world but means service to God and witness to the gospel.

FOR FURTHER STUDY

Robert Lowry Calhoun, *God and the Common Life* (Hamden, Conn.: Shoe String Press, 1935). Robert Lowry Calhoun, *God and the Day's Work: Christian Vocation in an Unchristian World* (New York: Association Press, 1943). Donald K. McKim, "The 'Call' in the Reformed Tradition," in *Major Themes in the Reformed Tradition*, ed. Donald K. McKim (Grand Rapids: Wm. B. Eerdmans, 1992), 335–43. Paul S. Minear, *To Die and to Live: Christ's Resurrection and Christian Vocation* (New York: Seabury, 1977).

The Witness of Jesus Christ

Christians are called to discipleship and, as Karl Barth interprets it, that means Christians are called to witness to God's grace in Jesus Christ. Christians are not "little Christs," and the church is not an extension of the incarnation; but Christians are called to witness to Christ before the world.

SOURCE

Barth, *Church Dogmatics*, IV/2:604–5.

The special fellowship of the Christian with Christ involves participation in the passion of His cross. As Christians take up and bear their cross, they do not suffer, of course, with the direct and original and pure obedience which for all its bitterness it was natural and self-evident for the Son of God who was also the Son of Man to render to His Father. Their obedience will never be more than the work of the freedom which they are given. It will always be subsequent. It will always be so stained by all kinds of disobedience that if in the mercy of God it were not invested with the character of obedience it would hardly deserve to be called obedience. Nor is their suffering even the tiniest of contributions to the reconciliation of the world with God. On the contrary, it rests on the fact that this has been perfectly accomplished, not by them but by God Himself in Christ, so that it does not need to be augmented by their suffering or by any lesser Calvaries. Among other men, Christians are simply those to whom its truth and perfection are revealed (not hidden). They arise only as its witnesses. What they suffer is not what Jesus suffered—the judgment of God on the man of unrighteousness, the divine rejection without which the election of man cannot be accomplished. This was suffered by Jesus for the whole world and therefore for them. They exist only—and this is quite enough—in the echo of His sentence, the shadow of His judgment, the after-pains of His rejection. In their cross they have only a small subsequent taste of what the world and they themselves deserved at the hand of God, and Jesus endured in all its frightfulness as their Head and in their place. It is true—and we shall have to return to this—that they too have to suffer rejection at the hands of men. But they do not have to suffer rejection by God. On the contrary they have the sure knowledge that they are His elect. Again, they will not find, as Jesus did, that they are rejected by all men. At the very worst they will be rejected only by many, perhaps a majority. And in this as in other respects they will never be quite innocent in their suffering. They will never suffer merely through the corruption and wickedness of others, or through the undeserved decrees and buffetings of fate or the cosmic process. There is always a very definite (if sometimes disguised) connexion between the sufferings which befall them and their own participation in the transgression and guilt in which all men are continually implicated. And whereas Jesus was quite alone as the One who was rejected and suffered in their place, they can always know that even if they are rejected by ever so many they suffer as members of His community and therefore in company with at least a few others, and can count on the support and intercession, or at least the remembrance, of many more. Finally, whereas the suffering of Jesus is obviously on behalf of all other men, and for their salvation, liberation and exaltation, it is only with serious qualifications that we can say of the suffering of a Christian that it is significant and effective for others, and takes place in their favour. What it means to lay down one's life for one's friends (Jn. 15:13) is only indicated from afar by any conceivable relationship of a human sufferer to others.

External and Internal Calling

Otto Weber describes the calling of the Christian as both external and internal. Although the Reformed tradition has emphasized the former and Weber agrees that calling begins with external proclamation, what the Spirit seeks by means of the outward Word is the "little yes" of the individual in response to the Yes of God.

SOURCE
Weber, *Foundations*, 2:501–3.

"*External and Internal Calling*" = *vocatio externa et interna*. In its extreme definition, proclamation is "external calling." It comes to us solely from outside ourselves, and inquiry into the qualification of the proclaimer must ultimately be answered with reference to the empowerment which is derived purely "from outside." Nevertheless, proclamation as it is empowered throught the Spirit is simultaneously "internal calling." This must now be discussed in greater detail.

The chief point here is to avoid a very easy misunderstanding. That would be to make "external calling" a mere means to the end of the "internal calling" which actually leads to the goal intended, which would be to dispute the empowerment given to "external calling." In contrast to that, it must be emphasized that the concept of "internal calling" is found very seldom in the Reformers, and is never of major influence in Orthodoxy. It would be understandable if it were used by the Reformed to place in question the power which is granted the proclaimed Word in favor of a "secret" *(arcanum)* residing in God or in man. But this never happens. It would also mean that a second mystery would emerge next to that of divine election, which would be the insoluble "secret" of human inwardness—and it would have been a major step to combine or integrate the two. This step was never taken on the Reformed side. In view of the fact that Lutheran Orthodoxy tended to regard the "means of grace" as an institution already realized and effectual in itself, it is clear that it could not even begin to move in this direction. But where some Reformed placed "internal calling," the Lutherans generally set "illumination" as the second step within a so-called "order of salvation" *(ordo salutis)*.

In any event, we must insist that the "efficaciousness" of "external calling" is by no means impinged upon by the idea of "internal calling." When the Heidelberg Catechism derives the assembling of the Community from the Son's "Spirit and Word" (Answer 54), then what is meant is clear: the spoken Word is empowered by the Spirit. It may be rather remarkable that Luther, at the comparable place in his Large Catechism, speaks of the calling together of the Community "only through the Holy Spirit," and totally fails to mention the Word here, although he is not, of course, disregarding it.

The decisive point is our emphasis on the fact that proclamation is empowered by the Spirit, but not relativized. This can be concluded when we carefully read the New Testament witness in John 20:22f.; Acts 4:8, 13:9; 1 Corinthians 2:4; Romans 15:19; and 1 Thessalonians 1:5. Proclamation does not start out as ambivalent and then later become distinct in the inward part of man. It is unified, and it is a valid event. Just as the validity of the Community's prayer and that of its members is granted by the Spirit (cf. Rom. 8:15; Gal. 4:6; Rom. 8:26f.), and just as their odes or hymns are empowered and infilled by the Spirit (Eph. 5:18f.; Col. 3:16), the proclaimed witness of the Community is valid and authoritative by virtue of the Spirit's power. This validity is not a power which automatically creates faith. And the older theology of both the Lutherans and the Reformed never held that. However, the Reformed did make proclamation the effectual instrument of the eternal divine decision, which was obviously terrifyingly twofold, whereas the Lutherans regarded the proclaimed Word as finally effectual only in combination with the faith with which men responded to it. Clearly the stronger emphasis on "subjectivity" is found on the Lutheran side. But even when the traditional views are dealt with critically, as we have done, and have been opposed with a Christological understanding of election, the result can scarcely be the deduction of the "security" of the one who merely hears (or is baptized as an infant), but rather that the divine decision made in Christ and announced to us in the calling of proclamation does effectually call forth our Yes—or effectually places us in the position of No, which cannot be further illuminated with any of the methods of dialectic. Paul accepts the possibility of this other effect (2 Cor. 2:16; 4:3), as does Acts (13:48), and likewise the rest of the Old and New Testaments (Calvin refers to Ezek. 2:3; 12:2; Jer. 1:10; Isa. 6:9, 10; John 12:39f.; Matt. 13:11). This impenetrable and puzzling No cannot be understood in terms of man's subjectivity. It is a part of the Word's character as a scandal. But that does not mean that the Word, which obviously does not automatically enforce "faith," is "hanging in mid-air," fluctuating between two possibilities. Its very unambiguity is what summons forth the No. The effector of proclamation is the Spirit, and thus God's decision which reaches man in proclamation does not impugn its efficaciousness but is rather its presupposition. Certainty about the decision about man, made in Jesus Christ, makes it impossible for the bearer of proclamation to appeal to election and then take no pains in regard to the form of his proclamation, since everything depends on the work of the Spirit which takes place in the inward man. The work of the Spirit resides first in the outward Word and the activities associated with it (the so-called sacraments). But it is directed toward the inward man. However, it does not make man's inwardness its criterion.

"Internal calling" is nothing other than the inconceivable miracle that the person called under the Yes of God then speaks his "little yes," not because some kind of irresistible force worked upon him, but in the freedom which the Spirit provides. This little Yes does not create something new. But it receives everything. The mystery of our relationship to God is not to be sought in our subjectivity nor in its exclusion, but rather in the fact that the freedom is instituted in us within which we ourselves do say yes, do give witness, do accede to the truth.

The Call to Love the Enemy

Jürgen Moltmann raises the question of what the gospel's call to love not only one's neighbor but also one's enemy means in the twentieth century in the context of "the politics of national security."

SOURCE

Jürgen Moltmann, "Discipleship of Christ in an Age of Nuclear War," in idem, *On Human Dignity: Political Theology and Ethics*, trans. M. Douglas Meeks (Philadelphia: Fortress, 1984), 126–27.

The love which Jesus puts in place of retaliation is the love of the enemy. Love of friends, mutual love, is nothing special; it is only retaliation of good for good. Love of the enemy, however, is not recompensing but is rather an anticipating, intelligent, and creative love. Whoever repays evil with good must be really free and strong. Love for the enemy does not mean surrendering to the enemy, submission to the enemy's will. Rather, such a person is no longer in the stance of reacting to the enemy, but seeks to create something new, a new situation for the enemy and for himself or herself. Such a person follows his or her own intention and no longer allows the law of actions to be prescribed by the foe. Jesus did not die with a curse upon his enemies but rather with a prayer for them. In his life, his passion, and his dying Jesus revealed the perfection of God: "Be perfect, even as your heavenly Father is perfect."

Of what does God's perfection consist? In no way is a moral perfectionism meant. It consists of that love which is long-suffering, friendly, and patient, which does not add to evil or carry a grudge, which bears all things, believes all things, and hopes all things (1 Corinthians 13). God's perfection lies in the fact that he loves his enemies, blesses them, does good to them, and does not return evil for their evil. It is precisely from this that we all live. The whole world lives from this divine reality, even if it does not know it. As Jesus said, God is like the sun rising on the evil and the good, or like the rain pouring down upon the just and the unjust. Hence, God bears all and maintains all because he hopes for each one. God's perfection is his limitless ability for suffering, his almightiness is his patient suffering for and with all things. God's uniqueness is his inexhaustible creative power of love.

In former times, we have asked only What serves our security, what serves our survival? But now, in listening to the Sermon on the Mount and seeking to experience God's love for the enemy, we must rephrase the basic question: What is the most helpful thing for the enemy? In what way can we best bless those who curse us? How do we do good for those who hate us? To remain concrete for my situation in Germany: Since we Germans fear the Russians (and otherwise almost nothing on the face of the earth), we must ask, What helps the Russian people to gain peace more, our further armament or our disarmament? In what way can we bless the communist who curses us? In what way can we do good for the peoples of the Third World who consider us their exploiter and enemy?

The politics of national security is, to a large degree, a politics of anxiety and fear. Because we have anxiety we demand security. Because we demand security, we increase our armaments. As we increase our arms we give terror to our adversaries. Therefore our adversaries also increase their arms. Quite to the contrary of this system, creative intelligent love arises out of freedom, out of the freedom to be a child of the eternal God (which means out of the freedom from the fear of temporal death). Out of this freedom can come love for the enemy and work for peace.

Can one, however, really become free from this anxiety? One can become at least a bit freer from it when one recognizes the danger and consciously enters into the risk. To the degree that the risk of the vulnerable, defenseless but creative life becomes conscious to us, the more free and patient we become. Only the unknown and the repressed make us really anxious. In this sense I am personally willing and ready to live without armaments.

CHRISTIAN FREEDOM

For much of its history the Reformed tradition discussed the nature of Christian freedom in relation to the category of law. The freedom Christians receive through God's forgiving and justifying grace in Jesus Christ was contrasted with the condemnation and indictment of human sin exposed by the law. In Calvin's theology, the three uses of the law (to condemn sin, to restrain sin and protect the community, and, principally, to urge the regenerate to obey God's will) were developed in conjunction with the three aspects of Christian freedom (freedom from the law, freedom to obey the law, and freedom in "things indifferent" or *adiaphora*). Calvin, however, separated his discussion of religious freedom (*Institutes* 3.19) from his analysis of the church's relation to the state and the nature of political freedom (*Institutes* 4.20).

In the nineteenth and twentieth centuries, the discussion of freedom in Reformed theology has been significantly influenced by historical events. America's Civil War and its struggle over slavery, the experience of the church in Germany during the Second World War, the civil rights movement in the United States during the 1960s, the policy of apartheid in South Africa, and the emergence of "base ecclesial communities" in Latin America during the last half of the twentieth century are only a few of the events that have shaped the theological interpretation of freedom. Particularly important and controversial has been the shift in idiom and paradigm from "freedom" to "liberation." Those theologians who have welcomed the change argue that freedom in the Western church has been a liberal notion that valued autonomy at the expense of justice. On the other hand, the criticism of the language of liberation has been that it uncritically identifies the gospel and the theological reality of freedom with a particular ideology and social agenda.

FOR FURTHER STUDY

Peter C. Hodgson, *New Birth of Freedom: A Theology of Bondage and Liberation* (Philadelphia: Fortress, 1976). Alexander J. McKelway, *The Freedom of God and Human Liberation* (London: SCM and Philadelphia: Trinity, 1990).

Freedom from and Freedom for

Karl Barth draws an important distinction between a human freedom which is "freedom from" and that freedom which is rooted in the freedom of God and is "freedom for." Although human beings never fully realize the latter, it is in God's freedom for the world that freedom is seen to be joyful.

SOURCE

Karl Barth, "The Gift of Freedom: Foundation of Evangelical Ethics," in idem, *The Humanity of God,* trans. John Newton Thomas and Thomas Wieser (Richmond: John Knox, 1960), 77–78.

As a gift of God, human freedom cannot contradict divine freedom. This leads to certain limitations regarding human freedom which are similar to those mentioned in our earlier attempt to define the freedom of God. We now make bold to say:

(1) Human freedom as a gift of God does not allow for any vague choices between various possibilities. The reign of chance and ambiguity is excluded. For the free God Himself, the giver of man's freedom, is no blind accident, no tyrant. He is the Lord, choosing and determining Himself unmistakably once and for all. He is His own law.

(2) Human freedom is not realized in the solitary detachment of an individual in isolation from his fellow men. God is *a se* (for Himself), but He is *pro nobis* (for us). For us! It is true that He who gave man freedom because He is man's friend, is also *pro me* (for me). But I am not Man, I am only *a man,* and I am a man only in relation to my fellow men. Only in encounter and in communion with them may I receive the gift of freedom. God is *pro me* because He is *pro nobis.*

(3) Human freedom is only secondarily freedom *from* limitations and threats. Primarily it is freedom *for.*

(4) Human freedom is not to be understood as freedom to assert, to preserve, to justify and save oneself. God is primarily free *for;* the Father is free for the Son, the Son for the Father in the unity of the Spirit. The one God is free for man as his Creator, as the Lord of the covenant, as the beginner and perfecter of his history, his *Heilsgeschichte.* God says "Yes." Only once this "Yes" is said, He also says "No." Thereby He reveals Himself to be *free from* all that is alien and hostile to His nature. Only once this "Yes" is said, is He free for Himself and for His own glory. Human freedom is freedom only within the limitations of God's own freedom.

And thus we can see that freedom is *being joyful.* Freedom is the great gift, totally unmerited and wondrous beyond understanding. It awakens the receiver to true selfhood and new life. It is a gift from *God,* from the source of all goodness, an ever-new token of His faithfulness and mercy. The gift is unambiguous and cannot fail. Through this gift man who was irretrievably separated and alienated from God is called into discipleship. This is why freedom is joy! Certainly, man does not live up to this freedom. Even worse, he fails in every respect. It is true enough that he does not know any longer the natural freedom which was bestowed upon him in creation; he does not know as yet the ultimate freedom in store for him at the completion of his journey, in the ultimate fulfillment of his existence. It is true enough that man may presently know and enjoy this freedom through the abiding Spirit of the Father and the Son only in spite of sin, flesh, and death; in spite of the world, his earthly anxiety and his worldly nature; and in spite of himself in his persistent temptation. This however, does not prevent man from being enabled to know and to live out this freedom in incomparable and inexhaustible joy, limited as his own awareness may be. Some may not want any part of it, and at times we all feel this way. But this does not change anything. God's gift is there for all. It is poured out at the beginning of our journey, at its destination, and most certainly also in our present plight. Freedom is waiting here and now to be received and lived out in joy, albeit a joy that is not without travail.

Freedom as Obedience

French Reformed theologian Jacques Ellul develops the paradox that true freedom is to be found in obedience to God's law. Such obedience is not primarily a matter of moral obligation but is derived from devotion to and worship of the God incarnate in Jesus Christ.

SOURCE

Jacques Ellul, *The Ethics of Freedom,* trans. Geoffrey W. Bromiley (Grand Rapids: Wm. B. Eerdmans, 1976), 122–23.

Freedom for God means that man becomes responsible before God. At a later point we shall have to examine responsibility as an expression of freedom. The first element in responsibility, however, is this responsibility towards God. God, the Creator, wills that man should be responsible before him because this responsibility itself is an expression of dialogue and communication. God speaks and we have to respond. Man finds himself questioned—although he is not, of course, responsible before being freed by God. This is a point which is often made in the New Testament epistles: If you had not known the law, you would not have committed sin (cf. Romans 7:7). Knowing the law surely means more than being set in a moral system, and committing sin means more than disobeying such a system.

The deeper meaning is that the law is the word of God. It is thus liberation. The aim of the commandment is to free, not to enslave. It is when I have the freedom to receive God's word, and to see in it a commandment which concerns me, that I know what it is to obey and I become responsible for my act. For it is then that I am free to reply to God's question. To be responsible is not to be crushed by an indefinite culpability. It is not having to bear the burden of all that takes place or is produced in the world. It is not having to accept the penalty of an inevitable fault which is the result of original sin. On the contrary, it is being questioned by the God who frees us so that we can freely respond to his question. This question is both the question: "What hast thou done?" (Genesis 4:10; cf. v. 9) and the question: "What wilt thou that I should do unto thee?" (Mark 10:51), or: "Wilt thou be made whole?" The two questions belong together. We become responsible the moment we hear at one and the same time this double question of God. At this moment what we traditionally call the law is transformed, for it ceases to be a pressing duty and becomes permission. Freedom for God is the permission which man is given to obey God and to serve him.

I realize that these statements sound paradoxical. We find it so hard to believe that God is truly the Father and that he is totally in Jesus Christ giving his life for us. Because of this lack of faith we continue to regard the law as morality, duty, constraint, and obligation. To read it thus is always the result of unbelief. If we have even a little understanding of the fact that God did seriously undertake to live with and for man in Jesus Christ, if we truly think of him as radically different, so that finally we cannot say anything about him at all but can only bow down and worship him in silence, as his undertaking demands if it is really taken seriously, then we can see that this unlikely and unheard of event represents a summons to the service of God, that it is in effect a permission that has been given us and not a constraint, an authorization and not a duty. For in this service we do something with God and even for God even though God does not finally need it and could get on quite well without it. In this service we have a part in the work that God does even though this is complete in itself and we have no right to have a part in it. In this service we discover a hidden and secret dimension which gives meaning to our lives. We lift the lid, and we are allowed to do it ourselves. Without us, as Baudelaire rightly says, the lid cannot be lifted. The authorization which God grants is for us a fulfilment and an accomplishment. The commandment of God which begins with this service of God is never a personal restriction and diminution.

Jesus Christ the Liberator

In Jesus Christ, argues Daniel L. Migliore, the Christian community sees the liberating activity of God and hears the call to participate responsibly and critically in movements of liberation. Migliore suggests three criteria for assessing responsible Christian participation.

SOURCE

Daniel L. Migliore, *Called to Freedom: Liberation Theology and the Future of Christian Doctrine* (Philadelphia: Westminster, 1980), 60–62.

First, in the light of Jesus the liberator, the cause of human liberation must be seen holistically rather than partially. There is a tendency among all liberation movements to claim ultimacy and exclusivity as the vanguard of the future. The question whether sexism or racism is the root cause of human alienation is pointless, for human beings need to be liberated from both. The debate whether exploitative capitalism or totalitarian socialism is the lesser of evils makes little sense, for both political rights and economic justice are essential to the development of free human life in a peaceful society. Liberation movements have a tendency to perpetuate the special-interest and group-bound consciousness that characterizes the old world of oppression. Jesus did not set people free by creating a kind of negative identity. To be sure, there is a partisanship in the ministry and proclamation of Jesus, a partisanship for the poor and the exploited, the sick and the dying, the sinners and the accursed. But this partisanship has the goal of new community. Jesus frees and reconciles. Christians will be characterized by their partisanship for the oppressed, but they will not identify the kingdom of God with the goals of a particular liberation movement. Their partisanship will be critical. . . .

Second, in the light of Jesus the liberator, true liberation means not the exchange of the power over others from one set of masters to another but the transformation of the meaning of power. The passion and death of Jesus at the hands of the established religious and political authorities creates a dangerous memory that stands opposed to all political idolatries, civil religion, nationalism, and militarism. To be crucified with Christ is to be freed from the bondage of these gods. The cross of Christ is the sign of God's identification with the victims of oppression in history. But it is also the expression of God's love which is greater than and different from the power possessed by masters and desired by slaves. Just as Jesus rejected the way of the Zealots, so Christians will resist the temptation to make revolutionary violence a *policy* by which the violence of the oppressors will be overcome. . . .

Third, in the light of Jesus the liberator, the human liberation we seek is acknowledged as a gift as well as a task. We are set free by the grace of God and called to the freedom of service. Freedom begins in joyful receptiveness of God's acceptance and affirmation of us. That is the basis of our call to solidarity with others. Openness to the grace of God is the foundation of active engagement in liberation struggles. Without the joy of the provisional gift of freedom in the Spirit of Christ, the call to promote freedom in the world becomes burdensome and legalistic. This has been the experience of many young people in recent years. If human liberation, including our own, is only a task and not also a gift, then discouragement, resignation, and cynicism eventually triumph. Faith in the lordship of Jesus the liberator is the basis of the joy and confidence of the Christian community. In the power of the Spirit of the crucified and risen Lord, perseverance in the service of God's justice, freedom, and peace is possible.

Freedom and Social Structures

In its Confession of Faith (1977), the Presbyterian-Reformed Church in Cuba affirms that Christians will know real freedom as they become advocates of love and justice in the structures of human society.

SOURCE

"Confession of Faith" (1977) of the Presbyterian-Reformed Church in Cuba, in *Reformed Witness Today*, 175–76.

FREEDOM:
A HUMAN RESPONSIBILITY

The Scriptures teach that the human being, different from any other creature, is a "free" being. Human freedom is, however, a "responsible, freedom." According to the Scriptures, human freedom is not doing what one wishes "out of whim or conceit." Neither is it the "free will" of the philosophers. The Bible teaches that human freedom is responsible, voluntary and conscious obedience of the Divine Will.

The Will of God—as it is described in the Bible—is a Will of loving grace for the creature. God's loving Grace for the human being is revealed concretely in the realization of Justice and Peace in the world, in the establishment of his Kingdom of Freedom and Love.

Therefore, the Church proclaims that the human being is "predestined to be free."

The Church teaches that we will be free to the extent which we obey the loving Will of God, serving effectively the cause of Justice and Peace among all human beings.

The Church lives in a real and concrete practice of human freedom on the part of the members as they become committed participants in the quantitative growth and the qualitative development of "love-justice" in the social-political economical structures of human society, including the very structure of the Church as a social-juridical institution.

CHRISTIAN MARRIAGE AND FAMILY

The interpretation of marriage is an example of the attempt by Reformed theology to remain faithful to its deepest convictions and also responsive to developments in society and culture. In the Reformed tradition the categories of covenant, faithfulness, and promise keeping have been used to describe God's relation to the world and the quality of relationships to which God calls human beings. Although the Westminster Confession of 1647 affirmed that "nothing but Adultery, or such wilfull assertion as can no way be remedied, by the Church, or Civil Magistrate, is cause sufficient of dissolving the bond of Marriage," theologians in the twentieth century, while still affirming the importance of marriage, have had to come to terms with the patriarchal character of most Western social institutions (including marriage), the widespread oppression and abuse of women, new discoveries about human sexuality, the rapid increase in divorce and single-parent families, and the struggle of gays and lesbians to find acceptance within society and the church. By the end of the twentieth century, the result was pervasive confusion and disagreement in most Christian denominations, including the Reformed, concerning the nature and acceptable practice of human sexuality, whether "marriage" referred only to heterosexual relationships, and whether gays and lesbians should be eligible for ordained positions in the life of the church.

FOR FURTHER STUDY

Elizabeth R. Achtemeier, *The Committed Marriage* (Philadelphia: Westminster, 1976). Geoffrey Bromiley, *God and Marriage* (Grand Rapids: Wm. B. Eerdmans, 1980). Shirley C. Guthrie, Jr., "Toward a Theology of Christian Marriage," in *Major Themes in the*

Reformed Tradition, ed. Donald K. McKim (Grand Rapids: Wm. B. Eerdmans, 1992), 326–31. James B. Nelson, *Between Two Gardens: Reflections on Sexuality and Religious Experience* (New York: Pilgrim, 1983). James B. Nelson, *Embodiment: An Approach to Sexuality and Christian Theology* (Minneapolis: Augsburg, 1978).

Marriage as Divine Institution

Charles Hodge's interpretation of marriage is typical of that of many theologians in the last half of the nineteenth century: Marriage is primarily a theological and not a social reality. Hence, Adam and Eve had no need of a justice of the peace (but notice the comparison of Eden with a desert island!). Marriage is not, in the first place, vows between two human beings, but vows by each to God.

SOURCE

Hodge, *Systematic Theology,* 3:376–77.

MARRIAGE A DIVINE INSTITUTION

Marriage is a divine institution. (1.) Because founded on the nature of man as constituted by God. He made man male and female, and ordained marriage as the indispensable condition of the continuance of the race. (2.) Marriage was instituted before the existence of civil society, and therefore cannot in its essential nature be a civil institution. As Adam and Eve were married not in virtue of any civil law, or by the intervention of a civil magistrate, so any man and woman cast together on a desert island, could lawfully take each other as husband and wife. It is a degradation of the institution to make it a mere civil contract. (3.) God commanded men to marry, when He commanded them to increase, and multiply and replenish the earth. (4.) God in his word has prescribed the duties belonging to the marriage relation; He has made known his will as to the parties who may lawfully be united in marriage; He has determined the continuance of the relation; and the causes which alone justify its dissolution. These matters are not subject to the will of the parties, or to the authority of the State. (5.) The vow of mutual fidelity made by husband and wife, is not made exclusively by each one to the other, but by each to God. When a man connects himself with a Christian Church he enters into covenant with his brethren in the Lord; mutual obligations are assumed; but nevertheless the covenant is made with God. He joins the Church in obedience to the will of God; he promises to regulate his faith and practice by the divine word; and the vow of fidelity is made to God. It is the same in marriage. It is a voluntary, mutual compact between husband and wife. They promise to be faithful to each other; but nevertheless they act in obedience to God, and promise to Him that they will live together as man and wife, according to his word. Any violation of the compact is, therefore, a violation of a vow made to God.

Marriage is not a sacrament in the sense which in baptism and the Lord's Supper are sacraments, nor in the sense of the Romish Church; but it is none the less a sacred institution. Its solemnization is an office of religion. It should, therefore, be entered upon with due solemnity and in the fear of God; and should be celebrated, i.e., the ceremony should be performed by a minister of Christ. He alone is authorized to see to it that the law of God is adhered to; and he alone can receive and register the marriage vows as made to God. The civil magistrate can only witness it as a civil contract, and it is consequently to ignore its religious character and sanction to have it celebrated by a civil officer. As the essence of the marriage contract is the mutual compact of the parties in the sight of God and in the presence of witnesses, it is not absolutely necessary that it should be celebrated by a minister of religion or even by a civil magistrate. It may be lawfully solemnized, as among the Quakers, without the intervention of either. Nevertheless as it is of the greatest importance that the religious nature of the institution should be kept in view, it is incumbent on Christians, so far as they themselves are concerned, to insist that it should be solemnized as a religious service.

Marriage as a Special Divine Calling

According to Karl Barth, marriage is not a necessity of nature, but a special divine calling. God calls some people to marriage and others to "the unmarried state." Marriage is a life-partnership, and as such is the proof of love but is also more comprehensive than love.

SOURCE

Barth, *Church Dogmatics*, III/4:183–87.

1. When marriage is seen in the light of the divine command, it is surely evident that the decision for the way of marriage is for some, as the choice of the unmarried state for others, the matter of a supremely particular divine vocation. It is no injustice to marriage, but rather an

appreciation of its true dignity, to observe that it is in no sense self-evident that man should settle in this centre of the whole sphere and thus reach in his own individual life the intersecting point of all the lines visible in it. There is no necessity of nature nor general divine law in virtue of which every man is permitted or commanded to take a wife, or every woman a husband. If this is permitted and commanded, it is a special distinction, a special divine calling, a gift and grace. A man enters and remains in the married state because he recognises that this is the divine will for him, and therefore obligatory. But this obviously means that God might have willed it differently. He has accepted marriage in obedience to the former realisation. He is thus free for this permission and obligation, not by nature, or from the very outset, or in his own right, but he is freed for it by God's calling, gift and grace. . . .

As marriage is the matter of a special divine calling, it is wholly subject to the divine command. A true and obedient marriage is one which in all its elements fulfils this special divine vocation. Just as man is a totality which as such, and not merely in certain relations, is subject to the divine command and is obedient or disobedient, so is it with marriage. Its component parts, as already indicated, are all interrelated and all count quite seriously. Where there is a vocation to marriage, it is a vocation to the venture and its fulfilment and realisation as a whole. And when we enquire concerning obedience to this vocation, we must do so in relation to this whole, asking with equal attention to each of its parts what obedience or disobedience implies. We do not treat the matter seriously if we isolate and abstract, i.e., select one of these elements, maintaining that this is where the question of good and evil is decided and ignoring all the other questions except a few chosen at random, or even stating quite expressly that they are indifferent from a Christian standpoint. To be sure, we may produce a doctrine of marriage which is apparently very solid and imposing because thoroughly examined from our selected standpoint. But we cannot do justice to the reality, or what is worse to the divine command to which it is subject. Serious moral insight is possible at this point, and serious moral instruction can be given, only when—precisely because it is a question of the divine command—we are prepared to consider marriage as a whole, at the very salutary risk of only then perceiving how difficult it is not to apply some principle but really to seek a command of God, and how little obvious the answer is. The answer is not obvious for the simple reason that in this connexion a whole series of serious questions emerges and a whole series of equally serious answers has to be given—answers which must be given one after the other, which, if they are really to be serious, can only be given in this way and not, as hasty tyros suppose, in the form of a closed system. Placed under the command of God, marriage is a tremendously big thing. It is full of meaning and promise in many directions. It is not merely two-edged, but many-edged. For it is a totality which consists of many coherent elements, all equally important, all equally decisive for good and ill, all subject in the same way to the divine command, all in the light of the command revealing its blessing but also its judgment, the goodness of the Creator and the failure of man. . . .

The proposition which, with all that it implies, must be fundamental is that marriage is the special life-partnership established and maintained between a particular man and a particular woman. Vocation to marriage is vocation to this life-partnership. To this extent marriage is more than love. It must spring from love if it is to take shape as a genuine life-partnership. It must always be fed and sustained by love if it is to have firm subsistence as such. But we shall have to speak of this later. The essence of marriage is more comprehensive than what we must understand by the term love in the sense of the special love of husband and wife. It consists essentially in the life-partnership established and subsisting between these two. As such it is the consummation of what is sought and striven for in genuine love. Marriage as a life-partnership is the touchstone whether or not this seeking and striving was and is that of genuine love. Marriage as a life-partnership is therefore the proof of love. In marriage as a life-partnership it is a matter of repeating in all seriousness the Yes of love. But "in all seriousness" means in a life which is the whole life of man, in toil and care, in joy and pain, in sickness and health, in youth and age, in wrestling with the many questions, small and great, inner and outer, individual and social, which lovers united in a common life can and may as little evade as other men, but all these things in the fellowship of their life, in some way or other together, in the special orientation of the one on the other, in the evenness of step between the two selected and willed for this purpose. "In all seriousness" means experiencing all this in the succession of unforeseeably many days of twenty-four hours and unforeseeably many years of fifty-two weeks, with the intimacy of an everyday and everynight companionship which discloses everything on both sides, in which each very soon gets to know the other with terrifying exactitude, and in which the greatest thing can become astonishingly small and the smallest astonishingly great. "In all seriousness" means to have become a collective, a We, a pair, and to live as such, not merely outwardly, but inwardly as the only possible basis of the outward, and not merely in the life of mutual relations, but in the thinking, willing, and feeling of both participants upon which these relations must rest if they are to be tenable. This seriousness of love is what we mean by marriage as a life-partnership. And when love stands the test of this seriousness, it means that marriage is a partnership which is fulfilled not merely according to the claims of duty, but gladly, joyfully and willingly, in repetition of the Yes of love. . . .

Sexuality and Partnership

Letty Russell argues that sexuality is best understood in terms of the categories of eschatology and partnership: There is no single pattern of sexuality in the Bible, and a church that believes in a God who is transforming the world must not absolutize one cultural form.

SOURCE

Letty M. Russell, *The Future of Partnership* (Philadelphia: Westminster, 1979), 95–98.

ESCHATOLOGICAL PERSPECTIVES

We are God's utopia: created to become full human beings in relation to God, others, and ourselves. In human beings sexuality is *omnipresent* but not *omnipotent*. What distinguishes us from animals is not genital sex or reproduction, but the ability to assign meaning to these actions. All our ways of being as male and female can be vehicles for relationships of love and growth as we develop in Christ toward a full human personhood (Eph. 4:13). But they can also be vehicles for broken relationships of hatred and alienation among persons.

In approaching New Testament *teachings on marriage* in an eschatological perspective, we must remind ourselves again that the Biblical patterns changed over the centuries and were not static. They included polygamy and extended families and did not reflect the pattern of small nuclear families. They did reflect a strong patriarchal structure in which females were honored as mothers and emphasis was on procreation for survival.

The only direct teaching of Jesus on marriage is that contained in the conflict story of Mark 10:2–12. This saying of Jesus is presented as a response to the challenge of the Pharisees and not as a new law. Jesus is challenged about the meaning of Deut. 24:1 which permits divorce of the woman by a man if she does something "objectionable." What was objectionable was a subject for debate among different schools of Pharisees. Instead of allowing himself to be drawn into this debate, Jesus points to the deepest intention of marriage as seen in Genesis 1 and 2.

221

Marriage is a gift of God as a relationship of solidarity and loyalty for the protection of family life and the life of the community. It appears that Jesus regarded marriage as an indissoluble union in which *both* the husband and the wife have equal responsibility.

How can we interpret this passage today through the leading of the Holy Spirit? First, by recognizing that Jesus' constant concern was not the "law" itself, but going behind it to God's intention and then applying it to actual persons. Thus, for instance, in his concern to defend the disciples' plucking of corn on the Sabbath he said, "This sabbath was made for [persons], not [persons] for the sabbath" (Mark 2:27).

Secondly, Jesus and Paul viewed the social order, like the natural order, as God given in a certain pattern. This is not as we usually view social order today, as a changing construct of human organization. Yet Jesus was willing to treat each situation contextually, and with concern for the persons involved. All things were viewed in the light of the breaking in of God's Kingdom and of the relationships of love, obedience, and integrity made possible by God's love.

Lastly, alongside this one brief conflict story in which Jesus points out the basic truth that God did not intend divorce and broken, unfaithful relationships, we have other indications that Jesus welcomed all the outsiders and sinners and reserved his sharpest criticism for those who were hypocrites in thinking about right actions and forgetting the orientation of their hearts (Matt. 5:28). If we keep in mind that marriage was made for man and woman, but not man and woman for marriage, we may be able to raise the deeper question of ways relationships between persons in our time can be supported as relationships of trust, mutuality, and responsibility.

Paul, like Jesus, follows the injunction that man and woman are not made for marriage. Both he and Jesus broke the customs of their times by refusing marriage for the sake of their work for the Kingdom of God and the good news of God's liberation. In 1 Cor. 7:10–31, Paul quotes Jesus' saying about divorce. Yet in his advice on marriage, divorce, celibacy, and slavery Paul is pointing toward an ethic of the New Age in which all such relationships are *hōs mē* (as if not), because they are at the disposal of the wider task of witnessing to the gospel. In Christ the established orders of creation have been decisively changed so that religious, racial, and sexual differences are not lost as a basis of our self-identity, but they are not counted of ultimate significance. All are set free to be accepted as equals in Christ's church (Gal. 3:28).

The use of the metaphor of marriage in Eph. 5:21–33 to illuminate the relationship of Christ and the church continues the Old Testament understanding of marriage as a sign of the covenant relationship between God and Israel. In this sense of mutual faithfulness and sacrifice the metaphor is very powerful for understanding the meaning of covenant partnership. However, in its usage in church tradition this text has served to reinforce the model of subjection of the wives (church) to their husbands (Christ). The result is that women are tied to the structures of fallen creation through sexist attitudes, and marriage is often unable to represent a true metaphor of deep mutuality.

Christian freedom stems from our justification by God's grace through faith and no outward circumstance can be said either to merit or to earn God's love, nor can it be considered a barrier to being welcomed into the fellowship of the body of Christ. Paul makes this clear in his struggles against the requirement that all male Gentile Christians be circumcised. This insistence seems to have raised as much controversy in the early churches as the issues of the ordination of woman or of homosexuals are raising in the churches of today (Acts 10—11; Gal. 2). For Paul, circumcision or no circumcision was not of ultimate importance except as it became a stumbling block for the understanding and acceptance of God's free gift of faith (1 Cor. 7:17–20). Similar struggles are constantly part of church life as human beings seek out ways to restrict and control God's grace, requiring converts to become "like me" before being allowed entrance into the church.

The circumstances of Paul's time and his expectation of the Parousia never provided occasion for Paul to work out fully and consistently his teachings in regard to slave and free, male and female. Nor did they provide occasions for our particular questions of today such as: Does a "secular" person have to become "religious" in order to share in church life; or an African become "European" before being a Christian; or a homosexual become "heterosexual" before being accepted by Christ?

All these questions are pressing in on us today. The questions themselves are signs of the New Age breaking into our lives, for the Spirit of Christ is manifested in the lives of those who formerly were not "qualified" to minister among us. When God's Spirit was manifested in the life of Cornelius, the centurion, Peter was led to see that "God shows no partiality," and to baptize him (Acts 10:34; Gal. 2:6). When challenged, Peter said,

> If then God gave the same gift to them as . . . to us when we believed in the Lord Jesus Christ, who was I that I could withstand God? (Acts 11:17)

God's Ordering of
the Interpersonal Life

The Confession of 1967 of the reunited Presbyterian Church (U.S.A.) was written in the midst of the so-called sexual revolution of the 1960s. The document recognizes that anarchy and alienation can damage sexual relationships and calls the church to be a community that encourages responsible freedom.

SOURCE

"The Confession of 1967," in *Book of Confessions*, 9.47.

The relationship between man and woman exemplifies in a basic way God's ordering of the interpersonal life for which he created mankind. Anarchy in sexual relationships is a symptom of man's alienation from God, his neighbor, and himself. Man's perennial confusion about the meaning of sex has been aggravated in our day by the availability of new means for birth control and the treatment of infection, by the pressures of urbanization, by the exploitation of sexual symbols in mass communication, and by world overpopulation. The church, as the household of God, is called to lead men out of this alienation into the responsible freedom of the new life in Christ. Reconciled to God, each person has joy in and respect for his own humanity and that of other persons; a man and woman are enabled to marry, to commit themselves to a mutually shared life, and to respond to each other in sensitive and lifelong concern; parents receive the grace to care for children in love and to nurture their individuality. The church comes under the judgment of God and invites rejection by man when it fails to lead men and women into the full meaning of life together, or withholds the compassion of Christ from those caught in the moral confusion of our time.

WORSHIP AND PRAYER

Theological classics such as Augustine's *Confessions* and Anselm's *Proslogion* were written in the form of prayers. In these texts the language of prayer was not simply a literary device. For Augustine and Anselm there was an important relation between what was written, to whom it was written, and the form in which it was written. That is, they understood theology to be "faith in search of understanding."

There are theologians in the modern period who have a similar understanding of the nature of theology and the importance of worship and prayer, but much of contemporary theology stands in striking contrast to the classical tradition. Not only is it unusual to find serious theology in the nineteenth and twentieth centuries written in the form of prayer, but modern theologians, especially those in universities, have sometimes written extensive systematic interpretations of Christian faith without discussing worship and prayer. In contemporary theology God is often an academic problem and an important cultural and political symbol rather than a living, personal, purposive reality in human history.

FOR FURTHER STUDY

Karl Barth, *Evangelical Theology: An Introduction* (Grand Rapids: Wm. B. Eerdmans, 1963), 159–70. Brunner, *Dogmatics*, 3:324–35. John E. Burkhart, *Worship: A Searching Examination of the Liturgical Experience* (Philadelphia: Westminster, 1982). Howard G. Hageman, *Pulpit and Table: Some Chapters in the History of Worship in the Reformed Churches* (Richmond: John Knox, 1962). James Hastings Nichols, *Corporate Worship in the Reformed Tradition* (Philadelphia: Westminster, 1968). Hughes Oliphant Old, *Worship That Is Reformed According to Scripture* (Atlanta: John Knox, 1984). Nicholas Wolterstorff, "The Reformed Liturgy," in *Major Themes in the Reformed Tradition*, ed. Donald K. McKim (Grand Rapids: Wm. B. Eerdmans, 1992), 273–304.

Prayer as an Encounter of Wills

P. T. Forsyth argues that prayer is not simply a spiritual exercise but "a cause acting on the course of God's world." His primary metaphor for understanding prayer is wrestling.

SOURCE

P. T. Forsyth, *The Soul of Prayer* (London: Independent Press, 1949), 82–84.

There are many plain obstacles to the deepening of spiritual life, amid which I desire to name here only one; it is prayer conceived merely, or chiefly, as *submission*, resignation, quietism. We say too soon, "Thy will be done"; and too ready acceptance of a situation as His will often means feebleness or sloth. It may be His will that we surmount His will. It may be His higher will that we resist His lower. Prayer is an act of will much more than of sentiment, and its triumph is more than acquiescence. Let us submit when we *must*, but let us keep the submission in reserve rather than in action, as a ground tone rather than the sole effort. Prayer with us has largely ceased to be *wrestling*. But is that not the dominant scriptural idea? It is not the sole idea, but is it not the dominant? And is not our subdued note often but superinduced and unreal?

I venture to enlarge on this last head, by way of meeting some who hesitate to speak of the power of prayer to alter God's will. I offer two points:

I. Prayer may really change the will of God, or, if not His will, His intention.

II. It may, like other human energies of godly sort, take the form of resisting the will of God. Resisting His will may be doing His will.

I. As to the first point. If this is not believed the earnestness goes out of prayer. It becomes either a ritual, or a soliloquy only overheard by God; just as thought with the will out of it degenerates into dreaming or brooding, where we are more passive than active. Prayer is not merely the meeting of two moods or two affections, the laying of the head on a divine bosom in trust and surrender. That may have its place in religion, but it is not the nerve and soul of prayer. Nor is it religious reverie. Prayer is an encounter of *wills*—till one will or the other give way. It is not a spiritual exercise merely, but in its maturity it is a cause acting on the course of God's world. It is, indeed, by God's grace that prayer is a real cause, but such it is. And of course there must be in us a faith corresponding to the grace. Of course also there is always, behind all, the readiness to accept God's will without a murmur when it is perfectly evident and final. "My grace is sufficient for thee." Yes, but there is also the repeated effort to alter its form according to our sanctified needs and desires. You will notice that in Paul's case the power to accept the sufficiency of God's grace only came in the course of an importunate prayer aiming to turn God's hand. Paul ended, rather than began, with "Thy will be done." The peace of God is an end and not a beginning.

"Thy will be done" was no utterance of mere resignation; though it has mostly come to mean this in a Christianity which tends to canonize the weak instead of strengthening them. As prayer it was a piece of active co-operation with God's will. It was a positive part of it. It is one thing to submit to a stronger will, it is another to be one with it. We submit because we cannot resist it; but when we are one with it we cannot succumb. It is not *a* power, but *our* power. But the natural will is not one with God's; and so we come to use these words in a mere negative way, meaning that we cease to resist. Our will does not accept God's, it just stops work. We give in and lie down. But is that the sense of the words in the Lord's Prayer? Do they mean that we have no objection to God's will being done? or that we do not withstand any more? or even that we accept it gladly? Do they not mean something far more positive—that we actively will God's will and aid it, that it is the whole content of our own, that we put into it all the will that there can be in prayer, which is at last the great willpower of the race? It is our heart's passion that God's will be done and His kingdom come. And can His kingdom come otherwise than as it is a passion with us? Can His will be done? God's will was not Christ's consent merely, nor His pleasure, but His meat and drink, the source of His energy and the substance of His work.

Prayer and the Holy Spirit

Prayer is sometimes understood to be pious language addressed to God. But such is not the case, insists Jacques Ellul. Properly understood, prayer is not something we say, but the intercession of the Holy Spirit who evokes sighs too deep for words.

SOURCE

Jacques Ellul, *Prayer and Modern Man*, trans. Edward Hopkin (New York: Seabury, 1970), 61–64.

THE ESSENCE OF PRAYER

In other words, prayer is not to be analyzed like a language. It has none of that form or content, for it receives its content, not from what I have to say, but from the One to whom it is spoken. It is from the Interlocutor that this speech receives its validity. That this prayer can be what it is meant to be—a prayer—depends on him and not on me, still less on my ability to speak the adequate language. For of course I can always pronounce a discourse supposedly addressed to God. I can arrange the sentences, but it is neither the harmony of the form, nor the elevation of the content, nor the fullness of the information which turns it into a prayer. Insofar as it remains a discourse, it is in fact subject to the language analysis with which we are familiar, but that is always as discourse, that is to say, as "nonprayer."

It becomes prayer by the decision of God to whom it is addressed, but then its nature undergoes a change. Henceforth there is a *quid* which eludes our grasp. Of course, insofar as it continues to be made up of words and sentences, I could pretend to treat it as language in spite of the difficulties emphasized above, but then we must understand that that takes place exactly in the degree in which I do not look upon it as prayer, in which that which I grasp in this manner is not what prayer is!

But ultimately under those conditions I am no longer analyzing anything, since I am unable to account for the transformation which the discourse has undergone, which alters it *in its entirety*. For henceforth it is known as a prayer of Christ or as a prayer of the Holy Spirit.

That is how we should understand the famous statement of Paul, in which he says that in the last analysis we do not know what the content of our prayer should be (Romans 8:26–27), but that the Holy Spirit himself "intercedes with sighs too deep for words." This phrase has too often been interpreted as though the Holy Spirit added a little something to our prayer. In short, we pray, but not very well. Our prayer is incomplete, unsatisfactory. Fortunately, the Holy Spirit helps the situation by completing what we are unable to say. That is quite incorrect. It is the entire prayer which is the prayer of the Holy Spirit. If we conceive of prayer as language it is then that we do not know what to put into the discourse. It is nothing because it cannot have a content. Only when the Holy Spirit intercedes, and in a way which *cannot be expressed*, that is, which transcends all verbalizing, all language, then is the prayer prayer, and it is a relationship with God. *Only* then "he who searches the hearts of men knows" (hence, not by a signifying language) "what is the mind of the Spirit, because the Spirit intercedes . . . according to the will of God." We are forced to the conclusion that prayer is a gift from God, and that its reality depends upon him alone.

But if that is the case we can see the extreme difficulty of our present situation. I believe that what we have just been saying is a true account of the profound reality of prayer. What, then, can prayer mean for the man of our Western world who looks upon it purely as a discourse? This false conception is undisputed, widespread, and habitual in all the churches. Now, as long as one is living in Christian security in a Christianized society, in Christianity, in a world in which to be a Christian is *normal, correct,* and taken for granted, one can continue to pronounce such discourses. They are not prayers. The sociologist can seize upon them as a certain kind of language. We are in the domain of custom, of ritual, of spiritual hygiene. Yet these prayers go on, without result surely, because the milieu presupposes them. When the milieu changes, becomes secularized, unchurched, then one perceives clearly that these discourses make no contact with reality.

From then on one gains the impression that prayer is disappearing, but in truth it disappeared long before, at the moment when it was transformed by man into a discourse, into a purely verbal operation, into a false communication with the Supreme Being, into a misunderstanding. Man in our society cannot understand prayer except as a discourse, a sort of pious language addressed to God, a mode of communication. Every other reality is closed to him. Now precisely because prayer is not that, he cannot pray in truth. That is the tragedy.

So in the process of this analysis we have been led to discern many true components of what prayer is, and of what it is not. There has emerged progressively a "being" of prayer, which is at the same time an ought-to-be. The theological components remain true, but as we went along we were led to realize that for man in our society prayer cannot be what it is. A whole set of misunderstandings, of obsolete images, of spurious identifications, rob prayer of all further justification and being, except as a counterfeit.

The Place of Prayer in Theology

George Hendry argues that what a theologian says (or does not say) about prayer is a "clue" concerning the value of his or her theology.

SOURCE

George S. Hendry, "The Life Line of Theology," *The Princeton Seminary Bulletin* 65, no. 2 (December 1972), 25–26.

For some time I have employed a simple device in forming a judgment on the systematic writings of theologians, new and old. I read what they have to say about prayer. It provides a significant clue. There are three things I look for.

1. I look to see how much space the theologian devotes to prayer. Not that the amount of space is important in itself, but it serves as an index of how seriously the theologian takes the subject. And if he takes prayer seriously, I take him seriously, even if I am not able to agree with him in everything. I am disappointed with the theologian who disposes of the subject briefly with a few commonplace observations or pious platitudes. I am impatient of those who omit the subject altogether (a group which contains some surprising names). And I am ambivalent toward those who show a serious concern to attach some real significance to prayer, but who reduce it to the practice of the presence of God or to some kind of sensitivity training.

2. I look to see whether the theologian thinks of prayer as an act of the individual wrestling with his lot in face of the mysterious workings of providence, or as an act of the community of Christ arising out of their faith in Christ. It has been customary for so long to treat prayer as

a problem of apologetics or philosophy or religion and to formulate it in terms of the individual pitting his will against nameless powers, that many theologians seem incapable of seeing it in any other way. I am not suggesting that that is not a genuine aspect of prayer. But I submit that in Christian theology prayer should be understood first as the act of the community of faith, in which that faith comes to its most characteristic expression. In other words, a Christian theology of prayer has to begin with the Christological fact (a fact which, however, has seldom received its due weight in Christology) that Jesus prayed, and we are invited to join with him in his prayers. It is only as people who have heard that invitation and learned to join with him in saying "Our Father" that we may retire—without breaking the circle of faith, each into his closet and pray to his Father who is in secret. The priority of common prayer in the community of faith was put rather forcefully by Jesus when he said, "If two of you agree on earth about anything they ask, it will be done for them by my Father in heaven" (Matt. 18:19).

3. I look to see what the theologian says about prayer as petition. For prayer is basically petition—asking, seeking, making requests. Of course, it is not all petition; there are other things—adoration, confession, thanksgiving, and so forth. But if these elements are so enlarged as to crowd out petition, prayer is denatured; for petition is the heart of prayer. This is the crucial point.

Prayer as Covenant Relationship

Hendrikus Berkhof interprets the meaning of prayer within the covenant relationship between God and humanity. Prayer is "the vertical dimension" of humanity which presupposes that a person has first experienced enough of life to be ready to listen and give thanks.

SOURCE
Berkhof, *Christian Faith*, 495–97.

One should also bear in mind that prayer is a universal religious phenomenon; the history and psychology of religion can teach us a great deal about that. Prayer as such is not yet a Christian act. Christian prayer is the expression of a specific covenant relationship, the response to a very specific knowledge of God and his deeds and plans.

But these demarcations do not take away the primary importance prayer has in the Christian's fellowship with God. At times other utterances may push prayer to the periphery. But where it disappears, faith itself ceases. For "covenant" means our adoption as sons and daughters who may call God "Father." We are not only objects of redemption. In fact, our redemption also "liberates" us from being objects, and changes us again into true subjects. God does not want us as objects, but as covenant partners, partners who can converse. He desires our conversational input, our spontaneous gratitude, and our free concurrence, but also our patient or impatient questioning; and even our vehement protest is dearer to him than a silent, unconvinced acquiescence (see Job).

But as the input of the partner of *this* God it is a restricted input. For in this covenant the partners are not equal. We are the second partner, redeemed by the great Partner unto partnership. All our actions—personal and creative—are a reaction to his. We follow his action, we follow in his steps. We accept his conditions. Our coming to him is determined by his coming to us. Therefore Christian prayer, notwithstanding its spontaneity and variety, is a speaking that is determined and informed by the One whom we address.

So prayer is the accentuated manifestation of what can be called the vertical dimension of our humanity. That is not the first dimension coming to development. Before a person is ready to listen, give thanks, and pray, he has to do a lot of eating and drinking, and do and experience many other things besides. But once that stage is reached, this vertical dimension proves not only to presume the other dimensions but to embrace them as well. In the posture of prayer, as *homo orans*, our humanity perfects itself. And in that posture of prayer we place life with all its heights and depths and in its full horizontality before the face of God. Prayer is indeed for the most part a personal matter, but it is never a private concern and certainly not just that of a purely inner "soul" that is lifted out of this world. In prayer, our total human existence in all its varied contexts and responsibilities and cares which we have in and for the world expresses itself.

This means that prayer is as extensive as the faith and life itself, and thus has and can have a great variety of content. As a matter of fact, that is already implied in the fact that prayer links up with the manner in which God comes to us. Prayer can thus be, and depending on the situation and circumstances will be: thanksgiving for what God does; adoration for who he is; losing oneself in his incomprehensible love; confession of guilt for my sinfulness and for my offending that love; prayer for faith and forgiveness; prayer for strength in the fight of the faith; outcry because of the lostness of our existence; prayer for help in need; for wisdom to make right decisions; for submission and surrender when we see that our will conflicts with God's. And because the believer does not exist only by and for himself, he cannot intercede for himself alone; together with the church and for the sake of the church he prays for the progress of the proclamation of the gospel and for the upbuilding, unity, and expansion of the church in whatever form. And because the church does not exist by and for itself, but for the sake of the world, the believer and the church pray representatively for a groaning world which does not know what it longingly looks forward to, for an increase in the knowledge of God, for a strengthening of the forces that can mitigate the endless suffering, for conversion or restraint of those who in their folly maintain and promote injustice in the world. And in and beyond that, as the all-inclusive basis and goal, there is the prayer for the renewal of all of existence, for the definitive and total coming of God's Kingdom.

Not only has prayer a variety of content, it also has a variety of forms. We think first of all of the liturgy in the congregational worship service which displays a diversity of types of prayer: the hymn of praise and of thanksgiving, confession of sin, prayer for the illumination of the Spirit, intercessory prayer. The hymns in the services are mainly prayers, ranging from the exuberant adoration of God's excellencies to the anxious prayer for the coming of the Kingdom. Beside the church service there is the prayer group, often spontaneously formed in response to special needs. Furthermore, there is family prayer, a prayer that can be of great significance as the intercession by the smallest unit of society for needs great *and* small, but one which suffers from routine or is abandoned out of an aversion to routine. There is the carefully phrased and regular personal prayer, for instance when getting up in the morning or at retirement at night, but also the "quick prayer" in moments of tension and fear. There is also the prayer—unfortunately suffering from misuse and overuse—at the opening of meetings and gatherings which in some way relate to the cause of the gospel. The forms are as extensive as the faith and life itself.

From what we said both about the content and about the form, it could be inferred that petition is the dominant form of prayer. It is not the only form, however. There is also the prayer of thanksgiving, of adoration, of confession, of surrender. But almost always they turn into petition. That happens in the Bible as well as in our own use of the term "prayer," whereby we think in the first place of asking and pleading. With our definition of prayer as "input" we already anticipated that. We defined that further as "restricted input." That cannot mean, however, a timidity and holding back in our asking, as if we were having an audience with a very important person: precisely in the father-child relationship there may and must also be spontaneity. Before the face of this God we dare to voice our deepest motives and all the shortcomings we sense in our life and in the world. Even the most superstitious who came to Jesus, asking for bread or healing, he did not send away unanswered. On the contrary, in fellowship with him they learned to ask for *more* than they had begun with, and to ask differently: no longer only from the standpoint of their own needs, but much more from the perspective of God's purposes of which their cares were a part. Particularly the disciples learned this new way of asking in a hard training school. But their master, Jesus, was not spared this training school either. The words of his agonizing prayer in Gethsemane: "Yet not what I will, but what thou wilt" (Mark 14:36) are, in our judgment, misunderstood if we hear in them only an acquiescence in the unavoidable that is going to happen. It is a real prayer, of the same nature as the third petition in the Lord's Prayer. Jesus asks of God that his own will and desires be made subordinate to the great goal in which he is of one mind with the Father, namely that the Father's will to save people and to establish his Kingdom be carried out—if necessary through the torture and the agonizing death of Jesus.

How to ask questions is something we must be taught. The disciples realized that when they saw Jesus himself pray; therefore they asked: "Lord, teach us to pray" (Luke 11:1). The answer was the Lord's Prayer (vv. 2–4), which in its very structure teaches us by example. First, with three actually synonymous petitions (a repetition necessary for us, not for God) man through prayer makes God's plans of salvation his own, so that his will submits itself to God's will and becomes one with it. Man's will is not thereby obliterated, however. Where God receives the priority, man's will can for that reason come into its own in the petitions for a decent life in the world and for forgiveness of sins, perseverance, and deliverance on the basis of redemption. This prayer does not use "I" and "me" but "we" and "us," because one who gives God the priority will want the same room for his neighbor as he desires for himself. Moreover, the plurals "we" and "us" are used because the believer always prays as a member of the total body of Christ.

Praise and Prayer as Equipment for the Church

The Confession of 1967 of the reunited Presbyterian Church (U.S.A.) describes praise and prayer as the means by which God equips the church to carry out its ministry of reconciliation.

SOURCE

"The Confession of 1967," in *Book of Confessions*, 9.48–50.

THE EQUIPMENT OF THE CHURCH

Jesus Christ has given the church preaching and teaching, praise and prayer, and Baptism and the Lord's Supper as means of fulfilling its service of God among men. These gifts remain, but the church is obliged to change the forms of its service in ways appropriate to different generations and cultures.

1. Preaching and Teaching

God instructs his church and equips it for mission through preaching and teaching. By these, when they are carried on in fidelity to the Scriptures and dependence upon the Holy Spirit, the people hear the word of God and accept and follow Christ. The message is addressed to men in particular situations. Therefore effective preaching, teaching, and personal witness require disciplined study of both the Bible and the contemporary world. All acts of public worship should be conducive to men's hearing of the gospel in a particular time and place and responding with fitting obedience.

2. Praise and Prayer

The church responds to the message of reconciliation in praise and prayer. In that response it commits itself afresh to its mission, experiences a deepening of faith and obedience, and bears open testimony to the gospel. Adoration of God is acknowledgement of the Creator by the creation. Confession of sin is admission of all men's guilt before God and of their need for his forgiveness. Thanksgiving is rejoicing in God's goodness to all men and in giving for the needs of others. Petitions and intercessions are addressed to God for the continuation of his goodness, the healing of men's ills, and their deliverance from every form of oppression. The arts, especially music and architecture, contribute to the praise and prayer of a Christian congregation when they help men to look beyond themselves to God and to the world which is the object of his love.

THE PERSEVERANCE OF THE SAINTS

Classical Reformed theology affirmed that those individuals elected and regenerated by God may experience setbacks and lapses of faith, but they can still be assured of God's eternal salvation. God will persevere with them even when they are unfaithful to God. Like the doctrine of election or predestination, the perseverance of the saints is a strong Reformed affirmation that human destiny is ultimately grounded in God's sovereign grace and not in human free will.

In the contemporary period, topics such as election and the freedom of the will have been reexamined and reinterpreted, but many Reformed theologians have continued to affirm God's perseverance of the saints, although in different ways and for different reasons than their classical predecessors.

FOR FURTHER STUDY

G. C. Berkouwer, *Faith and Perseverance*, trans. Robert D. Knudsen (Grand Rapids: Wm. B. Eerdmans, 1958). Jürgen Moltmann, *Prädestination and Perseveranz: Geschichte und Bedeutung der reformierten Lehre "de perseverantia sanctorum"* (Neukirchen: Neukirchener Verlag, 1961).

Faith in Christ as the Basis for Perseverance

In *Church Dogmatics* Karl Barth argued that John Calvin's interpretation of election was both unbiblical and insufficiently christological. Barth did not believe that Calvin's theology provided Christians any real assurance that they are eternally elect. The only sound basis for such assurance, Barth argued, is faith in Jesus Christ, not self-examination.

SOURCE

Barth, *Church Dogmatics*, II/2:339–40.

The need for a total revision of the dogma is plainly shown by the history of this subsidiary problem. If Jesus Christ, rather than the absolute decree, is regarded as the real basis of the election of each elected individual, and the community of God as the medium through which there are elected individuals, then Calvin—and also Beza and the rest—are justified to the extent that the question of the personal assurance of the individual is actually put and must be answered. Individuals as such are godless; elect only in Jesus Christ and through the medium of the community, and therefore directed continually to grasp their election in faith ("to make sure," 2 Pet. 1:10), as they hear and receive the testimony of Jesus Christ, holding it before them as their own testimony. They have need of assurance. And if that about which they have to assure themselves can only be the election of Jesus Christ, and the power with which they do so can only be the power of that Christian faith and life which is mediated to them on the basis of His election, then they are not merely permitted but commanded continually to assure themselves of their election, as it has taken place in Jesus Christ, by themselves being its witnesses—living as the elect by their faith. From this point of view, to be elect means to be oneself a witness of one's election, living by one's faith. This must be said even more emphatically than it was said by Calvin. But if Jesus Christ is the real basis of election, the following points must be made in opposition to the interpretation of Beza and the rest, and in answer to the scruples of other Calvinist theologians, as a foolproof version of the reservation of Calvin.

First, the fact that the elect is himself a witness to his election means that he himself may witness to the election of Jesus Christ, and to his own election in and with it. Similarly, the *consideratio operum* in which he himself accepts this testimony can be understood only as the *consideratio operum Christi;* the consideration of the grace which for the sake of Christ, and through Him, is vouchsafed to him as one of the godless threatened with rejection; of the redemptive act of Christ of which he is the subject as His elect. It is obvious, then, that although he participates in this witness as a bearer as well as a recipient, he does so simply as *adminiculum inferius* of the testimony itself, and even as such only by its own inner power, in the inexpressible wonder of the grace of Jesus Christ. And it is also obvious that this participant, the godless man threatened with rejection, who through grace alone has become a bearer and recipient of this witness, cannot possibly understand the difference between his situation and that of the godless alongside him as one of absolute antithesis.

Second, his participation in this witness and therefore his assurance about himself, can have absolutely nothing to do with self-examination and self-evaluation. What can self-examination mean except that the godless considers the godless, and how can this in itself be adequate even for self-condemnation, not to mention the self-justification which is presupposed as possible in the *minor* of the syllogism? It is not in self-examination or self-evaluation, but exclusively in faith, that he may be and is active as the bearer and recipient of this witness: as he is in fact the elect of Jesus Christ; as he leaves his godlessness behind him in faith, and therefore lives in acknowledgment of the grace of Jesus Christ vouchsafed to him as a godless man; as his works are the works of this faith; as he actually witnesses to the election of Jesus Christ by what he is. It is obvious that the syllogism is not a form which we can use to describe this process. But above all it is obvious that the elect man cannot possibly receive this witness if he gives it only to himself, if as he gives it to himself he does not also give it to his "rejected" neighbour, if he does not permit the contradiction of the rejection that threatens him to benefit this other man as it has benefited him. How can he be the elect of Jesus Christ if the operation of faith by which he is assured that he is elect is not immediately and primarily a work of hope and proclamation to his neighbour also, a participation in the work of the community of God in the world?

Third, as the elect man is in this way assured of his election, he is indeed aware of a mysterious correspondence (even identity), not between the hidden counsel of God and the condition of his own piety and morality, but between the election of Jesus Christ and the miracle of the actual fulfilment of his faith; between the inner power of the witness, whose bearer and recipient (and messenger) he may be, and the miracle of the fact that he actually finds himself enabled to be the bearer and recipient (and messenger) of this witness. It is obvious that he will not rejoice in himself because of this correspondence (even identity), but solely "in the Lord," solely in the grace that encounters him in this relationship. It is also obvious—in consequence—that he will manifest this joy of his as a promise and hope, especially to his "rejected" neighbour, the godless one. The *sancta voluptas* of the individual assurance of the elect is that he may hand on the Word by which he himself lives to those who do not yet, or any longer, live by it.

Our conclusion is, then, that Calvin's problem of the self-assurance of the elect can and actually must be tackled, but that the caution with which Calvin dealt with it can and actually must be maintained. In the setting of the classical doctrine the one could take place only at the expense of the other. But in a setting of the doctrine of predestination which has a christological basis there is room for both and both are needed.

The Syllogism of Faith

Like Karl Barth, G. C. Berkouwer believed that a Christian should not seek assurance about salvation by looking to personal experience or good works. There can be no empirical or rational demonstration of God's grace, no *syllogismus practicus*, because that grace is a gift that can only be known by faith alone, by a *syllogismus fidei*.

SOURCE

G. C. Berkouwer, *Divine Election*, trans. Hugo Bekker (Grand Rapids: Wm. B. Eerdmans, 1960), 291–93.

We now approach the core of the problem concerning the *syllogismus practicus* in connection with election. How, and in which sense, have man's good works significance for one's assurance of salvation? Can they really become an unambiguous indication of election, or do they rather lead to more doubt? How is it possible to look solely unto the goodness and mercy of God—without regarding one's works—and still, for the confirmation and strengthening of our faith, attach significance to good works?

It is quite understandable that on the basis of the *sola fide* the *syllogismus practicus* has at times been abandoned. For the dangers of moralism threaten in connection with the *syllogismus practicus*, and of mysticism in connection with the *syllogismus mysticus*. And the "signs" have often been more esteemed than God's revelation and trustworthy promise. Does it not betray a lack of courage of faith to reserve a place for this function of good works along with the *sola fide*? And is it indeed possible to ascribe such a function to good works, which after all, according to our Christian confession, are polluted with sin (Heidelberg Catechism, Q. 24)? Has not this confession its implications for the problem of certainty? Is it not rather true that our works will again make the certainty uncertain? Can certainty ever be evoked and strengthened apart from belief in the forgiveness of sins? How can our good works become a witness, even a secondary witness? Do they not remain witnesses on the debit side rather than on the credit side? All these questions arise automatically when we discuss the *syllogismus practicus*, and they can be summarized in these words: (1) Can good works have this function? (2) Is such a function of good works indeed necessary for the certainty, which after all issues from the indisputable trustworthiness of God's promises and the convincing power of the Holy Spirit?

First of all we wish to point out that it is impossible to accept the *syllogismus practicus* if it is understood as a logical conclusion, made apart from faith, and based on a neutral analysis of one's life, whether mystical or practical.

So understood, it shifts the emphasis from *sola fide*, and therefore can never bring about true certainty of salvation. Schilder was correct when he pointed out in this connection that Scripture even speaks of pagans who by nature do what the law requires, which shows that we can never conclude that we are elected on the basis of a neutral analysis of our works which conform to the law. Man can easily overestimate himself in such a neutral self-analysis and reach a conclusion that could not stand before God.

Man's heart is deceitful above all things, and exceedingly corrupt.

Who can know it? (Jer. 17:9). This is true especially regarding the analysis of one's own life. For that reason, such an analysis can never lead to certainty. It would only be the rationalistic form of the *syllogismus practicus,* which is in flagrant contradiction to the teaching of the Reformation and especially of Scripture. It is, apart from faith and promise, utterly impossible to come to the conclusion: I believe. Besides, a peculiar reasoning here takes place, namely, reasoning from the content of faith proper, which then has to be examined as to its presence (or absence) and its activity. This process of thinking resembles the Roman Catholic reasoning when it draws rational conclusions from the creation. The rationalistic *syllogismus practicus* draws a causal conclusion very similar to the conclusion of the *theologia naturalis.*

This kind of syllogism is merely a reasoned conclusion, and it is understandable that it leaves man's heart cold and untouched, and that it presently evolves into a new *tentatio,* when the question arises—must arise—whether the "conclusion" is correct or maybe based on self-deception and illusion.

Over against that it must be posed that the *syllogismus practicus* is possible only if it is understood as the syllogism of faith. To be sure, that evokes other questions, but at any rate it is clear that this principle puts us on an altogether different basis than the one of rational conclusions drawn from the observed empirical reality of our lives.

The Certainty of Salvation and the Glory of God

Otto Weber argues that the certainty of salvation must not be separated from the theme of the glory of God. Furthermore, he says, Jesus Christ is not simply the means or the image, but the concrete reality of both salvation and God's freedom.

SOURCE
Weber, *Foundations,* 2:429–30.

The Certainty of Salvation. Experience, as we have discussed up to now, opens up primarily the negative, delimiting aspect of the doctrine of election. The positive aspect, which both corresponds to it and surpasses it, is that of the certainty of salvation. Wherever faith is accompanied by certainty (and it is an essential property of faith), it is based on the fact that "our salvation may be taken entirely out of our hands and put in the hand of God alone. . . . For we are so weak and uncertain that if it depended on us, not even a single person would be saved; the devil would surely overpower us all. . . ." "The doctrine of predestination is the dogma used to describe God as the living and active God, whose activity transcends the possibilities of human awareness." The certainty of salvation is an aspect which had already concerned Augustine: "perseverance" in faith is based solely on the fact that faith is derived from a reality which is absolutely superior to it, and lives out of God's electing act. Every ethical or phenomenological description of faith confronts its limitations here—in faith I exist on the basis of that which I do not comprehend in faith. It is only when that is true that certainty is given to faith. All of the Reformers could be summoned as witnesses for this insight—their opposition to the idea of the "free will" *(liberum arbitrium)* as well as to the thesis (related to it) of the self-efficiency of the "means of grace" distributed by the Church is not derived from speculation but emerged essentially from the area of pastoral responsibility. And it has certainly not been erroneous to describe the doctrine of election in the Formula of Concord, which particularly emphasizes the motif of the certainty of salvation, as ultimately understandable in pastoral terms, whatever else might be said against it. And finally, it is to the point when Paul Althaus in his dogmatics devotes a special section to the problem of the certainty of salvation. In general, Lutheran doctrine emphasizes the motif of the certainty of salvation more strongly, and Reformed doctrine the motif of the "glory of God." Both belong together. On the basis of our discussion up to now, it ought to be agreed that the doctrine of election corresponds to the "motif" of salvation-history only when it proclaims that God's honor is revealed as his gracious freedom, and that conversely the honor of God is properly proclaimed only when God"s freedom is described as the freedom of his gracious turning to man. Thus, we cannot speak of the certainty of salvation where, as in the doctrine of Trent, man is ascribed on one hand the capacity for preparing himself independently for the reception of grace, and on the other hand is not granted "perseverance." Along those lines, the question must also be asked whether the Formula of Concord really says what it wants to say, which is that God's election can provide the Christian comfort in times when he is tested. If it ascribes to man the capacity of "closing" *(praecludere)* to the Holy Spirit the "ordinary way" *(via ordinaria;* the way through the Word), then we must ask if that does not in fact imply that God is not able to work apart from the will of man, so that no one can know whether he will always have the necessary will-power throughout the future, leaving every believer in a state of uncertainty. In these first two views of predestination, which have only been briefly discussed, God's gracious freedom is seen in too minimal a fashion; that being the case, the converse question must be raised whether the objection of the older Lutherans that the Calvinist doctrine (in the sense of the so-called "absolute decree") made the certainty of salvation impossible was not well based, since in this instance the divine offer of grace can apply to all but is not in fact valid for all. Is not God's freedom another kind than that of his grace? And is not then the doctrine of predestination basically a totally comprehensive reservation in favor of the absolute freedom of God? When this consideration is allowed, then it applies most pointedly to Luther, who formulated this reservation with an acuteness which is not to be found in Calvin. The significant thing is that here two positions confront each other which, at least as a general tendency, lead to the result of confronting God and man abstractly, and it is just as significant that in this case Jesus Christ is ultimately spoken of only in the sense of a "means" or an "image" *(medium, speculum)*. The question then is whether this states what is right and necessary.

6

THE CHURCH

Although Reformed theology has never understood the church to be a sacrament, it has consistently held that Christian life cannot be lived privately and in isolation. To be baptized into the name of Jesus Christ is to become a participant in the body of Christ. Christian faith is both personal and communal, but it is never private.

The church believes it receives its identity from the God who has called it into being and in whose grace it lives. Because that God is a living reality, the church must struggle in every situation with the question of what God is calling it to be and to do. In the nineteenth century, many Reformed churches in Western Europe and North America believed God was calling them to take the gospel to nations and cultures where there were few, if any, Christians. In the twentieth century, one of the fruits of that missionary work has been the creation of the World Alliance of Reformed Churches. Many of these churches, especially those in Africa, Asia, and Central and South America, along with African American and Hispanic churches in the Western world, have begun to develop their own interpretations of the meaning of the gospel for their respective cultures.

Some Reformed churches also have been deeply influenced by recent developments in Roman Catholic theology. Following the Second Vatican Council (1962–65), many Roman Catholic theologians decided that questions about the nature and mission of the church could not be resolved without first reexamining what the church believes about Jesus Christ; that is, Christology is the necessary presupposition of ecclesiology. Influenced by the liberation theology emerging from Central and South America, some Christian communities concluded that the gospel story reveals a God who has a preferential option for the poor and that if the church is to be faithful to that God it must live in solidarity with the poor and oppressed.

Both the church as an institution in society and the distinctive activities of the church have been carefully reexamined in contemporary theology. The

243

sacraments of baptism and the Lord's Supper have also been the subject of significant theological reconstruction.

FOR FURTHER STUDY

James Gustafson, *Treasure in Earthen Vessels: The Church as a Human Community* (New York: Harper & Brothers, 1961). Peter C. Hodgson, *Revisioning the Church: Ecclesial Freedom in the New Paradigm* (Minneapolis: Fortress, 1988). Eric G. Jay, *The Church: Its Changing Image Through Twenty Centuries*, 2 vols. (Richmond: John Knox, 1980; London: SPCK, 1977). Hans Küng, *The Church* (New York: Image Books, 1976). Geddes MacGregor, *Corpus Christi: The Nature of the Church According to the Reformed Tradition* (Philadelphia: Westminster, 1958). Paul Minear, *Images of the Church in the New Testament* (Philadelphia: Westminster, 1960). Trutz Rendtorff, *Church and Theology: The Systematic Function of the Church Concept in Modern Theology* (Philadelphia: Westminster, 1962). Alan P. F. Sell, "The Reformed Family Today: Some Theological Reflections," in *Major Themes in the Reformed Tradition*, ed. Donald K. McKim (Grand Rapids: Wm. B. Eerdmans, 1992), 433–41.

THE CALLING AND MISSION OF THE CHURCH

Given the political and social contexts in which many Reformed churches found themselves in the sixteenth and seventeenth centuries, it is not surprising that the theological documents of that era are concerned primarily with the internal structure and life of the church in the midst of a hostile world. In the twentieth century, many theologians recognized that there had been little discussion in the Reformed tradition of the mission of the church. One of the major features, therefore, of recent Reformed theology has been the discussion of the mission of the church. While mission was understood by many theologians in the nineteenth century to be the task of taking the gospel to the non-Christian world, in the latter half of the twentieth century some have suggested that Western Europe and North America may now be the new mission fields.

FOR FURTHER STUDY

Barth, *Church Dogmatics*, IV/3a:481–901. Brunner, *Dogmatics*, 3. Hendrik Kraemer, *The Christian Message in a Non-Christian World* (Grand Rapids: Kregel Publications, 1938). John H. Leith, *The Reformed Imperative: What the Church Has to Say That No One Else Can Say* (Philadelphia: Westminster, 1988). Lesslie Newbigin, *The Gospel in a Pluralist Society* (Grand Rapids: Wm. B. Eerdmans; Geneva: WCC Publications, 1989).

The Church as the Continuation of Christ's Activity

Friedrich Schleiermacher argues that the threefold office of Jesus Christ (as prophet, priest, and king) is perpetuated in the "the essential activities" of the church, including prayer and the forgiveness of sins (the office of king), the scriptures and preaching (the office of prophet), and the sacraments (the office of priest).

SOURCE

Schleiermacher, *Christian Faith*, 589–91.

That we have here given a complete view of the elements on which the unity and identity of the Christian Church rest in every time and place is best seen if we recur to the relation of the Church to Christ. On the one hand, as the organism of Christ—which is what Scripture means by calling it His Body—it is related to Christ as the outward to the inward, so that in its essential activities it must also be a reflection of the activities of Christ. And since the effects produced by it are simply the gradual realization of redemption in the world, its activities must likewise be a continuation of the activities of Christ Himself. These we have reduced to the scheme of the Threefold Office; and in the same way it must be possible to show that the three offices of Christ are reflected and carried on in the essential activities of the Church as stated above.

Prayer in the Name of Jesus, embracing as it does the full vocational activity of each individual Christian, is a reflection of Christ's kingly activity, both as it is in itself and as concerns the relation between His rule and that of the Father. It is the latter, inasmuch as it concludes with the reverently submissive utterance of the thoughts of each regarding the extension of the Kingdom of God or the assaults of the world. It is the former, inasmuch as it comprehends all purposes flowing from the energies of the God-consciousness. And in the Power of the Keys there is attached to the forgiveness of sins, rightly understood, all that has to do with Church order and the estimate of persons in the Church which flows from the common consciousness. Thus we have here the continuation of that kingly activity of Christ which began with His choice of the disciples and His giving of ordinances for the fellowship that was to be.

Further, since the prophetic activity of Christ consists in His self-presentation and His invitation to enter the Kingdom of God, the Holy Scriptures are the permanent reflection of His prophetic activity, inasmuch as in their composition and preservation, regarded as the work of the Church, they form the most direct exhibition of Christ. The Ministry of the Word we cannot but regard as also a continuation of His prophetic work, for it essentially consists in the applied presentation of Christ and invitation in His name.

If, finally, the essential element in Christ's priestly office—to distinguish this as clearly as possible from the prophetic and kingly offices—lies supremely in this, that He mediates the fellowship of men with God, there will be no difficulty in acknowledging that both sacraments have a relation thereto. In this sense, that baptism owing to its more symbolical character is related more as a reflection, the Lord's Supper owing to its more real content as a continuation.

This arrangement also shows that everything essentially belonging to Christ's activity has its reflection and continuation in the Church, for the first three features pertain to His redemptive, the other three to His reconciling, activity. Nor in our Evangelical interpretation of Christianity shall we have to indicate any other feature of the Church which could claim to stand on the same level as these institutions. On the contrary, we shall neither place tradition beside Scripture nor subordinate the Ministry of the Word to any kind of symbolical rites; we shall neither acquiesce in the multiplication of sacraments nor by attributing magical effects to them destroy the analogy they bear to the other features of the Church; we shall neither limit Prayer in the Name of Jesus by invocation of the saints nor permit any special representation of Christ—whether individual or collegial—to usurp the place of the Power of the Keys.

Believing in the Visible Church

Karl Barth warns those who believe in the church as an ideal community, but do not believe in the visible reality they encounter in the daily world, that ecclesiastical docetism (the denial of the church's worldly and human reality) is just as much a danger as christological docetism (the denial of Christ's humanity).

SOURCE
Barth, *Church Dogmatics*, IV/1:653–54.

There is an ecclesiastical Docetism which will not accept this, which paradoxically tries to overlook the visibility of the Church, explaining away its earthly and historical form as something indifferent, or angrily negating it, or treating it only as a necessary evil, in order to magnify an invisible fellowship of the Spirit and of spirits. This view is just as impossible as christological Docetism, not only in point of history, but also in point of substance. For the work of the Holy Spirit as the awakening power of Jesus Christ would not take place at all if the invisible did not become visible, if the Christian community did not take on and have an earthly-historical form. The individual Christian can exist only in time and space as a doer of the Word (Jas. 1:22) and therefore in a concrete human form and basically visible to everyone. Similarly the Christian community as such cannot exist as an ideal commune or universum, but—also in time and space—only in the relationship of its individual members as they are fused together by the common action of the Word which they have heard into a definite human fellowship; in concrete form, therefore, and visible to everyone. If we say with the creed *credo ecclesiam*, we do not proudly overlook its concrete form; just as when we confess *credo resurrectionem carnis* we cannot overlook the real and whole man who is a soul and yet also a body, we cannot overlook his hope as though the resurrection was not also promised to him. Nor do we look penetratingly through this form, as though it was only something transparent and the real Church had to be sought behind it; just as we cannot overlook or look through the pleasing or less pleasing face of the neighbour whom we are commanded to love. We look at the visible aspect of the Church—this is the state of it. And as we look at what is seen—not beside it or behind but in it—we see what is not seen. Hence we cannot rid ourselves in this way of the generally visible side of the Church. We cannot take refuge from it in a kind of wonderland. The *credo ecclesiam* can and necessarily will involve much distinguishing and questioning, much concern and shame. It can and necessarily will be a very critical *credo*. In relation to the side of the Church which is generally visible it can and necessarily will express what does not amount to much more than a hope and yearning. But it does take the Church quite seriously in its common visibility—which is its earthly and historical existence. It confesses faith in the invisible aspect which is the secret of the visible. Believing in the *ecclesia invisibilis* we will enter the sphere of labour and conflict of the *ecclesia visibilis*. Without doing this, without a discriminate but serious participation in the historical life of the community, its activity, its upbuilding, its mission, in a kind of purely theoretical and abstract churchliness, no one has ever seriously repeated the *credo ecclesiam*. Those who try to repeat it in a way which looks above the Church, only dreaming of its existence in time and space, must see to it that they are not secretly pandering to a christological Docetism as well, or, at any rate, that they are really taking seriously the true humanity of Jesus Christ. Faith in His community has this in common with faith in Him, that it, too, relates to a reality in time and space, and therefore to something which is at bottom generally visible. If, then, we believe in Him, we cannot refuse—however hesitantly or anxiously or contentiously—to believe in His community in its spatiotemporal existence, and therefore to be a member of it and personally a Christian. We will return to the implications of this in the second part of the doctrine of reconciliation under the title of the true humanity of Jesus Christ. For the moment it is enough to point to it by way of demarcation.

The Goal of the Church:
Love of God and Neighbor

The goal or purpose of the church, argues H. Richard Niebuhr, is to increase the love of God and neighbor among people.

SOURCE

Niebuhr, *The Purpose of the Church*, 31–33.

Is not the result of all these debates and the content of the confessions or commandments of all these authorities this: that no substitute can be found for the definition of the goal of the Church as the *increase among men of the love of God and neighbor?* The terms vary; now the symbolic phrase is reconciliation to God and man, now increase of gratitude for the forgiveness of sin, now the realization of the kingdom or the coming of the Spirit, now the acceptance of the gospel. But the simple language of Jesus Christ himself furnishes to most Christians the most intelligible key to his own purpose and to that of the community gathered around him. If the increase among men of love of God and neighbor is the ultimate objective may it not be that many of our confusions and conflicts in churches and seminaries are due to failure to keep this goal in view while we are busy in the pursuit of proximate ends that are indeed important, but which set us at cross-purposes when followed without adequate reference to the final good?

Any adequate discussion of the theme of love of God and neighbor and of its relevance to Church and school requires all the resources of the theological curriculum from study of the Scriptures through systematic theology, the philosophy, psychology and history of religion, Christian and social ethics to pastoral theology, Christian education and homiletics. Yet in relative brevity some things can be said about this theme which, one hopes, will invite the assent of many members of the community, however great their dissent because of the incompleteness of the statement and because differences of emphasis are inevitable. The statement of a final end can never be a final statement until the whole community confesses it in the moment of its achievement.

In the language of Christianity love of God and neighbor is both "law" and "gospel"; it is both the requirement laid on man by the Determiner of all things and the gift given, albeit in incompleteness, by the self-giving of the Beloved. It is the demand inscribed into infinitely aspiring human nature by the Creator; its perversion in idolatry, hostility and self-centeredness is the heart of man's tragedy; its reconstruction, redirection and empowerment is redemption from evil. Love of God and neighbor is the gift given through Jesus Christ by the demonstration in incarnation, words, deeds, death and resurrection that God is love—a demonstration we but poorly apprehend yet sufficiently discern to be moved to a faltering response of reciprocal love. The purpose of the gospel is not simply that we should believe in the love of God; it is that we should love him and neighbor. Faith in God's love toward man is perfected in man's love to God and neighbor. We love in incompleteness, not as redeemed but in the time of redemption, not in attainment but in hope. Through Jesus Christ we receive enough faith in God's love toward us to see at least the need for and the possibility of a responsible love on our part. We know enough of the possibility of love to God on our part to long for its perfection; we see enough of the reality of God's love toward us and neighbor to hope for its full revelation and so for our full response.

The Dissimilarity Between the Church and the Incarnation

Claude Welch echoes a long-standing reservation in the Reformed tradition about identifying Jesus Christ with the church. The relation between Jesus Christ and the church is at best analogical and neither literal nor ontological.

SOURCE

Claude Welch, *The Reality of the Church* (New York: Charles Scribner's Sons, 1958), 122–23.

Again, as in the incarnation a true and concrete human existence is brought forth which has its true humanness just in its union with God, so in a similar way the church has its dependence on God as real historically immanent center and life. Or, more positively, Christ expresses his lordship over the church in the concrete reality of its temporal being and form.

So far, we can speak of the analogy of Christ and the church as determinative likeness and congruity. The community of which he is Lord reflects in its life the pattern of his being. But this is only an analogy, or better, it *is* an *analogy* and therefore implies difference as well as likeness. The church is not incarnation, and the duality of divinity and humanity in the person of Christ is *not* the same as the polarity of the church's being (it is certainly misleading, and in the strict sense, improper, to speak of the church as "divine"). For Christ is the first-born of brethren, yet he alone is Son "by nature" and he is Head and Lord of the church, present to it and in it as ground of its life. Thus the terms inseparable, unconfused, unchangeable and indivisible cannot mean quite the same thing with reference to the church that they mean in relation to Christ. Moreover, the servant-form of the church is not identical with the new humanity in Christ, and the mystery of the church's holiness is not the same as the sinlessness of Christ. In its obedience and suffering, the church shares in the experience of Christ, but its obedience is imperfect and its suffering ambiguous. The church awaits fulfillment, depending on the Christ who not only was and is, but is to come. The Head is victorious, but the struggle continues fiercely in the body. . . .

This contrast may be put another way by saying that, while the historical figure of Jesus Christ is such as to make intelligible to faith the conviction that he is the Incarnate Word, the historical life of the church is not evidently such as to make intelligible many of the claims made for it. Certainly it is *called* to be the people of God and the body of Christ, and it is affirmed to be a *holy* nation and a *royal* priesthood, but the call seems to have met with distorted response and the theological claim seems quite inconsistent with the facts of its life. In the church we meet rebellious rejection of the "servant-form," and idolatrous desire for the "lord-form." Thus in insisting on the truly historical being of the church as human community, we seem to have deepened the problem. If we are able to illuminate one side of the dialectic (or one of the "paradoxes") of the church's being by seeing it in the light of the incarnation, we at the same time expose the more sharply the other side of the dialectic, its real dissimilarity to the incarnation and the inconsistency of its life.

Ubi Christus, Ibi Ecclesia

On the basis of his interpretation of Matt. 25:31 ff., Jürgen Moltmann argues that it is not the church who makes Christ present to the world. Christ is present in the poor and oppressed, and the church is called to join him in solidarity with them.

SOURCE

Moltmann, *The Church*, 128–29.

If we introduce Matthew 25 into ecclesiology, then an unheard-of tension arises for the church, which finds its truth in the presence of Christ. Where is the true church? In the fellowship manifest in word and sacrament, or in the latent brotherhood of the Judge hidden in the poor? Can the two coincide? If we take the promises of Christ's presence seriously, we must talk about a brotherhood of believers and a brotherhood of the least of his brethren with Christ. "He who hears you hears me"—"He who visits them, visits me." The two have seldom been successfully combined in the church's history. The Christian church in its manifest form has always appealed to the exalted Christ's promises of authority, interpreting itself as the body of the exalted Lord. The apocalyptic Christ, the poor, hungry, forsaken Judge, has generally remained outside the door of church and society. The only people who have asked about him have been the Christian religions of the oppressed and Christian communities which were themselves pushed out of society and church as sects. But if the church, in appealing to the exalted Christ's promises of authority, understands itself as his earthly presence, must it not also, and with equal emphasis, seek the presence of the world's humiliated Judge? Evidently there are two brotherhoods of Christ, the professed and professing brotherhood which is the community of the exalted one; and the unknown and disowned brotherhood of the least of men with the humiliated Christ. If the church appeals to the crucified and risen Christ, must it not represent this double brotherhood of Christ in itself, and be present with word and Spirit, sacrament, fellowship and all creative powers among the poor, the hungry and the captives? Then the church would not simply be a "divinely human mystery" but the mystery of this double presence of Christ. Then the church with its mission would be present where Christ awaits it, amid the downtrodden, the sick and the captives. The apostolate says what the church is. The least of Christ's brethren say where the church belongs.

If Matthew 25 is applied to the teaching and practice of the church, then the conflict between a "dogmatic" and an "ethical" Christianity must be resolvable. Statements about the "manifest" and the "latent" church could also be understood in the sense of the double presence and brotherhood of Christ. Admittedly one could not then simply talk about a "Christianity outside the church" or about "the workings of the Spirit outside the church." For then the question is not how people or happenings outside the church respond to the church, but how the church responds to the presence of Christ in those who are "outside," hungry, thirsty, sick, naked and imprisoned. It is not a question of the integration of Christians outside the church into Christianity in its ecclesiastical form; it is a matter of the church's integration in Christ's promised presence: *ubi Christus, ibi ecclesia*.

Missionaries to the Western World

Lesslie Newbigin, who spent nearly forty years as a missionary in India, identifies "seven essentials" necessary for the church in the Western world to become an authentic witness to God in its own culture. One of these "essentials" is that the church must listen to the voices of Christians in other parts of the world who have different interpretations of the meaning of the gospel.

SOURCE

Lesslie Newbigin, *Foolishness to the Greeks: The Gospel and Western Culture* (Grand Rapids: Wm. B. Eerdmans, 1986), 146–48.

As the fifth condition for a missionary encounter with our culture, I would list the necessity for help in seeing our own culture through Christian minds shaped by other cultures. Paul says that we need all the saints to comprehend the greatness of Christ (Eph. 3:14 ff.). We need the witness of the whole ecumenical family if we are to be authentic witnesses of Christ to our own culture. I referred in an earlier chapter to the impression we receive when we look at the portraits of Jesus painted in different cultures. They make vividly clear how much our vision of Jesus is shaped by our culture. It cannot be otherwise. The fact that Jesus is much more than, much greater than our culture-bound vision of him can only come home to us through the witness of those who see him with other eyes. Asian and African Christians who received the gospel from European and American missionaries and therefore were invited to see Jesus as our culture saw him now struggle through their own study of Scripture and their own obedience in their own time and place to articulate a form of Christian believing and behaving in terms of their own cultures. We need their witness to correct ours, as indeed they need ours to correct theirs. At this moment our need is greater, for they have been far more aware of the dangers of syncretism, of an illegitimate alliance with false elements in their culture, than we have been. But whether it is we or they, we imperatively need one another if we are to be the faithful witnesses of Christ in our many different cultures.

For this reason the churches in the Western world must recognize that they cannot do without the World Council of Churches. When that Council held its second Assembly in Evanston in 1954, it was a great media event. There was immense enthusiasm throughout the nation, and even the secular press and radio were full of it. Today the World Council of Churches is widely regarded with deep suspicion in many parts of the Western world. The reason is obvious.

Thirty years ago the ecumenical movement was perceived as the worldwide triumph of our kind of Christianity. The colored and colorful representatives of the Asian and African churches were hailed and photographed as trophies of our missionary success. Today the ecumenical movement is perceived as a threat, and the theologies coming out of the younger churches call our own certainties into question. Of course, a theology is not true just because it comes from Buenos Aires or Jakarta. But we cannot faithfully discharge our missionary responsibility to our own people unless we are willing to listen for what the living God says to us through his servants in other cultures. We need all the saints, and the foreign missionary is not a temporary but an abiding necessity for the life of the church, provided always that the movement of missionaries is multidirectional, all churches both sending and receiving. The word of God is to be spoken in every tongue, but it can never be domesticated in any. The contemporary campaign of abuse directed against the World Council of Churches is certainly predictable and perhaps even to be welcomed as a sign that the sharp sword of the word of God is piercing our complacence and challenging the comfortable syncretism in which our Western Christianity has been living for so long.

The Mission of Reconciliation

One of the most important aspects of The Confession of 1967 of the reunited Presbyterian Church (U.S.A.) is its emphasis on the church's mission. The church does not exist as an end in itself; it exists in order to serve God's purposes in the world. In the 1960s, the United Presbyterian Church in the U.S.A. discerned God calling it to a ministry of reconciliation in the church and in the world.

SOURCE

"The Confession of 1967," in *Book of Confessions*, 9.31.

DIRECTION

To be reconciled to God is to be sent into the world as his reconciling community. This community, the church universal, is entrusted with God's message of reconciliation and shares his labor of healing the enmities which separate men from God and from each other. Christ has called the church to this mission and given it the gift of the Holy Spirit. The church maintains continuity with the apostles and with Israel by faithful obedience to his call.

The life, death, resurrection, and promised coming of Jesus Christ has set the pattern for the church's mission. His life as man involves the church in the common life of men. His service to men commits the church to work for every form of human well-being. His suffering makes the church sensitive to all the sufferings of mankind so that it sees the face of Christ in the faces of men in every kind of need. His crucifixion discloses to the church God's judgment on man's inhumanity to man and the awful consequences of its own complicity in injustice. In the power of the risen Christ and the hope of his coming the church sees the promise of God's renewal of man's life in society and of God's victory over all wrong.

The church follows this pattern in the form of its life and in the method of its action. So to live and serve is to confess Christ as Lord. . . .

RECONCILIATION IN SOCIETY

In each time and place there are particular problems and crises through which God calls the church to act. The church, guided by the Spirit, humbled by its own complicity and instructed by all attainable knowledge, seeks to discern the will of God and learn how to obey in these concrete situations. The following are particularly urgent at the present time.

a. God has created the peoples of the earth to be one universal family. In his reconciling love he overcomes the barriers between brothers and breaks down every form of discrimination based on racial or ethnic difference, real or imaginary. The church is called to bring all men to receive and uphold one another as persons in all relationships of life: in employment, housing, education, leisure, marriage, family, church, and the exercise of political rights. Therefore the church labors for the abolition of all racial discrimination and ministers to those injured by it. Congregations, individuals, or groups of Christians who exclude, dominate, or patronize their fellowmen, however subtly, resist the Spirit of God and bring contempt on the faith which they profess.

Called to Serve a Socialist Society

The Presbyterian-Reformed Church in Cuba confesses that in its historical context it is called to participate in God's reconstruction of humanity by serving a socialist society that demonstrates "sacrificial, solidary and effective love."

SOURCE

"Confession of Faith" (1977) of the Reformed-Presbyterian Church in Cuba, in *Reformed Witness Today*, 184–85.

THE INTEGRAL HUMAN BEING:
THE CENTER OF THE CHURCH'S INTEREST
IN HISTORY

The church is interested specifically in human History not only because, for almost 2000 years, it has been an important part of its development, but, principally because it is precisely within the process of human history where God in Jesus Christ has proposed to reconstruct the human being integrally. To cut up that reconstruction into sections has been the temptation the Church has fallen into as a consequence of the ideological captivity in which it has been engulfed for centuries, putting itself at the service of the exploiting classes, especially in the period of Monopolistic Capitalism.

The Church proclaims that there is only one History, and there it is not so much concerned about guaranteeing its own interests in the institutional-ecclesiastical order, inherited from the past, as about assuring the readiness and willingness of its members to respond freely "with the glorious freedom of the children of God" to the historical demands that God makes of them in the conquest of a society in which the integrally reconstructed human being—which is the purpose of the Gospel—can emerge little by little.

The Church teaches that the "atheism" of the ideology sustained by the Social Revolution, makes more clearly evident the atheism of the "believers" who are not capable of "discerning the signs of the times" in the midst of the new society being constructed, in which the radical transformations of the unjust structures make possible the creation of a more integrally reconstructed human being. The most important thing, in this case, is that the atheist-communists serve as an inspiration to us because of their readiness and willingness to live sacrificial, solidary and effective love.

The Church should be juridically separated from the State. This does not mean however that the Church relinquishes its historical-political responsibility nor that the Christian believers should withhold their most decided contribution to the construction of the new Socialist society.

The Church lives this new situation without fears, proclaiming the truth of the Gospel, confiding only in its Lord and captive only of Jesus Christ. In that way it finds its place in the human-historical process of integral recuperation. To do this the Church does not begrudge any sacrifices that may be necessary to fulfill its mission, the special characteristics of which vary in accordance with the moment and the place it has to live in.

The Church lives through the concrete love practiced by its members when they serve the socialist society without hostility, trusting the divine-human sense of History and trusting the future which envisions a more effective peace among nations and a more real justice among human beings.

THE MARKS OF THE CHURCH

In addition to the classical Nicene marks of an authentic church (one, holy, catholic, and apostolic), the Reformed tradition has emphasized three more functional criteria. For Calvin, where the Word of God is "purely preached and heard" and the sacraments "administered according to Christ's institution," a church of God undoubtedly exists. Other classical Reformed documents add "ecclesiastical discipline" as a third sign, or note, of an authentic church.

In the twentieth century, some Reformed theologians have argued that a church that is not engaged in mission is not faithful to the gospel. Furthermore, some theologians have suggested that the traditional marks, both Nicene and Reformed, should be reinterpreted in light of the theme in liberation theology of God's preferential option for the poor.

FOR FURTHER STUDY

Brunner, *Dogmatics*, 3:117–33. Weber, *Foundations*, 2:530–66.

How Many Marks?

G. C. Berkouwer discusses the question of whether there are more than four marks of the church. He points out the dangers of thinking of the church only in terms of one mark or of so emphasizing one that the others are diminished.

SOURCE

G. C. Berkouwer, *The Church*, trans. James E. Davison (Grand Rapids: Wm. B. Eerdmans, 1976), 24–25.

WHY FOUR ATTRIBUTES?

When we deal successively with the four well-known attributes, the question could be asked whether this approach allows the whole reality of the Church to come into view. In fact, some difference still exists with respect to the number of the Church's attributes. Sometimes other attributes have been added to the four, especially indefectibility and infallibility. According to Bavinck, these two also belong to the attributes of the Church. Obviously, it is not a matter of a closed number of four attributes seen as exhaustively and adequately describing the reality of the Church. However, it is reasonable to ask whether various newer words do not simply bring to light implications of these four words. For instance, has the confession of the Church concerning, respectively, her apostolicity and catholicity not contained essentially what is intended by infallibility and indefectibility? Yet one must always be open to all the revealing light that falls on the reality of the Church. Here we cannot help thinking of the many images and characterizations of the Church in the Scriptures, especially in the New Testament. From the nature of the case, it is impossible to add up all such images to arrive at a total sum. Each points to a different aspect of the one Church, and all need to be considered seriously. This multiplicity itself can guard us from onesidedness. Repeatedly, one particular aspect has been isolated from the whole or, at least, has been designated as the most central and primary aspect. The dangers of such centralizing are obvious. Other aspects can recede into the background and interest in them can lessen. It is good to remember this when we reflect on the attributes of the Church, since the whole life of the Church is at stake in the pure understanding of the *credo ecclesiam*, the one reality of the Church.

By dealing first with the unity and catholicity of the Church—so much in the center of interest at present—we do not mean to attach priority to these attributes at the expense of apostolicity and holiness. All aspects are so closely connected that any such priority is unthinkable. It is never possible to isolate the different aspects, and it would be possible to put unity and apostolicity or holiness and catholicity together at the beginning. Only from the way in which one deals with the one Church of Jesus Christ in all her aspects can it be clear whether or not the temptation to give priority to one of the attributes has been overcome. So, starting from the mystery of the Church, we call attention to what is undeniably obvious: unity and catholicity, or, phrased differently, the catholicity of the one Church.

Old Marks and New Signs

Jürgen Moltmann argues that theology is not restricted to a particular list of marks of the true church or to a specific interpretation of the meaning of those marks. He borrows themes from liberation theology in order to reinterpret the classical Nicene marks for the life of the church today.

SOURCE

Moltmann, *The Church*, 339–41.

(iv) If the characteristics of the church are statements of faith and hope, they also lead to *statements of action*. Because in Christ the church is one, it ought *to be* one. Those who receive its unity in Christ ought to seek its unity. The one people of the one kingdom ought to lay the foundations of unity among men. Because in Christ the church is holy, its members ought to fight sin and sanctify its life through righteousness. Because they are sanctified through the Spirit, they ought in obedience to sanctify all things for the new creation. Because in Christ it is open to the world, it ought to be catholic, testifying everywhere to the all-embracing kingdom. As the church of the Spirit, the one church is the unifying church. The holy church is the church that sanctifies or makes holy. The catholic church is the peace-giving, and so the all-embracing, church. The apostolic church is—through the gospel—the liberating church in the world.

The church's essential nature is given, promised and laid upon it in the characteristics we have named. Faith, hope and action are the genesis of the form of the church visible to the world in unity, holiness, catholicity and apostolicity. That is why theology cannot withdraw to "the invisible church," "the church of the future," or "the church of pure demands." The church lives in the one, holy, catholic and apostolic rule of Christ through faith, hope and action.

(v) Although the creed limits itself to these three or four marks of the church, this has never been seen in history as a restriction, but always as a pointer to the essentials. Theological doctrines of the church therefore include a wealth of other signs. Luther, for example, named seven: (i) the preaching of the true word of God; (ii) the right administration of baptism; (iii) the right form of the Lord's supper; (iv) the power of the keys; (v) the rightful calling and ordination of the church's ministers; (vi) prayer and hymn-singing in the vernacular; (vii) suffering and persecution. The church's creeds, however, always stopped short at the four classical attributes. These are undoubtedly the essential ones. But it must be noted that they were formulated and laid down for the first time at the great imperial synods of the early church and we therefore have to see them in the context of the church's development into the church of the empire. At that period there was considerable political pressure for the church's unity and universality, so that it might be in a position to administer the unified religion for the Roman empire. To make this historical observation is not to deny the truth of these statements about the church. But it gives us liberty to move other marks of the true church into the foreground in a changed world situation, and to link these with the traditional ones.

Theological recognition is not in itself a creed. It is not therefore bound to the formulated creed either. We shall permit ourselves to add other characteristics to the theological interpretation of the classical marks of the true church and to show their essential connection with the latter today. The church's unity is its *unity in freedom*. The church's holiness is its *holiness in poverty*. The church's apostolicity bears *the sign of the cross*, and its catholicity is linked with its *partisan support for the oppressed*.

Orthodoxy and Orthopraxis

Jan Lochman interprets the marks of the church by means of the theme "the service of God." An authentic church, one which is faithful to the gospel, is a church that both serves God in its worship and serves God in the world by means of its ministry. A faithful church is as concerned about right practice, or orthopraxis, as it is about correct doctrine, or orthodoxy.

SOURCE
Lochman, *The Faith We Confess*, 202–6.

MARKS OF THE TRUE CHURCH

The tension between these two aspects of the single reality of the church, this dialectic of the invisible in the visible, raises the question: if the church is a composite entity, where are we to look for the criterion that can point us in the right direction theologically and in practice? What direction is our commitment to the church to take? Here we come upon the frequently debated question about the marks of the true Church. The Apostles' Creed is somewhat sparing on this point. It names only two marks of the true church—it is holy, and it is catholic.

Holiness is not a demonstrable characteristic of the church. To take this biblically minted concept as denoting the quality of life of members of the church would be to misunderstand it completely. The term "holy," which we shall have to consider more fully later, emphasizes on the contrary that the church is the people "sanctified" by God, called and commissioned by him for special service. Knowledge of this special summons, call, and commission, however, knowledge of this the church's "holiness," inspires at once a commensurate effort to move in the direction indicated by Christ's work of salvation—in other words—an effort to sanctify our lives as individual Christians and as the church.

Catholicity, the other mark of the church named here—which in many Protestant churches is rendered by the pallid word "universal"—denotes what we should call today the "ecumenicity" of the church, its all-inclusive range. This is a quality of undoubted significance and import. But here again it has to be soberly acknowledged that none of the visible churches, not even the Roman Catholic Church, has any monopoly on catholicity, though it is certainly true that the Roman Catholic Church has pioneered further in this direction than others. The basis of catholicity, like that of holiness, lies not within us but outside ourselves—in the foundation which is Christ, in his Holy Spirit, who crosses all frontiers and divisions and sets them all in motion, who is the hope of all human beings. On this foundation we are called to oppose every kind of selfish isolation and to make visible true catholicity and ecumenicity.

It should be noted that both these marks of the church point beyond the empirical state of existing ecclesial institutions. Neither holiness nor catholicity is a possession; they represent rather the church's mission and task. How is this task to be defined? As the two terms themselves indicate—comprehensively: multi-faceted and all-inclusive. The two terms relate to the whole of human life sanctified by the triune God; they are aimed at the whole of the people of God and every aspect of its life. They therefore reject any singling out of certain areas as "holy," any selection of certain groups as "elites."

One reality, however, one concept, must be set very firmly in the center, namely, the service of God. And this means first of all the service of God in the sense of the church service—worship, the liturgical assembly of the Christian community gathered for praise and proclamation, for intercession and edification. In his Gifford Lectures on "The Knowledge of God and the Service of God" Karl Barth had this to say about the church service:

> The church service is the most important, momentous, and majestic thing that can possibly take place on earth, because its primary content is not the work of man but the work of the Holy Spirit and, consequently, the work of faith.

So lofty a claim may seem somewhat of an exaggeration when we remember the poverty of our liturgical life and our church services. Yet it accords with the view of the ancient church for which the Creed also speaks. For the ancient church, the liturgy was the real contemporization of Christ, the making present and contemporary of Christ's history, the particularization in time and space of the presence of the Holy Spirit. This can be seen most impressively even today in the great liturgies of the Eastern church. Nor was it entirely forgotten even at the time of the Reformation. The definition of the church given in Article VII of the Augsburg Confession, for example, points unmistakably to the church service: the church is "the assembly of saints in which the gospel is taught purely and the sacraments are administered rightly."

It is here, at this specific point—the church service—that the heartbeat of the church is to be found and heard even today. We must never forget that. Here, in this action, this event, the church is really in its own element, doing its own thing. Here the church truly comes into its own. If it were to abandon this "point," it would abandon itself. Here in particular the warning about having the rose and having its thorns must be heeded—especially by the theologians. Even today we have no more important and pertinent service to perform than this struggle for a living Christian liturgy, an authentic church service.

But the Reformation view of the service of God cannot be restricted to this central point alone. From this center, the lines radiate outwards. This center becomes the focal point for the whole of life. Indeed it is our *whole* life—in the widest sense—that constitutes the service of God.

It was primarily the Swiss and Czech Reformers who championed this comprehensive view of the service of God, as can be seen from their expansion of the marks of the true church. To the two main Lutheran marks of the church—proclamation of God's Word in its purity and the right administration of the sacraments—the Reformed churches added a third, the godly discipline, that is, the duty of the individual Christian and of the Christian community to live according to the gospel. The

Czech Reformers went even further. From the beginning the Czech Reformation put great emphasis on the normative character of apostolic practice, and hence on the life style of the poor Christian community as over against the Constantinian church's lust for power. Five sure and infallible marks of the true church are listed in the Bohemian Confession of 1575. In addition to the two classic Reformation marks, it mentions: (3) obedience to Christ's gospel and law, with special emphasis on love between Christians; (4) suffering (cross) and persecution for the truth and kingdom of God; and (5) a disciplined ordering of church life (church discipline).

An important aspect is underscored by "these additions." In the Christian life, in the struggle for the church, it is not just "orthodoxy" (correct doctrine) that matters but also a related "orthopraxy" (correct practice), that is, the maintenance of the Christian faith in all aspects of life, in all our dealings with other human beings; the willingness to act and to suffer for God's kingdom and justice; a disciplined discipleship. The church is the company of those who are gathered around this service of God and for this service of God. As Calvin would say, it is "the company of the faithful." Only in union with this company of the faithful, only as we share in its spiritual struggle does our confession of the church ring true. The church has never been a gathering of neutrals and mere spectators. It is no accident that in the "Letters to the Seven Churches" in the Book of Revelation it is "lukewarm" Christians rather than avowed opponents of the church who are identified as its real source of danger: "Would that you were cold or hot! So, because you are lukewarm and neither cold nor hot, I will spew you out of my mouth" (Rev. 3:15f.). In Christ's army a noncombatant is a dubious Christian!

These emphases point to a fundamental ecclesiological truth: the church, in the sense intended in the Creed, is not an end in itself. It exists in the active service of God, meaning both God's service to the world and the Christian's service of God and the world. In both senses, the church is assigned an all-embracing horizon which cannot possibly be called "ecclesiocentric." On the contrary, the church is essentially an "ex-centric" community or it is not the church.

All the terms employed in this credal clause—church, holy, catholic—point in this same direction. Understood in their biblical sense, all three terms make audible a summons to service within the horizon of the whole world, a call to cross our own frontiers and to go into all the world. This was how the Old Testament people of God was understood by its own prophets: Israel is an elect people, a holy nation. It is so, however, in a quite precise sense. It had been chosen and sanctified not in and for itself but in the midst of all the other nations and for their sake. This comes out even more forcefully and with extremely practical and tangible effects in the apostolic church. Its members do not remain in a huddle behind closed doors; in the power of the risen Christ and the Holy Spirit they move out into the world, there to take up their world-transforming venture of missionary witness and compassionate service.

SACRAMENTS AND THE MEANS OF GRACE

Although classical Reformed theology discussed the nature of a sacrament, usually defining it in Augustinian fashion as a visible sign of an invisible grace, contemporary theology has been more reticent and less inclined to approach the issue abstractly. Like their predecessors in the tradition, Reformed theologians today acknowledge two sacraments—baptism and the Lord's Supper. What has been vigorously debated in twentieth-century theology, however, is the meaning and appropriate practice of baptism and the Lord's Supper. Several prominent Reformed theologians, such as Karl Barth and Jürgen Moltmann, recently have raised questions about the baptism of the children of believers. Far-reaching questions also have been raised about the significance of the Lord's Supper for the church's life and ministry in the world.

FOR FURTHER STUDY

Baptism, Eucharist, and Ministry (Geneva: World Council of Churches, 1982). G. C. Berkouwer, *The Sacraments*, trans. Hugo Bekker (Grand Rapids: Wm. B. Eerdmans, 1969). Geoffrey W. Bromiley, *Sacramental Teaching and Practice in the Reformation Churches* (Grand Rapids: Wm B. Eerdmans, 1957). P. T. Forsyth, *The Church and the Sacraments* (London: Independent Press, 1953). Robert S. Paul, *The Atonement and the Sacraments: The Relation of the Atonement to the Sacraments of Baptism and the Lord's Supper* (New York: Abingdon, 1960).

The Nature of Sacrament

The Sacraments as Means of Grace

Writing in the last half of the nineteenth century, Princeton Seminary theologian Charles Hodge described the main themes in the Reformed understanding of the nature of a sacrament.

SOURCE

Hodge, *Systematic Theology*, 3:499–500.

DOCTRINE OF
THE REFORMED CHURCH

The first point clearly taught on this subject in the Symbols of the Reformed Church is that the sacraments are real means of grace, that is, means appointed and employed by Christ for conveying the benefits of his redemption to his people. They are not, as Romanists teach, the exclusive channels; but they are channels. A promise is made to those who rightly receive the sacraments that they shall thereby and therein be made partakers of the blessings of which the sacraments are the divinely appointed signs and seals. The word grace, when we speak of the means of grace, includes three things. 1st. An unmerited gift, such as the remission of sin. 2d. The supernatural influence of the Holy Spirit. 3d. The subjective effects of that influence on the soul. Faith, hope, and charity, for example, are graces.

The second point in the Reformed doctrine on the sacraments concerns the source of their power. On this subject it is taught negatively that the virtue is not in them. The word virtue is of course here used in its Latin sense for power or efficiency. What is denied is that the sacraments are the efficient cause of the gracious effects which they produce. The efficiency does not reside in the elements, in the water used in baptism, or in the bread and wine used in the Lord's Supper. It is not in the sacramental actions; either in giving, or in receiving the consecrated elements. Neither does the virtue or efficiency due to sacraments reside in, or flow from the person by whom they are administered. It does not reside in his office. There is no supernatural power in the man, in virtue of his office, to render the sacraments effectual. Nor does their efficiency depend on the character of the administrator in the sight of God; nor upon his intention; that is, his purpose to render them effectual. The man who administers the sacraments is not a worker of miracles. The Apostles and others at that time in the Church, were endued with supernatural power; and they had to will to exercise it in order to its producing its legitimate effect. It is not so with the officers of the Church in the administration of the sacraments. The affirmative statement on this subject is that the efficacy of the sacraments is due solely to the blessing of Christ and the working of his Spirit. The Spirit, it is to be ever remembered, is a personal agent who works when and how He will. God has promised that his Spirit shall attend his Word; and He thus renders it an effectual means for the sanctification of his people. So He has promised, through the attending operation of his Spirit, to render the sacraments effectual to the same end.

The third point included in the Reformed doctrine is, that the sacraments are effectual as means of grace only, so far as adults are concerned, to those who by faith receive them. They may have a natural power on other than believers by presenting truth and exciting feeling, but their saving or sanctifying influence is experienced only by believers.

All these points are clearly presented in the standards of our own Church. The sacraments are declared to be means of grace, that is, means for signifying, sealing, and applying the benefits of redemption. It is denied that this virtue is in them, or in him by whom they are administered. It is affirmed that their efficiency in conveying grace, is due solely to the blessing of Christ and the coöperation of his Spirit; and that such efficiency is experienced only by believers.

The One Sacrament Jesus Christ

In the context of discussing the meaning of baptism, Karl Barth argues that baptism is not a sacrament because baptism is not "a divine work and word." Baptism is not the bearer of grace, but the acknowledgment of the one sacrament, that which alone is God's grace, the history of Jesus Christ.

SOURCE

Barth, *Church Dogmatics*, IV/4:101–2.

To begin with a critical observation, the praise of baptism is not served but fatefully damaged if the sanctity of this action is sought, not in the true and distinctive thing which characterizes it as a human action, but in a supposedly immanent divine work. The presumed better becomes an enemy of the good, and one misses the meaning, if one regards it as too mean a thing to focus attention on that which is willed and done in baptism by the men whom God has liberated for it. If the true and distinctive thing in baptism is sought in a divine work and word which takes place in, with and under what men will and do, then we are impaled on the horns of a dilemma. On the one side, that which men will and do is completely overshadowed and obscured by the immanent divine work and word. It is thus robbed of significance and interest, and cannot be the proper theme of independent study. On the other side, that which men will and do becomes as such the will and accomplishment of the divine work and word. The human action as such is also a divine action. Water baptism is integrated into the baptism of the Spirit, and renders the latter superfluous. Either way, Christian baptism is treated docetically. It is divested of its character as the water baptism which is distinct from the baptism of the Spirit, as the human decision which corresponds to the divine turning to man. It thus ceases to be a truly human work and word which proceeds from that basis, which hastens to that goal, and which is done in the freedom that God has given to men. At the commencement of the Christian life there is, then, no free human answer to the act and call of the free God. The subordination of baptism to its basis and goal also disappears; its meaning is identical with its basis and goal. It is a strangely competitive duplication of the history of Jesus Christ, of His resurrection, of the outpouring of the Holy Spirit.

All this, and the implied understanding of the meaning of baptism, has to be resolutely rejected. Nor is this rejection surprising in view of what has had to be thought and said already about the basis and goal of baptism. Baptism relates to the one divine work which took place in Jesus Christ, to the one divine word which was spoken in Him. It is not itself, however, a divine work and word. It is the work and word of men who have become obedient to Jesus Christ and who have put their hope in Him. Baptism, as water baptism, takes place in the light of the baptism of the Spirit, and with a view to it. As such, however, it is not itself the baptism of the Spirit; it is always water baptism. Baptism takes place in active recognition of the grace of God which justifies, sanctifies and calls. It is not itself, however, the bearer, means, or instrument of grace. Baptism responds to a mystery, the sacrament of the history of Jesus Christ, of His resurrection, of the outpouring of the Holy Spirit. It is not itself, however, a mystery or sacrament.

Sacraments "Between the Times"

Donald M. Baillie discusses the significance of the sacraments for Christians who live "between the times," that is, between those events in the first century which are the basis of Christian faith and hope and that eschatological event which hovers on the horizon of history. Because they both look backward and anticipate God's future, sacraments are eschatological signs.

SOURCE

Donald M. Baillie, *The Theology of the Sacraments* (New York: Charles Scribner's Sons, 1957), 69–71.

As a background to the particular sacraments, theology in our time has begun in a new way to speak of the eschatological nature of the Church, or of the Church as an eschatological entity. What does that mean? It is bound up with the rediscovery that the Christian message is a *Heilsgeschichte*, a sacred story, running on from eternity through history to eternity again, with Christ as its central and determinative point. There is no doubt about the presence of that idea in the New Testament. And it has been worked out by writers like Barth and Cullmann so as to yield what we may call a time-scheme, a temporal process divided into successive periods, one of which, the period between the ascension of Christ and His second coming, is the period in which we are living. It is an interim period, the "time between the times," and it is the "time of the Church." It is a period in which we may say that the Kingdom has come (since it came with the coming of Christ) and yet has still to come because the final consummation is not yet. Christ is present with us, yet not in the way in which He was present in the days of His flesh, and again not in the way in which we shall enjoy His immediate presence in the final consummation. In this interim period He is present with us through the Holy Spirit in the Church. And in this interim period the Church is always looking back and looking forward.

That is why the Church needs sacraments. And in both baptism and the Lord's supper, the Church looks both back to the death and resurrection of Christ, which have to be reproduced in us, and forward to the full enjoyment of the Kingdom, of which the Holy Spirit given in baptism is an earnest and seal, and whose messianic banquet we rehearse and anticipate in the sacrament of the Lord's supper. When the Kingdom comes, or when we reach heaven, we shall no longer need sacraments, because we shall have passed *ex umbris et imaginibus in veritatem*, we shall be living in the immediate presence of God, we shall be *in patria*. But meanwhile we are *viatores*, present in the body and absent from the Lord, able to see only "in a mirror and in a riddle"; and a sacrament is a kind of mirror, the kind of mirror of eternal things required by creatures of flesh and blood in a fallen world which has been redeemed but whose redemption is not yet complete. That is our situation, of which and to which the sacraments speak; and that is why we call them eschatological signs.

Finally, lest we should fall into a fashionable jargon which is remote from the common man, we must in a few words try to relate this to our common life.

Even the most untheological minds know sometimes what it means to feel that we are "strangers and pilgrims" journeying through a world in which we have to walk by faith and not by sight. We have a certain sense of separation, our fellowship is never complete, or even our reconciliation with each other; and the same is true of our relationship to God.

Our very bodies seem to separate us, and we long for a fuller life in which we should be not disembodied spirits, but in some sense "all one body" in God, and in which faith and love would be as natural as the air we breathe. We cannot be satisfied with a merely "spiritual" union. We love the bodies of our friends as well as their souls, and when we are separated from them we long to hear the sound of their voices, to see their faces and familiar gestures, and to feel the touch of their hands. And yet even when we have all these things, we know that our isolation has not been quite overcome. It has been overcome in Christ, and in Him we are all one with God and one with each other; and yet our unity will never be complete until we see God face to face. And thus we stand between looking back and looking forward.

"And I saw the holy city, new Jerusalem . . . and I heard a great voice out of the throne saying: Behold, the tabernacle of God is with men, and He shall dwell with them, and they shall be His people, and God Himself shall be with them and be their God . . . and I saw no temple therein: for the Lord God Almighty and the Lamb are the temple thereof."

When that comes true, there will be no more need of temples and altars, signs and symbols, services and sacraments. But it has not yet come true; and meanwhile we are creatures of flesh and blood in this spoilt and fallen world, and do need the helps which God in His kindness has provided for us in the sacraments of the Gospel.

Baptism

In the twentieth century, several theologians have challenged the traditional Reformed interpretation of baptism. Classical Reformed theology interpreted baptism in terms of the covenant of grace, the cleansing of sin, and the biblical imagery of circumcision (Col. 2:11–12). Recently some theologians have argued that it is not cleansing and circumcision but participation in Christ's death and resurrection and the call to discipleship that are the New Testament's primary interpretations of baptism. This emphasis on discipleship has led some theologians to question the traditional Reformed practice of baptizing the children of believers. The issue, they argue, is whether the baptism of infants renders God's costly grace in Jesus Christ "cheap" and deemphasizes the call to discipleship. Those theologians who continue to support the traditional practice of baptizing infants argue that to give it up would violate the biblical and Reformed understanding of baptism as a celebration of God's prevenient grace.

FOR FURTHER STUDY

Karl Barth, *The Teaching of the Church Regarding Baptism*, trans. Ernest A. Payne (London: SCM, 1948). Markus Barth, *Die Taufe, ein Sacrament?* (Zurich: Evangelischer Verlag, 1951). Alexander A. Campbell, *Scripture Baptism Defined According to the Revealed Church of God, and the Doctrine of Justification by Faith; Its Origin, Design, Mode and Subject* (Cincinnati: A. Pugh and Company, 1844). Church of Scotland Report on Baptism, *The Biblical Doctrine of Baptism* (Edinburgh: St. Andrew, 1960). Oscar Cullmann, *Baptism in the New Testament*, trans. J. K. S. Reid (Chicago: Allenson, 1950). Paul K. Jewett, *Infant Baptism and the Covenant of Grace: An Appraisal of the Argument That As Infants Were Once Circumcised, So They Should Now Be Baptized* (Grand Rapids: Wm. B. Eerdmans, 1978). Hodge, *Systematic Theology*, 3:526–611.

Faith as a Precondition for Baptism

Friedrich Schleiermacher argued that faith is a necessary precondition for baptism and that without it baptism is wrongly received and given. Furthermore, baptism should not be administered before preaching has awakened faith.

SOURCE

Schleiermacher, *Christian Faith*, 629–31.

From what has now been said regarding the nature of the action, and especially from the fact that the baptized person is asked to give a confession of the Word joined to the action, it follows very clearly that the baptized person's faith is a precondition of the action really being what it is intended to be. So much lies before us in Christ's two sayings about baptism. For even if in the first saying we seek to combine "making disciples" and baptizing as closely as possible, what we there have is a later elaboration which only reached its final stage in the second saying, and which from the outset could only represent an approximation to faith; and even in baptism this approximation could only be fully realized if the baptized person were prepared to make confession of the Word that accompanies baptism. Similarly, the faith which in the other passage Christ makes an antecedent of baptism must be the very faith of which we have been speaking all along. Peter, indeed, seems to demand merely repentance, not faith, before baptism; still, it was repentance for the part which his hearers, as members of the Jewish nation, had had in the rejection of Christ, a repentance which had only been rendered possible through the acknowledgment of Christ and adoption of His cause which they owed to Peter's address; and this of itself must involve faith. Peter brings in this demand at the close of his sermon; he must therefore have started with the same assumption as Paul, and been convinced that his preaching had already produced faith in every case where this was a possibility. Similarly, our thought of the Church, as constantly engaged in preaching, must be that it ought to conclude preaching by baptism, but not interrupt preaching to baptize. Now in the quoted credal passages it is also stated that baptism is proper and complete even without faith, and it tallies with this that other thinkers represent faith as the fruit and consequence of baptism. But against both views we must enter a protest. Baptism is received wrongly if it be received without faith, and it is wrongly given so. True, the ordinance loses none of its significance, whether considered as originally an institution of Christ or in its more definite form as an ordinance of the Church; but this is so only because the Church can never have laid down that it is a matter of indifference whether those baptized are believers or not. For the same reason, baptism as an act of the mere individual has never been such that the Church could approve of it and regard it quite as its own; in any case such acts of baptism fall under the head of imperfect Church administration. But if this only means that even in such cases baptism need not be repeated, the point is one which requires to be stated more emphatically, lest we should seem to be ignoring what are manifest imperfections. Baptism, that is to say, is ineffectual only when it is imparted prematurely, before the work of preaching is complete and has awakened faith. It is different with the assertion that faith springs from baptism as its fruit. This is obviously in contradiction to the whole practice of the Apostles and the whole experience of the Church as it grew in consequence of mass-baptism; nay, even in the individual case, where one who is still an unbeliever has been baptized too early, the Church does not rely on baptism alone but carries on the work of preaching in the full sense of the word; and if in these circumstances faith arises later, no simple Christian mind will ascribe this to the wrongly administered baptism, but to what subsequently to baptism has been done by the Church.

The Case for Infant Baptism

Geoffrey W. Bromiley repeats some of the basic convictions of Reformed theology in making the case for the continued practice of baptizing the children of believers: Baptism is a sign of God's grace, and children in covenant communities who participate in that reality should not be denied the sign.

SOURCE

Geoffrey W. Bromiley, *Children of Promise: The Case for Baptizing Infants* (Grand Rapids: Wm. B. Eerdmans, 1979), 107–9.

When we consider the positive aspects we find first that the baptism of infants in a covenant setting is consonant with God's dealings with his people in both the Old Testament and the New. This does not prove, of course, that infants have to be baptized. Parents are not disobeying any clearcut command if they withhold baptism from their children. On the other hand they are assuming that the extension of the covenant promise to the nations has brought a discontinuity with God's mode of covenant dealing with families and peoples. No evident support can be found for this in the New Testament. Indeed, all the evidence that we have points the other way. Christians still live within a family structure and a church structure. The one covenant of grace still obtains. The covenant signs have been changed, but they still are signs. The types of baptism continue to bear witness to God's work in family and people. The church is the Israel of God but not to the exclusion of God's Old Testament people and not as its spiritualization.

We also find positively that baptism, like the word itself, bears first and final testimony to the work of God on which any response of our own must be grounded. If baptism tells us what we ourselves are to do, it bases this imperative on the indicative of what God has done, does, and will do for us. Hence baptism does not arise *out of* any work of ours. It is baptism *into* the work of God on our behalf. Naturally, if no knowledge of this work is available, baptism can have no meaning. For this reason its administration is dependent on the presence of the word which tells us of the divine work. Adult converts from unbelief are baptized when the word has come to them and they have heard and received it. Their children are baptized because they are already in the sphere of the word and are to hear it as soon as possible. They belong to the people of the word. The electing, reconciling, and regenerating work of God forms the basis of their life and the primary theme of their upbringing. Since the word which tells of this work is with them from the very first, they may properly receive the sign, seal, and testimony of God's sovereign activity before them, for them, and in them.

Also positively, we find that even our own response is the work of God. In this area two points can easily be overlooked. The first is that regeneration is not a human possibility, and the second that it does not stand alone but is part of that total renewing in Christ's image which embraces sanctification and glorification as well. When these truths are appreciated, the difference between adult and infant baptism is set in its proper perspective. It is relativized both by the distinction between divine and human possibility and also by the discrepancy between human achievement and divine purpose and perfecting. Even the adult has neither reached that which baptism signifies nor begun to grasp what its consummation will be. By coming to personal repentance and faith he may be a little further on the road of entry into the divine work. But the Spirit who has brought him thus far is the Spirit who works in infants too—and both he and they have a long way to go before they are brought by the Spirit into the fullness of the baptismal work.

On the positive side we see finally that children cannot be denied a part in the divine work of salvation. The witness of scripture is surely conclusive enough here. If, then, baptism signifies what God does in election, reconciliation, and renewal, infants who enjoy the thing signified cannot properly be denied the sign so long as they are brought up within the covenant and with an assurance that they will hear the gospel promises. This does not mean automatic salvation for the baptized any more than it means automatic perdition for the non-baptized. What it does mean is that salvation extends to infants too and that where the means are present by which the Spirit does his gracious work of calling the sign of salvation may also be extended.

Inherited Faith?

Karl Barth's last volume in his *Church Dogmatics* evoked controversy and considerable debate in Reformed communities. He was well known throughout the theological world for emphasizing God's grace in Jesus Christ as the central theme of the gospel (one commentator described Barth's theology as "the triumph of grace"), but it came as a surprise to many people to learn that Barth advocated "believer's baptism": Because the Christian life cannot be inherited, baptism should be left to that event in which an individual professes faith in the prevenient grace of God.

SOURCE

Barth, *Church Dogmatics*, IV/4:183–84.

The New Testament undoubtedly does provide for the singling out of children who are born and brought up in the community of Jesus Christ which is gathered, built up and sent out by the Holy Spirit. Since they live from the very first with parents who are summoned to this people, who live with some degree of truth and power in its faith, who take part in its prayer and witness, their situation is certainly very different from that of children who do not have this privilege. The fact that the promise which is given to this people and the claim to which it is subjected are from the very first (to varying degrees) presented to them and brought to their attention, means that they enjoy a very special *praevenire* of the grace of God. Even for these children, however, it cannot be cheap grace. They have still to enter in at the strait gate and tread the narrow way. No one is a true and living member of this people, to be taken seriously as such, merely by living in its midst. A man can be this only when he is awakened to be such a member by the Holy Spirit who is the power of the work and word of Jesus Christ, only when he is born again, created anew. The Christian life cannot be inherited as blood, gifts, characteristics and inclinations are inherited. No Christian environment, however genuine or sincere, can transfer this life to those who are in this environment. For these, too, the Christian life will and can begin only on the basis of their own liberation by God, their own decision. Its beginning— this is no part of their distinction but would run contrary to it—cannot be made for them by others through the fact that, without being asked about their own decision, they received baptism. How can one expect any growth of the living community of the living Lord Jesus Christ in this way?

A New Baptismal Practice

Jürgen Moltmann proposes a new practice of baptism for the church. Parents would not be compelled to have their children baptized, nor would they be prevented from having their children baptized. Those parents who choose not to have their children baptized would participate in a service in which the children would be blessed and the parents and the congregation commissioned for service to the children. Baptism would be postponed until a later date when the individual would be commissioned for service in the world.

SOURCE

Moltmann, *The Church*, 240–42.

SUGGESTIONS FOR
A NEW BAPTISMAL PRACTICE

The way to a new, more authentic baptismal practice will be the way from infant to adult baptism. By adult baptism we mean the baptism of those who believe, are called and confess their faith. The usages of centuries cannot be suddenly altered. The path proposed means a learning process for the Christian church which has many implications.

As a first step the time of baptism should be made a matter of free decision and left to the parents. Church law and church order would have to be altered in this sense. The clergy and the church's "full-time workers" should not be forced to have their children baptized either. But for their part they must not compel anyone to postpone baptism, or prevent parents from having their children baptized. They should preach and teach the Christian meaning of baptism and make it comprehensible, and not only at baptismal services themselves. Responsibility for children lies in the parents' hands in the first instance. This responsibility must be impressed on the parents as regards baptism, but it cannot be taken from them.

Infant baptism should be replaced by the blessing of the children in the congregation's service of worship and by the "ordination"—the public and explicit commissioning of parents and congregation—for their messianic service to the children. The baptism of parents is a call covering their family, social and political relationships as well. The Christian ought to follow his call in his secular profession too, and act accordingly. That is why it is important to make this call clear in the vocation of parenthood. Parenthood is a charisma, and becomes a living charisma in faith. The calling of the community is then realized in missionary service to the children and in their instruction. "Confirmation" classes can then be directed towards baptism, which people approach when they feel able to confess their faith before the congregation and desire the assurance of their calling. Through the birth of children to Christian parents, the church is called to the service of reconciliation and liberation on their behalf. This progression from infant baptism to baptism as a call cannot be pursued unless we note the implications for the history of the individual life and for the church of Christ.

In the history of the individual life the religious festival of birth and name-giving would be replaced by a call event, which would make clear the believer's Christian identity. The person's natural identifications through family, nation and society then recede into the background. The new identity of Christ's fellowship frees the believer from those natural identifications for representative, liberating service on their behalf. So-called voluntary baptism does not really make baptism a matter of choice, but is essentially a baptism into the liberty of Christ. It is a liberating event. In the history of a person's life this means the pain of alienation from his present associations and groups, and often enough an exodus like the exodus of Abraham. But it leads him into a freedom in which he can "be there for others." In baptism as a call, the important thing is to stress not merely the alienation from the existing groups and associations of life, but even more the commission to service for their reconciliation and liberation. This baptism must not become the symbol of inner emigration and resignation in the face of "the wicked world." It is the sign of the dawn of hope for this world and of messianic service in it. It is a missionary sign. Through a baptism of this kind the meaning of one's own life is comprehended in the wider framework of God's history with the world. Baptism joins a fragmentary and incomplete human life with the fullness of life and the perfect glory of God.

Without new fellowship in a supporting group, this way cannot be pursued by individuals. It is only in the degree in which the church ceases to be a non-committal religious society and turns into a recognizable messianic fellowship of service for the kingdom of God that individuals can realize their calling in the sense we have described. Conversely, however, such a fellowship only develops out of professing believers. Here we are concerned with a reciprocal relationship which has to be given effect from the individual and the social side simultaneously. If individuals go over to vocational baptism from infant baptism, then the church must develop at the same time from the religious welfare institution to a social body built up on firm fellowship. It must stop being a church of ministers functioning on behalf of laymen, and become a charismatic fellowship in which everyone recognizes his ministry and lays hold on his charisma. People then become "subjects" within the church, losing their position as "objects" of religious welfare. Just as believers' baptism can lead to inner emigration, so a confessing community of this kind can of course turn into an introvert group in a self-made ghetto. That is why this development must be accompanied by increased stress on the individual's call to liberating service for society and on the fellowship's openness to the world. If a "worldly" church were merely to become an "unworldly" one, nothing would be gained. The church's detachment from worldly influence must lead to the "church for the world," which renders service to society and the individual out of the things that are its own: the proclamation of the gospel and the new turning to the future. Common baptism binds together the fragmentary form of this church with the perfection of the coming kingdom of God. Baptism as the calling event in the life of the individual person corresponds only to a church that follows Christ's call, the "call to freedom." Baptism as the liberating event in a person's life corresponds only to a church which spreads the liberty of Christ. This must not be confused with a liberalization of religious usages in a "Christian society." A liberal church may make adult baptism "voluntary." A church of liberation lives from baptism as liberating event. That is something different.

The Lord's Supper

Beginning with John Calvin, one of the central features of Reformed theology has been its understanding of the real, spiritual presence of Christ in the Lord's Supper, or Eucharist. Although Reformed communities have from time to time strayed from that conviction, its recovery has often marked a revitalization of the church. The challenge for modern theologians has been to interpret the significance of the real presence of Christ for the life of the church in the world. Two of the themes that have been prominent in recent discussions of the Lord's Supper are eschatology and social ethics.

The Lord's Supper is not simply an exercise in *anamnesis* or the actualization in the present of the redemptive power of Christ's death and resurrection. It is also an exercise in eschatology, "for as often as you eat this bread and drink this cup you do show forth the Lord's death until he comes." The Lord's Supper, therefore, is a celebration and an anticipation of the messianic banquet.

In addition, what the church celebrates when it gathers at the Lord's table must also be lived and enacted in the world. Because it is God's grace alone which calls people to the messianic feast, so too they are called to be witnesses in society to God's justice and love.

FOR FURTHER STUDY

Donald M. Baillie, *The Theology of the Sacraments* (New York: Charles Scribner's Sons, 1957), 91–124. G. C. Berkouwer, *The Sacraments*, trans. Hugo Bekker (Grand Rapids: Wm. B. Eerdmans, 1969), 188–296. Alasdair I. C. Heron, *Table and Tradition: Toward an Understanding of the Eucharist* (Philadelphia: Westminster, 1983). Hodge, *Systematic Theology*, 3:611–92. Schleiermacher, *Christian Faith*, 638–57. Weber, *Foundations*, 2:614–47.

The Recovery of Real Presence

One of the most important movements in nineteenth-century Reformed theology in the United States was Mercersburg theology, led by Philip Schaff (1819–93) and John Williamson Nevin (1803–86). Mercersburg, Pennsylvania, was the educational center of the German Reformed Church in the United States, and it was here that Schaff and Nevin began to teach in 1844. In 1846 Nevin attacked what he perceived to be a widespread retreat by Reformed churches from the understanding of the Lord's Supper in the Reformed confessions. Nevin called for a recovery of a Calvinist understanding of the real, spiritual presence of Christ in the Supper and the rejection of both rationalist and Roman Catholic interpretations.

SOURCE

John Williamson Nevin, *The Mystical Presence: A Vindication of the Reformed or Calvinistic Doctrine of the Holy Eucharist*, in *The Mercersburg Theology*, ed. James Hastings Nichols (New York: Oxford University Press, 1966), 200–204.

FOR FURTHER STUDY

Theodore Appel, *The Life and Work of John Williamson Nevin* (Philadelphia: Reformed Church Publication House, 1889). B. A. Gerrish, *Tradition and the Modern World: Reformed Theology in the Nineteenth Century* (Chicago: University of Chicago Press, 1978), 49–70. James Hastings Nichols, *Romanticism in American Theology: Nevin and Schaff at Mercersburg* (Chicago: University of Chicago Press, 1961).

To obtain a proper view of the original doctrine of the Reformed Church on the subject of the Eucharist, we must have recourse particularly to Calvin. Not that he is to be considered the creator, properly speaking, of the doctrine. It grew evidently out of the general religious life of the Church itself, in its antagonism to the Lutheran dogma on the one hand and the low Socinian extreme on the other. Calvin, however, was the theological organ by which it first came to that clear expression, under which it continued to be uttered subsequently in the symbolical books. His profound, far-reaching, and deeply penetrating mind drew forth the doctrine from the heart of the Church, exhibited it in its proper relations, proportions, and distinctions, gave it form in this way for the understanding, and clothed it with authority as a settled article of faith in the general creed. He may be regarded, then, as the accredited interpreter and expounder of the article for all later times. A better interpreter in the case we could not possibly possess. Happily, too, his instructions and explanations here are very full and explicit. He comes upon the subject from all sides, and handles it under all forms, didactically and controversially, so that we are left in no uncertainty whatever, with regard to his meaning, at a single point.

Any theory of the Eucharist will be found to accord closely with the view that is taken at the same time of the nature of the union generally between Christ and his people. Whatever the life of the believer may be as a whole in this relation, it must determine the form of his communion with the Saviour in the sacrament of the Supper as the central representation of its significance and power. Thus, the sacramental doctrine of the primitive Reformed Church stands inseparably connected with the idea of an inward living union between believers and Christ, in virtue of which they are incorporated into his very nature, and made to subsist with him by the power of a common life. In full correspondence with this conception of the Christian salvation as a process by which

277

the believer is mystically inserted more and more into the person of Christ till he becomes thus at last fully transformed into his image, it was held that nothing less than such a real participation of his living person is involved always in the right use of the Lord's Supper. The following distinctions may serve to define and explain more fully the nature of the communion which holds between Christ and his people, in the whole view now mentioned, as taught by Calvin and the Reformed Church generally in the sixteenth century.

1. The union of *believers* with Christ is not simply that of a common humanity, as derived from *Adam*. In this view, all men partake of one and the same nature, and each may be said to be in relation to his neighbor bone of his bone and flesh of his flesh. So Christ took not on him the nature of angels but of men. He was born of a woman, and appeared among us in the likeness and fashion of our own life, only without sin. But plainly our relation to his nature, and through this to his mediatorial work, as Christians, is something quite different from this general consanguinity of the human race. Where we are said to be of the same life with him, "members of his body, of his flesh and of his bones" (Eph. 5:30), it is not on the ground merely of a joint participation with him in the nature of Adam, but on the ground of our participation in his own nature as a higher order of life. Our relation to him is not circuitous and collateral only; it holds in a direct connection with his person.

2. In this view, the relation is more again than a simply *moral* union. Such a union we have where two or more persons are bound together by inward agreement, sympathy, and correspondence. Every common friendship is of this sort. It is the relation of the disciple to the master whom he loves and reveres. It is the relation of the devout Jew to Moses, his venerated lawgiver and prophet. It holds also undoubtedly between the believer and Christ. The Saviour lives much in his thoughts and affections. He looks to him with an eye of faith, embraces him in his heart, commits himself to his guidance, walks in his steps, and endeavors to become clothed more and more with his very mind itself. In the end the correspondence will be found complete. We shall be like him in all respects, one with him morally in the fullest sense. But Christianity includes more than such a moral union, separately considered. This union itself is only the result here of a relation more inward and deep. It has its ground in the force of a common life, in virtue of which Christ and his people are one even before they become thus assimilated to his character. So in the sacrament of the Lord's Supper; it is not simply a moral approach that the true worshipper is permitted to make to the glorious object of his worship. His communion with Christ does not

consist merely in the good exercises of his own mind, the actings of faith, and contrition, and hope, and love, the solemn recollections, the devotional feelings, the pious resolutions, of which he may be himself the subject during the sacramental service. Nor is the sacrament a sign only, by which the memory and heart may be assisted in calling up what is past or absent, for the purposes of devotion; as the picture of a friend is suited to recall his image and revive our interest in his person, when he is no longer in our sight. Nor is it a pledge simply of our own consecration to the service of Christ, or of the faithfulness of God as engaged to make good to us in a general way the grace of the new covenant, as the rainbow serves still to ratify and confirm the promise given to Noah after the flood. All this would bring with it in the end nothing more than a moral communication with Christ, so far as the sacrament itself might be concerned. It could carry with it no virtue or force more than might be put into it in every case by the spirit of the worshipper himself. Such, however, is not the nature of the ordinance. It is not simply an occasion by which the soul of the believer may be excited to pious feelings and desires; but it embodies the actual presence of the grace it represents in its own constitution; and this grace is not simply the promise of God on which we are encouraged to rely, but the very life of the Lord Jesus Christ himself. We communicate, in the Lord's Supper, not with the divine promise merely, not with the thought of Christ only, not with the recollection simply of what he has done and suffered for us, not with the lively present sense alone of his all-sufficient, all-glorious salvation, but with the living Saviour himself, in the fullness of his glorified person, made present to us for the purpose by the power of the Holy Ghost.

3. The relation of believers to Christ, then, is more again than that of a simply *legal* union. He is indeed the representative of his people, and what he has done and suffered on their behalf is counted to their benefit, as though it had been done by themselves. They have an interest in his merits, a title to all the advantages secured by his life and death. But this external imputation rests at last on an inward, real unity of life, without which it could have no reason or force. Our interest in Christ's merits and benefits can be based only upon a previous interest in his person; so, in the Lord's Supper, we are made to participate not merely in the advantages secured by his mediatorial work, the rewards of his obedience, the fruits of his bitter passion, the virtue of his atonement, and the power of his priestly intercession, but also in his true and proper life itself. We partake of his merits and benefits only so far as we partake of his substance.

4. Of course, once more, the communion in question is not simply with Christ in his *divine nature* separately taken, or with the *Holy Ghost* as the representative of his presence in the world. It does not hold in the influences of the Spirit merely, enlightening the soul and moving it to holy affections and purposes. It is by the Spirit, indeed, we are united to Christ. Our new life is comprehended in the Spirit as its element and medium. But it is always bound in this element to the person of the Lord Jesus Christ himself. Our fellowship is with the Father and with his son Jesus Christ, *through* the Holy Ghost. As such it is a real communion with the Word made flesh, not simply with the divinity of Christ but with his humanity also, since both are inseparably joined together in his person, and a living union with him in the one view implies necessarily a living union with him in the other view likewise. In the Lord's Supper, accordingly, the believer communicates not only with the Spirit of Christ, or with his divine nature, but with Christ himself in his whole living person, so that he may be said to be fed and nourished by his very flesh and blood. The communion is truly and fully with the *man* Christ Jesus, and not simply with Jesus as the Son of God.

These distinctions may serve to bound and define the Reformed doctrine of the Eucharist on the side towards *rationalism*. All pains were taken to guard it from the false tendency to which it stood exposed in this direction. The several conceptions of the believer's union and communion with Christ which have now been mentioned, were explicitly and earnestly rejected as being too low and poor altogether for the majesty of this great mystery. In opposition to all such representations, it was constantly affirmed that Christ's people are inserted by faith into his very life; and that the Lord's Supper, forming as it does an epitome of the whole mystery, involves to the worthy communicant an actual participation in the substance of his Person under this view. The participation is not simply in his Spirit, but in his flesh also and blood. It is not figurative merely and moral, but *real*, *substantial* and *essential*.

The Politics of the Lord's Supper

The Lord's Supper has unmistakable implications for politics and society, even if Christians have not always acknowledged them. How Christians live in the world either confirms or invalidates what they say they believe about the Lord's Supper. This is reflected, Hendrikus Berkhof points out, in how Christians regard the poor and how they treat Christians from other denominations.

SOURCE
Berkhof, *Christian Faith*, 368.

Where the meal is understood in its full breadth and strength as representing the grace of God, it turns out that, in spite of its stable conventional form and its symbolic character, it can exercise an incisively sifting function in politics and society. Already Paul warns of the possibility of eating and drinking judgment to oneself in the celebration of the holy meal if one persists with the gap between the well-to-do and the needy and thereby shows that he does not "discern the body" (of the Lord and of the church) (1 Cor. 11:20–34). From the struggle of the Confessing Church under the Nazis we remember how the open admission of Christian Jews to the Lord's Supper became the first test in the clash of the spirits. In our day the meal serves a similar disclosing function in the *apartheid* problematic in South Africa. But it functions as such in ecumenical relations as well; if a church denies to believers not belonging to its particular community access to the meal, it looks at itself, not at Christ as the host, and renders his presence doubtful (cf. Matt. 18:20 and 1 Cor. 11:20).

An Open Table?

Jürgen Moltmann raises the question of whether admission to the Lord's Supper should be open only to believers or whether, following Jesus' practice, the table should be open to everyone.

SOURCE

Moltmann, *The Church*, 259–60.

(c) Because of Christ's prevenient and unconditional invitation, the fellowship of the table cannot be restricted to people who are "faithful to the church," or to the "inner circle" of the community. For it is not the feast of the particularly righteous, or the people who think that they are particularly devout; it is the feast of the weary and heavy-laden, who have heard the call to refreshment. We must ask ourselves whether baptism and confirmation ought to go on counting as the presuppositions for "admittance" to the Lord's supper. If we remember that Jesus' meal with tax-collectors and sinners is also present in the Lord's supper, then the open invitation to it should also be carried "into the highways and byways." It will then lose its "mystery" character, but it will not become an ordinary, everyday meal for all that, because the invitation is a call to the fellowship of the crucified one and an invitation in his name to reconciliation with God (1 Cor. 11:27).

(d) In a congregation which sees itself as a messianic fellowship, one person will offer another bread and wine with Christ's words of promise. Everyone who tells the gospel story and proclaims faith will distribute the bread and wine as well. The celebration of the supper is not bound to any particular ministry, though it is bound to the "ministry" in the sense of the calling and mission of the whole congregation and every individual Christian.

(e) The meal's character of fellowship is brought out when the person performing the liturgy stands behind the altar, so making it the table, and celebrates facing the people. It is demonstrated even more clearly when the congregation sits round a table. But for this the body of the church has to be altered; the traditional church form, designed for a number of people facing the front, has to be changed to a "common room" in which the participants can see and talk to one another.

(f) This will also make it externally possible to celebrate divine worship as the assembly of the community, to follow the Lord's supper by a common meal, and the proclamation of the gospel by a common discussion of people's real needs and the specific tasks of Christian mission. The *agape* meal that follows shows the Lord's supper's openness to the future. Between the feast with Christ and the great banquet of the nations in the kingdom of God lies the world's hunger and misery. In this tension we become aware of this and accept it as our task in the hope for the kingdom founded on the fellowship of Christ. This means that the *agape* will not be a friendly appendage to the Lord's supper; it will be a *shalom* meal to express, in the promises of the prophets, the eschatological hope which is the ground for the Lord's supper.

As a feast open to the churches, Christ's supper demonstrates the community's catholicity. As a feast open to the world it demonstrates the community's mission to the world. As a feast open to the future it demonstrates the community's universal hope. It acquires this character from the prevenient, liberating and unifying invitation of Christ.

The Real Presence of the Whole Christ

Scottish theologian Thomas F. Torrance argues that the real presence of Christ in the Eucharist is not just the presence of the Spirit, but the presence of the crucified and resurrected Christ. Consequently, salvation is not simply a possibility or an idea but a present reality.

SOURCE

Thomas F. Torrance, "The Paschal Mystery of Christ and the Eucharist," in *Theology in Reconciliation* (Grand Rapids: Wm. B. Eerdmans, 1975), 119–20.

We have now come to the point where we must consider more carefully the *real presence of Christ*, the *eucharistic parousia*. This is not directly, at any rate, the *parousia* of the Lord either in the historical form that was his in the days of his flesh or in the glorified form that is his now at the right hand of the Father. But it is nevertheless the real presence (*parousia*) of the whole Christ, not just the presence of his body and blood, nor just the presence of his Spirit or Mind, but the presence of the actual Jesus Christ, crucified, risen, ascended, glorified, in his whole, living and active reality and in his identity as Gift and Giver. How he is thus present is only explicable from the side of God, in terms of his creative activity which by its very nature transcends any kind of explanation which we can offer. That is what is meant by saying that he is really present *through the Spirit*, not that he is present only as Spirit, far less as some spiritual reality, but present through the same kind of inexplicable creative activity whereby he was born of the Virgin Mary and rose again from the grave. Because it really is the presence of the Lord Jesus Christ in his living, creative reality, in his personal self-giving to us, it is a presence over which we have no kind of control, ecclesiastical, liturgical or intellectual. It is the kind of presence that confronted the disciples on the first Easter morning at Emmaus or in the upper room at Jerusalem, and indeed it is the same presence except that now it takes another form, the eucharistic form specifically appointed by Jesus as the particular empirical form in which he has promised as the risen and glorified Christ to meet his people in the closest and most intimate way, throughout all history, in anticipation of his unveiled form when he will come again in great power and glory. It is the whole Jesus Christ who makes himself specifically and intensely present to us in this eucharistic form in his oneness as Gift and Giver, the whole Jesus Christ in the fulness of his deity and in the fulness of his humanity, crucified and risen, not a bare or naked Christ, far less only his body and blood, but Jesus Christ clothed with his Gospel and clothed with the power of his Spirit, who cannot be separated from what he did or taught or was in the whole course of his historical existence in the flesh. What he has done once and for all in history has the power of permanent presence in him. He is present in the unique reality of his incarnate Person, in whom Word and Work and Person are indissolubly one, personally present therefore in such a way that he creatively effects what he declares, and what he promises actually takes place: "This is my body broken for you," "This is my blood shed for many for the remission of sins." The real presence is the presence of the Saviour in his personal being and atoning self-sacrifice, who once and for all gave himself up on the Cross for our sakes but who is risen from the dead as the Lamb who has been slain but is alive for ever more, and now appears for us in the presence of the Father as himself prevalent eternally propitiation.

The Means of Grace

The sacraments are not the only means by which a gracious God provides for the sustenance of faith. The Bible, proclamation, the confessions and catechisms, and the fellowship of the church are only some of the "means" God gives to Christians in order that they might grow in their faith and in their service of God in the world.

Characteristics of the Means of Grace

Louis Berkhof (1873–1957) acknowledges that the term "means of grace" has been defined in very different ways by Reformed theologians. He argues for a narrow definition that would restrict the term to the Word and the sacraments as "objective channels which Christ has instituted in the Church."

SOURCE

Louis Berkhof, *Systematic Theology* (Grand Rapids: Wm. B. Eerdmans, 1941), 604–5.

THE MEANS OF GRACE

I. The Means of Grace in General

A. The Idea of the Means of Grace

Fallen man receives all the blessings of salvation out of the eternal fountain of the grace of God, in virtue of the merits of Jesus Christ and through the operation of the Holy Spirit. While the Spirit can and does in some respects operate immediately on the soul of the sinner, He has seen fit to bind Himself largely to the use of certain means in the communication of divine grace. The term "means of grace" is not found in the Bible, but is nevertheless a proper designation of the means that are indicated in the Bible. At the same time the term is not very definite and may have a far more comprehensive meaning than it ordinarily has in theology. The Church may be represented as the great means of grace which Christ, working through the Holy Spirit, uses for the gathering of the elect, the edification of the saints, and the building up of His spiritual body. He qualifies her for this great task by endowing her with all kinds of spiritual gifts, and by the institution of the offices for the administration of the Word and the sacraments, which are all means to lead the elect to their eternal destiny. But the term may have an even wider scope. The whole providential guidance of the saints, through prosperity and adversity, often becomes a means by which the Holy Spirit leads the elect to Christ or to an ever closer communion with Him. It is even possible to include in the means of grace all that is required of men for the reception and the continued enjoyment of the blessings of the covenant, such as faith, conversion, spiritual warfare, and prayer. It is neither customary nor desirable, however, to include all this under the term "means of grace." The Church is not a means of grace alongside of the Word and the sacraments, because her power in promoting the work of the grace of God consists only in the administration of these. She is not instrumental in communicating grace, except by means of the Word and of the sacraments. Moreover, faith, conversion, and prayer, are first of all fruits of the grace of God, though they may in turn become instrumental in strengthening the spiritual life. They are not objective ordinances, but subjective conditions for the possession and enjoyment of the blessings of the covenant. Consequently, it is better not to follow Hodge when he includes prayer, nor McPherson when he adds to the Word and the sacraments both the Church and prayer. Strictly speaking, only the Word and the sacraments can be regarded as means of grace, that is, as objective channels which Christ has instituted in the Church, and to which He ordinarily binds Himself in the communication of His grace. Of course these may never be dissociated from Christ, nor from the powerful operation of the Holy Spirit, nor from the Church which is the appointed organ for the distribution of the blessings of divine grace. They are in themselves quite ineffective and are productive of spiritual results only through the efficacious operation of the Holy Spirit.

B. Characteristics of the Word and the Sacraments as Means of Grace

The fact that one can speak of means of grace in a rather general sense makes it imperative to point to the distinctive characteristics of the means of grace in the technical or restricted sense of the word.

1. They are instruments, not of *common* but of, *special* grace, the grace that removes sin and renews the sinner in conformity with the image of God. It is true that the Word of God may and in some respects actually does enrich those who live under the gospel with some of the choicest blessings of common grace in the restricted sense of the

word; but it, as well as the sacraments, comes into consideration here only as a means of grace in the technical sense of the word. And the means of grace in this sense are always connected with the beginning and the progressive operation of the special grace of God, that is redemptive grace, in the hearts of sinners.

2. They are *in themselves*, and not in virtue of their connection with things not included in them, means of grace. Striking experiences may, and undoubtedly sometimes do, serve to strengthen the work of God in the hearts of believers, but this does not constitute them means of grace in the technical sense, since they accomplish this only in so far as these experiences are interpreted in the light of God's Word, through which the Holy Spirit operates. The Word and the sacraments are in themselves means of grace; their spiritual efficacy is dependent only on the operation of the Holy Spirit.

3. They are *continuous* instruments of God's grace, and not in any sense of the word exceptional. This means that they are not associated with the operation of God's grace merely occasionally or in a more or less accidental way, but are the regularly ordained means for the communication of the saving grace of God and are as such of perpetual value. The Heidelberg Catechism asks in Question 65, "Since, then, we are made partakers of Christ and all His benefits by faith only, whence comes this faith?" And the answer is, "From the Holy Spirit, who works it in our hearts by the preaching of the holy gospel, and confirms it by the use of the holy sacraments."

4. They are the *official* means of the Church of Jesus Christ. The *preaching* of the Word (or, *the Word preached*) and the *administration* of the sacraments (or, *the sacraments administered*) are the means *officially instituted in the Church*, by which the Holy Spirit works and confirms faith in the hearts of men. Some Reformed theologians limit the idea of the means of grace still more by saying that they are administered only within the visible Church, and that they presuppose the existence of the principle of the new life in the soul.

Institutional Activities as Means of Grace

In addition to the three traditional means of renewal—sermon, baptism, and the Lord's Supper—Hendrikus Berkhof lists six additional means of nurture in the faith: instruction in the faith, religious discussion, the diaconal ministry of Christian mercy, worship services, church offices, and church order.

SOURCE

Berkhof, *Christian Faith*, 349–51.

THE CHURCH AS INSTITUTE

For many centuries the study of the faith started this theme on a high note, in the spirit of: the church is the God-established, Christ-directed, and Spirit-animated institute of salvation. It was conveniently overlooked that "church" refers to many different communities and "institute" to many different organizations. It did not take long before reflection on the church was far removed from everyday reality where the ecclesiastical institutes are found. We do well therefore to begin from that empirical reality. Then the beginning must look something like this: the Christian churches are forms of organization that belong to the genre of the institutes. Like all institutes, their right to existence is based on the interpersonal activities they bring about and maintain. The uniqueness of the churches lies in the nature of those activities. That nature can be described from the perspective of their origin as well as from their goal. Seen from the vantage point of origin, those activities aim to extend through time and space that which has once taken place in history, in Israel, and in Christ. Seen from the standpoint of goal, those activities aim at the renewal of people by means of that history, by bringing them into a relationship with God and Christ and so into a new relationship with each other, to life, and to the world. The concern of this institute is thus participation in the covenantal event, which in paragraph 37 we came to know as the work of the Spirit.

What are the activities which make such participation possible, which are as it were "mediating"? It is clear that such a general question also evokes a general answer. If one were to ask different believers which activities were or are mediating for the origination or building up of their faith, he could expect a wide variety of answers, such as the reading of certain books, the singing of certain hymns, participation in certain groups, and contact with certain persons. The Spirit blows where he wills and the participation is as varied as life itself. Many of these means to pass on the faith are not institutionalized, nor are they susceptible of it. A closer look will usually show, however, that the incidental means, regular or irregular, are also in one way or another linked to and fed by other means of a more constant and institutionalized character (for example: the songs are found in an ecclesiastical hymnal, the books are written by leading churchmen or other members of the church). In the study of the faith we search for the enduring and institutionalizable means of transmission that are essential to the ecclesiastical communities. Protestant dogmatics usually distinguishes three: the sermon, baptism, and the Lord's Supper. In our opinion these should be augmented by instruction in the faith, religious discussion, and the diaconal task or the ministry of Christian mercy as intentional and indispensable media of transmission. These elements are partly embedded in and partly supported by the regular gatherings of the congregation in the worship services, in which other elements, intentionally or unintentionally, also have a mediating character (confession of sin, proclamation of pardon, song, prayer). To make all these activities happen, people are necessary who hold particular offices. And they, with their functions and responsibilities, together with the whole community, must operate within a clearly defined set of agreements which we call a church order. So we arrive at nine elements that are essential to the church as transmission institute, seven of which are themselves transmission instruments, while the last two are intended to facilitate the work of the instruments of transmission, and for that reason are closely and necessarily linked to them. We thus come to a total of nine institutional elements: instruction, baptism, sermon, discussion, Lord's Supper, diaconate, worship service, office, and church order.

Special Features of the Church's Life

The Congregational Church in England and Wales in "A Declaration of Faith" (1967) lists several "special features" of the church's life which it considers to be "particular means of grace." Especially interesting are the document's comments on tradition as a means of grace.

SOURCE

"A Declaration of Faith" (1967) of the Congregational Church in England and Wales, in *Reformed Witness Today*, 139–42.

GOD IS SOVEREIGN OVER THE CHURCH

1. God Has Means of Grace in the Church

God draws Christian believers into the community of his Church and makes them glad in his service. In the sovereignty of grace he is present to the Church with living authority and power; the true life of the Church is awakened, reformed and renewed in love and obedience corresponding to God's grace. There are special features of the Church's life used by God as particular means of grace and we declare our understanding of them in gratitude and faith.

2. The Bible

God calls the Church to love and obedience through the Bible. The Bible is a series of historical documents. We seek to understand them in their ancient setting and find that they often reflect habits of life and thought which have passed away. Yet through them God speaks to us about our own life with him, in our own world which is his. For these documents are the record of God's revelation of himself in the life of ancient Israel, where there was true knowledge of him; of his revelation in the life, death and resurrection of Jesus Christ, where in our fellow-man he was personally and uniquely present among us; of his revelation in the testimony of Christ's apostles through which the Church was first formed.

In this revelation the living and eternal God discloses the truth about himself which is to be found in all his dealings with mankind. By knowing this record and steeping itself in the details the Church is able to hold fast to the revelation of God which has authority over all its life and thought. The Bible is not wholly free from error, confusion and contradictions; it must be read with fully critical attention if the Church is to discern the truth which is binding and not be in bondage to what is not binding. The Bible is trustworthy, not in the sense that it is impervious to criticism but in the sense that through its record we can trust God with reliable knowledge. It testifies faithfully to his wonderful works; but it is not, as a whole or in any part, identified with his deity.

By means of this trustworthy record God brings us to worship him and to obey him. Through its words God in Christ speaks personally to believers and carries home to their lives and to the life of the Church the reality of his claims and promises. There are in the Church other means and agencies which help to illuminate, guard and renew its thought and life; but all of them are rooted in God's revelation of himself in the Bible and by it they are also to be judged.

3. Tradition

God directs his Church through the study of its own past history. We look to the past with open historical vision and are ready to consider the experience of any who have claimed the Christian name, whether or not they satisfied particular theological standards for being the Church. Our task is to discern where in past times Christian communities were obedient and where they were disobedient. Scrutiny of the past will include expressions by the Church of its faith and of its thinking, the institutions of the Church and its standards of action, the decisions of Councils and the practice of piety, together with the patterns of eventful development which display the Church's course not only in periods of vitality and expansion but also in dull or dead periods. No one period has an over-riding claim upon the attention of the contemporary Church; all periods have some claim. As we come to appreciate the questions which earlier generations met and answered in their own way, and also become aware of questions still vexing us which they did not answer, we believe that we are open to guidance and help from God, preparing us for the decisions which present obedience requires of us.

4. Creeds, Confessions and Catechisms

We acknowledge with particular thankfulness the great affirmations of Christian faith which come down to us from the past: the Apostles' Creed, the Nicene Creed, and the Te Deum, together with the notable Confessions and Catechisms given to us from the Reformation period. We listen to them carefully as we make our witness in the present day. They direct us to the Bible's whole message and we follow them in so far as they lead us to God in Christ. We have been insufficiently attentive to affirmations of Christian faith which have come to us from other Churches of East and West, and pray that God will open our minds and enrich our spirits by what is in them.

5. Present Obligations

In its own present situation the Church must find what God wants it to think and to do. It is no surprise to the Church that it must do this in times marked by uncertainty and confusion. It does not look for results which are spectacular in human eyes, its own or those of unbelievers. It seeks so to discern God's will that in retrospect it is plain, even to hostile observers, that what has been sought is the will and purpose of the everlasting God and not the Church's own self-will. The Church seeks grace so to decide and so to act, that because of what is done and how it is done, it is easier and not harder for men and women to worship God and to persist in faithful and confident Christian living. Channels must be open, within each church and within all wider associations for Church life, for the free action of God's grace; and liberty of conscience must be preserved to men and women so that the fullest response of obedience to God may be offered in love and freedom.

CHRISTIAN MINISTRY

Ministry in the Reformed tradition has been understood to be God's call to all Christians to serve God in the church and the world. At the same time, Reformed churches have acknowledged that there are specific tasks in the life of the church which should be recognized by ordination—the teaching of doctrine, the proclamation of the Word and the administration of the sacraments, the government of the church, and service to the sick, the poor, and the needy.

Several important developments in society and in the life of the church in the twentieth century have led theologians to reexamine traditional interpretations of ministry. In the first place, many "parish ministers" are no longer simply leaders of worship. They are also counselors and administrators. Because of the church's changing needs in the contemporary world, new images and interpretations of ministry have recently been proposed. In addition, the "offices" of ordained ministry in many but, unfortunately, not all Reformed denominations have been opened to women. Furthermore, the church has struggled to listen to an emerging feminist theology and its critique of traditional forms of ministry and church order as hierarchical, exclusive, and oppressive.

FOR FURTHER STUDY

Ray S. Anderson, ed., *Theological Foundations for Ministry: Selected Readings for a Theology of the Church in Ministry* (Edinburgh: T. & T. Clark; Grand Rapids: Wm. B. Eerdmans, 1979). John H. Leith, *From Generation to Generation: The Renewal of the Church According to Its Own Theology and Practice* (Louisville: Westminster/John Knox, 1990). H. Richard Niebuhr and Daniel D. Williams, eds., *The Ministry in Historical Perspective* (San Francisco: Harper & Row, 1956). Robert S. Paul, *Ministry* (Grand Rapids: Wm. B. Eerdmans, 1965). Thomas F. Torrance, *Royal Priesthood* (Edinburgh: Oliver & Boyd, 1955).

The Call to Ministry

H. Richard Niebuhr identifies four elements that are at least implicitly acknowledged by most traditions to be a part of a call to ministry: the call to be a Christian, the secret call, the providential call, and the ecclesiastical call.

SOURCE

Niebuhr, *The Purpose of the Church*, 63–66.

The Call to the Ministry. A definite understanding of the ministerial office also includes a relatively clear-cut conception of what constitutes the call to the ministry. How and by whom are men appointed to this office? Once more, differences in historic definitions of the ministry are less due to exclusive insistence on some one interpretation of what constitutes a call than to variations in the emphasis placed on the various elements present in every call. Christians of all ages and churches have encountered in their reading of Scriptures socially appointed, institutionally recognized priests, prophets and apostles, but also extraordinary, "natural" or "charismatic" leaders—non-Levitical priests, prophets without human appointment and apostles chosen like Paul. In their contemporary experience they have dealt with both types of ministers and have found virtues and vices attached to both types. Even the most highly organized churches which insist on the importance of "legitimate" orders recognize with the Church of England that "there always remains the power of God to give to the Church prophets, evangelists and teachers apart from the succession," and even the most spiritualistic groups will elect certain men to interpret the sense of meetings in which anyone moved by the spirit is allowed to speak.

It appears that there is general though only implicit recognition of the fact that a call to the ministry includes at least these four elements: (1) *the call to be a Christian*, which is variously described as the call to discipleship of Jesus Christ, to hearing and doing of the Word of God, to repentance and faith, et cetera; (2) *the secret call*, namely, that inner persuasion or experience whereby a person feels himself directly summoned or invited by God to take up the work of the ministry; (3) *the providential call*, which is that invitation and command to assume the work of the ministry which comes through the equipment of a person with the talents necessary for the exercise of the office and through the divine guidance of his life by all its circumstances; (4) *the ecclesiastical call*, that is, the summons and invitation extended to a man by some community or institution of the Church to engage in the work of the ministry. At no time have the Church and the churches not required of candidates for the ministry that they be first of all men of Christian conviction, however such conviction and its guarantees were interpreted. The Church everywhere and always has expected its ministers to have a personal sense of vocation, forged in the solitariness of encounter with ultimate claims made upon them. It has also generally required that they show evidence of the fact that they have been chosen for the task by the divine bestowal upon them, through birth and experience, of the intellectual, moral, physical and psychological gifts necessary for the work of the ministry. Finally, in one form or another, it has required that they be summoned or invited or at least accepted by that part of the Church in which they undertake to serve. But ideas of the ministry have varied as Christian call, secret call, providential call and church call have been related to one another in varying orders of importance and modes of relationship. In the cases of the pastoral ruler of Gregory the Great and of Chrysostom's priest the summons of the church to men whom it found divinely chosen by Christian and providential call was of the first importance. The secret call, the summons and decision that occurred in solitariness, usually came after the public or church call. In the case of the evangelist, however, the order of these calls was reversed. "I allow," said John Wesley, "that it is highly expedient, whoever preaches in his name should have an outward as well as inward call; but that it is *absolutely necessary* I deny." More extremely, early Friends not only maintained that the "inward call, or testimony of the Spirit" was "essential and necessary to a minster" but denied the validity of the church call and seemed indifferent to the providential call, at least insofar as they discounted the significance of "birth-right" Christianity. Whatever the variations, it seems true that when a clear idea of the ministry prevailed there was also a clear idea of what constituted a call to the ministry and for the most part such a clear idea took into account the necessity of all four calls and ordered their relations.

Modern vagueness in thought about the ministry appears in the uncertainty of the churches, the minsters themselves, of boards and schools about the nature of the call. This vagueness doubtless is partly due to the conflict of traditions—a conflict in which exponents of the primacy of the "secret call" may take the position that it alone is adequate while others who emphasize the first importance of church call come to the indefensible position of renouncing the importance of command and obedience enacted in solitariness. It may be due also to the inapplicability to the Christian experience of young persons in our time of a theory of call developed in another age of Christian experience—the age of revivalism and evangelicalism. Whatever the reasons for the uncertainty, there is evidence that a new idea of call is emerging among Protestant churches and is contributing its share to the emerging new concept of the ministry. The idea is not a simple one but an idea of order and relation in the complex action and interaction of person, community and God, governing providentially, working by his spirit, active in history.

The Theologian as Minister

Karl Barth appeals to Calvin's description of ministry and argues that the theologian is a part of the church's ordained ministry. From this perspective the theologian's work is service in and for the needs of the church.

SOURCE

Karl Barth, *Evangelical Theology: An Introduction*, trans. Grover Foley (Grand Rapids: Wm. B. Eerdmans, 1963) 184–85.

Theological work is service. In general terms, service is a willing, working, and doing in which a person acts not according to his own purposes or plans but with a view to the purpose of another person and according to the need, disposition, and direction of others. It is an act whose freedom is limited and determined by the other's freedom, an act whose glory becomes increasingly greater to the extent that the doer is not concerned about his own glory but about the glory of the other. Such a serving act is the work of the theologian, whether this work is prayer or study or both simultaneously. Once again defined in general terms, it is *ministerium Verbi divini*, which means, literally, "a servant's attendance on the divine Word." The expression "attendance" may call to mind the fact that the New Testament concept of *Diakonos* originally meant "a waiter." The theologian must wait upon the high majesty of the divine Word, which is God himself as he speaks in his action. There is no better description of the freedom and honor of the theologian's action than the notable image in Psalm 123: "Behold, as the eyes of servants look to the hand of their master, as the eyes of a maid to the hand of her mistress, so our eyes look to the Lord our God, till he have mercy upon us." Theological work is a concentrated action by the very fact that it is also eccentrically oriented toward its *telos*, or goal. We must now attempt to understand it with respect to this inalienable and characteristic orientation.

In Calvin's famous classification of the ecclesiastical ministry the "deacon" occupies only the fourth and last place; what is allotted him is "only" to provide for the community's poor and sick. The "presbyter" precedes him and is responsible for the external conduct of the life of the community. He, in turn, is preceded by the "pastor," who is the preacher, instructor, and community parson. At the head of Calvin's ecclesiastical hierarchy, however, there is the "doctor," the teacher of the Church who, *ex officio*, interprets and explains the Scriptures. Obviously, he is, in particular, the theologian. Calvin certainly did not intend this classification to be as static as it appears or as it has frequently been understood and practiced. In any case, the *doctor ecclesiae* and the theologian, as the leading figures, will find it not only advisable but also necessary to become speedily, according to the Gospel, the last figure— the servant, waiter, and "deacon" for all the others. On the other hand, a fact also worthy of note is that the "waiting" of the martyr Stephen and of a certain Philip—those two "deacons" who are the only ones to be frequently mentioned in the Acts of the Apostles—seems to have consisted, according to the presentation of Luke, in searching and interpreting the Scriptures (Acts 6—8).

If, then, theological work is a special service which may technically precede all others, it cannot, all the same, wish to be more than service or ministry. It is not fit for anything unless it also, though in quite a special way, is provision for the poor and sick in the community. The corresponding truth is that Christian ministry of this practical type would also not be possible without a minimum of serious theological work.

New Models of Ministry

Letty M. Russell proposes three new images, or models, of ministry. All three presuppose that all the people of God are ministers and that "women and Third World people should assume roles of competence in proportion to their numbers in the church and societies where they serve."

SOURCE

Letty M. Russell, *Human Liberation in a Feminist Perspective—A Theology* (Philadelphia: Westminster, 1974), 180–81.

Any *new models of ministry* developed from the perspective of open ecclesiology would have to begin from God's Mission of liberation in the world. Such models would thus stress the importance of learning as a continuing participation in action (service) and reflection (doing theology). They would move toward such a variety of specialization that minsters would not be professional clergy, but those involved in servanthood who have many different professional and nonprofessional skills which are needed in today's world. New models would begin with the assumption that all the people of God are ministers, and each one needs help in finding ways to develop his or her gifts for service. And, of course, they would grow out of the premise that women and Third World people would assume roles of competence in proportion to their numbers in the church and societies where they serve. The "laying on of hands" would not set apart only those with certain degrees, but whatever members of a congregation who have a particular calling and ability to perform the service or mission needed in the life and mission of that witnessing community. Some new models that might be explored are that of *advocate, mother,* and *layperson*.

In a church that is open for the world, *advocates* would be those with special abilities to help in bringing signs of liberation and blessing into a particular situation or need. Such people would need to have special training in their area of competence, as well as a grounding in theology as a basis for carrying out the praxis of freedom as advocates. One example of this role is that of social scientists aiding in the process of conscientization among Latin-American groups. These people are called *militant observers, coordinators,* or *animators*. They are not neutral gatherers of data. Rather they live and work with the people, gathering "the unorganized elements which already exist in the group and giving them back in organized form" in order to help clarify the direction of the liberation struggle.

In a church that is open for others, another model might be that of *mother,* or nurturer. This role would be quite different from the accustomed dominant position of the *Father* in church life. The minister today who is genuinely seeking to nurture a congregation to its highest potential of growth is already exercising an enabling function that is related to the cultural role usually associated with women. Both *men and women* would learn to specialize in this nurturing, enabling, and mediating role as they seek to equip others of service and dialogical action in the world.

A third model of ministry, for a church open to the future, would be that of riotous pluralism. Here the role model would be that of the *layperson,* not in the old sense of laity conceived as "domesticated clergy," but quite the reverse. Those who wish to serve in a variety of roles, using their gifts in many ways, could look to models of laypersons who have accomplished this feat even against the heavy odds of the existing clergy line. The key to independence and flexibility would be self-support. Such economic independence, already possessed by laypersons, could open the way to large numbers of people who would be free to subvert the heretical structures of the church into new forms of open ecclesiology. It would also open the way to the inclusion of all groups, men and women alike, in the direction and service of the church.

7

POLITICS, SOCIETY, AND CULTURE

Christians in the Reformed tradition have seldom attempted to live apart from the rest of society. They have believed that God calls them to live out their faith in their daily lives. Their belief in the sovereignty of God, the goodness of creation, and the calling of God has led them to work for and witness to God's transformation of creation. Consequently, Reformed theology has often adopted a "transformationist" posture in relation to the world. Instead of uncritically identifying the gospel with their culture or withdrawing from an "evil" world in order to maintain their spiritual purity, Reformed churches have sought a "third way," a path between the two, by participating in the life of society as a witness to the grace of God in Jesus Christ.

Is this traditional Reformed posture a faithful reflection of the call of the gospel, or is it an easy compromise which enables Christians to evade the radical claims of the gospel? Recently, some theologians have begun to question whether this "transformationist" perspective does not unwittingly mask an uncritical acceptance of middle-class Western values and, in so doing, supports institutions and social policies that are contrary to Christian faith.

CHRISTIAN ETHICS

One principle of Reformed theology has been that truth is in order to goodness. In other words, truth is not an abstraction that has nothing to do with human life. The truth of the gospel cannot be separated from the living of it. Christian faith and theology, therefore, are inseparably related to Christian ethics; these are not two distinct disciplines but different perspectives on one reality.

Although this general principle has characterized the Reformed tradition, Christian ethics in the twentieth century has debated whether theological ethics is simply a subset of the larger field of general or philosophical ethics or whether Christian perceptions of truth and goodness give Christian ethics a distinctive form and content.

In addition, the emergence of liberation theology, with its criticism of the concept of "practice" (as the application of theory) and its affirmation of "praxis" (as reflection based on prior commitment and action) has raised further questions about traditional Reformed interpretations of the relation between truth and goodness.

FOR FURTHER STUDY

Karl Barth, *Ethics*, ed. Dietrich Braun and trans. Geoffrey W. Bromiley (New York: Seabury, 1981). Emil Brunner, *The Divine Imperative: A Study in Christian Ethics*, trans. Olive Wyon (New York: Macmillan, 1937). Jacques Ellul, *The Ethics of Freedom*, trans. Geoffrey W. Bromiley (Grand Rapids: Wm. B. Eerdmans, 1976). Richard J. Mouw, *The God Who Commands* (Notre Dame: University of Notre Dame Press, 1990). Friedrich Schleiermacher, *An Introduction to Christian Ethics*, trans. John C. Shelley (Nashville: Abingdon, 1989).

Ethics and the Command of God

Karl Barth rejects the notion that the starting point for Christian ethics can be the question of the good. Christian ethics begins and ends with the command of God. Only in God's revealed Word—that is, only in Jesus Christ—does the Christian discover "the good." In response to God's command, the issue is human obedience.

SOURCE

Barth, *Church Dogmatics*, II/2: 515–17.

Our contention is, however, that the dogmatics of the Christian Church, and basically the Christian doctrine of God, is ethics. This doctrine is, therefore, the answer to the ethical question, the supremely critical question concerning the good in and over every so-called good in human actions and modes of action.

It is the *answer*—this must be our starting-point. But we must be more exact and say that it is the attestation, the "tradition," the repetition of the answer. For the answer is not theology, or the doctrine of God, but their object—the revelation and work of the electing grace of God. But this, the grace of God, *is* the answer to the ethical problem. For it sanctifies man. It claims him for God. It puts him under God's command. It gives predetermination to his self-determination so that he obeys God's command. It makes God's command for him the judgment on what he has done and the order for his future action. The ethical task of the Christian doctrine of God is to attest this answer to the ethical problem. The ethical problem as such, in the sense of that general definition or conception of ethics, is something with which we are not here concerned.

We are not, of course, surprised at the existence of that general conception. We are not surprised that in every age and place—for all the many and varied attempts which have been made—men have never been able to acquiesce in an equation of the good with all the other different continuities in human behaviour. We are not surprised that the question of the good had and has still to crop up as a specific question which transcends the question of these other conformities. And therefore we are not surprised at the different attempts made by man to give himself a human answer to this specific question—with varying degrees of insight into its special nature and in greater or less correspondence to its actual openness compared with all other questions. We are not surprised because by revelation and the work of God's grace this question is actually put as the inescapable question of human existence which is quite incomparable with other questions in weight and urgency and which the answers to others are quite unable to silence. For it is as he acts that man exists as a person. Therefore the question of the goodness and value and rightness, of the genuine continuity of his activity, the ethical question, is no more and no less than the question about the goodness, value, rightness and genuine continuity of his existence, of himself. It is his life-question, the question by whose answer he stands or falls. "To be, or not to be, that is the question." Why? Because with its answer there is put into effect the decision of the power which disposes absolutely of his existence or non-existence, the power of God. For it is the electing grace of *God* which has placed man under His command from all eternity. The command of God is therefore the truth from which—whether he knows and wants to know it or not—man derives, and which he will not evade. By the decree of the divine covenant with man, the ethical question as the question of human existence is put from all eternity as the question to which, on the basis of revelation and the work of grace, man will himself in some way be the answer. That is why it is such a necessary, a burning question. And that is also why all possible attempts to answer it, all forms of ethics, are so pressing.

Man derives from the grace of God, and therefore he is exposed from the very outset to this question. Before he was, before the world was, God drew him to Himself when he destined him to obedience to His command. But, strangely enough, it is just because of this that the impossible—sin—presses so insistently. For man is not content simply to *be* the answer to this question by the grace of God. He wants to be like God. He wants to know of himself (as God does) what is good and evil. He therefore wants to *give* this answer himself and of himself. So, then, as a result and in prolongation of the fall, we have "ethics," or, rather, the multifarious ethical systems, the attempted human answers to the ethical question. But this question can be solved only as it was originally put—by the grace of God, by the fact that this allows man actually to *be* the answer. Revelation and the work of God's grace are just as opposed to these attempts as they are to sin. From all eternity it is not the will of God to acquiesce in man's presumption and therefore to let man fall into the perdition which is the necessary consequence of his presumption. The grace of God protests against all man-made ethics as such. But it protests positively. It does not only say No to man. It also says Yes. But it does so by completing its own answer to the ethical problem in active refutation, conquest and destruction of all human answers to it. It does this by revealing in Jesus Christ the human image with which Adam was created to correspond and could no longer do so when he sinned, when he became ethical man. This human image is at the same time God's own image. The man Jesus, who fulfills the commandment of God, does not *give* the answer, but by God's grace He *is* the answer to the ethical question put by God's grace. The sanctification of man, the fact that he is claimed by God, the fulfillment of his predetermination in his self-determination to obedience, the judgment of God on man and His command to him in its actual concrete fulfillment—they all take place here in Jesus Christ. The good is done here—really the good as understood critically—beyond all that merely pretends to be called good. But it is not done because, like Hercules at the cross-roads, this man chooses between good and evil and is good on the basis of His choice of the good. The Son, who is obedient to the Father, could not possibly want to ask and decide what is good and evil. He could not possibly regard as the good that which He had chosen for Himself as such. No, it is as He is elected by the grace of God that the good is done. As this Elect, quite apart from any choice of His own between good and evil, He is concerned only with obedience. He does not crave to be good of and for Himself. And so in all His acts He is subject only to the will and command of the God who alone is good. This is how the good is done here. This is how the ethical question is answered here—in Jesus Christ. What has taken place in this way—in antithesis and contrast to all human ethics—is divine ethics.

Christian Realism: Between Orthodoxy and Liberalism

The position of "Christian realism" is identified with Reinhold Niebuhr, who carved out a third position for Christian theology and ethics between orthodoxy, on the one hand, and liberalism, on the other. A basic theme in Niebuhr's ethics is the relation between love and justice, and how neither orthodoxy nor liberalism adequately deals with that relation. Orthodoxy usually inclines toward a legalism that sacrifices love for justice, and liberalism tends toward antinomianism that degenerates into sentimentality.

SOURCE

Reinhold Niebuhr, *An Interpretation of Christian Ethics* (New York: Seabury, 1979), 71–74.

If the relevance of the love commandment must be asserted against both Christian orthodoxy and against certain types of naturalism, the impossibility of the ideal must be insisted upon against all those forms of naturalism, liberalism, and radicalism which generate utopian illusions and regard the love commandment as ultimately realizable because history knows no limits of its progressive approximations. While modern culture since the eighteenth century has been particularly fruitful of these illusions, the logic which underlies them was stated as early as the fourth century of the Christian faith by Pelagius in his controversy with Augustine. He said:

> We contradict the Lord to his face when we say: It is hard, it is difficult; we cannot, we are men; we are encompassed with fragile flesh. O blind madness! O unholy audacity! We charge the God of all knowledge with a two-fold ignorance, that he does not seem to know what he has made nor what he has commanded, as though forgetting the human weakness of which he is himself the author, He imposed laws upon man which he cannot endure.

There is a certain plausibility in the logic of these words, but unfortunately, the facts of human history and the experience of every soul contradict them. The faith which regards the love commandment as a simple possibility rather than an impossible possibility is rooted in a faulty analysis of human nature which fails to understand that though man always stands under infinite possibilities and is potentially related to the totality of existence, he is, nevertheless, and will remain, a creature of finiteness. No matter how much his rationality is refined, he will always see the total situation in which he is involved only from a limited perspective; he will never be able to divorce his reason from its organic relation with the natural impulse of survival with which nature has endowed him; and he will never be able to escape the sin of accentuating his natural will-to-live into an imperial will-to-power by the very protest which his yearning for the eternal tempts him to make against his finiteness.

There is thus a mystery of evil in human life to which modern culture has been completely oblivious. Liberal Christianity, particularly in America, having borrowed heavily from the optimistic credo of modern thought, sought to read this optimism back into the gospels. It was aided in doing this by the fortuitous circumstance that the impossibility of an impossible possibility was implicit rather than explicit in the thought of Jesus. It became explicit only in the theology of Paul. Modern Christianity could thus make the "rediscovery of Jesus" the symbol and basis of its new optimism. The transcendent character of the love ideal was covert rather than overt in the words of Jesus because of the eschatological mould in which it was cast. Jesus thus made demands upon the human spirit, which no finite man can fulfill, without explicitly admitting this situation. This enabled modern liberalism to interpret the words of Jesus in terms of pure optimism. The interpretation of Jesus' own life and character was also brought into conformity with this optimism. For liberal Christianity Christ is the ideal man, whom all men can emulate, once the persuasive charm of his life has captivated their souls. In Christian theology, at its best, the revelation of Christ, the God-man, is a revelation of the paradoxical relation of the eternal to history, which it is the genius of mythical-prophetic religion to emphasize. Christ is thus the revelation of the very impossible possibility which the Sermon on the Mount elaborates in ethical terms. If Christian orthodoxy sometimes tends to resolve this paradox by the picture of a Christ who has been stripped of all qualities which relate him to man and history, Christian liberalism resolves it by reducing Christ to a figure of heroic love who reveals the full possibilities of human nature to us. In either case the total human situation which the mythos of the Christ and the Cross illumines, is obscured. Modern liberalism significantly substitutes the name of "Jesus" for that of "Christ" in most of the sentimental and moralistic exhortations by which it encourages men to "follow in his steps." The relation of the Christ of Christian faith to the Jesus of history cannot be discussed within the confines of this treatise in terms adequate enough to escape misunderstanding. Perhaps it is sufficient to say that the Jesus of history actually created the Christ of faith in the life of the early church, and that his historic life is related to the transcendent

Christ as a final and ultimate symbol of a relation which prophetic religion sees between all life and history and the transcendent. In genuine prophetic Christianity the moral qualities of the Christ are not only our hope, but our despair. Out of that despair arises a new hope centered in the revelation of God in Christ. In such faith Christ and the Cross reveal not only the possibilities but the limits of human finitude in order that a more ultimate hope may arise from the contrite recognition of those limits. Christian faith is, in other words, a type of optimism which places its ultimate confidence in the love of God and not the love of man, in the ultimate and transcendent unity of reality and not in tentative and superficial harmonies of existence which human ingenuity may contrive. It insists, quite logically, that this ultimate hope becomes possible only to those who no longer place their confidence in purely human possibilities. Repentance is thus the gateway into the Kingdom of God.

The real crux of the issue between essential Christianity and modern culture lies at this point. The conflict is between those who have a confidence in human virtue which human nature cannot support and those who have looked too deeply into life and their own souls to place their trust in so broken a reed. It is out of such despair, "the godly sorrow which worketh repentance," that faith arises.

Revelation as the Point of Departure

Like Barth, Paul Lehmann denies that Christian ethics is concerned with the good. Its starting point is reflection upon Jesus Christ by those who live in the church.

SOURCE

Lehmann, *Ethics*, 45.

In our thinking about Christian ethics everything depends upon the point of departure. This is really what makes Christian thinking about ethics different from the ethical thinking of other religious traditions and different from philosophical ethics. It is the point of departure which also fundamentally differentiates one interpretation of Christian ethics from another.

When Christian ethics is defined as *the disciplined reflection upon the question and its answer: What am I, as a believer in Jesus Christ and as a member of his church, to do?*, the point of departure is neither vague nor neutral. It is not the common moral sense of mankind, the distilled ethical wisdom of the ages. Not that we can ignore this ethical wisdom, but we do not start with it. Instead, the starting point for Christian thinking about ethics is the fact and the nature of the Christian Church. To put it somewhat too sharply: Christian ethics is not concerned with *the good,* but with what I, as a believer in Jesus Christ and as a member of his church, am to do. *Christian ethics, in other words, is oriented toward revelation and not toward morality.*

Ethics as Discernment

James Gustafson describes ethics as the practice of discernment in response to the question, "What is God enabling and requiring us to be and to do?"

SOURCE

Gustafson, *Ethics,* 1:327–29.

The practical moral question in a theocentric construal of the world is, as I have noted, "What is God enabling and requiring us to be and to do?" The most general answer is that we are to relate ourselves and all things in a manner appropriate to their relations to God. . . .

The process of discernment, as I shall describe it, reasonably follows from what I have written. It coheres with the principal lines of my interpretation of persons and communities, of the possibilities and limitations of knowledge of the divine governance, and with what we can claim about that governance.

While to discern something sometimes means that we simply perceive what is difficult to behold, such as the profile of a human face in a natural rock formation, discerning normally bears a qualitative meaning. A discerning person is one who has a certain keenness of mind, hearing, sight, and so forth. The discerning critic of literature, art, or music is one who can describe, interpret, and evaluate things in such a way that their readers' perceptions, understandings, and evaluations become keener and more discriminating. To discern is not merely to see or to hear; it is to discriminate. Description of the process of discernment requires that attention be given to some of its facets, and this is best done with an example.

Think of different biographers, and their works. One expects every biographer to master the available information about his subject, about the times and events in which he or she lived, and so forth. If the subject was personally known to the author, one expects sound observations of the actions, relations, and events that are significant. The word "signifi-cant" begins to be one criterion by which we distinguish a discerning biographer from one who, in a positivistic way, simply gathers all avail-able facts and arranges them chronologically. What is deemed signifi-cant is related to the author's sensitivity to the salient features of the subject's life: the important relationships, the critical events. Differences between biographers in part are differences in their sensitivities and their empathic capacities. The discerning author has insight into the important features of the subject; attention is not given to all available information but to that which sheds light on the subject's actions, char-acter, and relationships. The interpretation, we say, is perceptive. It is subtle, and does not cram information into a simple general causal thesis about human life and activity. Yet its perceptiveness is in part due to the author's awareness of various factors that, if they do not deter-mine life and action, establish certain conditions, explain certain desires and purposes of the subject, illuminate the subject's conflicts of motives, and so forth. A biographer who violates simple rules of accuracy for the sake of an explanatory thesis would not count as discerning. The deter-mination of the salient features involves discrimination, a keenness of perception, subtlety, and imagination. It involves judgments about what is of greatest importance in understanding the life of the subject. Biogra-phy is not merely the collection of facts but the interpretation of a life: its motives, its decisions, its perceptions of the world of which it was a part, its responses to events, its conflicts and its aspirations, its effects on others and on events in which it participated. A discerning biogra-pher gives the reader an understanding of the subject that is not only insightful but can be tested by others for its accuracy and explanatory power.

Discerning what the divine governance enables and requires obviously is different in important respects from discerning the character and qualities of a human life. But there are some common elements in both processes. What does the person who discerns (in both a descriptive and evaluative sense) bring to the process? There is one's own nature; one's desires, appetites, and natural capacities. There is the particularity of one's life experiences and interests. A biographer of the last czar and his family who experiences hemophilia in his own family can shed insight on their actions that another biographer cannot. Sensitivities, affectivi-ties, capacities for empathy, and imagination are important. Imagining possibilities of motives, aspirations, and responses plays an important part. But what has been imagined must be tested; a biography is not a novel. There is a drive for the greatest possible degree of accuracy of knowledge; the biographer who believes that human character and action are explainable by a relatively single-minded theory casts the writing in ways coherent with such a belief. Principles of analysis are important; at least at some stages the fair-minded biographer is willing to test alternative principles of explanation of the life and actions of the subject. Synthetic principles or capacities are needed to bring some measure of coherence and wholeness to what is known and observed. Irrelevant principles of analysis and synthesis are discarded, yet there must be sufficient openmindedness to avoid premature foreclosure: capacities for judgment are informed by all these and other elements. They go into establishing the perspective and the point of vision that bring the "reality" responded to and acted upon into a coherent and manageable whole. All of these go into making discerning choices and judgments, not only in the writing of biographies, but also in many other areas of human experience, including moral experience.

THEOLOGY AND POLITICS

Reformed theologians have taken different positions on the question of the relationship between the Christian and the state. On the one hand, John Calvin urged Christians to be content with their stations in life and to serve God in the roles to which they had been called. Moreover, Calvin allowed Christians to participate in rebellion against their government in only the most extreme of circumstances (for example, when the government made it impossible for Christians to worship God). On the other hand, the Reformed tradition includes John Knox and the Scottish revolution, the Puritans and the English Revolution, and John Witherspoon and the American Revolution.

In the nineteenth century, Presbyterians in the southern United States affirmed "the spirituality of the church." They argued that the church is a spiritual community which should not be stained by involvement in secular political debates such as the struggle over slavery. Other Presbyterians actively participated in the movement to abolish slavery.

In the twentieth century, a significant number of Reformed communities have understood faithfulness to the gospel to require their opposition to oppression and injustice in society.

FOR FURTHER STUDY

Eberhard Busch, "Church and Politics in the Reformed Tradition," in *Major Themes in the Reformed Tradition*, ed. Donald K. McKim (Grand Rapids: Wm. B. Eerdmans, 1992), 180–95. C. D. Cloete and D. J. Smit, eds., *A Moment of Truth: The Confession of the Dutch Reformed Mission Church* (Grand Rapids: Wm. B. Eerdmans, 1984). Arthur C. Cochrane, *The Church's Confession Under Hitler* (Philadelphia: Westminster, 1962).

Helmut Gollwitzer, *The Christian Faith and the Marxist Criticism of Religion*, trans. David Cairns (New York: Scribner's Sons, 1962). John de Gruchy and Charles Villa-Vicencio, eds., *Apartheid Is a Heresy* (Cape Town: David Philip; Grand Rapids: Wm. B. Eerdmans, 1983). John W. de Gruchy, *Liberating Reformed Theology: A South African Contribution to an Ecumenical Discussion* (Grand Rapids: Wm. B. Eerdmans, 1991). George L. Hunt, ed., *Calvinism and the Political Order* (Philadelphia: Westminster, 1965). David Little, "Reformed Faith and Religious Liberty," in *Church and Society*, May/June 1986: 5–28. Jürgen Moltmann, *On Human Dignity: Political Theology and Ethics*, trans. M. Douglas Meeks (Philadelphia: Fortress, 1984). E. T. Thompson, *The Spirituality of the Church* (Richmond: John Knox, 1961). Nicholas Wolterstorff, *Until Justice and Peace Embrace* (Grand Rapids: Wm. B. Eerdmans, 1983).

The Provisionality of All Political Systems

Christians should not identify any particular political theory or system with the kingdom of God, insists Karl Barth. All political systems are human creations and as such are incommensurable with God's kingdom.

SOURCE

Karl Barth, "The Christian Community and the Civil Community," in *Community, State, and Church* (Garden City, N.Y.: Doubleday & Co., 1960), 160–61.

FOR FURTHER STUDY

George Hunsinger, ed., *Karl Barth and Radical Politics* (Philadelphia: Westminster, 1976). Friedrich-Wilhelm Marquardt, *Theologie und Sozialismus: Das Beispiel Karl Barths* (Munich: Chr. Kaiser, 1972).

In making itself jointly responsible for the civil community, the Christian community has no exclusive theory of its own to advocate in face of the various forms and realities of political life. It is not in a position to establish one particular doctrine as *the* Christian doctrine of the just State. It is also not in a position to refer to any past realisation of the perfect State or to hold out any prospect of one in the future. There is but one Body of Christ, born of the Word of God, which is heard in faith. There is therefore no such thing as a Christian State corresponding to the Christian Church; there is no duplicate of the Church in a political sphere. For if, as the effect of a divine ordinance, as the manifestation of one of the constants of divine Providence and of the historical process which it governs, the State is in the Kingdom of Christ, this does not mean that God is revealed, believed, and perceived in any political community as such. The effect of the divine ordinance is that men are entrusted (whether or not they believe it to be a divine revelation) to provide "according to the measure of human insight and human capacity" for temporal law and temporal peace, for an external, relative, and provisional humanisation of man's existence. Accordingly, the various political forms and systems are human inventions which as such do not bear the distinctive mark of revelation and are not witnessed to as such—and can therefore not lay any claim to belief. By making itself jointly responsible for the civil community, the Christian community participates—on the basis of and by belief in the divine revelation—in the human search for the best form, for the most fitting system of political organisation; but it is also aware of the limits of all the political forms and systems which man can discover (even with the co-operation of the Church), and it will beware of playing off one political concept— even the "democratic" concept—and *the* Christian concept, against all others. Since it proclaims the Kingdom of God it has to maintain its own hopes and questions in the face of all purely political concepts. And this applies even more to all political achievements. Though the Christian will be both more lenient and more stern, more patient and more impatient towards them than the non-Christian, he will not regard any such achievement as perfect or mistake it for the Kingdom of God—for it can only have been brought about by human insight and human ability. In the face of all political achievements, past, present, and future, the Church waits for "the city which hath foundations, whose builder and maker is God" (Hebrews 11:10). It trusts and obeys no political system or reality but the power of the Word, by which God upholds all things (Hebrews 1:3; Barmen Thesis No. 5), including all political things.

A Yes to Communism?

Czechoslovakian theologian Joseph L. Hromádka was forced to leave his country prior to the Second World War. He taught at Princeton Theological Seminary but returned to Czechoslovakia after the war. There he served on the Central Action Committee and worked with the communist government. At Lund, Sweden, in August 1952, Hromádka addressed the Third Conference on Faith and Order on some of the social and cultural barriers that divided delegates to the meeting.

SOURCE

Joseph L. Hromádka, "Social and Cultural Factors in Our Divisions," in *Theology Today* 9, no. 4 (January 1953): 467–71.

Our conference is taking place in a time of profound shifts and changes in the very structure of our life and history, and we look at one another with apprehension, distrust, and, at times, even suspicion. What I say may be an exaggeration, and yet let us not be too optimistic. We may speak the same doctrinal, dogmatic, and theological language, and be separated from one another by such a gulf or barrier that we urgently have to ask ourselves whether our common doctrine has not degenerated to an empty shell, meaningless for the present history of the Church. Our division cuts across our church organizations, common worship, and sacramental forms. I have had—just as many of you—a depressing experience that my—hypothetically speaking—most provocative dogmatic heresies would be tolerated, overlooked, or leniently listened to, whereas my Christian loyalty would be (or better, has been) questioned on account of my political and social point of view and decisions. What is, at times, happening in our congregations or local discussions may be true also in such a gathering as the present one. What is it that cements and integrates members of this conference into one organic unity? What are the ultimate, deepest, invisible, imperceptible, and at the same time the most real motives and norms by which we are guided and which determine the way of our mutual approach? What formed and shaped our preparations for Lund? What is forming and shaping our preparations for Lucknow and Evanston? We may be very sincere in emphasizing with vigor our definite theological and Biblical approach to any particular issue. And yet, somewhere at the bottom of our inward life, of our theological thought, may be a hidden ulterior driving force. Our struggle for an adequate understanding of the Word of God, of the Prophets, of the Gospel, of the Church, of her functions, may be, in a perilous way, colored and transformed by our unconscious, or almost unconscious, social, political, cultural fears, anxieties, and desires.

But let us look at it also from the opposite side. If we disagree among ourselves in our theological perspective, in either our Catholic or Protestant emphases, we must carefully scrutinize our approach, our personal or ecclesiastical predilections and hobbies to see to what extent and in what measure they might have been prompted by some unavowed political or sociological pressure. There are people who use the Church and Christian ideology for a social or cultural self-protection. There exists a static orthodoxy as a trench or as a Maginot line of political fear, of social anxiety and conservatism. But the dangers are everywhere.

It is here that I may call your attention to a serious situation we in our countries are confronted with. The tremendous changes in the very structure and the very formation of our social life have made our theology and Church much more watchful and responsible than they used to be before. All is at stake. We are realizing what it means (*theologically* speaking) to walk between life and death. Every word and category, every traditional church activity has to be re-thought, re-interpreted, re-evaluated as to its integrity and relevance. Many of us have rejected the notion that we can hibernate behind the old walls of confession, doctrine, or Church constitution. The tremendous challenge which comes from the revolutionary socialistic ideology has a salutary effect. We have to go to where the Prophets heard the Word, where the Church of the Apostles had to walk—between Jerusalem with her devastated Temple and Rome, the old Rome, the new center of the world. We have to give up all the myths, superstitions, empty speculations, and idealistic illusions inherited from the past. We have to combat a self-pitying self-righteousness and to understand in what the *real* freedom of the Church consists. We have to give up many altars and idols. But we have to be on the alert lest we misread the signs of our times and lest we exchange new myths for the old ones.

II

In what way can we help one another? We are constantly tempted to sit in judgment over one another and do it in a wrong way. Political prejudices, fixed cultural ideas, and social loyalties are so strong that we are unaware of them. The more vigorously we identify ourselves with a given social structure, political regime, and cultural tradition, the more uneasy and irritated we get if anybody questions the purity and integrity of our actions, of our theology and faith. We have become servants and slaves of our social and cultural traditions and use the most sacred theological and Church formulae to protect them. It is discouraging and depressing to see how profoundly our interpretation and evaluation of the contemporary social and international events differ. They contradict one another. All the momentous problems of our time (Communism, the Korean war, the new China, the unification and neutralization of Germany, the North Atlantic Pact, European federation, the peace movement) stand like colossal blocks between us. To what extent are these differences and contradictions an indication of our theological disagreements, of our disunity in faith and hope?

All of us agree that the prophetic function is one of the two or three essential aspects of the Church of Christ. All of us, as we are gathered here, long and desire to proclaim a real prophetic message, a prophetic word straight into a given situation. But all of us are in danger of self-illusion. The prophetic Word defies all *our* theological patterns of prophecy. "Spiritus ubi vult spirat" (John 3:8). The prophetic word deprives man of all his human treasures, political, national, social, and cultural, makes him naked, takes away his self-assurance, self-righteousness, self-complacency, drags him against his own will to the place where the genuine fire of the divine presence burns until a servant of God stands without any pious weapon or prop and human support, as a beggar and a lost sheep. "Ah, Lord God! behold, I cannot speak: for I am a child" (Jer. 1:6).

When do we speak actually, genuinely, in the name of the Lord, and not in the interest of *our* way of life, of our culture, of our political, social, and economic vested interests? There exists among theologians and churchmen a curious idea that a prophetic word is regularly a negative word, a word of defiance and protest. Furthermore, there are Christians whose eyes are charmed and horrified, even stupefied by the dark shadow of Communism. They project all the corruptions and ideas they hold of Satanic, devilish destruction into the advance of communistic power. They almost identify the present prophetic function of the Church with her anti-communistic proclamation, with her resounding "No" against Communism. It is exactly this that we—who are, behind the Iron Curtain, at present responsible for the affairs of our Churches—reject. Yes, indeed, there are inevitable "No's" to be proclaimed as in any human situation. But we insist that our first prophetic word must be a "Yes," a persistent as well as a joyful "Yes" to the Lord Crucified and Risen, who has put us into our situation.

III

I wish to stress most emphatically that this does not imply a "Yes" to any system, to any official ideology or to everything that goes on. It means simply that we have to make decisions in the sovereignty of faith, no matter how difficult and questionable they might appear to a traditional churchman or to our brethren who are not on the spot and cannot understand always what we do. What does it mean if we so deeply differ in practical application of what we call the prophetic mission of the Church? Is it not a challenge to re-examine our Christological doctrines and to search in what way and to what extent political, social, and cultural interests have penetrated into our theological thought and ecclesiastical action? Is it not a challenge to help one another to a real Christian liberty, to a real sovereignty of faith, and to a real unity?

My questions and comments may have sounded a little pessimistic and cynical. However, I am neither a pessimist nor a cynic. In all humility and love, I desire to contribute to the success, *real* success, of our Conference. It was a salutary suggestion to start with what we call non-theological factors. It is a kind of self-purification. But it must be a true *theological* self-examination. It must be a struggle within ourselves. The Church must remove—under the guidance of the Holy Spirit—all her idols and false altars. She must struggle with the Antichrist in her own sanctuary and not look for devils where they are nothing more than creations of our fear and our human phantasy.

Black and Reformed

Allan Boesak, one of the leaders in the struggle against apartheid in South Africa and a former president of the World Alliance of Reformed Churches, argues that black South African Christians should reinterpret the Reformed tradition and appropriate it for their own.

SOURCE

Allan Boesak, "Black and Reformed: Contradiction or Challenge," in *Black and Reformed: Apartheid, Liberation and the Calvinist Tradition,* ed. Leonard Sweetman (Maryknoll, N.Y.: Orbis, 1984), 95–99.

It is my conviction that the reformed tradition has a future in this country only if black Reformed Christians are willing to take it up, make it truly their own, and let this tradition once again become what it once was: a champion of the cause of the poor and the oppressed, clinging to the confession of the lordship of Christ and to the supremacy of the word of God. It will have a future when we show an evangelical openness toward the world and toward the worldwide church so that we shall be able to search with others for the attainment of the goals of the kingdom of God in South Africa. I do not mean that we should accept everything in our tradition uncritically, for I indeed believe that black Christians should formulate a Reformed confession for our time and situation in our own words.

Beginning with our own South African situation, we should accept our special responsibility to salvage this tradition from the grip of the mighty and the powerful who have so shamelessly perverted it for their own ends and let it speak once again for God's oppressed and suffering peoples. It is important to declare apartheid to be irreconcilable with the gospel of Jesus Christ, a sin that has to be combatted on every level of our lives, a denial of the Reformed tradition, a heresy that is to the everlasting shame of the church of Jesus Christ in the world.

To accept the Reformed confession is more than a formal acknowledgment of doctrine. Churches accepting that confession thereby commit themselves to show through their daily witness and service that the gospel has indeed empowered them to live in this world as the people of God. They also commit themselves to accept in their worship and at the table of the Lord the brothers and sisters who accept and proclaim the lordship of Christ in all areas of life, and to work ceaselessly for that justice, love, and shalom that are fundamental to the kingdom of God and the kingly rule of his Son. Confessional subscription should lead to concrete manifestation in unity of worship and cooperation in the common tasks of the church. In South Africa adherence to the Reformed tradition should be a commitment to combat the evil of apartheid in every area of our lives and to seek liberation, peace, justice, reconciliation, and wholeness for all of God's children in this torn and beloved land.

We must be clear. It is one thing when the rules and laws of unjust and oppressive governments make it impossible for the church to carry out its divine task. But it is quite another thing when churches purposely reject this unity and this struggle, as the white Reformed churches of South Africa have consistently done. Apartheid is not simply a political ideology. Its very existence has depended and still depends on a theological justification by these same white Reformed churches. This, too, is part of our task: in struggling *against* apartheid, we struggle *for* liberation; *against* an oppressive and inhuman ideology, but also *for* the sake of the gospel and the integrity of the church of Jesus Christ. Christians and churches purporting to serve the gospel by the justification of apartheid on biblical grounds do so only at the risk of blasphemy.

I am also convinced that in this struggle some Reformed expressions of faith, now centuries old, and for many redundant, can provide us with both prophetic clarity and pastoral comfort. Lord's Day 1 of the Heidelberg Catechism asks the question: "What is your only comfort in life and death?" The answer is:

> That I, with body and soul, both in life and death, am not my own, but belong to my faithful Savior Jesus Christ; who with his precious blood has fully satisfied for all my sins, and delivered me from all the power of the devil, and so preserves me that without the will of my heavenly Father not a hair can fall from my head; yea, that all things must be subservient to my salvation, wherefore by his Holy Spirit he also assures me of eternal life, and makes me heartily willing and ready, henceforth, to live unto him.

This is one of the most powerful statements of faith I have ever encountered. In our situation, when black personhood is thoroughly undermined, when our God-given human dignity is being trampled underfoot, when our elderly are uprooted and thrown into the utter desolation of resettlement camps, when even the meager shelter of a plastic sheet is brutally taken away and mothers and their babies are being exposed to the merciless winter of the Cape, when young children are terrorized in the early hours of the morning, when the prophetic voices of our youth are teargassed into silence, when the blood of our children flows in the streets of our townships—what *then* is our comfort in life and in death? When we are completely at the mercy of those for whom our humanity does not exist, when our powerlessness against their ruthless rule becomes a pain we can no longer bear, when the stench of our decaying hope chokes us half to death, when the broken lives and silent tears of our aged show the endlessness of our struggle, when the power of the oppressor is arrogantly flaunted in the face of all the world—what *then* is our comfort in life and death? That I, with body and soul, both in life and death, am not my own, but belong unto my faithful Savior, who is Jesus the Liberator; Christ the Messiah and *Kyrios*, the Lord.

Is this excessive spiritualization? No, it is not. But it is a revolutionary spirituality without which our being Christian in the world is not complete, and without which the temptations that are part and parcel of the liberation struggle will prove too much for us. Furthermore, in the situation in which we find ourselves, it is of vital importance that we be able to resist the totalitarian claims of the powers that rule South Africa so harshly. The most frightening aspect of apartheid is the totality of control that the government seeks to exercise over human lives—from the subtle and not so subtle propaganda to the harsh, draconian laws designed to ensure the "security" of the country. Apartheid is a false god whose authoritarian audacity allows no room for the essence of meaningful humanity: freedom under God. It is of vital importance that we never forget to whom our ultimate allegiance and obedience are due.

In this country, the government will come to expect more and more unquestioning submission for the sake of "national security." More and more the government will expect the church to participate in its "total strategy." Such participation could only take the form of theological justification of the national security ideology, the sanctification of the militarization of our society, and the motivation of South African soldiers for the "holy war" against communism. The church will be expected to applaud the kind of theology expounded by the state president at the centenary celebrations of the Nederduitse Gereformeerde Sendingkerk in October 1981: "The total onslaught against South Africa is a total onslaught against the kingdom of God."

Furthermore, as the situation of violence and counterviolence develops and the fear of whites that they will lose their overprivileged position grows, the courage of those who seek justice will be challenged.

So the confession that Jesus Christ is Lord of my life is not spiritual escapism. It is a confession with profound implications for the whole of life. It is a fundamental theological affirmation of the place of the Christian in this world, and it firmly sets the limits of the powers of this world. It places us within the best tradition of the Christian church through the ages, opening our eyes and ears to the inspiration of the "great cloud of witnesses on every side of us." It is a reminder, in the midst of the struggle, that our lives have meaning only when they are in the hands of the one who has given his life for the sake of all others. And although he is the Lamb who is slaughtered, for those who call him Lord he is also "Jesus Christ, the faithful witness, the firstborn from the dead, the ruler of the kings of the earth" (Rev. 1:5).

It is comfort, but it is more: it is the quiet, subversive piety that is quite indispensable for authentic Christian participation in the struggle for liberation. And in this struggle I am inspired by the words of the Belgic Confession:

> The faithful and elect shall be crowned with glory and honor; and the Son of God will confess their names before God his Father and his elect angels; all tears shall be wiped from their eyes; *and their cause, which is now condemned by many judges and magistrates as heretical and impious, will then be known to be the cause of the Son of God.*

This, also, is our tradition and is worth fighting for.

God's Special Concern for the Minjung

Minjung theology is the Korean version of liberation theology. The Minjung are the poor, oppressed masses, not the rich and the powerful. The goal of Minjung theology is a more just society in which the oppressed will be enabled to break the vicious cycle of oppression.

SOURCE

Hyun Young-hak, "A Theological Look at the Mask Dance in Korea," in *Minjung Theology: People as the Subjects of History,* ed. Commission on Theological Concerns of the Christian Conference of Asia (Maryknoll, N.Y.: Orbis, 1983), 53–54.

Thus, today, in the streets and on university campuses, ordinary people, intellectuals, laborers, and even poets have begun to proclaim the relevant messages of the Bible in the current economico-socio-political context of Korea. This movement has challenged the church in general. Some of those who have responded to the challenge have gone to prison willingly. We have been forced to formulate a theology of the *minjung* in order to furnish a biblical basis for the situation of the *minjung* who have been subjected to oppression and contempt. This theology can be truly called an indigenous, "grass-roots" theology, for it grew, and continues to grow, directly out of Christian experiences in the political struggle for justice. Moreover, *minjung* theology is Korean theology; it begins with the Korean *minjung*, their suffering and struggle. It is a theology of the oppressed in the Korean political situation, a theological response to the oppressors, and is for both the Korean church at large, as well as any who share in the struggle for liberation. This is what *minjung* theology is all about.

The main objectives of *minjung* theologians are several. First, we wish to learn the truth about humanity, history, and God through the age-old experience of the *minjung*. We believe that truth becomes most apparent when it is looked at from the vantage point of the oppressed, and most comprehensive when it is searched for through the long history of the *minjung*. One's sense of the value of self becomes keener, the ability to discern good and evil becomes sharper, and the aspiration for a new and just society becomes firmer when one is oppressed and one's human rights are unjustly trampled upon.

We are also aware that God is revealed to us at this point of struggle in our lives, confirming our self-worth, justifying our discernment, encouraging our aspiration for a new tomorrow, and leading us to that future which is the destination of human history. This truth has been revealed to us little by little throughout the centuries as the *minjung* have struggled for their humanization. Therefore, the task of theologians is to examine the nature of the *minjung's* experiences, discover the hidden activities of God in them, and discern the significance of the discovery for our attempts to create a new and just society.

Finally, we want to formulate a theology which will help the *minjung's* struggle for a better tomorrow. This can be accomplished by clarifying the nature of the *minjung's* struggle and charting directions and guidelines for them to follow. Therefore, we believe that through the study of *minjung* theology we can learn not only about ourselves, but also about our adversaries, which is absolutely necessary if our work is to be effective. Furthermore, through the in-depth study of the *minjung's* experience in the Old Testament, we can discern the direction of human history which is important for the charting of our struggle.

What are our goals? First and foremost is equality. *Minjung* theology describes this equality as the unification of two elements: the renewal of human rights and the revolutionary change for justice in the social structure. In order to establish a society of equality, the *han*-ridden *minjung* must effect a drastic, systemic change in the existing order. In other words, the *minjung*, with the help of the insight derived from the Old Testament, must assume a new responsibility. This will strengthen their awareness of their bondage and offer them hope for liberation. Historically, such awareness often generates struggle and confrontation. Korea is already in the midst of some struggle but this new, conscientized struggle will have the proper direction, along with the lasting strength needed to reach its goals.

At the same time, it would be idealistic of us to assume that changes leading to true equality will come about easily. There will always be a stumbling block in our way—the pervasiveness of greed. This greed touches not only the oppressor but also the oppressed, and leads to the vicious cycle of imbalance and inequality. We can see this so clearly in the history of Korea and in the story of Solomon which we examined in previous chapters. The cycle of the oppressed becoming the oppressor or the exploited taking on the role of the exploiter seems never-ending. But is it?

One possible answer to this question lies in the Korean concept of "dan." This is a Chinese word meaning "a cutting off" and represents the attempt to destroy the greed which is at the center of the oppressor-oppressed cycle. The cutting of the cycle of revenge would finally establish harmony in the political and social order. For the oppressors, it means that they should stop being greedy and oppressive. For the oppressed, it means that they should stop wishing to be like their masters and wanting to take revenge. Needless to say, we have discovered that neither of these transformations is easy to accomplish. Indeed, through cries and demonstrations the oppressed *minjung* have urged and demanded that the oppressors act in the spirit of *dan* and be fair. As demonstrations have escalated, however, the hearts of the rulers have hardened, and they have regressed further in the direction of evil. *Dan* is not easy for the oppressed either. Once liberation is achieved, it is difficult to resist the temptation to be like their masters and enjoy all the pleasure and comfort which they have been craving for so long. As a result, our hopes turn to the arrival of a Messiah to undertake this necessary exorcism. In fact, the messianic expectation is a common characteristic of all oppressed peoples. And the history of the Korean *minjung* is no exception, being full of such expectations.

Reformed Confessions

All Areas of Life Belong to Jesus Christ

One of the most important events in the life of the Reformed church in the twentieth century was the writing of The Theological Declaration of Barmen in Germany in 1934 in response to the attempt by the Nazi government to dictate the life of the church.

SOURCE

"The Theological Declaration of Barmen," in *Book of Confessions*, 8.13–18, 8.22–24.

2. "Christ Jesus, whom God made our wisdom, our righteousness and sanctification and redemption." (1 Cor. 1:30.)

As Jesus Christ is God's assurance of the forgiveness of all our sins, so in the same way and with the same seriousness he is also God's mighty claim upon our whole life. Through him befalls us a joyful deliverance from the godless fetters of this world for a free, grateful service to his creatures.

We reject the false doctrine, as though there were areas of our life in which we would not belong to Jesus Christ, but to other lords—areas in which we would not need justification and sanctification through him.

3. "Rather, speaking the truth in love, we are to grow up in every way into him who is the head, into Christ, from whom the whole body [is] joined and knit together." (Eph. 4:15, 16.)

The Christian Church is the congregation of the brethren in which Jesus Christ acts presently as the Lord in Word and sacrament through the Holy Spirit. As the Church of pardoned sinners, it has to testify in the midst of a sinful world, with its faith as with its obedience, with its message as with its order, that it is solely his property, and that it lives and wants to live solely from his comfort and from his direction in the expectation of his appearance.

We reject the false doctrine, as though the Church were permitted to abandon the form of its message and order to its own pleasure or to changes in prevailing ideological and political convictions.

The Gospel and National Security

When The Confession of 1967 was being considered for adoption by the United Presbyterian Church (U.S.A.), one of the most controversial lines in the document declared that nations should pursue peace "even at risk to national security."

SOURCE

"The Confession of 1967," in *Book of Confessions*, 9.45.

God's reconciliation in Jesus Christ is the ground of the peace, justice, and freedom among nations which all powers of government are called to serve and defend. The church, in its own life, is called to practice the forgiveness of enemies and to commend to the nations as practical politics the search for cooperation and peace. This search requires that the nations pursue fresh and responsible relations across every line of conflict, even at risk to national security, to reduce areas of strife and to broaden international understanding. Reconciliation among nations becomes peculiarly urgent as countries develop nuclear, chemical, and biological weapons, diverting their manpower and resources from constructive uses and risking the annihilation of mankind. Although nations may serve God's purposes in history, the church which identifies the sovereignty of any one nation or any one way of life with the cause of God denies the Lordship of Christ and betrays its calling.

The Responsibility of Creating Goods

The Presbyterian-Reformed Church in Cuba in its 1977 Confession of Faith describes the right of creating goods, a phrase that has a strong Marxist ring to it, as "the essential principle" of human spirituality.

SOURCE

"Confession of Faith" (1977) of the Presbyterian-Reformed Church in Cuba, in *Reformed Witness Today*, 172–73.

SECTION II:
THE HUMAN BEING: AN "ECONOME"

The Scriptures teach us that the human being is characterized by being an "econome" of all things, God's "steward." All goods, material and spiritual, that we obtain as persons or as nations, cannot be considered in the final analysis as "individual" or "national" property in an exclusive way, be it individualistic, classist, elitist or nationalistic. Much less can they have a transcendent value which, by reason of the "natural law" or "divine law," has been given goods as private ownership of the means of production.

To make human spiritual essentiality depend on the exercising of the so-called "right to private property," constitutes one of the most tragic aberrations—because of its consequences—that human spirituality has suffered to this day.

The Scriptures teach us that the human being will be whatever he is able to do and become as an "econome." The word "econome" (*oikóno-mos*) is the one most used in the New Testament when it is a matter of judging the achievements of human life. In the Old Testament the term "econome" (*menshala*) is given equal importance.

When the Marxists insist on the "economical" as the basic element, fundamental for interpreting the significance of human life as it is developed in history, they make the Church—one of those ironies of history—reconsider the Biblical criterion of the human being as an "econome."

The Church proclaims that the human vocation is that of being a "good econome." The "house" that the human creature administers is the whole world of Creation; and each person is responsible for it to his fellow creatures and to God.

The responsibility of creating goods and administrating them is the first right of every human being, the essential principle of his spirituality. The Church teaches that each and every human being should share responsibly in the mutual exercise of that right. To violate that right is the first criminal act against human dignity and decorum.

The most perfect social system will be the one that guarantees the responsible participation of all citizens in the matters of "public administration." The effective respect for that right is necessary in order for the society to be made up of persons and not infrahuman individuals. Such is the real principle of true "demo-cracy."

The Church teaches that the committed participation of its members in public life, in the administration of its economy, is not something one can choose to add or not to add to his condition of believer; on the contrary, the responsible exercise of this right is an integral and inseparable part of the loving practice of the Christian faith.

Therefore the Church teaches that it is an integral part of the life of the Christian believer to exercise his rights and to fulfill his duties as a citizen, especially in our case, where democracy is made effective through the constitution of the Popular Power and the participation in labor unions in the different places of work.

The aberrations of a "faith" which calls itself "a-political" are of such consequence for the falsification of human spirituality and the meaning of the social nature of life, that the Church, indignant, rejects them and combats them as "heretical." Only an interested distortion of the faith— against all argumentation grounded on scriptural truth—can make the simple Christian believer renounce the struggle and effort to find, together with his fellow countrymen, the most adequate solutions to the problems patent in the neighborhood, in the city or in the nation, and keep him from enriching the life of all and making it more decorously human through a better "economy" of his time, his abilities, his knowledge and the goods he produces.

THEOLOGY AND ECONOMICS

One of the most spirited debates in twentieth-century theology concerned the relation between Calvinism and capitalism. The debate began with the publication in 1904–5 of an essay by Max Weber entitled *The Protestant Ethic and the Spirit of Capitalism*. The Calvinist doctrines of predestination and vocation, argues Weber, laid the foundation for the development of capitalism. Not all theologians, however, have found Weber's thesis compelling. Weber was unable to demonstrate that Calvin or any other Reformed theologian actually advocated anything resembling capitalism. One individual he did cite was Benjamin Franklin, who was not widely recognized to be a Calvinist!

In the twentieth century, several Reformed theologians and churches have argued that the gospel is more compatible with socialism than with capitalism. That point of view is found, for example, in the 1977 Confession of Faith of the Presbyterian-Reformed Church in Cuba.

FOR FURTHER STUDY

Helmut Gollwitzer, *The Rich Christians and Poor Lazarus*, trans. David Cairns (New York: Macmillan, 1970). Douglas John Hall, *The Steward: A Biblical Symbol Come of Age* (New York: Friendship Press, 1982). M. Douglas Meeks, *God the Economist: The Doctrine of God and Political Economy* (Minneapolis: Fortress, 1989). Max L. Stackhouse, *Public Theology and Political Economy: Christian Stewardship in Modern Society* (Grand Rapids: Wm. B. Eerdmans, 1987). R. H. Tawney, *Religion and the Rise of Capitalism: A Historical Study* (Gloucester, Mass.: Peter Smith, 1962). Max Weber, *The Protestant Ethic and the Spirit of Capitalism*, trans. Talcott Parsons (New York: Charles Scribner's Sons, 1958).

Calvinism and Capitalism

Like Max Weber, Ernst Troeltsch argued that the theological convictions of Calvinism made it hospitable to the development of capitalism. The Calvinist understanding of vocation, or "calling," made work an end in itself and led to "our present-day bourgeois way of life."

SOURCE

Ernst Troeltsch, *The Social Teaching of the Christian Churches*, 2 vols., trans. Olive Wyon (New York: Harper & Brothers, 1960), 2:644–46.

CALVINISM AND CAPITALISM

Thus this economic practice of Geneva became the starting-point from which Capitalism was incorporated into the Calvinistic ethic all over the world, though with caution and under certain limitations. Conditions among the French Huguenots, in the Netherlands, and in England, each with their own characteristics, also helped to adjust modern business life to the religious point of view. One very important aspect of the situation is the fact that the Calvinists in France and England, and at the outset also in the Netherlands, and, above all, during their period of exile on the Lower Rhine, as minorities were forced out of public life and official positions in the State; they were thus obliged, in the main, to go into business life. Apart from this, however, the Calvinists displayed a strong tendency in this direction, even in circumstances which were not particularly favourable to business life; their industrious habits, their detachment from the world, and their rational and utilitarian spirit certainly strengthened this tendency.

The economic situation in Geneva, however, contained the germ of logical developments which went beyond the intention of Calvin and the Genevese. Once Capitalism had been accepted, even with many precautions, given the right *milieu*, everywhere it led to results which increased its power; while the specifically Calvinistic habits of piety and industry justified its existence and helped to increase its strength, which gave it in the Calvinistic communities a special character and a peculiar intensity. The exhortation to continual industry in labour, combined with the limitation of consumption and of luxury, produced a tendency to pile up capital, which for its part—in the necessity of its further utilization in work and not in enjoyment—necessitated an ever-increasing turnover. The duty of labour, coupled with the ban on luxury, worked out "economically as the impulse to save," and the impulse to save had the effect of building up capital. To what extent these developments took place everywhere is a separate question. Upon the whole, however, this result belonged to the very nature of the case, and it is the general opinion that this is what actually took place among the most important Calvinistic peoples.

This, however, is not the main point at issue. The contribution of Calvinism to the formation of the Capitalist system itself is not the most important aspect of the question. This only becomes clear when, with Weber and Sombart, we inquire into the ethical "spirit" and the world outlook, or the "economic temper" which gave the system its firm hold over the minds of men, and which, in spite of its opposition to natural human instincts, has been able to strike root in human minds as a firm conviction. Economic traditionalism, interrupted by unscrupulous individuals who are simply out for gain, is much more in line with ordinary human instincts than the concrete and abstract dominion of labour and profit, as ends in themselves, the continual increase of work produced by every fresh profit from labour. It is here that we perceive the importance (together with the related, yet different, effects of Judaism) which the peculiar Calvinistic type of the inward ethical attitude has gained towards the performance of labour in business life, and its religious estimate of the earning of money. The Protestant ethic of the "calling," with its Calvinistic assimilation of the Capitalist system, with its severity and its control of the labour rendered as a sign of the assurance of election, made service in one's "calling," the systematic exercise of one's energies, into a service both necessary in itself and appointed by God, in which profit is regarded as the sign of the Divine approval. This conception of the "calling" and of labour, with its taboo on idleness of every kind, with its utilization of every chance of gain, and its confidence in the blessing of God, now, however, to a great extent approached the commercial professions and the business of making money. It laid the foundation of a world of specialized labour, which taught men to work for work's sake, and in so doing it produced our present-day bourgeois way of life, the fundamental psychological principles which gave it birth, which, however, it was not bound to perpetuate once this way of life had become the constitution of the modern world.

Thus there arose a current—definite, particularly powerful, and influential—of the bourgeois capitalistic spirit, which was pre-eminently typical of the bourgeois way of life in general. This was the predominance of labour and of the "calling," of industry for its own sake, a process of objectifying work and the results of work, which was only possible where work was exalted by means of an ascetic vocational ethic of that kind, into the sphere of that which is *necessary in itself* by means of the underlying religious conception. Calvinism, which in its early days included a good many groups of the aristocracy, was at first indifferent to social questions, but in the course of the political development in various countries it became bourgeois; this social transformation, however, was entirely in line with certain elements in its spirit.

The significant point which is important even to-day for our subject is this: that in these Christian circles, and in them alone, was it possible to combine modern economic activity with Christian thought, and, indeed, that down to the present day it is possible to do this with a clear conscience. In this connection we only need to recall the circumlocutions with which Catholicism tries to make this modern form of economic life tolerable, and how, at bottom, it continually attempts to restrain it, or the revulsion with which early Lutheranism and contemporary German Conservatism officially regard Capitalism. Seen in this light, the significance of this new Calvinistic form of Christianity for the whole modern development, and especially for the position of Protestantism within it, becomes plain. It is the only form of Christian social doctrine which accepts the basis of the modern economic situation without reserve. The reason for this does not lie in any supposed "greater insight" into the essence of the economic processes, but in the fact that here the super-idealistic and Pietistic hindrances in the fundamental ethical idea have fallen away, which would have otherwise hindered or restrained this development; because, on the contrary, the Calvinistic ethic contains energies which directly further this economic development.

Capitalism Is Un-Calvinistic

Jürgen Moltmann argues that Weber's thesis cannot be supported historically: Calvinism was not the seedbed for capitalism but, rather, was an advocate for "a just social order in freedom."

SOURCE

Jürgen Moltmann, "The Ethic of Calvinism," in *The Experiment Hope*, trans. M. Douglas Meeks (Philadelphia: Fortress, 1975), 124–27.

Since its beginnings in Zurich and Geneva, Reformed Christianity has been alive predominantly in the great cities. It was spread in France by merchants and was carried into other countries by emigrants. Thus it formed a certain alliance with the freedom struggles of the middle class against the medieval structures of feudalism and ecclesiastic domination. It is a fact that the modern mastery of the world through science and industry was accomplished more quickly among peoples and groups with a Protestant, and to be more exact a Reformed tradition, than it was in other places. From this fact the German social and economic historian Max Weber developed his famous thesis of the "congeniality" between *Calvinism and capitalism*. This thesis is disseminated by many today with the defamatory slogans that Calvinism is the "religion of capitalism" or that it mixes *Geist und Geld* (Spirit and money).

This contention however lacks any factual proof and Max Weber's thesis can scarcely hold up any longer historically. The actual figure whom Weber adduces to prove his theory is the American inventor and statesman Benjamin Franklin who lived from 1706 to 1790 in the period of mercantilism, that is, two hundred years after Calvin. In Franklin, Weber found maxims with religious and ethical overtones, such as: ceaseless work is an end in itself and the increase of capital is the highest aim. Weber thought he had detected the connection between religion and the accumulation of capital in the Calvinistic doctrine of unmerited election. It isolates man from society, deprives him of all sacramental and churchly mediations between himself and God, and makes him entirely dependent upon himself. How shall he become certain of his election? Since, according to the New Testament, only the good tree brings forth good fruit, the isolated soul must make itself certain of its election by constantly producing new good works. Good works are no longer a means to purchase one's salvation. Rather they are the means of ridding oneself of anxiety about one's salvation. Because one must constantly be able to see one's good works, the results of one's work may not be consumed, but must be capitalized.

Weber called this religious life-style, which he believed he had discovered in the Puritans of the seventeenth century, "inner worldly asceticism." In it Weber thought he recognized that spirit which has formed modern capitalism: the accumulation of capital through ascetic economizing. At the "cradle of the modern businessman" stood the Puritan anxiously tending to his own election. Here were "bred those self-certain 'saints,' which we see again in the hard-as-steel Puritan merchants of the heroic periods of capitalism and in individual examples down to the present." But as historical evidences Weber could cite only late Puritan texts, such as Richard Baxter's *Christian Directory or Body of Practical Divinity* (1673) and Richard Steele's *The Tradesman's Calling* (1684). And even from their writings he quoted only half the truth. He suppressed such themes as responsibility for the community, care for the weak, and education for the common good which are expressed in these pastoral writings and belonged to the reality of Puritan life.

Is there in the writings of Reformed theologians a recognizable connection between faith in election and zeal for business? Weber's thesis sounds quite plausible, but it cannot be supported by historical evidence. He himself excluded Calvin. According to Calvin, Christ is first and foremost the "mirror of election." In the knowledge of Christ's representative suffering and dying the believing person becomes sure of his call and election. There are for Calvin signs which accompany this, namely, the fear of God in one's heart and the community of the church which is gathered around the Word and the Lord's Supper. Calvin does not refer to the fruits of one's occupational labor. The Calvinist Synod of Dordrecht (1618) speaks of Christ as the revelation of God's election through grace, then of the self-witness of true, persevering faith, next of childlike fear of God and distress over one's sin, and only in the last place of zeal for a good conscience and good works. That these "good works" should consist of ceaseless work at one's job and the egoistic accumulation of capital is nowhere said, not even in the late Puritan literature of devotion and edification. Only the prosaic morality of a businessman in the Victorian period could speak in this way. An inner connection between Calvinist-Puritan faith in election and the spirit of capitalism cannot be demonstrated.

The history of the rise of capitalism is much more complex than Weber's one-dimensional thesis can account for. Capitalistic economic forms arose in the period of the Renaissance in the Lombardian cities. The business policies of the Fuggers, Welsers, Paumgartners, and other merchants belonging to the Catholic confession were clearly a form of "early capitalism." Even the mercantilist absolute princes, such as the Catholic Sun-King Louis XIV of France (1643–1715), may be described as "capitalistic." It may be the case that, in the eighteenth century, capitalistic forms of economy together with the first great industries developed faster in Protestant-Calvinist regions than elsewhere. But if this was so, it was due to the changed economic and geographical circumstances. The discovery of America and the sea routes to Asia had displaced the centers of trade to Northern and Western Europe. It has been shown that the predominance of Calvinism actually hindered rather than promoted capitalism in Geneva itself. In 1568 and again in 1580 the pastors successfully prevented the establishment of a bank.

But how did the Calvinist economic ethic appear if Max Weber's thesis cannot hold? The Reformation in Geneva was a renewal of faith but it included the whole life of the church, society, and politics. Calvin had a substantial part in refashioning the *ordre civil* (1543). He condemned the mercenary system and Genevan nationalism and he inspired a new openness toward refugees. With the establishment of the diaconate a new system of providing for the poor and the operation of hospitals was devised. Calvin took over from Luther the Reformation understanding of every worldly means of earning a livelihood as a *calling (Beruf)*. Whereas in the Middle Ages this word was reserved exclusively to the calling of the priests and the *vita contemplativa* stood higher than the *vita activa*, Luther and Calvin paved the way for a fundamentally new understanding of calling. In the "universal priesthood of all believers" every Christian has his calling. All work, in whatever calling, stands under the command and promise of God.

Precisely for this reason Calvin, in particular, persistently stressed the community-related character of one's vocational work. "Work is necessary so that all may live and it is to be done in such a way that there will be no exploitation of the poor by the rich, strangers by local citizens, the weak by the strong" (Max Geiger). Calvin followed the same tendency in his judgments about the *charging of interest*. Applying the Old Testament prophetic pronouncements against the taking of interest to his own situation, Calvin prohibited interest in the following case: no interest was to be taken from the poor. Capital investments which yield interest may be undertaken only insofar as they do not prejudice aid to those in need. Contracts for interest must be made according to the Golden Rule of Christ (Matt. 7:12).

Calvin set aside the rules of canon law and placed economic life under the command of God. Accordingly "the rights of the neighbor," especially of the weak and the fugitives, were decisive for him. In the economic ethic both of Calvin himself and of the Calvinist traditions one's work and possessions are to serve the neighbor, for "God is an advocate of the poor, the aliens, and the fugitives." The Reformed congregations have usually distinguished themselves through their exemplary social institutions and methods of caring for the poor. That capitalism in which every man preys like a wolf on every other man is utterly un-Calvinistic. In Germany the "Elberfelder system" of the Dutch Reformed congregations became a model for the state's welfare system. This was also the case in Switzerland, Holland, and England. The Calvinist economic ethic abandoned the class society of the old church; it did not, however, become the precursor of capitalism but rather of a just social order in freedom.

The Cause of the World's Poor

The Confession of 1967 of the reunited Presbyterian Church (U.S.A.) takes a clear position against poverty. A church that is indifferent to poverty, it argues, cannot offer acceptable worship to God.

SOURCE

"The Confession of 1967," in *Book of Confessions*, 9.46.

The reconciliation of man through Jesus Christ makes it plain that enslaving poverty in a world of abundance is an intolerable violation of God's good creation. Because Jesus identified himself with the needy and exploited, the cause of the world's poor is the cause of his disciples. The church cannot condone poverty, whether it is the product of unjust social structures, exploitation of the defenseless, lack of national resources, absence of technological understanding, or rapid expansion of populations. The church calls every man to use his abilities, his possessions, and the fruits of technology as gifts entrusted to him by God for the maintenance of his family and the advancement of the common welfare. It encourages those forces in human society that raise men's hopes for better conditions and provide them with opportunity for a decent living. A church that is indifferent to poverty, or evades responsibility in economic affairs, or is open to one social class only, or expects gratitude for its beneficence makes a mockery of reconciliation and offers no acceptable worship to God.

Salvation as the Abolishment of Private Property

The 1977 Confession of Faith of the Presbyterian-Reformed Church in Cuba affirms that a society organized on socialist structures is more just than capitalist societies.

SOURCE

"Confession of Faith" (1977) of the Presbyterian-Reformed Church in Cuba, in *Reformed Witness Today*, 180–83.

SALVATION: THE HISTORY OF THE
SOCIAL-ECONOMICAL RECONSTRUCTION
OF THE HUMAN BEING

Salvation for Scriptures means the reconstruction of the human being as "co-heir of all things"; that is, of those goods which, in faithfulness to his vocation as "econome," he has, with his work, co-created or recreated. Salvation is also, thus, the history of the reconstruction of his being in community.

The "creation" of a "new man" means the establishment of a new community life in the new society, where there is no place for the exploitation of the work of another, nor for racial discrimination nor the subjection of women as objects of mercantile, commercial or sexual consumption; nor will there be tolerance for the self-interested use of the legitimate values of family life in benefit of the false interests of the classist and discriminatory society.

The Scriptures teach us that salvation necessarily includes the emerging of a new fraternal solidarity that is made concrete in a "community of goods" where "private property" is abolished in order for all of us to be able to enjoy the goods produced.

The Bible teaches us, in the Old Testament, that a liberating process involves "as is written, that he who gathers much has nothing left over nor he who gathers little has lack." In the New Testament, we are shown in a reliable way that the liberating fact of the Gospel, accepted fully, has as an inevitable consequence that, "uniting us all" ideologically, we "have all things in common," receiving "each one according to his need."

The Church proclaims, following the Biblical-prophetic line carried to its final expression in Jesus Christ, that the entrance to the Kingdom is closed to the "rich," to the extent that their riches are the products of violence and injustice; and, in a specific way, it points out to all and especially to the Christian believers, the fact that the Capitalistic System of social organization, in order to endure, has to maintain a manipulated and enslaving education that produces egoists who distort the meaning of human life and see as the supreme ideals of human life, unending consumption, insatiable satisfaction of getting rich, materialistic fetichism [sic] and the drive for luxury and ostentation. As a result, this brings about a dehumanized society where most ferocious competition is of utmost importance and in which its victims are inculcated social evasions by means of drugs, sexual excesses, gambling and alienating religiosity.

The Church teaches, according to its best reformed tradition, that "God desires that there be such identification and equality among us that each help . . . according to his capacities, so that some do not have things left over while others are in need . . . that possessions and other goods be distributed according to the needs of each one."

The Church teaches that in the stability of the government—in spite of its necessary ambiguities—we can find a guarantee for the administration of justice and the maintenance of peace when it is a case of "non-classist" societies, where the power of the state is not in the hands of exploiting and oppressing classes, but in the hands of the workers.

The Church lives in the same measure in which each one of its members works for the social-economical reconstruction of the human being within the Socialist State; because, of all the historical forms of State known and experienced to this day, it is the society organized with such (socialist) structures which offers the most concrete possibilities for making workable a more and more fairly distributive justice, which progressively reaches all citizens with greater efficiency.

SALVATION: THE HISTORY OF THE
ECOLOGICAL RECONSTRUCTION
OF THE HUMAN BEING

"Sin," according to the Bible, distorts the human being's relationship with nature. The human being converted into an unscrupulous pillager of natural resources, not only has abused them, but also has made a diabolic use of them, making them a part of exploitation, oppression and domination of his fellow creatures.

The human being has pathologically altered the development of nature and has become, not its guardian, but its perverter. Doing this, he has upset and damaged his own human nature from a biological point of view. As a psycho-social-somatic unit, given the complexity of his nature, the human being has found himself affected in biological development as well as in his psychic health and social promotion.

Nevertheless the Church affirms that the technical-scientific activities of the human being, in his eagerness to dominate and control nature, do not work against God's redeeming purpose which proposes—according to the Scriptures—"to put all things under his feet." The "way" of salvation that God works in Jesus Christ includes the full realization of that domination and control. The Bible uses the same word "health" (salud) for "salvation" and for "liberation." We can not overlook the fact that in order to achieve a better human "health," both in the biological and in the psychic and social sense, it is necessary to control nature more perfectly and dominate its "mysteries" more completely.

The Church proclaims that although it is an extremely secularizing society we are dealing with, this does not mean that God would be absent from it; rather it would mean the opposite. To believe in the doctrine of Incarnation means we believe in a God radically secularized in Jesus of Nazareth as the only way to the possibility of human redemption.

The Church teaches that the human technological undertaking serves to help create a new humanity to the extent it makes achievable a greater deepening of human spirituality with the disappearance of work as "exploitation."

The Church teaches that modern technology, when it is at the service of the interests of exploiting classes, has produced a series of false idols, such as utilitarian logic, the cosificación of human beings (cosa = thing, cosificación = making into a thing) and technocratic nihilism. All Christian believers should fight committedly—together with those who strive to eradicate such idols—for the disappearance of their "creators."

The Church teaches that, when our people chose the Marxist-Leninist way of development through a social-political revolution, a more human relationship with nature has been brought about as well as a primary concern for the health of the people. The Marxist-Leninist revolution has proved to be the only way which makes the technological and ecological development possible and which successfully puts an end to underdevelopment. This phenomenon of underdevelopment has produced infrahuman beings, victims of exploitation and oppression with the World Capitalistic and Imperialistic System.

The Church joyfully lives in the midst of the Socialist revolution, since the revolution has concrete and historically inaugurated a series of values in human relations that make it possible for the whole technical-scientific development to be at the service of the full dignity of human beings.

An Ethic of Justice

In 1984 the Presbyterian Church (U.S.A.) produced a study paper entitled "Christian Faith and Economic Justice." It examined the strengths and weaknesses of both democratic capitalism and democratic socialism, and it developed six guidelines for determining what faithfulness to God requires in matters of economic justice.

SOURCE

Christian Faith and Economic Justice (Louisville: Office of the General Assembly of the Presbyterian Church [U.S.A.], 1989), 31–32.

AN ETHIC OF JUSTICE

29.309

Of all the biblical and theological themes that we reviewed in our search for clues as to what faithfulness to God requires of us here and now, none seemed more relevant than the one that witnesses to the justice that God does and expects. Thus, we sought to discern with care the kind of justice that God does and that we are to do. The biblical word is that God's justice is inseparable from God's love and compassion, that God's justice is a liberating and saving justice, that God's justice lifts up the fallen, cares for the helpless, empowers the powerless, and restores human community.

29.310

Drawing on the biblical witness to God's justice and other theological convictions about God, ourselves, and our neighbors, we discerned six guidelines for action. Faithfulness to the God of justice, we said, requires us (1) to allow equal respect and concern for all; (2) to demonstrate special concern for the poor and oppressed; (3) to respond to human needs; (4) to respect human freedom; (5) to contribute to the well-being of the community; and (6) to fulfill our obligations to future generations.

29.311

In light of these requirements, we projected a vision of a just economy and set forth six moral norms for evaluating the justice and thus the moral legitimacy of economic systems, structures, and situations. Our vision and norms are these:

29.312

(1) A just economic arrangement is one which honors and respects the equal worth of all members of the human family. It demonstrates that respect and concern with a presumption toward a distribution of economic goods and services which will enable an enhancement of the dignity of each member of the community. Borrowing from the work of John Rawls, we concluded that economic inequalities can be justified only if they are to the greatest benefit of the least advantaged, and if they go with positions or appointments which are open to all under conditions of fair equality of opportunity.

29.313

(2) A just economic arrangement is one that shows special concern for the vulnerable. In a just arrangement, society seeks to realize the biblical mandate, "There shall be no poor among you" (Deut 15:4). A just system gives particular concern to honoring the dignity and worth of the sick, the aged, the very young, the poor.

29.314

(3) A just economic arrangement is one which enables people to meet their basic needs such as food, water, clothing, shelter, health care, education, meaningful work, and participation in decisions that most significantly affect their life. For those who because of illness, age, or for other reasons are unable to provide for their own needs, the just society will make provisions in ways which honor human dignity, as a matter of right.

29.315

(4) A jus: economic arrangement is one which honors and respects human freedom and provides opportunities for the responsible exercise of liberty. A just society will recognize that in some circumstances respect for human freedom requires noninterference by the state, and it will create means to protect the individual from abuse by the state. A just society will also recognize that in other circumstances positive action by the state is necessary to make possible human freedom and enable it to flourish, and it will support such positive action.

29.316

(5) A just economic arrangement is one which requires and enables persons to contribute to the common good according to their abilities. A just society will recognize in law and practice that to whom much is given, of that one is much required. It will accept responsibility for providing job opportunities for each member of society who is able to work, so that each may contribute to the production and distribution of economic goods and services.

29.317

(6) A just economic arrangement is one which exercises responsible stewardship of natural resources, mindful of its obligations to generations unborn. A just society will aim for ecological sustainability. It will recognize that pollution and the depletion of nonrenewable resources are issues of justice, and it will operate in the solemn awareness that either the sins or the virtues of the parents will be the legacy of their children and their children's children.

29.318

We believe that faithfulness to God in our time requires us not only to be just and to show compassion in our interpersonal relations, but also to join with all others of good will in seeking to construct a more just political economy in both our own nation and the whole interdependent world. That the construction of a more just society will require not merely modest reforms but major transformations seems obvious to us. That the struggle will be long and painful is apparent. That we ourselves who are so relatively privileged and who enjoy what is so ironically called a "high standard of living" will be tempted to resist mightily the changes required is also quite likely. But the cause of justice is God's cause. The call to justice is God's call. And it is in responding to God's call that we discover what life is all about.

CHRISTIANITY AND CULTURE

In addition to contributing to politics and economics, the Reformed tradition has played an important role in the development of culture. Because of its emphasis on the knowledge of God and the importance of education for the service of God, the Reformed tradition has usually fostered a deep respect for the achievements of human intellect and creativity. Because early Reformed theology emphasized simplicity in all things and prohibited the use of images, there has been a certain reserve concerning the visual arts. Reformed Christians have promoted literature and, to an even greater extent, music. Karl Barth's enthusiasm for Mozart is a well-known example of the appreciation for culture in Reformed theology.

An important development in the twentieth century has been the attempt by many non-Western Reformed churches to interpret the gospel in the context of their own cultures. Both Western and non-Western theologians now have to struggle with what, if anything, is of the essence of the gospel and what is a cultural accretion.

FOR FURTHER STUDY

Emil Brunner, *Christianity and Civilization* (New York: Charles Scribner's Sons, 1948). David Baily Harned, *Theology and the Arts* (Philadelphia: Westminster, 1966). Julian N. Hartt, *A Christian Critique of American Culture: An Essay in Practical Theology* (New York: Harper & Row, 1967). George S. Heyer, *Theology and the Arts: Theological Essays on Art in the Twentieth Century* (Grand Rapids: Wm. B. Eerdmans, 1980). H. Richard Niebuhr, *Christ and Culture* (New York: Harper & Row, 1951). Henry R. Van Til, *The Calvinist Concept of Culture* (Grand Rapids: Baker Book House, 1959). Nicholas Wolterstorff, *Art in Action: Toward a Christian Aesthetic* (Grand Rapids: Wm. B. Eerdmans, 1980).

The Reaching of the Heart
toward the Eternal

Many theologians would argue that the period of modern theology began in 1799 with the publication of Friedrich Schleiermacher's *On Religion: Speeches to Its Cultured Despisers*. Schleiermacher addressed himself to a circle of well-educated non-Christians and argued that religion is important not because it serves some other end, but because it is based on piety, which has its own special province in the mind.

SOURCE

Friedrich Schleiermacher, *On Religion: Speeches to Its Cultured Despisers*, trans. John Oman (New York: Harper & Row, 1958), 18–21.

FOR FURTHER STUDY

Jack Forstman, *A Romantic Triangle: Schleiermacher and Early German Romanticism* (Missoula, Mont.: Scholars Press for The American Academy of Religion, 1977).

I ask, therefore, that you turn from everything usually reckoned religion, and fix your regard on the inward emotions and dispositions, as all utterances and acts of inspired men direct. Despite your acquirements, your culture and your prejudices, I hope for good success. At all events, till you have looked from this standpoint without discovering anything real, or having any change of opinion, or enlarging your contemptuous conception, the product of superficial observation, and are still able to hold in ridicule this reaching of the heart towards the Eternal, I will not confess that I have lost. Then, however, I will finally believe that your contempt for religion is in accordance with your nature, and I shall have no more to say.

Yet you need not fear that I shall betake myself in the end to that common device of representing how necessary religion is for maintaining justice and order in the world. Nor shall I remind you of an all-seeing eye, nor of the unspeakable short-sightedness of human management, nor of the narrow bounds of human power to render help. Nor shall I say how religion is a faithful friend and useful stay of morality, how, by its sacred feelings and glorious prospects, it makes the struggle with self and the perfecting of goodness much easier for weak man. Those who profess to be the best friends and most zealous defenders do indeed speak in this way. Which of the two is more degraded in being thus thought of together, I shall not decide, whether justice and morality which are represented as needing support, or religion which is to support them, or even whether it be not you to whom such things are said.

Though otherwise this wise counsel might be given you, how could I dare to suppose that you play with your consciences a sort of fast and loose game, and could be impelled by something you have hitherto had no cause to respect and love to something else that without it you already honour, and to which you have already devoted yourselves? Or suppose that these Speeches were merely to suggest what you should do for the sake of the people! How could you, who are called to educate others and make them like yourselves, begin by deceiving them, offering them as holy and vitally necessary what is in the highest degree indifferent to yourselves, and which, in your opinion, they can again reject as soon as they have attained your level? I, at least, cannot invite you to a course of action in which I perceive the most ruinous hypocrisy towards the world and towards yourselves. To recommend religion by such means would only increase the contempt to which it is at present exposed. Granted that our civil organizations are still burdened with a very high degree of imperfection and have shown but small power to prevent or abolish injustice, it would still be a culpable abandonment of a weighty matter, a faint-hearted unbelief in the approach of better things, if religion that in itself is not otherwise desirable must be called in.

Answer me this one question. Could there be a legal constitution resting on piety? Would not the whole idea that you hold so sacred vanish as soon as you took such a point of departure? Deal with the matter directly, therefore, if it seems to be in such an evil plight. Improve the laws, recast the whole constitution, give the state an iron hand, give it a hundred eyes if it has not got them already. At least do not allow those it has to sleep veiled in delusion. If you leave a business like this to an intermediary, you have never managed it. Do not declare to the disgrace of mankind that your loftiest creation is but a parasitic plant that can only nourish itself from strange sap.

Speaking from your standpoint, law must not even require morality to assure for it the most unlimited jurisdiction in its own territory. It must stand quite alone. Statesmen must make it universal. Now quite apart from the question whether what only exists in so far as it proceeds from the heart can be thus arbitrarily combined, if this general jurisdiction is only possible when religion is combined with law, none but persons skilled to infuse the spirit of religion into the human soul should be statesmen. And in what dark barbarousness of evil times would that land us!

Just as little can morality be in need of religion. A weak, tempted heart must take refuge in the thought of a future world. But it is folly to make a distinction between this world and the next. Religious persons at least know only one. If the desire for happiness is foreign to morality, later happiness can be no more valid than earlier; if it should be quite independent of praise, dread of the Eternal cannot be more valid than dread of a wise man. If morality loses in splendour and stability by every addition, how much more must it lose from something that can never hide its foreign extraction.

All this, however, you have heard of sufficiently from those who defend the independence and might of the moral law. Yet let me add, that to wish to transport religion into another sphere that it may serve and labour is to manifest towards it also great contempt. It is not so ambitious of conquest as to seek to reign in a foreign kingdom. The power that is its due, being earned afresh at every moment, satisfies it. Everything is sacred to it, and above all everything holding with it the same rank in human nature. But it must render a special service; it must have an aim; it must show itself useful! What degradation! And its defenders should be eager for it!

At the last remove, morality and justice also must conduce to some further advantage. It were better that such utilitarians should be submerged in this eternal whirlpool of universal utility, in which everything good is allowed to go down, of which no man that would be anything for himself understands a single sensible word, than that they should venture to come forward as defenders of religion, for of all men they are least skilled to conduct its case. High renown it were for the heavenly to conduct so wretchedly the earthly concerns of man! Great honour for the free and unconcerned to make the conscience of man a little sharper and more alert! For such a purpose religion does not descend from heaven. What is loved and honoured only on account of some extraneous advantage may be needful, but it is not in itself necessary, and a sensible person simply values it according to the end for which it is desired. By this standard, religion would be valueless enough. I, at least, would offer little, for I must confess that I do not believe much in the unjust dealings it would hinder, nor the moral dealings it would produce. If that is all it could do to gain respect, I would have no more to do with its case. To recommend it merely as an accessory is too unimportant. An imaginary praise that vanishes on closer contemplation, cannot avail anything going about with higher pretensions. I maintain that in all better souls piety springs necessarily by itself; that a province of its own in the mind belongs to it, in which it has unlimited sway; that it is worthy to animate most profoundly the noblest and best and to be fully accepted and known by them. That is my contention, and it now behoves you to decide whether it is worth your while to hear me, before you still further strengthen yourselves in your contempt.

Calvinism and Science

Abraham Kuyper gave the L. P. Stone Lectures at Princeton Seminary in 1898–99 on the topic of Calvinism. He argued that Calvinism had made important contributions to the development of science and cited as an example the founding of the University of Leyden.

SOURCE

Abraham Kuyper, *Calvinism* (New York: Fleming H. Revell Co., n.d.), 143–46.

CALVINISM AND SCIENCE

In my fourth lecture allow me to draw your attention to the nexus between *Calvinism and Science*. Not, of course in order to exhaust in one lecture such a weighty subject. Four points of it only I submit to your thoughtful consideration; first, that Calvinism fostered and could not but foster *love for science;* secondly, that it restored to science *its domain;* thirdly, that it delivered science from *unnatural bonds;* and fourthly in what manner it sought and found a solution for the unavoidable *scientific conflict.*

First of all then: There is found hidden in Calvinism an impulse, an inclination, an incentive, to scientific investigation. *It is a fact,* that science has been fostered by it, and its principle demands the scientific spirit. One glorious page from the history of Calvinism may suffice to prove the fact, before we enter more fully upon the discussion of the incentive to scientific investigation found in Calvinism as such. The page from the history of Calvinism, or let us rather say of mankind, matchless in its beauty, to which I refer, is the siege of Leyden, more than three hundred years ago. This siege of Leyden was in fact a struggle between Alva and Prince William about the future course of the history of the world; and the result was, that in the end Alva had to withdraw, and that William the Silent was enabled to unfurl the banner of liberty over Europe. Leyden, defended almost exclusively by its own citizens, entered the lists against the best troops of what was looked upon at that time as the finest army of the world. Three months after the commencement of the siege, the supply of food became exhausted. A fearful famine began to rage. The apparently doomed citizens managed to live on dogs and rats. This black famine was soon followed by the black death or the plague, which carried off a third part of the inhabitants. The Spaniard offered peace and pardon to the dying people; but Leyden, remembering the bad faith of the enemy in the treatment of Narden and Harlem, answered boldly and with pride: If it is necessary, we are ready to consume our left arms, and to defend with our right arms our wives, our liberty and our religion against thee, o tyrant. Thus they persevered. They patiently waited for the coming of the Prince of Orange, to raise the siege, . . . but . . . the prince had to wait for God. The dikes of the province of Holland had been cut through; the country surrounding Leyden was flooded; a fleet lay ready to hasten to Leyden's aid; but the wind drove the water back, preventing the fleet from passing the shallow pools. God tried his people sorely. At last however, on the first of October, the wind turned towards the West, and, forcing the waters upward, enabled the fleet to reach the beleaguered city. Then the Spaniards fled in haste to escape the rising tide. On the 3rd of October the fleet entered the port of Leyden, and the siege being raised, Holland and Europe were saved. The population, all but starved to death, could scarcely drag themselves along, yet all to a man, limped as well as they could to the house of prayer. There all fell on their knees and gave thanks to God. But when they tried to utter their gratitude in psalms of praise, they were almost voiceless, for there was no strength left in them, and the tones of their song died away in grateful sobbing and weeping.

Behold what I called a glorious page in the history of liberty, written in blood, and if you now ask me, what has this to do with *science*, see here the answer: In recognition of such patriotic courage, the States of Holland did not present Leyden with a handful of knightly orders, or gold, or honour, but with a *School of the Sciences*,—The University of Leyden, renowned through the whole world. The German is surpassed by none in pride of his scientific glory, and yet no less a man than Niebuhr has testified, "that the Senate chamber of Leyden's University is the most memorable hall of science." The ablest scholars were induced to fill the amply endowed chairs. Scaliger was conveyed from France in a man-of-war. Salmasius came to Leyden under convoy of a whole squadron. Why should I give you the long list of names of the princes of science, of the giants in learning, who have filled Leyden with the lustre of their renown, or tell you how this love for science, going forth from Leyden, permeated the whole nation? You know the Lipsii, the Hemsterhuizen, the Boerhaves. You know that in Holland were invented the telescope, the microscope and the thermometer; and thus empirical science, worthy of its name, was made possible. It is an undeniable fact, that the Calvinistic Netherlands *had* love for science and fostered it. But the most evident, the most convincing proof is doubtless found in the establishment of Leyden's University. To receive as the highest reward a University of the Sciences in a moment, when, in a fearful struggle, the course of the history of the world was turned by your heroism is only conceivable among a people, in whose very life-principle love for science is involved.

Mozart's Place in Theology

In the context of discussing creation and chaos, Karl Barth pauses and acknowledges the beauty and order of the music of Wolfgang Amadeus Mozart.

SOURCE

Barth, *Church Dogmatics*, III/3: 297–99.

I must again revert to Wolfgang Amadeus Mozart. Why is it that this man is so incomparable? Why is it that for the receptive, he has produced in almost every bar he conceived and composed a type of music for which "beautiful" is not a fitting epithet: music which for the true Christian is not mere entertainment, enjoyment or edification but food and drink; music full of comfort and counsel for his needs; music which is never a slave to its technique nor sentimental but always "moving," free and liberating because wise, strong and sovereign? Why is it possible to hold that Mozart has a place in theology, especially in the doctrine of creation and also in eschatology, although he was not a father of the Church, does not seem to have been a particularly active Christian, and was a Roman Catholic, apparently leading what might appear to us a rather frivolous existence when not occupied in his work? It is possible to give him this position because he knew something about creation in its total goodness that neither the real fathers of the Church nor our Reformers, neither the orthodox nor Liberals, neither the exponents of natural theology nor those heavily armed with the "Word of God," and certainly not the Existentialists, nor indeed any other great musicians before and after him, either know or can express and maintain as he did. In this respect he was pure in heart, far transcending both optimists and pessimists. 1756–1791! This was the time when God was under attack for the Lisbon earthquake, and theologians and other well-meaning folk were hard put to it to defend Him. In face of the problem of theodicy, Mozart had the peace of God which far transcends all the critical or speculative reason that praises and reproves. This problem lay behind him. Why then concern himself with it? He had heard, and causes those who have ears to hear, even to-day, what we shall not see until the end of time—the whole context of providence. As though in the light of this end, he heard the harmony of creation to which the shadow also belongs but in which the shadow is not darkness, deficiency is not defeat, sadness cannot become despair, trouble cannot degenerate into tragedy and infinite melancholy is not ultimately forced to claim undisputed sway. Thus the cheerfulness in this harmony is not without its limits. But the light shines all the more brightly because it breaks forth from the shadow. The sweetness is also bitter and cannot therefore cloy. Life does not fear death but knows it well. *Et lux perpetua lucet (sic!) eis*— even the dead of Lisbon. Mozart saw this light no more than we do, but he heard the whole world of creation enveloped by this light. Hence it was fundamentally in order that he should not hear a middle or neutral note, but the positive far more strongly than the negative. He heard the negative only in and with the positive. Yet in their inequality he heard them both together, as, for example, in the Symphony in G-minor of 1788. He never heard only the one in abstraction. He heard concretely, and therefore his compositions were and are total music. Hearing creation unresentfully and impartially, he did not produce merely his own music but that of creation, its twofold and yet harmonious praise of God. He neither needed nor desired to express or represent himself, his vitality, sorrow, piety, or any programme. He was remarkably free from the mania for self-expression. He simply offered himself as the agent by which little bits of horn, metal and catgut could serve as the voices of creation, sometimes leading, sometimes accompanying and sometimes in harmony. He made use of instruments ranging from the piano and violin, through the horn and the clarinet, down to the venerable bassoon, with the human voice somewhere among them, having no special claim to distinction yet distinguished for this very reason. He drew music from them all, expressing even human emotions in the service of this music, and not *vice versa*. He himself was only an ear for this music, and its mediator to other ears. He died when according to the worldly wise his life-work was only ripening to its true fulfillment. But who shall say that after the "Magic Flute," the Clarinet Concerto of October 1791 and the Requiem, it was not already fulfilled? Was not the whole of his achievement implicit in his works at the age of 16 or 18? Is it not heard in what has come down to us from the very young Mozart? He died in misery like an "unknown soldier," and in company with Calvin, and Moses in the Bible, he has no known grave. But what does this matter? What does a grave matter when a life is permitted simply and unpretentiously, and therefore serenely, authentically and impressively, to express the good creation of God, which also includes the limitation and end of man.

I make this interposition here, before turning to chaos, because in the music of Mozart—and I wonder whether the same can be said of any other works before or after—we have clear and convincing proof that it is a slander on creation to charge it with a share in chaos because it includes a Yes and a No, as though orientated to God on the one side and nothingness on the other. Mozart causes us to hear that even on the latter side, and therefore in its totality, creation praises its Master and is therefore perfect. Here on the threshold of our problem—and it is no small achievement—Mozart has created order for those who have ears to hear, and he has done it better than any scientific deduction could. This is the point which I wish to make.

Christian Gratitude for Secularism

In 1937 Reinhold Niebuhr gave a lecture entitled "The Christian Church in a Secular Age." Although modern Christians sometimes understand secularism to be the enemy of Christian faith, Niebuhr argued that secularism and not the church has at times been the defender of truth and the search for knowledge.

SOURCE

Reinhold Niebuhr, "The Christian Church in a Secular Age," in *The Essential Reinhold Niebuhr: Selected Essays and Addresses,* ed. Robert McAfee Brown (New Haven: Yale University Press, 1986), 88–91.

SECULARISM AS A REACTION AGAINST A PROFANE CHRISTIANITY

Modern secularism was forced to resist a profanization of the holiness of God both in the realm of the truth and in the realm of the good, in both culture and ethics. In the realm of culture the Christian religion was tempted to complete the incompleteness of all human culture by authoritative dicta, supposedly drawn from Scripture. It forgot that theology is a human discipline subject to the same relativities as any other human discipline. If modern culture was wrong in regarding the Anselmic axiom *"Credo ut intelligam"* as absurd because it failed to understand that reason cannot function without the presuppositions of faith, Christian culture was wrong in insinuating the specific insights and prejudices of a particular age into the *"credo."* While modern science was wrong in assuming that its descriptions of detailed historical sequences in nature and history offered an adequate insight into the meaning of life, Christian culture was wrong in regarding its knowledge of the transhistorical sources of the meaning of life as adequate explanations of detailed sequences and efficient causation.

Thus we have been subjected for centuries to a conflict between a theology which had become a bad science, and a science which implied an unconscious theology, a theology of unconscious presuppositions about the ultimate meaning of life. These presuppositions were doubly wrong. They were wrong in content and erroneous in being implicit rather than explicit. But surely the responsibility for this confusing conflict rests as much with a theology which had become a bad science as with a science which is a bad theology. In one sense all orthodox Christian theology has been guilty of the sin of profanity. It has insisted on the literal and historic truth of its myths, forgetting that it is the function and character of religious myth to speak of the eternal in relation to time, and that it cannot therefore be a statement of temporal sequences.

No Christian theology, worthy of its name, can therefore be without gratitude to the forces of modern secularism inasfar as their passion for truth was a passion for God. They failed indeed to recognize that every search for truth begins with a presupposition of faith. They did not know for this reason how vulnerable they were to the sneer of Pilate: "What is truth?"; and they could not consequently appreciate the affirmation of Christ: "I am the truth" (cf. John 14:6). But this secularization of truth is no more culpable than the religious profanization of truth which blandly appropriates the truth in Christ for every human vagary and prejudice, for every relative insight and temporal perspective.

The profanity of historic Christianity in regard to the problem of righteousness has been even more grievous than in regard to the problem of truth. Every human civilization is a compromise between the necessities and contingencies of nature and the Kingdom of God with its absolute love commandment. This is as true of a Christian as of an unchristian civilization. In a Christian, as well as in an unchristian civilization, the strong are tempted to exploit the weak, the community is tempted to regard itself as an end in itself, and the rulers are tempted to use their power for their own advantage. When the welter of relative justice and injustice, which emerges out of this conflict and confluence of forces, is falsely covered with the aura of the divine, and when the preservation of such a civilization is falsely enjoined as a holy duty, and when its rebels and enemies are falsely regarded as enemies of God, it is only natural that those who are most conscious of the injustices of a given social order, because they suffer from them, should adopt an attitude of cynical secularism toward the pretensions of sanctity made in behalf of a civilization. A profanization of the holiness of God leads inevitably to an effort to eliminate the sacred from human life. Invariably this effort is partially informed by a covert and implicit sense of the sacred, morally higher than the historic sanctity against which it protests. One need only study the perverted religious intensity of the nineteenth-century Russian nihilists to understand how a warfare against God may be prompted by a prophetic passion for God and scorn for the dubious political divinities which seek to borrow His holiness.

It is impossible to understand the secularism of either the commercial classes or the radical proleterians of the past hundred and fifty years, if it is not appreciated to what degree this secularism represents a reaction to the too intimate and organic relation of Christianity with a feudal society. The priest of religion and the landlord of an agrarian society were too closely related to each other and the former was too ·frequently the apologist and auxiliary gendarme of the latter.

It may seem that this charge falls more heavily upon Catholicism than upon Protestantism, not only because of the historic relation of the former with a medieval culture and feudal civilization, but also because the latter is less prone to identify itself with the detailed economic and political arrangements of any society. But with its higher degree of detachment, Protestantism has sometimes also revealed a higher degree of social irresponsibility. It has allowed its pessimism to betray it into a negative sanctification of a given social order, on the assumption that any given order is preferable to anarchy and that the disturbance of the status quo might lead to anarchy.

Thus Catholicism and Protestantism, between them, have exhausted the possibilities of error in Christianity's relation to society. In either case peace and order through power were estimated too highly and the inevitable injustice of every stabilization of power was judged too leniently. Frequently Christianity was content to regard deeds of personal generosity and charity as adequate expressions of the Christian love commandment within a civilization in which every basic relationship was a complete denial of that commandment.

The secularism both of our modern bourgeois civilization and of the more proletarian civilizations which threaten to replace it, is therefore something more than the religion of self-glorification. It combines this sin with a passion for justice which frequently puts the historic church to shame. If the Christian church is to preach its gospel effectively to men of such a culture, it must understand the baffling mixture of a new profanity and resistance to an old profanity which is comprehended in this culture.

8

ESCHATOLOGY

One of the most difficult tasks for theology in the modern period has been the reinterpretation of eschatology—the Bible's claim that the resurrection of Jesus Christ is but the "first fruits" of a consummation yet to come, when Christ will return and God will transform all creation.

Many modern theologians have argued that eschatology must be demythologized or reinterpreted in order to make it intelligible to a post-Enlightenment world that does not believe in a sudden end to history or in the possibility of a supernatural God who intervenes in history. Protestant liberalism in the nineteenth and twentieth centuries stumbled over eschatology and either ignored the doctrine altogether or reduced it to a moralism about hope in the future. The disillusionment following the First World War and the emergence of neo-orthodoxy led to a recovery of the importance of the resurrection of Jesus Christ and the reaffirmation of the conviction that Christian hope in the final triumph of God must not be confused with a bland and mistaken confidence about moral progress within history.

In the last half of the twentieth century, theologians such as Jürgen Moltmann and Wolfhart Pannenberg made eschatology a central theme in their interpretation of Christian faith. Eschatology is not some distant goal toward which history is moving but is the reign of God moving toward the present. Eschatology is not a philosophy of history, not a theory about the future, but hope in the advent of God's kingdom.

THE REIGN OF GOD AND
THE LAST THINGS

According to the New Testament, the central symbol in Jesus' preaching and teaching was the kingdom of God. Jesus came preaching repentance and the nearness of God's kingdom. Theology in the nineteenth and twentieth centuries has struggled with the task of interpreting the relation between contemporary understandings of history and the Bible's eschatological depiction of God's kingdom. Some Christians have understood the kingdom of God to be utterly discontinuous with human history and to have nothing to do with this life except to be a release from it. Most contemporary theology, however, has pointed out that the eschatological reality of God's kingdom has immediate implications for how Christians live in relation to one another and what they do in the world. There is a "politics" to God's kingdom as it is described in Jesus' parables, and that politics weighs heavily on the church as it seeks to discern what God is calling it to do.

FOR FURTHER STUDY

Hendrikus Berkhof, *Christ the Meaning of History,* trans. Lambertus Buurman (Grand Rapids: Baker Book House, 1979). G. C. Berkouwer, *The Return of Christ* (Grand Rapids: Wm. B. Eerdmans, 1972). Jürgen Moltmann, *The Experiment Hope,* trans. M. Douglas Meeks (Philadelphia: Fortress, 1975). Reinhold Niebuhr, *Beyond Tragedy: Essays on the Christian of History* (New York: Charles Scribner's Sons, 1937). Wolfhart Pannenberg, *Theology and the Kingdom of God* (Philadelphia: Westminster, 1969). Dietrich Ritschl, *Memory and Hope: An Inquiry Concerning the Presence of Christ* (New York: Macmillan, 1967).

The Danger of Insufficient Eschatology

Reinhold Niebuhr argues that it is dangerous for the church to be insufficiently eschatological. Eschatology is the basis of Christian hope, and it is hope that leads Christians to responsible participation in the world.

SOURCE

Reinhold Niebuhr, *Faith and History: A Comparison of Christian and Modern Views of History* (New York: Charles Scribner's Sons, 1949), 238–39.

The Christian church is a community of hopeful believers, who are not afraid of life or death, of present or future history, being persuaded that the whole of life and all historical vicissitudes stand under the sovereignty of a holy, yet merciful, God whose will was supremely revealed in Christ. It is a community which does not fear the final judgement, not because it is composed of sinless saints but because it is a community of forgiven sinners, who know that judgement is merciful if it is not evaded. If the divine judgement is not resisted by pretensions of virtue but is contritely accepted, it reveals in and beyond itself the mercy which restores life on a new and healthier basis.

Ideally the church is such a community of contrite believers. Actually the church is always in danger of becoming a community of the saved who have brought the meaning of life to merely another premature conclusion. It is in danger of becoming a community of the righteous who ask God to vindicate them against the unrighteous; or, even worse, who claim to vindicate God by the fruits of their own righteousness. In that case the church loses the true love of Christ, which is the fruit of a contrite heart, by claiming that love as a secure possession.

In short, the church is always in danger of becoming Anti-Christ because it is not sufficiently eschatological. It lives too little by faith and hope and too much by the pretensions of its righteousness. There is a modern form of eschatological Christianity, particularly upon the European continent, which goes to the length of disavowing the Christian's responsibility for the weal of the world in its frantic flight from the moral pretension of the Pharisaic church. Ideally the faith and hope by which the church lives sharpen rather than annul its responsibility for seeking to do the will of God amid all the tragic moral ambiguities of history. This faith and hope are the condition of a true love "which seeketh not its own." They are the condition for a courageous witness against "principalities and powers," which is untroubled by punitive strength in the hands of these powers and which does not mistake the judgements of the church as an historic institution for the final judgement of God.

Without such a faith and hope the church seeks to vindicate itself by the virtue of its martyrs and its saints. This vindication never avails in the end because the "godless" are always able to find for every martyr and saint in the church a score of pious frauds or religiously inspired bigots or self-righteous Pharisees. Without the final eschatological emphasis the church claims to be the Kingdom of God. Actually it is that community where the Kingdom of God impinges most unmistakably upon history because it is the community where the judgement and the mercy of God are known, piercing through all the pride and pretensions of men and transforming their lives.

Christianity Is Eschatology

The 1965 publication of Jürgen Moltmann's *Theology of Hope* was an important event in twentieth-century theology. Moltmann placed eschatology at the center of Christian faith and argued that theology must not end with the doctrine but must begin with it.

SOURCE

Moltmann, *Theology of Hope*, 15–17.

WHAT IS THE "LOGOS" OF
CHRISTIAN ESCHATOLOGY?

Eschatology was long called the "doctrine of the last things" or the "doctrine of the end." By these last things were meant events which will one day break upon man, history and the world at the end of time. They included the return of Christ in universal glory, the judgment of the world and the consummation of the kingdom, the general resurrection of the dead and the new creation of all things. These end events were to break into this world from somewhere beyond history, and to put an end to the history in which all things here live and move. But the relegating of these events to the "last day" robbed them of their directive, uplifting and critical significance for all the days which are spent here, this side of the end, in history. Thus these teachings about the end led a peculiarly barren existence at the end of Christian dogmatics. They were like a loosely attached appendix that wandered off into obscure irrelevancies. They bore no relation to the doctrines of the cross and resurrection, the exaltation and sovereignty of Christ, and did not derive from these by any logical necessity. They were as far removed from them as All Souls' Day sermons are from Easter. The more Christianity became an organization for discipleship under the auspices of the Roman state religion and persistently upheld the claims of that religion, the more eschatology and its mobilizing, revolutionizing, and critical effects upon history as it has now to be lived were left to fanatical sects and revolutionary groups. Owing to the fact that Christian faith banished from its life the future hope by which it is upheld, and relegated the future to a beyond, or to eternity, whereas the biblical testimonies which it handed on are yet full to the brim with future hope of a messianic kind for the world,—owing to this, hope emigrated as it were from the Church and turned in one distorted form or another against the Church.

In actual fact, however, eschatology means the doctrine of the Christian hope, which embraces both the object hoped for and also the hope inspired by it. From first to last, and not merely in the epilogue, Christianity is eschatology, is hope, forward looking and forward moving, and therefore also revolutionizing and transforming the present. The eschatological is not one element *of* Christianity, but it is the medium of Christian faith as such, the key in which everything in it is set, the glow that suffuses everything here in the dawn of an expected new day. For Christian faith lives from the raising of the crucified Christ, and strains after the promises of the universal future of Christ. Eschatology is the passionate suffering and passionate longing kindled by the Messiah.

348

Hence eschatology cannot really be only a part of Christian doctrine. Rather, the eschatological outlook is characteristic of all Christian proclamation, of every Christian existence and of the whole Church. There is therefore only one real problem in Christian theology, which its own object forces upon it and which it in turn forces on mankind and on human thought: the problem of the future. For the element of otherness that encounters us in the hope of the Old and New Testaments—the thing we cannot already think out and picture for ourselves on the basis of the given world and of the experiences we already have of that world— is one that confronts us with a promise of something new and with the hope of a future given by God. The God spoken of here is no intra-worldly or extra-worldly God, but the "God of hope" (Rom. 15:13), a God with "future as his essential nature" (as E. Bloch puts it), as made known in Exodus and in Israelite prophecy, the God whom we therefore cannot really have in us or over us but always only before us, who encounters us in his promises for the future, and whom we therefore cannot "have" either, but can only await in active hope. A proper theology would therefore have to be constructed in the light of its future goal. Eschatology should not be its end, but its beginning.

But how can anyone speak of the future, which is not yet here, and of coming events in which he has not as yet had any part? Are these not dreams, speculations, longings and fears, which must all remain vague and indefinite because no one can verify them? The term "eschato-*logy*" is wrong. There can be no "doctrine" of the last things, if by "doctrine" we mean a collection of theses which can be understood on the basis of experiences that constantly recur and are open to anyone. The Greek term *logos* refers to a reality which is there, now and always, and is given true expression in the word appropriate to it. In this sense there can be no *logos* of the future, unless the future is the continuation or regular recurrence of the present. If, however, the future were to bring something startlingly new, we have nothing to say of that, and nothing meaningful can be said of it either, for it is not in what is new and accidental, but only in things of an abiding and regularly recurring character that there can be log-ical truth. Aristotle, it is true, can call hope a "waking dream," but for the Greeks it is nevertheless an evil out of Pandora's box.

But how, then, can Christian eschatology give expression to the future? Christian eschatology does not speak of the future as such. It sets out from a definite reality in history and announces the future of that reality, its future possibilities and its power over the future. Christian eschatology speaks of Jesus Christ and *his* future. It recognizes the reality of the raising of Jesus and proclaims the future of the risen Lord. Hence the question whether all statements about the future are grounded in the person and history of Jesus Christ provides it with the touchstone by which to distinguish the spirit of eschatology from that of utopia.

The Politics of Resurrection

Brazilian theologian Rubem Alves, in his book *A Theology of Human Hope*, describes the resurrection in terms of the politics of liberation. The resurrection represents the "ongoing politics of God in history."

SOURCE

Rubem Alves, *A Theology of Human Hope* (Washington, D.C.: Corpus Books, 1969), 131–32.

Resurrection, hence, is the language of the ongoing politics of God in history. It is the language of hope. It points to what we can expect. "In this hope we were saved," Paul states (Rom. 8:24). As hope, it cannot be verified by handling the events that became past. The past events can be the "aperitif"; they do not, however, offer any ground for verification. This is why no historical research is able to "verify" the resurrection. It could verify a fact, but not a factor. The field of the verification of hope is not, therefore, the past, but the future. Hope is verified to the extent to which man is made open for the future, the structures of oppression are broken, and the future is made open for man. And each of these events is a new celebration of hope, a new enjoying of the "aperitif" of liberation.

The language of resurrection, therefore, refers to what we can expect from history, as being penetrated, liberated, made alive by God's freedom for history. It points to the possibility of the event of the *novum*, of the creation of the new. In this context it is possible to hope. To live in the light of the resurrection is to live in eschatological tension, in the expectation of the event of the new subject and of the new tomorrow. But is must be said that resurrection is radically opposed to any type of triumphalism, because the power of the resurrection is the dynamics of the cross. Therefore, man is compelled to participate in God's sufferings in the world. Wherever man is being oppressed and destroyed, there God is being crucified and killed. But in the context of hope, suffering loses its power to draw man to despair, and becomes the fertilizing No from which the powers of bondage are destroyed for the sake of a new tomorrow of liberation.

Songs of Hope

African-American theologian Gayraud S. Wilmore does not accept the description of black spirituals as "otherworldly." On the contrary, he believes those spirituals are filled with what he refers to as "the down-to-earth concreteness of black eschatology."

SOURCE

Gayraud S. Wilmore, *Last Things First* (Philadelphia: Westminster, 1982), 83–85.

In both African and Afro-American religion the idea of the next world, which is to say the Kingdom of God, is not some highly mystical, spiritualized realm that floats over the real world and has no connection with it. It is peopled with the ancestors who are ever near, with people we have known and loved, and it contains the things of this world wonderfully transformed. In that important sense it is the criterion of the present world, a model of perfection which stands in judgment upon it. What we have too glibly called the "otherworldliness" of slave religion was the eschatological vision that made it possible not only to experience that world ecstatically in the present but to make it visible and tangible in materialistic terms in the daily realities of the believer's life. Thus, as Miles Mark Fisher and other interpreters of the slave bards tell us, "Steal Away to Jesus" often was used as a signal on the Underground Railroad; "Crossing the Jordan" and "Wade in the Water, Children" sometimes meant getting across the Ohio River to free territory; "Going to the Promised Land" not only meant heaven, but the dawn of Emancipation Day on January 1, 1863.

The hope that is expressed in the spirituals and in some of the later gospel songs of the contemporary black church is rooted in the desire for freedom and a better chance in this world—under the pressure of the "next one." The images called forth, therefore, are materialistic— expressing the deprivation of slavery but also a profound sense of the possibility of a different experience in this life when Christ is Lord, although his Lordship is frustrated by evil men.

Marc Connelly's parody of a black heaven in *The Green Pastures* is fatuously extravagant, but there are aspects of the play that do convey the worldliness and concreteness of the black religious imagination. Given the thin line between the sacred and the secular that is characteristic of African and Afro-American world views, it is not surprising that Father Divine, Daddy Grace, and other "black gods of the metropolis," with their heavens and retinues of flesh-and-blood angels, had mass appeal in the black urban communities during the 1920s and 1930s. The familiar spiritual "All God's Chillun" is a good example of the down-to-earth concreteness of black eschatology:

I got a robe, you got a robe,
All God's chillun got a robe,
When I get to Heav'm, goin' put on my robe,
Goin' to shout all over God's Heav'm,
Heav'm, Heav'm,
Everybody talking' 'bout Heav'm ain't goin' dere,
Heav'm, Heav'm,
Goin' to shout all over God's Heav'm!

The verse speaks of robes, shoes, crown, wings, harps, and songs. With the exception of crowns and wings, all of these images used by the slave poet refer to worldly things. They are not mystical accessories to the heavenly existence. To the contrary, they are understood to be basic to it—the fundamental earthbound rights and requirements of personal fulfillment, justice, freedom, and autonomy. With them in his or her possession the believer can "shout all over God's Heav'm" without the inhibition experienced in daily life. But what is represented here is not only what the believer has been denied on earth but the values by which the world is weighed in the balance and found wanting, by which it is called to account for not making life what God intended it to be in the first place—fulfilling, just, free, and autonomous.

During the civil rights movement the folk on the marches and at rallies sometimes added votes, schools, and seats (acceptance in places of public accommodation) to the traditional robes, shoes, and crowns. The notion of using votes "when I get to Heav'm" cannot be mistaken for an example of "compensatory religion" when those doing the singing are walking a voter registration picket line in open defiance of angry whites with guns. Something else is obviously at work here.

Jesus Is Lord

A Declaration of Faith of the former Presbyterian Church in the United States concludes by grounding Christian hope in the lordship of Jesus Christ.

SOURCE

Declaration of Faith, 22–24.

HOPE IN GOD

(1) God keeps his promises and gives us hope.
In the life, death, and resurrection of Jesus
    God kept his promises.
All that we can ever hope for
    was present in Christ.
But the work of God in Christ is not over.
God calls us to hope for more than we have yet seen.

The hope God gives us is ultimate confidence
    that supports us when lesser hopes fail us.
In Christ God gives hope for a new heaven and earth,
    certainty of victory over death,
        assurance of mercy and judgment beyond death.
This hope gives us courage for the present struggle.

(2) All things will be renewed in Christ.
In Christ God gave us a glimpse of the new creation
    he has already begun and will surely finish.
We do not know when the final day will come.
In our time we see only broken and scattered signs
    that the renewal of all things is under way.
We do not yet see the end of cruelty and suffering
    in the world, the church, or our own lives.
But we see Jesus as Lord.
As he stands at the center of our history,
    we are confident he will stand at its end.
He will judge all people and nations.
Evil will be condemned
    and rooted out of God's good creation.
There will be no more tears or pain.
All things will be made new.
The fellowship of human beings with God and each other
    will be perfected. . . .

(5) Hope in God gives us courage for the struggle.
The people of God have often misused God's promises
    as excuses for doing nothing about present evils.
But in Christ the new world has already broken in
    and the old can no longer be tolerated.

We know our efforts cannot bring in God's kingdom.
But hope plunges us into the struggle
    for victories over evil that are possible now
    in the world, the church, and our individual lives.
Hope gives us courage and energy
    to contend against all opposition,
    however invincible it may seem,
    for the new world and the new humanity
    that are surely coming.

Jesus is Lord!
He has been Lord from the beginning.
He will be Lord at the end.
Even now he is Lord.

DEATH AND ETERNAL LIFE

Question 86 of the Larger Catechism of Westminster asks, "What is the communion in glory with Christ, which the members of the invisible Church enjoy immediately after death?" The answer states that as soon as Christians die their souls are "made perfect in holiness, and received into the highest heavens, where they behold the face of God in light and glory." Their bodies, however, rest in their graves awaiting the last coming of Jesus Christ when they will be raised and reunited with their souls.

Many twentieth-century theologians have concluded that Westminster's affirmation of "the immortality of the soul" rather than "the resurrection of the body" is more a reflection of Plato than of the gospel. It suggests a bifurcation of human beings between soul and body, a denigration of the physical, a denial of the full reality of death, and a realized eschatology. Careful study of the New Testament, especially 1 Corinthians 15, has led theologians to argue that when Christians die they "sleep" in Jesus Christ (to whom they belong in life and in death) and, along with the rest of creation, await the coming of Christ and the resurrection of the dead, which is not something that happens only to individuals at the moment of death, but is an event awaited by the whole of creation.

FOR FURTHER STUDY

Karl Barth, The *Resurrection of the Dead* (London: Hodder & Stoughton, 1933). P. T. Forsyth, *This Life and the Next: The Effect on This Life of Faith in Another* (London: Independent, 1953). John Hick, *Death and Eternal Life* (London: Collins, 1976). Hans Küng, *Eternal Life: Life After Death as a Medieval, Philosophical, and Theological Problem,* trans. Edward Quinn (Garden City, N.Y.: Doubleday, 1984).

The First and Second Death

Karl Barth, like many other recent theologians, argues that the Bible's understanding of death is both more realistic and more subtle than many Christians have understood. On the one hand, the Bible accepts and affirms that to be a creature is not to be God; it is natural death that separates God from creature. On the other hand, there is a second death that would separate a person from God. It is the sting posed by this second death that is addressed by the resurrection of Jesus Christ.

SOURCE

Barth, *Church Dogmatics*, III/2:637–40.

As regards the situation in the New Testament, we have already called attention to the idea of the "second death" which figures so prominently in the Apocalypse. The assumption is that there is a "first" death without the evil, corruptive and unnatural character of the "second." In Heb. 9:27 the sacrifice of Christ, offered once for all to take away the sins of many, is both formally and materially brought into relation with this notion. We are told in this sense that "it is appointed (ἀπόκειται) unto men once to die, but after this the judgment." From this it would seem that the phrase ἅπαξ ἀποθανεῖν does not of itself signify judgment, but an event which is general and neutral even though in contrast with the sacrificial death of Christ and its uniqueness it also seems to have a higher necessity. Again, the phrase ἄχρι θανάτου in Rev. 2:10: "Be thou faithful unto death," and Rev. 12:11: "They loved not their lives unto the death," cannot imply that death is the last enemy, but only the *terminus ad quem* of their faithfulness and unselfish devotion coinciding with the boundary of their life. Again it is no less clear that when in 1 Thess. 5:10, 1 Cor. 3:22, Rom. 8:38 and 14:7f. and Phil. 1:20 life and death are associated under the superior dominion of Christ, death does not signify an armed and powerful foe but the approaching end of human life contrasted with the possibility of its further continuation. There is a dying which throws no doubt on man's participation in the resurrection and life of Jesus Christ. Death in this sense is not ruled out by man's hope in a resurrection. This is expressly shown by Jn. 11:25: "I am the resurrection, and the life; he that believeth on me, though he die, yet shall he live." In the New Testament, too, the "death" in death can be abolished. It is never supposed, of course, that this possibility lies in human control. When it happens, it is always the result of God's extraordinary intervention. The concrete form of this is the appearance, death and resurrection of Jesus Christ: "He that heareth my word, and believeth him that sent me, hath everlasting life, and shall not come into condemnation, but is passed from death unto life" (Jn. 5:24). In these circumstances the "second death" is abolished and man is freed from unnatural death. But this obviously means that, as he is freed for eternal life, he is also freed for natural death. The New Testament, like the Old, speaks of this natural death.

It is worth noting that the New Testament fully matches the sober realism of the Old in this matter. It is striking, indeed, that it offers no parallels to such hints as we have in the stories of the end of Enoch and Moses or the disappearance of Elijah. The New Testament authors are content to refer to these occasionally without adding similar occurrences from their own historical sphere. These remarkable exceptions were obviously regarded in the New Testament age as types which, once fulfilled in the end of Jesus Christ, in His resurrection and ascension, did not need and were not capable of further multiplication. The Roman Catholic Church definition of the assumption of Mary as a dogma of the faith, quite apart from anything else, is an additional proof of its profound lack of understanding of the basic difference between the situation and order of the New Testament and that of the Old. In the New Testament order the exaltation of the one man Jesus Christ, in which the exaltation of His own is already latently accomplished, is followed by only one assumption of which nothing can be said because it has not yet happened, namely, the assumption of the community to meet its Lord when He comes again at the final revelation in which the exaltation which has already occurred in Jesus Christ will be made manifest. In this assumption the dead will share no less than the living (1 Thess. 4:16f.). There now are and may be those who have fallen asleep "in Christ" (1 Cor. 15:18) or "in Jesus" (1 Thess. 4:14), or who are even "dead in Christ" (1 Thess. 4:16). They are not lost (1 Thess. 4:15) even though they have not yet been assumed. And no one, not even Mary, can anticipate their assumption with a private one of his own. Death now wears a guise in which we can look it in the face. We can now face it as a natural prospect.

"To fall asleep" (κοιμᾶσθαι) is the characteristic New Testament term for the death which is freed from the "second" death by the death of Jesus Christ and is therefore a wholly natural thing for the Christian. "Our friend Lazarus sleepeth" (Jn. 11:11). Some of the witnesses of the resurrection of Jesus "are fallen asleep" (1 Cor. 15:6). "The fathers (i.e., those who belonged to the first Christian generation) have fallen asleep," say the false teachers in 2 Pet. 3:4. Similarly, the Corinthian church can

356

look back on not a few of its members who have fallen asleep (1 Cor. 11:30). It is noticeable that even David is now said to have fallen asleep (Ac. 13:36). Indeed, a violent death like that of Stephen (Ac. 7:60) is described almost euphemistically in these mild terms. What does this imply? It relates to the process of dying, or rather to the impression, designated, defined and shaped by faith and love, which the survivors have of what is finally perceptible in the death of a brother or sister. They see him falling asleep. What lies beyond they cannot see. For the Christians of the New Testament Jesus Christ Himself intervenes at once and absolutely on the far side of this event. His death and resurrection avail for those who have now "fallen asleep," as well as for those who survive. The hope in Him is a hope for the former too. The final thing to be said of them (apart from Jesus Christ Himself) is that they have fallen asleep. The expression is deliberately mild. It may be euphemistic, but it conveys an impression of peace. It is a striking expression of the freedom of New Testament Christians—the freedom of their faith and love. As they contemplate the dead they are able to use this peaceful term and keep their memory before their eyes in the form of this peaceful process. The decisive thing is not that they suffered or endured the agony of death. The real conflict with death was fought out long ago. All they had to do was to fall asleep. Even Stephen could simply fall asleep under the hail of stones. The term thus signifies the genuine reality visible in the light of Christian faith and love, of what is finally perceptible to those who remain in the dying of their friends. Their recollection of the dead is riveted to this term. The deduction that the dead are in a state of sleep is an ancient exaggeration. Κοιμᾶσθαι does not mean to be asleep but to *fall* asleep. Those who have fallen asleep means those whom we saw fall asleep, and whom we now recollect as those who then fell asleep and were therefore delivered from death even in dying. Looking back on them, we really look back on Jesus Christ who, as "the first fruits of them that slept" (1 Cor. 15:20), robbed their death of its sting and brought life and immortality to light even when they were *in extremis,* so that this death could not be anything but a falling asleep. The deduction that they are now actually asleep may seem to be logical, but it has no material basis. What special revelation did the New Testament Christians enjoy to persuade them that when the departed had fallen asleep their being was one of sleep? This inference was first drawn when Christians again began to derive their knowledge (in this as in other matters) from sources other than their knowledge of Jesus Christ. The term "fall asleep" shows that the New Testament Christians never asked independently concerning the being or state of man in death, or tried to find an answer in the postulate of an intermediate state. They simply held fast to the confession: "I am the resurrection and the life," and in the light of this hope they came to see in the visible process of dying the last conclusive symptom of a life surrounded by the peace of God.

If hope in Christ is a real liberation for natural death, this rests on the fact that by divine appointment death as such belongs to the life of the creature and is thus necessary to it. Adamic man was created a ψυχὴ ζώσα (1 Cor. 15:45), and therefore a being which has only its own span of time. His definitive relationship to God as the end and goal of human life demands that this life itself should be defined and therefore limited. On this limit there is made in its favour the divine decision which is the substance of the New Testament message of salvation. On this limit it was made in the life of the man Jesus. He had to die, to submit to the judgment of God and thus restore the right of God and that of man. "Except a corn of wheat fall into the ground and die, it abideth alone; but if it die, it bringeth forth much fruit" (Jn. 12:34). We cannot try to love and maintain finally and absolutely our life in this time; otherwise we shall lose it. We must give it up in order to save it (Mt. 16:25). In the harsh terms of Jn. 12:25 we must actually "hate" our "life in the world" in order to preserve it to eternal life. That is why Paul can also say: "Thou fool, that which thou sowest is not quickened, except it die" (1 Cor. 15:36). If we did not have to do with the definitive end of human life, we should not have to do with its resurrection and definitive co-existence with that of God. Anxious defiance of one's end could only mean the forfeiture of one's destiny. Since Jesus did not love His life and thus rescued our life from destruction, we are invited to accept the limit of the life which He has rescued, and therefore to acquiesce in the fact that we must have an end, and to set our hope wholly and utterly in Him.

In conclusion, however, it is worth noting that, while the New Testament reminds us of the necessity of death and exhorts us not to love our life or seek to save it, it never suggests that we ought to yearn for death or rejoice in it, even in the case of martyrdom, as often happened later. Death is never idealised or made into something heroic. That he should lose his life for Christ's sake is a possibility for which the New Testament Christian is always doubly prepared, but which he never desires or seeks, merely accepting it as a reality when it comes, as Stephen did. Like life itself, the loss of it is in itself a possibility qualified only by the fact that it takes place "in the Lord." In 2 Cor. 5:1–10 Paul contrasts our present life in a perishable tent with the divinely prepared and eternal house with which we shall be clothed; our pilgrimage in time with our being at home in the Lord. He makes no attempt to conceal his longing and sighing for the latter. Yet he finds only a relative and not an absolute place for this desire. And from this train of thought he draws the conclusion: "Wherefore we labour, that, whether present or absent, we may be accepted of him. For we must all appear before the judgment seat of Christ; that every one may receive the things done in his body, according to that he hath done, whether it be good or bad." Again, what he says in Philippians 1:20f. is similar. That Christ should be glorified in his body, whether by life or death, is the prospect which elates him (παρρησία). He again makes no secret of the fact that it is better for him to die. He has "a desire to depart, and to be with Christ." This is preferable. But he again qualifies his desire. For him to live is Christ. And this, as he puts it bluntly in v. 22, is "fruit" (καρπὸς ἔργου) in His service. Though dissolution would be preferable, his "abiding in the flesh" is thus more necessary for the sake of his communities (v. 24). Faced by this dilemma, with pressing arguments on both sides, he decides in this most important passage for life rather than death. The New Testament Christian does not fear death. But he never hopes for it. He hopes for the One who has delivered him from death. It is because he hopes for Him, and expects to be with Him when he dies, that he is willing to die "gladly" like Jacob. Death is the preferable alternative. But he does not will it. He wills the life bounded by it as the sphere of the decisions in which he moves towards Christ as his Judge. He wills it as the opportunity to serve the One who will be his only hope in his end. And it is because he can already serve in his life the One who even in death will be his Lord that he rejoices in this perfect form of His lordship, in the prospect of being definitely with Him. He does not rejoice in the prospect of being freed from His service, of having his time behind him. On the contrary, the definitive prospect in which he rejoices is for him an authorisation and command to serve God in his allotted span with all the preliminary joy without which his joy in his end and new beginning with Him would be purely imaginary. He affirms Jesus Christ as his beyond. And it is for this reason that he understands his life here and now as one which is affirmed by his beyond.

The Negation of the Negative

What is the significance of the resurrection of Jesus Christ for Christian hope? Jürgen Moltmann describes Jesus' death as "god-forsakenness" and his resurrection as a conquest of the deadliness of death.

SOURCE

Moltmann, *Theology of Hope*, 210–11.

The hope of resurrection does not overcome the deadliness of death by regarding living and dying as mere summary expressions for the transience of all things and as such unimportant, but by proclaiming the victory of praise and therewith of life over death and over the curse of god-forsakenness, by announcing the victory of God over the absence of God.

What is the significance of the death and resurrection of Jesus Christ in the context of these expectations?

In the context of these expectations of life, his death on the cross implies not only the end of the life which he had, but also the end of the life which he loves and in which he hopes. The death of Jesus was experienced as the death of him who had been sent as the Messiah of God, and therefore implies also the "death of God." Thus his death is experienced and proclaimed as god-forsakenness, as judgment, as curse, as exclusion from the promised life, as reprobation and damnation.

In the context of these expectations of life, his resurrection must then be understood not as a mere return to life as such, but as a conquest of the deadliness of death—as a conquest of god-forsakenness, as a conquest of judgment and of the curse, as a beginning of the fulfillment of the promised life, and thus as a conquest of all that is dead in death, as a negation of the negative (Hegel), as a negation of the negation of God.

It is then understandable, further, that Jesus' resurrection was not seen as a private Easter for his private Good Friday, but as the beginning and source of the abolition of the universal Good Friday, of that god-forsakenness of the world which comes to light in the deadliness of the death of the cross. Hence the resurrection of Christ was not understood merely as the first instance of a general resurrection of the dead and as a beginning of the revelation of the divinity of God in the nonexistent, but also as the source of the risen life of all believers and as a confirmation of the promise which will be fulfilled in all and will show itself in the very deadliness of death to be irresistible.

To recognize the event of the resurrection of Christ is therefore to have a hopeful and expectant knowledge of this event. It means recognizing in this event the latency of that eternal life which in the praise of God arises from the negation of the negative, from the raising of the one who was crucified and the exaltation of the one who was forsaken. It means assenting to the tendency towards resurrection of the dead in this event of the raising of the one. It means following the intention of God by entering into the dialectic of suffering and dying in expectation of eternal life and of resurrection. This is described as the working of the

Holy Spirit. The "Spirit" is according to Paul the "life-giving Spirit," the Spirit who *"raised up* Christ from the dead" and *"dwells* in" those who recognize Christ and his future, and *"shall* quicken their mortal bodies" (Rom. 8:11).

Not Safety but Sanctity

What does Christian faith say about life on the other side of death? According to Hendrikus Berkhof, what is promised in the gospel is that Christians will be conformed to Jesus Christ, but only through the process of judgment and renewal.

SOURCE

Berkhof, *Christian Faith*, 491–92.

Only now, finally, can we raise the main question of this paragraph: What can we know by faith about the content of the perfection on the other side of the boundary of death? In any case, that knowledge is limited to what we, in virtue of the coherence between this side and the other side, can derive or surmise from our experience of the faith. We know that Christ's Spirit, who here takes possession of people and partially transforms them, on the other side completes that process in this sense, that we, using a few New Testament designations, "shall be with Christ," "shall be made like his image," so that "God may be all in all." All that lies so far beyond our present experience, also beyond our faith experience, and it is so unimaginable, that we are inclined to think of it as being the product of an instantaneous re-creative act of God, so that from death man suddenly awakes to a totally changed life. But then we detract from the close tie between life on both sides of the death crisis. The same New Testament speaks about the completion as "fruit," "harvest," and "wages" of the sowing and struggling in this life.

That tie has first of all a negative consequence: on the other side, in the light of the all-exposing light of God's presence, we shall become aware of our culpable failure in respect of his covenant faithfulness as we never did or could within the confines of our earthly existence. Death does not instantaneously and automatically transfer us into the consummation. The connection with our former life is first of all expressed in what in the language of the Christian faith is called "the judgment." There can be no deep and joyful awareness of the renewal without an equally deep sense of obstruction. The radical renewal does not im-*media*-tely follow upon our earthly life, but it is mediated by the judgment that bridges the chasm. Only in the way of an exposure that puts us utterly to shame can we, as people with an *earlier* existence and with an earlier existence in which we were *different,* receive the renewal as God's marvelous gift.

But if that is so, we can hardly stop at this negative mediation. In the judgment we are shown how great the distance that separates us from the goal and which must still be bridged is. Will that distance suddenly, as if by magic, be bridged by a re-creative act of God? Or is there on the other side of death something like purification and maturing? Will we on the other side be required to lose ourselves in still more and new processes of death, in order to become completely ourselves relative to God? On this point we can do nothing else than ask questions. But these are questions that must be raised if we are serious about the tie between life here and beyond. If renewal here is no magical metamorphosis—and nowhere in creation do we observe such a discontinuous transformation—then we may not and should not expect it for the future. What awaits us beyond death may rather prove to be a continuing road, be it on a higher level and with the goal more clearly in view.

Taking this idea into consideration may also keep us from seeing the consummation first of all as a fulfillment of our own earthly desires. It is not a matter of safety, but of sanctity. Only through radical surgery are we made ready for a world in which God is all in all and in which he, as our God, satisfies all the desires he has created in us.

There is thus a goal which in virtue of God's intention is going to be reached. Its content can be variously described. In the New Testament and in church history we find many descriptions: "vision of God," "eternal rest," "be with Christ," etc. We prefer "conformity with Christ," for the reason set forth in paragraph 43. In the context in which we speak about it here this description has the advantage that it clearly maintains the connection with Christ's earthly work and that of the Spirit. It also has this advantage over "vision" and "rest," that it lacks the overtones of individualism and passivism. For to resemble Christ means that like him we are totally oriented toward God and the neighbor. Therefore this conformity is possible only in a fellowship. Hence the New Testament portrays the consummation as the consummated covenant communion of God in Christ with those who have become conformed to Christ's image; as a banquet, a city, a celebrating magnitude. The dimensions of the vision of God and of resting are aspects that are implicitly included. More we cannot say in this context about the great consummation.

Whatever more can be said about our eternal future will have to be postponed until, in the final chapter, we can also include history, culture, and nature in our expectations.

It remains yet to refer to the practical import of this belief in consummation. Only the outsider will think that this faith deprives our earthly life of its importance. The opposite is true: this perspective lends an eternal importance to our earthly life. For judgment and consummation tell us how seriously God takes this life and how great a responsibility he has given us in this life. At the same time, this seriousness does not crush us, because he guarantees its consummation. And because this earthly life is no goal but a road, we need not demand and expect everything from it. So the expectation of consummation liberates us *from* our passion for happiness now and *unto* the free service of God and man.

Life After Death as Reincarnation

Theologian John Hick typifies a long-standing tradition of rationalism in British interpretations of Christian faith. Hick describes traditional Christian beliefs about life after death as "unrealistic" and argues on the basis of "observable fact" that there must be "further time beyond death in which the process of perfecting can continue." Hick believes that that raises the possibility of one self having many lives in order to achieve self-transcending perfection.

SOURCE

John Hick, *Death and Eternal Life* (New York: Harper & Row, 1976), 455–58.

THE PARESCHATON

Although in the end the individual cannot be saved in isolation from the society of which he is ultimately a part, yet still society is composed of individuals and it is individual people who are to be saved. For the development of civilization has involved the breakdown of the closely knit tribal group whose members thought of themselves more as parts of a larger whole than as autonomous individuals. According to our hypothesis, the ultimate development of human life is to come full circle, though on a higher level, culminating in a new corporateness in which egoity has been transcended. But in the present age it is the now existing individuals who must freely transcend their own egoity.

The main weight of the christian tradition has insisted that this earthly life is the only environment in which the individual can either come of his own volition, or be brought by divine grace, to the "saved" relationship with God; and thereafter his individual existence is to be perpetuated in heaven (perhaps via purgatory) or in hell. I have argued that this scheme is unrealistic both as regards what is to happen before death and as regards what is to happen after death. If salvation in its fullness involves the actual transformation of human character, it is an observable fact that this does not usually take place in the course of our present earthly life. There must, then, be further time beyond death in which the process of perfecting can continue. The traditional scheme is equally unsatisfactory on its post-mortem side. I have argued that the doctrine of hell is morally intolerable; and that in any case the notion of the immortal ego, the finite person continuing endlessly through time, involves profound conceptual difficulties.

There is nevertheless an important insight behind the traditional christian insistence that the time of grace, in which we may respond to God, is limited by the boundary of death. For it is the prospect of termination that gives urgency and meaning to our life in time. This fact does not however necessitate the doctrine of one short life followed by an eternity in heaven or hell. The same fact is taken up into the alternative schemes of eastern thought in the idea of reincarnation, with many successive lives, each ended by its own death. Here the spiritual urgency of life is in one sense relaxed, in that our present existence is not regarded as the only one; and a welcome consequence of this has been that the religions of indian origin have never felt a need to convert anyone by force to their beliefs—for people will come to the truth when they are ready for it, if not in this life then in another. But these faiths have insisted, in agreement here with the christian tradition, that it is only in incarnate lives on this earth, and not in the many heavens and hells beyond it, that karma can be worked out and progress made towards final liberation. However, I have argued for yet a third possibility, other than eternal-heaven-or-hell or repeated earthly reincarnations, namely that of a series of lives, each bounded by something analogous to birth and death, lived in other worlds in spaces other than that in which we now are. This hypothesis accepts both the insistence upon the need for life to be lived within temporal limits and the conviction that the soul can only make progress in the incarnate state towards its final goal. But it differs from the western tradition in postulating many lives instead of only one, and from the eastern tradition in postulating many spheres of incarnate existence instead of only one. The hypothesis has been presented more fully—though still necessarily only as a possibility glimpsed in outline—in chapter 20.

But if we are to live many lives in the future, may we not have lived many lives in the past? I have already acknowledged that there are forms of the reincarnation doctrine—according to which we have indeed lived many times before—that cannot be disproved. But the broad conception of many successive lives can be held in different forms; it may affirm a first life or it may assume a beginningless infinity of existences. Both theories have their advantages and disadvantages. According to hindu belief the reincarnating *jiva* is eternal. The universe forms, develops, dissolves and then forms again in a cyclical movement which has no beginning or end. The *jivas* or souls are part of this eternal process and thus have no beginning. Within such a picture the future immortality of the soul presents no problems. There is however the very different problem of meaninglessness. The cosmic process, infinite into both past and future, serves no purpose and moves toward no fulfillment. For even when the *jivas* have at last become one in the eternal consciousness of Brahman the process begins again in an endless breathing out and breathing in of the realm of emanated being. If, on the other hand, we affirm a divine creation, then the human individual has a beginning and it is entirely possible that the present life is in fact—as it appears to be— his first life. But then it is his immortality that becomes problematic. If he began at birth, why should he not end at death? As Santayana said, "the fact of having been born is a bad augury for immortality." But although a bad augury, it may nevertheless not be a fatal one. And in favour of this being each person's first life there is both the positive fact that the individual does *seem* to be formed *ab initio* in the womb from which he is born to this present life, and the negative fact that human beings do not normally remember any previous existence. Admittedly neither of these arguments is decisive. But we have seen that the more popular conception of reincarnation, according to which the *same* person or self lives again and again, readily becomes diffused into the conception of a continuity of spiritual life being expressed in a series of different empirical selves—an idea which is far removed from the notion that *I* have lived many times before and shall live many times again. On the other hand something like the more "solid" conception of reincarnation can apply to the idea, outlined in chapter 20, of future lives in other worlds. This theory thus has the advantage of allowing for the moral and spiritual growth of one and the same self through many lives towards its final self-transcending perfection. It is mainly for this reason that it seems to me the more acceptable form of many-lives doctrine.

But if we do not postulate previous lives, how do we account for the glaring inequities and inequalities of human birth? I have already pointed out that this problem cannot be met by tracing it back into a regression of previous existences. If there is any "solution" to the problem of evil, it must be one which looks to the future rather than to the past; and I have suggested above, and have tried to develop more fully elsewhere, a theodicy based upon the final creation of infinite good out of the ambiguities and contradictions of life as we know it.

INDEX